AWS IoT With Edge ML and Cybersecurity

A Hands-On Approach

Syed Rehan

Foreword by Yasser Alsaied VP of AWS IoT

Apress®

AWS IoT With Edge ML and Cybersecurity: A Hands-On Approach

Syed Rehan
Stalybridge, UK

ISBN-13 (pbk): 979-8-8688-0010-8 ISBN-13 (electronic): 979-8-8688-0011-5
https://doi.org/10.1007/979-8-8688-0011-5

Managing Director, Apress Media LLC: Welmoed Spahr
Acquisitions Editor: Spandana Chatterjee
Development Editor: Spandana Chatterjee
Project Manager: Jessica Vakili

Cover designed by eStudioCalamar

Distributed to the book trade worldwide by Springer Science+Business Media New York, 1 New York Plaza, Suite 4600, New York, NY 10004-1562, USA. Phone 1-800-SPRINGER, fax (201) 348-4505, e-mail orders-ny@springer-sbm.com, or visit www.springeronline.com. Apress Media, LLC is a California LLC and the sole member (owner) is Springer Science + Business Media Finance Inc (SSBM Finance Inc). SSBM Finance Inc is a **Delaware** corporation.

For information on translations, please e-mail booktranslations@springernature.com; for reprint, paperback, or audio rights, please e-mail bookpermissions@springernature.com.

Apress titles may be purchased in bulk for academic, corporate, or promotional use. eBook versions and licenses are also available for most titles. For more information, reference our Print and eBook Bulk Sales web page at http://www.apress.com/bulk-sales.

Any source code or other supplementary material referenced by the author in this book is available to readers on the Github repository: https://github.com/Apress/AWS-IoT-With-Edge-ML-and-Cybersecurity. For more detailed information, please visit https://www.apress.com/gp/services/source-code.

Paper in this product is recyclable

For mum and dad, who gave me roots; for my wife,
who gave me wings; and for my daughters,
who gave me reasons to fly – with all my love, always.

Table of Contents

About the Author

Syed Rehan has established himself as a luminary in the world of cloud technologies during his career spanning over 18 years in the fields of development, IoT, and cybersecurity. Having joined AWS in 2017, Syed has been at the forefront of their initiatives, consistently driving innovation and contributing to the platform's evolution. His rich portfolio includes numerous insightful blogs, workshops, and authoritative whitepapers for AWS, showcasing his deep expertise and thought leadership in the industry.

Syed has graced the stage as a speaker at AWS re:Invent and numerous global conferences, shedding light on the rapidly evolving landscapes of cybersecurity, IoT, and cloud technologies.

Presently, Syed serves as a Senior Global Cybersecurity Specialist in the AWS IoT Core Security Foundation team. His collaborative spirit has been reflected in his instrumental role within the product teams in launching pivotal services such as AWS IoT Device Defender and AWS IoT Greengrass.

Syed's trailblazing journey is marked with several firsts. He was among the initial cohort of specialist solution architects for AWS IoT in EMEA; he also earned the honor of being the first specialist Solution Architect for Amazon Connect.

Syed's legacy in AWS and the cloud domain is a blend of vast experience, innovation, unwavering passion, and leadership, a legacy that continues to inspire and guide the next generation of tech enthusiasts.

Connect with him on LinkedIn: `www.linkedin.com/in/iamsyed/`.

About the Technical Reviewer

Ali Benfattoum is a Product Manager for AWS IoT at Amazon Web Services. With over 15 years of experience in IoT and smart cities, Ali brings his technical expertise to design and build innovative products and enable and help customers to accelerate their IoT and smart cities projects. Ali also holds an Executive MBA, giving him the ability to zoom out and help customers and partners at a strategic level.

Acknowledgments

First and foremost, I want to express my deepest gratitude to my mother, my father, my loving wife Shajna, and my precious daughters Maryam and Zahra; your unwavering patience and support while I was immersed in this project meant more to me than words can express. The countless hours and weekends I dedicated to this book were made possible because of your understanding and encouragement. I couldn't have achieved this without you by my side. From the bottom of my heart, thank you, I love you all dearly.

A special thank you to Yasser Alsaied, the VP of AWS IoT, truly one of the most genuine and humble leaders I've had the privilege to work with. My gratitude also extends to Ali Benfattoum for his pivotal role as a reviewer and supporter, ensuring this book offers insightful and practical value to all AWS IoT enthusiasts and practitioners. Your collective wisdom and support have been instrumental.

I would also like to express my sincere appreciation to the dedicated team at Apress. Your commitment and meticulousness have been invaluable in bringing this vision to reality.

To you, the reader, who chose to embark on this journey with me through the pages of this book, I extend my heartfelt gratitude. Your quest for knowledge and your trust in this work as a guide are deeply appreciated. It's my sincere hope that this book serves as a valuable resource to you, enlightening your path and enriching your understanding. Here's to your continued success and growth.

Introduction

In the world of rapidly evolving technologies, the Internet of Things (IoT) and cloud computing have become the symbol of innovation and efficiency. This book is designed to cater for all experience levels with a comprehensive guide to the AWS IoT ecosystem, valuable insights, and hands-on experiences.

What This Book Offers

You will have the opportunity to learn about AWS IoT platform setup and configuration of virtual devices, with the flexibility to use EC2-based virtual environments such as AWS Cloud9 or Raspberry Pi. Deep dive into AWS services by utilising AWS CLI (Command Line Interface) tool, explorations across diverse development SDKs, and a comprehensive emulation and utilization of the virtual environment to replicate hardware.

As the narrative progresses, you'll gain an all-encompassing view of AWS IoT services, delve into the intricacies of device software, and explore the vast landscapes of edge and industrial IoT (IIoT). Journey deeper to familiarize yourself with the crucial aspects of policy and security certificates, reinforcing your IoT initiatives with robust security and streamlined efficiency. Discover the transformative powers of Just-in-Time Provisioning (JITP) and Just-in-Time Registration (JITR) for device provisioning and registration, and sharpen your skills in telemetry data management using MQTT topics.

Practical Applications and Harnessing Data and Security

The journey then takes a riveting turn toward edge development with AWS IoT Greengrass, elucidating Interprocess Communication (IPC) and guiding you in setting up simulated home hubs for an enriching hands-on experience. And as the narrative evolves, you'll be introduced to the mesmerizing blend of machine learning and IoT, with a spotlight on image classification through a deep learning algorithm with a neural network model of 50 layers, ResNet-50, expanding the horizons of what IoT devices can perceive and achieve.

You will have the opportunity to acquaint yourself with the Zero Trust model, the ML Detect, and understanding the data analytics and business intelligence through Amazon's QuickSight and Timestream data.

Hope you have a warm and wonderful journey into AWS cloud services.

Foreword

In our modern digital landscape, the inevitability of technological progression is clear; the real challenge lies in navigating its intricacies. At first, "AWS IoT and ML" appears to dive deep into the technical nuances. Yet, as pages turn, it emerges as a lighthouse, illuminating the convergence of IoT's vast potential with the analytical prowess of machine learning, all housed within the AWS ecosystem.

Syed Rehan unravels this intricate tapestry with the clarity of a seasoned expert and the passion of a dedicated educator. He positions AWS IoT and machine learning not as mere tools but as fundamental pillars propelling digital transformation. Beyond the codes and configurations, this book resonates with a profound truth: embedded within these technologies are solutions to tangible, real-world challenges that, when unlocked, can catalyze transformative progress.

This work surpasses a mere introduction to AWS IoT or ML. It serves as a compass, guiding its readers from abstract ideas to tangible executions – from setting up an AWS account to harnessing the power of AWS IoT. Syed's meticulous progression from basic AWS CLI commands to nuanced telemetry data handling using MQTT is a testament to his mastery.

Digital transformation, as explored here, is more than the introduction of new tools or platforms. It demands a recalibration of an enterprise's foundational elements, a rethinking of business strategies, and the evolution of systems, all while engaging and enlightening its stakeholders. Such comprehensive transformation, reflecting both top-down and grassroots perspectives, echoes the depth and structure of this book.

What stands out distinctly is the book's harmonized focus on both IoT and ML. The depth and breadth of topics – from AWS IoT Greengrass and AWS IoT SiteWise to leveraging Amazon QuickSight for BI and drawing ML inferences – underscore its holistic approach. Syed's work is not just informative; it's an invitation – to question, to innovate, and, most importantly, to act.

Prepare to embark on an immersive journey. It promises to be a tapestry of technical depth interwoven with enlightening insights. Beyond being a guide, it represents a call to shift paradigms, urging readers to embrace the future's digital promise.

Yasser Alsaied, VP of AWS IoT

September 2023

CHAPTER 1

Setting Up Your AWS IoT Development Environment

Welcome to the fascinating realm of AWS IoT services. In this opening chapter, we'll embark on an in-depth exploration of these services, highlighting their distinctive use cases and scenarios. Our mission is to ensure that you, the esteemed reader, are well acquainted with the unique strengths and advantages that each service brings to the table.

As we progress, we'll guide you meticulously through the setup of your AWS account. This journey will encompass insights into the AWS Command Line Interface (AWS CLI) and the essential SDKs that will be a recurrent theme throughout the book. Moreover, we'll delineate the crucial steps to configure your development environment, making certain it stands ready for an efficient and smooth experience.

The world of development environments offers a plethora of choices. Whether your inclination leans toward the EC2-backed AWS Cloud9, an EC2 instance running a Linux-driven OS like Ubuntu or Amazon Linux, or hands-on hardware such as the Raspberry Pi, rest assured, we have curated insights just for you. Our narrative begins with a tutorial on creating a virtual device using AWS Cloud9, masterfully simulating the operations of a real-world device. For those with a penchant for hands-on exploration, a Raspberry Pi or any hardware with a comprehensive Linux OS (Debian or RHEL based), outfitted with Python 3, pip3, AWS CLI, and the associated SDKs, will serve as an impeccable guidepost.

Drawing from my expertise as an AWS IoT and cybersecurity specialist, I'll weave in practical insights throughout our journey. By spotlighting genuine use cases, I aim to underscore how different enterprises have optimally leveraged AWS services to boost adaptability, strengthen reliability, and achieve cost-effectiveness. Beyond the foundational knowledge available on the AWS website and other platforms, this book uniquely offers firsthand insights and in-depth examinations into the real-world applications of these services across a spectrum of customer scenarios.

S. Rehan, *AWS IoT With Edge ML and Cybersecurity*, https://doi.org/10.1007/979-8-8688-0011-5_1

AWS IoT Services Overview

In the realm of AWS IoT, the services are categorized into the following segments for a comprehensive learning perspective:

1. **Device Software:** This segment focuses on software solutions tailored for IoT devices. It covers development kits, SDKs, and tools that assist in building and managing device applications.
2. **Edge and IIoT:** This segment delves into services designed to support edge computing and Industrial IoT (IIoT) use cases. It includes services that enable intelligent data processing and analytics at the edge and solutions for managing large fleets of connected devices.
3. **IoT Services on Cloud:** This segment encompasses the core cloud-based services provided by AWS IoT. These services serve as the foundation for IoT deployments, offering features such as device connectivity, message routing, and integration with other AWS services.
4. **Security and Analytics Services for IoT:** Security and analytics are crucial aspects of any IoT system. This segment focuses on services that help secure IoT deployments, such as device authentication and threat detection. Additionally, it covers analytics services that enable data-driven insights and decision-making.

Device Software

There are software options available for running on devices, such as FreeRTOS, which is an open source real-time operating system designed for constrained devices like microcontroller units (MCUs). FreeRTOS allows devices to connect seamlessly with AWS IoT, providing a flexible and cost-effective solution for IoT deployments.

In addition to FreeRTOS, there is an add-on module called AWS IoT ExpressLink developed by silicon vendors. This module is specifically designed to accelerate the onboarding process for customers into the AWS IoT environment. It streamlines the initial setup and configuration, allowing customers to quickly and efficiently connect their devices to AWS IoT.

These software options, including FreeRTOS and AWS IoT ExpressLink, play a vital role in simplifying the device connectivity and integration process, enabling customers to establish a secure and reliable connection with AWS IoT services.

Edge and IIoT

In the context of AWS IoT, the term "edge" refers to devices deployed in the field, which can be microcontroller units (MCUs) or compact devices with CPUs. These edge devices can further be classified into a subcategory known as industrial gateways, which are extensively utilized in Industrial IoT (IIoT) environments, particularly in connected factories.

AWS provides a range of services dedicated to edge computing and IIoT:

- **AWS IoT Greengrass:** This service, available as open source, is compatible with Windows, Linux, and containerized environments. It enables local computing and data processing on edge devices, bringing AWS services and functionality closer to the data source. AWS IoT Greengrass empowers organizations to run applications and perform analytics at the edge, reducing latency and enhancing operational efficiency.
- **AWS IoT SiteWise Edge:** Designed to run on edge gateways, such as those found in connected factories, AWS IoT SiteWise Edge enables local data processing without the need for constant connectivity to the cloud. It facilitates efficient data transformation and analysis at the edge, allowing businesses to derive valuable insights and make real-time decisions.
- **AWS IoT FleetWise Edge Agent:** While AWS IoT FleetWise is primarily a cloud-based service for connected vehicles, the FleetWise Edge Agent operates at the edge, acting as a communication bridge between the physical device (in this case, a connected vehicle) and the cloud-based AWS IoT FleetWise service. This component facilitates secure and reliable data transmission, enabling efficient fleet management and insights.

These AWS edge and IIoT services empower organizations to extend their capabilities to the edge, enabling local processing, analytics, and communication. By leveraging these services, businesses can enhance their operational efficiency, reduce latency, and gain valuable insights from their edge devices and connected factories.

IoT Services on the Cloud

- **AWS IoT Core:** The central pillar of AWS IoT services. Serving as an MQTT gateway, it acts as the primary connection hub for all integrated devices. While the Message Broker is an integral subset of IoT Core, other services synergize with IoT Core to execute a myriad of tasks effectively.
- **AWS IoT Device Management:** This comprehensive service empowers users to remotely manage their connected devices. It offers a range of features to simplify device management operations.
- **AWS IoT Device Defender:** Working hand in hand with IoT Core, this security service plays a crucial role in auditing, validating, and enforcing rules on connected devices. It leverages machine learning capabilities to enhance device security. If you have a fleet of connected devices, this service is essential for monitoring their status effectively.
- **AWS IoT FleetWise:** Designed to work alongside the edge component installed on connected vehicles, this service provides intelligent insights into vehicle data in near real time. It enables businesses to make informed decisions based on the data collected from their fleet.
- **AWS IoT Analytics:** Dedicated to extracting value from raw data generated by connected devices, this service offers a wide range of features. Additionally, it facilitates seamless integration with other AWS services, such as Amazon QuickSight, for advanced data analysis and visualization.

- **AWS IoT Events:** Similar to Amazon EventBridge, this service focuses specifically on IoT devices. It enables the creation of actionable items based on events generated by these devices, enhancing automation and response capabilities.
- **AWS IoT SiteWise:** Tailored for industrial customers, this service provides comprehensive insights by transforming data from IIoT edge gateways. It offers features such as creating an OEE (Overall Equipment Effectiveness) dashboard, allowing businesses to optimize their operations effectively.
- **AWS IoT TwinMaker:** This service enables the creation of 3D visual representations of real-world assets using models derived from the physical devices. For example, it can generate a 3D representation of a power plant or factory, aiding in visualization and monitoring.
- **Amazon Kinesis Video Streams:** This service, commonly used in conjunction with other services like AWS IoT TwinMaker, allows the relay of live video streams from edge devices to the cloud. It is particularly useful for applications where visual data is essential, such as generating real-time 3D asset representations on a web page.

Environment Setup

Before we dive into the contents of this book, it's important to note that we assume you have a basic understanding of AWS and already have access to the AWS Console.

If you do not yet have access to the AWS Console, please follow the steps outlined here to set up your account and configure the AWS CLI.

AWS Account Setup

Visit the following website: `https://aws.amazon.com/`.

Here are the steps on how to set up an AWS account:

1. Go to the AWS website and click on the "Create an AWS Account" button.
2. Enter your email address and AWS account name.

3. You will receive an email with a verification code. Enter the verification code and click on the "Verify" button.
4. Create a strong password (16 characters or more).
5. I suggest using a Personal plan selection to go through this book and provide your contact details.
6. Read and accept the AWS Customer Agreement, provide billing details, confirm your identity, and click on the "Create Account" button.
7. You will be taken to the AWS Management Console. You can now start using AWS services.

Here are some additional tips for setting up your AWS account:

- Choose a strong password and do not share it with anyone.
- Enable multifactor authentication (MFA) for your account.
- Create a billing alert so that you are notified when your spending reaches a certain threshold.
- Use the AWS Free Tier to try out AWS services for free.

Book's Source Code

All source code related to this book can be conveniently accessed by visiting the official product page on Apress at `www.apress.com/ISBN`. Additionally, the code is hosted and available for download from the book's dedicated GitHub repository.

Type of Environment

After gaining access to the AWS Console, you can begin setting up your development environment. While we've chosen a virtual environment to bypass the need for specific hardware like the Raspberry Pi 4 Model B 4GB, you're welcome to use it if you have one on hand. Both setups are compatible and can be used interchangeably throughout this book.

- Virtual device environment
- Hardware device environment

Virtual Environment Choice

We've chosen the EC2-backed AWS Cloud9 setup for our virtual environment due to its beginner-friendly interface and comprehensive built-in features. However, if you already possess an EC2 instance and wish to use it, feel free to set it up as your virtual device.

Follow the steps and create an AWS Cloud9 environment in the US East (N. Virginia) region, as shown in Figure 1-1.

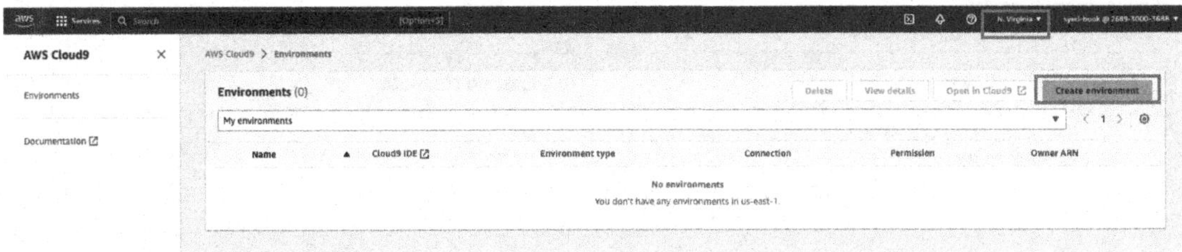

Figure 1-1. *Setting up AWS Cloud9 environment*

In the next step, you will need to select and populate details as follows (see Figure 1-2):

- Name: *VirtualDeviceEnvironment*
- Description: My AWS IoT Book virtual environment
- Environment type: New EC2 instance
    - Instance type: *t3.small*
- Platform:
    - *Ubuntu Server 22.04 LTS (at the time of writing this, we used the latest version. However, feel free to use the most recent Ubuntu version if it's available)*
    - Timeout: *30 minutes*
- Network settings:
    - *Secure Shell (SSH)*
- Select "*Create*"

Name
VirtualDeviceEnvironment
Limit of 60 characters, alphanumeric and unique per user.
Description – optional
My AWS IoT Book virtual environment
Limit 200 characters.
Environment type Info
Determines what the Cloud9 IDE will run on.
New EC2 instance
Cloud9 creates an EC2 instance in your account. The configuration of your EC2 instance cannot be changed by Cloud9 after creation.
Existing compute
You have an existing instance or server that you'd like to use.
New EC2 instance
Instance type Info
The memory and CPU of the EC2 instance that will be created for Cloud9 to run on.
t2.micro (1 GiB RAM + 1 vCPU)
Free-tier eligible. Ideal for educational users and exploration.
t3.small (2 GiB RAM + 2 vCPU)
Recommended for small web projects.
m5.large (8 GiB RAM + 2 vCPU)
Recommended for production and most general-purpose development.
Additional instance types
Explore additional instances to fit your needs.
Platform Info
This will be installed on your EC2 instance. We recommend Amazon Linux 2.
Ubuntu Server 22.04 LTS
Timeout
How long Cloud9 can be inactive (no user input) before auto-hibernating. This helps prevent unnecessary charges.
30 minutes

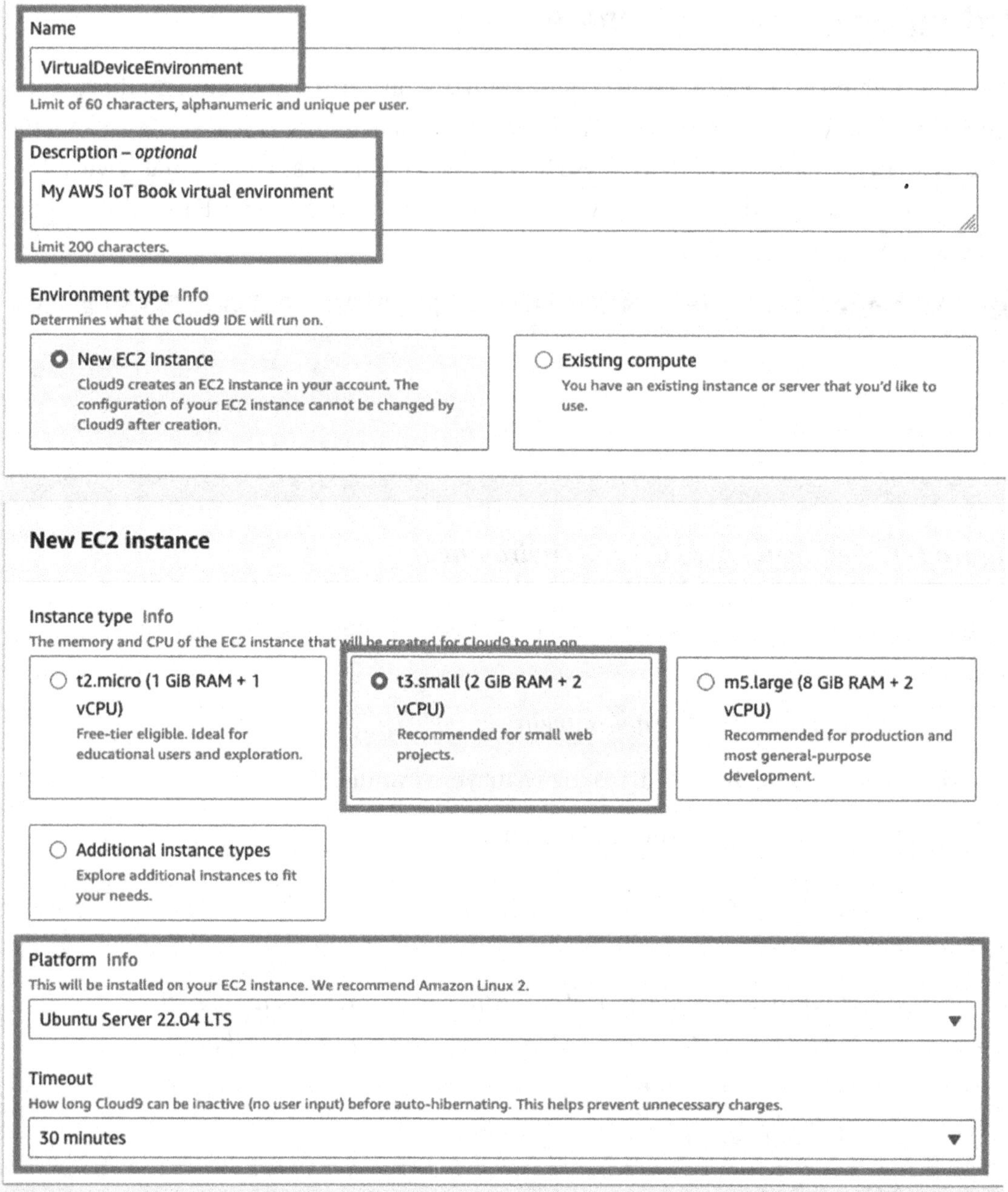

Figure 1-2. *Environment selection and details*

Once our environment is set up, we should be able to open the Cloud9 IDE and see developer tools and the Terminal window at the bottom.

While we are setting the environment, please select the "*cog*" and select "*Show Home in Favorites*" (see Figure 1-3).

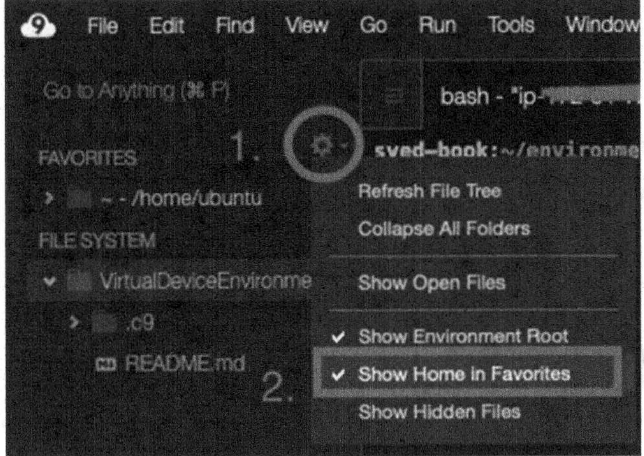

Figure 1-3. *Show Home in Favorites, to make development easier*

Going forward in the book, we will interact using the "AWS Cloud9" terminal and Cloud9 in-built editor.

Disk Size

The initial disk size of the environment is 10GB; we will increase to 50GB to run through the book.

Upload the file "*resize.sh*" obtained from Chapter 1 of the book's GitHub repository and place it in your home folder.

Select "*/home/ubuntu/environment*" on the left pane and choose *File ➤ Upload Local Files* (refer to Figures 1-4 and 1-5). Throughout this book, you'll use this method to upload various files, certificates, and source codes into their designated folders.

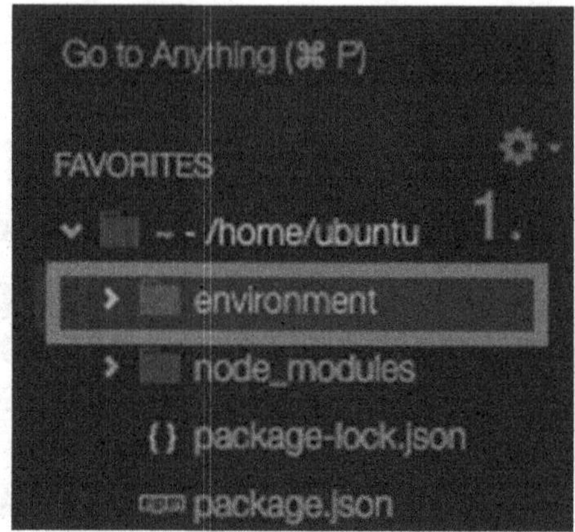

Figure 1-4. *Selecting the folder*

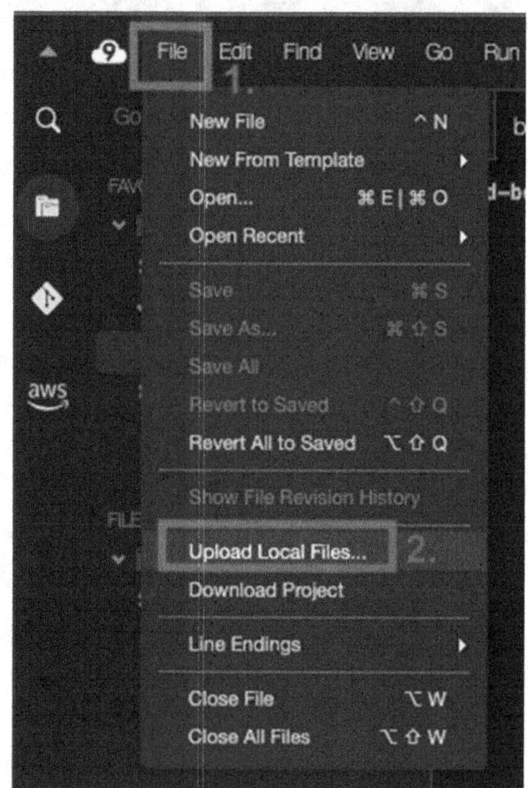

Figure 1-5. *Uploading local files*

Once you have the script in place, run the following command to increase disk size:

```
chmod +x resize.sh
./resize.sh
```

This script will adjust the disk size and then initiate a reboot. After this, you'll be primed to configure the AWS CLI. Upon setting up our environment, you should be greeted with the Cloud9 IDE, showcasing developer tools and a Terminal window positioned at the bottom.

Setting Up AWS CLI

The AWS Command Line Interface (CLI) is a fundamental tool we'll frequently engage with in this book. For a seamless learning journey and efficient interfacing with AWS services, it's imperative to have the AWS CLI integrated into your environment.

By default, the AWS Cloud9 environment should come with the AWS CLI pre-installed. To verify its presence and check the version, use

```
aws --version
```

If you're operating within a Raspberry Pi, another EC2 instance, or any other environment running a Linux OS and need to install or update the AWS CLI, execute the command provided here (for first-time installations, omit the --update flag):

```
curl "https://awscli.amazonaws.com/awscli-exe-linux-x86_64.zip" -o
"awscliv2.zip"
unzip awscliv2.zip
sudo ./aws/install --update
```

Executing this will either update the AWS CLI to the latest version, if it's already installed, or install the most recent version for you.

To set up your AWS CLI configuration, use the following command:

```
aws configure
```

You'll require the AWS Access Key ID, Secret Access Key, and region (set to us-east-1). These can be procured through the outlined process (refer to Figure 1-6).

- **AWS Access Key ID and Secret Access Key:**
    - Navigate to the AWS Management Console.
        1. Click on your username at the top right of the page.
        2. Click on the "*My Security Credentials*" link from the drop-down menu.
    - Here, you can find or create your "Access Key ID" and "Secret Access Key" under the "*Access keys*" section. Remember to store them securely; the Secret Access Key will not be shown again.

Important Ensure you store these credentials securely and never expose them in scripts or other public places. They provide access to your AWS resources and should be kept confidential.

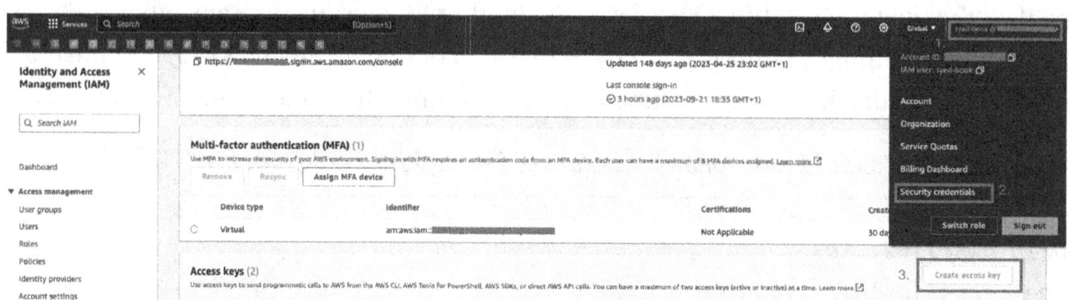

***Figure 1-6.** Obtaining credentials for AWS configure (to set up AWS CLI)*

Once you have the following:

- AWS Access Key ID
- Secret Access Key
- Region (use *us-east-1*)

Run AWS CLI again and populate it using the values obtained previously:

```
aws configure
```

If the prompt comes up for Force update, please select "*Force update*".

Development SDKs

Throughout this book, we'll utilize several SDKs. Here are the installation instructions for each:

Python IoT SDK

Install using the following commands:

```
python3 -m pip install awsiotsdk
python3 -m pip install AWSIoTPythonSDK
python3 -m pip install awscrt awsiot
```

Boto3 (Python)

Install with the following command:

```
python3 -m pip install boto3
```

jq Tool

Command for our AWS Cloud9 setup and for those on Debian/Ubuntu-derived OSes:

```
sudo apt-get update && sudo apt-get install jq -y
```

What You Have Learned

In this foundational chapter, we traversed multiple crucial terrains. We began by dissecting the myriad AWS IoT services, scrutinizing their distinct functionalities and capabilities to offer insights into their applicability for specific use cases. Alongside this, we enriched our understanding with real-world examples, showcasing how various AWS customers have adeptly harnessed these services to realize their IoT objectives.

Our journey commenced with establishing an AWS cloud account, the bedrock of your forthcoming IoT exploration. Following that, we delved into the nuances of configuring your development environment, making sure it's well armed with the requisite tools and settings for effective AWS service interactions.

Furthermore, we directed our attention to preparing the device environment, the locus where your IoT "thing" will come to life and communicate with the cloud. This phase is pivotal in building the vital link between your physical devices and AWS IoT services.

By meticulously covering these key facets, this chapter has set the stage for your IoT venture, empowering you with the essential know-how and toolset to confidently navigate the chapters ahead.

Summary

In this introductory chapter, we embarked on an enlightening journey into the vast world of AWS IoT services. We dissected various services, understanding their unique functionalities and real-world applications, as demonstrated by AWS customers.

Beginning with the essentials, we established an AWS cloud account, laying the groundwork for future IoT endeavors. Our focus then shifted to configuring the development environment, ensuring it's equipped for optimal AWS interactions. Moreover, we emphasized the importance of preparing the device environment and bridging the gap between physical devices and AWS IoT services. In essence, this chapter provided a comprehensive foundation, arming you with the knowledge and tools necessary for the upcoming chapters in the realm of IoT.

CHAPTER 2

MQTT in Action: Understanding IoT Policies, Just-In-Time Provisioning (JITP), and Just-In-Time Registration (JITR)

In this chapter, our focus will be on the crucial aspects of connectivity when connecting your IoT device to AWS IoT Core. We will dive deeper into the fundamentals of AWS IoT policies and certificates, understanding their significance in establishing secure and authenticated connections.

We will explore how AWS IoT policies and certificates play a pivotal role in device connectivity and how they enable devices to connect securely to AWS IoT Core.

Furthermore, we will examine the concept of Just-in-Time Registration (JITR) and Just-in-Time Provisioning (JITP) and their practical applications in real-life scenarios. These concepts highlight the dynamic and scalable nature of device onboarding and provisioning within AWS IoT, where JITP and JITR are not an option; we will discuss how you can leverage fleet provisioning options or use the manual registration process.

S. Rehan, *AWS IoT With Edge ML and Cybersecurity*, https://doi.org/10.1007/979-8-8688-0011-5_2

To conclude this chapter, we will explore the process of sending sample telemetry data using MQTT, a lightweight messaging protocol widely utilized in IoT communication. Through this practical exercise, we will delve into MQTT topics and gain a hands-on understanding of how message publishing and subscription function.

By thoroughly understanding connectivity aspects, policies, certificates, and telemetry data transmission, you will gain a solid foundation to build upon in subsequent chapters as we delve further into the realm of AWS IoT and its capabilities.

Fundamentals of AWS IoT Policy and Security Certificates

Securing and managing connectivity and permissions within an AWS IoT environment hinges on two foundational components: AWS IoT policy and security certificates.

AWS IoT Policy

This is a JSON document that outlines permissions and access control rules for devices and clients interfacing with AWS IoT Core. It governs MQTT client actions on specific resources, such as topics, rules, and shadow documents. AWS IoT identities, whether they're devices or roles, get these policies attached to dictate their interactions with the IoT Core service.

Key Concepts in AWS IoT Policies

Action: The permitted operations on an AWS IoT resource

Effect: Dictates if the policy grants or denies access to the desired action

Condition: Optional parameters that refine the policy's access control rules

Security Certificates

Used to authenticate and safeguard the communication between devices and AWS IoT Core, certificates validate the identity of a device or client and encrypt the data transferred across the network. AWS IoT Core leverages X.509 certificates, standard in SSL/TLS protocols.

Types of Certificates in AWS IoT

Device Certificates: Unique to individual devices or things. A Certificate Signing Request (CSR) containing the public key and additional details is generally created to procure a device certificate. Upon the CSR's approval by a Certificate Authority (CA), the device certificate is issued. Paired with its respective private key, this certificate becomes pivotal for cryptographic tasks and identity checks.

CA (Certificate Authority) Certificates: Emanating from a trusted Certificate Authority, these certificates are pivotal for trust establishment in a network. AWS IoT Core employs CA certificates to verify the authenticity of device certificates by checking if they're signed by a recognized CA.

By meshing AWS IoT policies with device certificates, a meticulous access control system is achieved, amplifying the security of device communications within your AWS IoT setting. These components are indispensable for erecting a robust and secure IoT framework.

AWS IoT Policies and Certificates: A Deep Dive

To ensure the robustness and security of the AWS IoT ecosystem, AWS IoT policies and certificates are paramount. Let's explore their intricacies and significance.

AWS IoT Policies: AWS IoT policies act as gatekeepers, dictating permissions for various resources within the AWS IoT platform, be it devices, topics, or rules. These JSON-formatted policies attach to identities like IoT things or groups, granting precise control over actions and resources.

Key aspects of AWS IoT policies

- **Policy Structure:** Comprising multiple "policy statements," an AWS IoT policy precisely determines the actions that are permitted or prohibited on specific resources. These statements encapsulate the "Effect" (allow/deny), "Action" (IoT operation), and "Resource" (affected IoT entity).
- **Granular Access Control:** With these policies, you can fine-tune permissions, such as allowing a device to publish data to a particular topic but denying subscription capabilities.
- **Dynamic Variables:** Variables like **${iot:Certificate.Subject.CommonName}** can be incorporated into policies to reference certificate values dynamically, enabling adaptive access control.
- **Hierarchical Approach:** The policies support a hierarchical structure, permitting the use of wildcards for broader permissions, such as granting access to an entire topic hierarchy or device group.

AWS IoT Certificates: These certificates bolster the secure communication pathway between devices and the AWS IoT cloud. They are instrumental in ensuring data protection, verification, and comprehensive security.

Key aspects of AWS IoT Certificates

- **X.509 Standard:** AWS IoT uses X.509 certificates and cryptographic standards essential for verifying device identities within the IoT domain. Every device should possess a unique certificate validated by a trusted Certificate Authority (CA) such as Amazon Trust Services (ATS).
- **Device Verification:** During the TLS handshake process, AWS IoT Certificates affirm device authenticity, permitting only recognized devices to connect with the AWS IoT cloud. This precaution prevents unauthorized access.
- **Certificate Management:** AWS IoT, in collaboration with Amazon Trust Services, provides a Certificate Authority service for generating, issuing, and managing certificates as the need arises.
- **Bidirectional Authentication:** Enabled by these certificates, mutual authentication ensures that both the device and the AWS IoT cloud validate each other's identities during the TLS handshake.
- **Device-Specific Permissions:** Associating AWS IoT policies with certificates allows for precise determination of actions and resources a device can access on the platform.

Together, AWS IoT policies and certificates constitute the foundation of a fortified IoT infrastructure on the AWS platform, facilitating meticulous access control and secure communication channels.

Understanding AWS IoT Policies Through Examples

To underscore the nuances of AWS IoT policies, let's examine two distinct policy examples and understand their ramifications:

1. **A resource-specific policy (tied to "client1" Thing Name):**

```
{
  "Version": "2012-10-17",
  "Statement": [
    {
      "Effect": "Allow",
      "Action": "iot:Connect",
```

```
      "Resource": "arn:aws:iot:us-east-1:123456789000:client/
      client1"
    }
  ]
}
```

This policy exemplifies a restrictive stance, zeroing in on a particular IoT resource, namely, "client1". By deploying the "iot:Connect" action, it exclusively authorizes the client with the designated ARN (Amazon Resource Name) to connect to the AWS IoT platform. Such pinpointed control ensures that only the named client can forge a connection.

2. **An open-ended policy (advised against in production settings):**

```
{
  "Version": "2012-10-17",
  "Statement": [
    {
      "Effect": "Allow",
      "Action": "*",
      "Resource": "*"
    }
  ]
}
```

This policy stands as a warning beacon, underscoring its unsuitability for production environments. Adopting a laissez-faire approach, it permits any conceivable action on every resource. While potentially viable for educational or specific testing phases, this liberal policy introduces formidable security vulnerabilities when integrated into live environments. It bestows unchecked access, granting carte blanche authority over the entirety of AWS IoT resources.

Navigating AWS IoT policy creation demands prudence and a security-centric perspective. By meticulously sculpting permissions tailored to your IoT implementation's precise demands, you fortify the security perimeter around your IoT assets and data.

Diving Deeper into Policy Action Types

The spectrum of policy actions is vast, with each action bearing unique implications:

- **Connect:** Regulates connections to the IoT platform.
- **Publish:** Determines the ability to broadcast messages to MQTT topics.
- **Subscribe:** Grants permission to subscribe to select MQTT topics and access associated messages.
- **Receive:** Concerned with the reception of messages from MQTT topics.
- **RetainPublish:** Manages the ability to dispatch messages bearing the "retain" flag. Such retained messages linger on AWS IoT Core, reaching subscribers upon their subscription.

For enhanced adaptability, these action types can undergo further customization. Such refinements can hinge on parameters like the Thing Name (denoting IoT devices), MQTT Topic, or Message type. Additional functionalities, such as message retention, can also be woven into the policy, providing augmented control and versatility.

Streamlining Device Provisioning and Registration

AWS IoT Core offers a variety of options for provisioning and onboarding a multitude of devices. The chosen approach depends on the device's capabilities and whether it possesses unique X.509 certificates and private keys prior to being purchased by the final customer.

When the manufacturing process or distribution chain enables the device manufacturer to embed unique credentials onto the device, they can opt for Just-in-Time Provisioning (JITP), Just-in-Time Registration (JITR), or Multi-Account Registration (MAR).

On the other hand, if embedding unique credentials on the device before its sale isn't feasible, manufacturers can turn to fleet provisioning as their onboarding solution.

JITP

JITP Overview

JITP, which stands for "Just-in-Time Provisioning" within AWS IoT, is a streamlined mechanism designed by AWS to facilitate the secure and efficient onboarding and provisioning of vast numbers of IoT devices.

Just-in-Time Provisioning Overview

Devices employing Just-in-Time Provisioning (JITP) are pre-equipped with certificates and private keys before integrating with AWS IoT. It's essential that these certificates are signed by a customer-specified CA, which needs to be registered in AWS IoT. AWS IoT–generated certificates aren't compatible with JITP. Prior to provisioning, the customer should determine the account the device will link to.

Setup Process

With JITP, devices link to AWS IoT Core where the certificate's signature is cross-checked with the registered CA. Post-validation, a provisioning template is utilized to register the Thing and certificate, and then a policy is assigned to the device. Device manufacturers must register the signer CA and attach a provisioning template to this CA.

Device Operation

On its inaugural connection to AWS IoT Core, the device's certificate needs to be transmitted during the TLS handshake. If the Server Name Indication (SNI) isn't sent by the device during this connection (TLS handshake), the signer CA must be transmitted. A failed TLS handshake is expected on the first attempt due to the absence of the certificate in the AWS IoT account. However, as part of the JITP, the device's certificate gets registered and activated in AWS IoT Core. It's crucial for devices to be programmed to reattempt connection to AWS IoT Core after a brief interval. Once provisioning is successful, devices can seamlessly connect to AWS IoT Core.

JITP Benefits

- **Scalability:** With dynamic credential and certificate generation, JITP optimizes provisioning for vast numbers of devices, bypassing individual pre-provisioning.
- **Security:** Unique credentials ensure that only authenticated devices communicate with AWS IoT.
- **Flexibility:** Provisioning templates allow for JITP customization to align with device-specific needs.

JITR

JITR Overview

JITR, or Just-in-Time Registration, is an AWS IoT feature designed for the effortless and secure automatic registration of IoT devices onto the AWS IoT platform, facilitating the smooth onboarding of newly introduced devices.

Just-in-Time Registration Overview

Use Just-in-Time Registration (JITR) when custom operations are needed during a device's registration on AWS IoT Core. Similar to JITP, devices should already have certificates and private keys before integration. Moreover, the signer CA should be preloaded in the AWS IoT account before the device's onboarding.

Setup Process

Upon its initial connection to AWS IoT Core, the device's certificate signature is cross-verified with the Certificate Authority, resulting in its registration in a dormant state. AWS IoT Core then triggers a life cycle event on the MQTT topic *"$aws/events/certificates/registered/<caCertificateID>"*. Manufacturers must implement an IoT Rule that prompts an AWS Lambda function when a message appears on this topic.

This Lambda function can execute tasks such as comparing against an approved list, checking against a revoked certificate list, associating the device with a specific user in the cloud, or kickstarting further onboarding processes. Once the supplementary verification is done, the Lambda function activates the certificate. Concurrently, it should instantiate the IoT thing, establish the Policy, and link both to the certificate.

Device Operation

Mirroring JITP, the device needs to forward the client certificate during the TLS handshake. In cases where the device lacks SNI support, the signer CA should be transmitted. The initial connection attempt to AWS IoT Core is expected to fail. Devices should have the capability to re-establish connection with AWS IoT Core post this initial connection. If the Lambda function validates and activates the certificate, the subsequent device connection will be successful.

JITR vs. JITP: When to Use Which?

Just-in-Time Registration (JITR) and Just-in-Time Provisioning (JITP) are both mechanisms for onboarding devices to AWS IoT Core, but they cater to different needs based on the customization and flexibility required during the registration process.

Why Use JITR?

1. **Custom Logic During Registration**: JITR is ideal for situations where additional, custom logic is necessary when registering a device. This can include tasks like the following:

    - Secondary validation against external databases or pre-approved lists
    - Special routing or assignment based on device type or certificate attributes
    - Instantiating user-specific resources based on device information or type of device

    Example: A company manufactures smart thermostats. When a thermostat connects for the first time, it should be linked to a user account based on its certificate attributes. Using JITR, the AWS Lambda function can cross-reference the certificate's metadata with a user database and bind the device to the right account.

2. **Greater Flexibility**: JITR provides granular control over the registration process, allowing for more intricate setups and validations.

    Example: A security company wants to ensure that only devices from certain manufacturers are registered. With JITR, they can cross-check the device's certificate against a pre-approved list of manufacturers during the registration process.

Why Use JITP?

1. **Streamlined Registration**: JITP is suitable for straightforward, automated device registrations without the need for additional custom logic.

    Example: A toy manufacturer creates thousands of Internet-connected teddy bears. Once sold, these teddies should connect to AWS IoT Core without any special routing or user-specific actions. JITP would be a perfect fit for such a bulk, uniform registration process.

2. **Less Overhead**: For scenarios where the registration process doesn't need to interface with other AWS services or external systems, JITP offers a quicker, less complex route to getting devices onboarded.

   Example: An agricultural firm deploys hundreds of soil sensors across multiple farms. All sensors are identical in function and only need to send data to a centralized system. Using JITP ensures a hassle-free, consistent registration process for all these sensors.

In Conclusion: The decision to use JITR or JITP largely hinges on the requirements of the device registration process. If there's a need for custom logic, advanced routing, or additional validation steps, JITR offers the flexibility to achieve that. On the other hand, for straightforward, bulk registrations without special requirements, JITP is the way to go.

Manual Registration Without a CA Overview

Devices can be manually registered to AWS IoT Core using existing client certificates, negating the need for a registered Certificate Authority (CA). This approach, often termed Multi-Account Registration (MAR), allows devices to connect to AWS IoT Core once they're provisioned with a unique certificate and private key. Though these certificates are generally signed with a CA, the CA doesn't need to be registered with AWS IoT Core for manual registration. Device makers can register certificates in any AWS Region or account they have access to.

Setup Process

Device manufacturers need to pre-configure the necessary AWS resources for every device before their inaugural connection to AWS IoT Core.

Some hardware vendors offer hardware security modules pre-loaded with a certificate and private key. These certificates, signed by the vendor's CA, come with a manifest provided to the device maker. It's the device maker's responsibility to register these certificates across desired accounts and regions, using resources like the AWS Management Console, the AWS IoT Control Plane API, or the AWS CLI.

Device Operation

Devices should have a TLS stack compatible with the SNI extension. For connection, the AWS IoT Core endpoint is included in the device's SNI string. No further device configurations are needed.

Use Cases for Manual Registration Without a CA

This registration method is ideal for those seeking flexibility in deciding the accounts and regions for device connection. Here's why:

- **Versatility Across AWS Accounts**: Device makers or service providers may maintain various AWS accounts for different purposes such as testing, sandboxing, or production. By pre-registering certificates in each account, devices can seamlessly transition between accounts during their life cycle, simply by adjusting the IoT endpoint on the device.
- **Global Sales and Multiple Regions**: Devices sold worldwide can have their certificates registered across numerous AWS Regions and even multiple accounts within a single region.
- **Collaborative Deployment**: This method empowers device manufacturers to share a device's public X.509 client certificate with IoT service providers. The providers can then manually register the device across their multiple accounts.

In essence, manual registration without a CA provides enhanced flexibility for device deployment across varied AWS environments, ensuring seamless connectivity regardless of the device's operational stage or geographical distribution.

Fleet Provisioning

Fleet Provisioning Overview

Fleet provisioning caters to scenarios where equipping devices with unique credentials during manufacturing isn't practical due to technical challenges, costs, or specific application needs. In such cases, generic devices are sold without a distinct identity. AWS IoT Core's fleet provisioning offers two methods to equip devices with unique credentials post-purchase: via trusted users or through claims.

Provisioning by Trusted User:

Using this method, AWS IoT Core introduces an API that empowers mobile applications to create temporary certificates and private keys. Devices are dispatched from the factory devoid of unique credentials, and only authenticated users can provision these devices with distinct credentials.

Here's how it works:

1. An installer accesses a mobile app (device maker provided), authenticating themselves with AWS.
2. The app triggers the CreateProvisioningClaim API call, which produces a short-lived (five-minute validity) temporary X.509 certificate and private key.
3. The installer transfers these temporary credentials to the device using the mobile app (i.e., using BLE).
4. Upon receipt, the device connects to AWS IoT and swaps the temporary credentials for a unique X.509 certificate, signed by a temporary AWS CA, along with a corresponding private key. During this exchange, AWS sets up the necessary resources such as Thing, Policy, and Certificate.

Setup Requirements

Manufacturers adopting the Trusted User method must

- Develop and oversee a mobile application integrated with the CreateProvisioningClaim API
- Configure and manage the fleet provisioning template in AWS IoT Core
- Optionally, integrate a pre-provisioning AWS Lambda function to provide enhanced authentication or extra logic during the provisioning phase

Device Requirements

Devices should

- Be able to receive temporary credentials via a secured channel, such as Bluetooth Low Energy (BLE), Wi-Fi, or USB
- Contain the necessary logic to interact with fleet provisioning MQTT topics, accept lasting credentials, and save these credentials securely

Use Cases for Trusted User Provisioning

This method is especially apt when

- Maximum security is paramount.
- The manufacturing process isn't entirely trusted.
- Device provisioning during manufacturing isn't feasible.

By utilizing trusted user provisioning, credentials remain shielded from the manufacturing pipeline. It's essential that only authorized users can carry out provisioning tasks, and devices used for generating temporary credentials should uphold strict security standards.

Fleet Provisioning Using Claims

In scenarios where devices lack the ability to securely create unique keys or when the manufacturing process isn't set up to provision devices uniquely, device manufacturers can resort to a shared claim certificate installed on the devices. AWS IoT Core facilitates these devices to acquire a distinct identity upon their first connection.

Provisioning by Claim Explained

Manufacturers use a shared claim certificate and key across devices. To enhance security, it's advised to have the claim certificate be unique for each batch, minimizing potential damage if a claim certificate's private key is compromised and necessitating revocation. If revoked, devices sharing this certificate can't proceed with the provisioning. The claim certificate firmware is integrated by the contract manufacturer, eliminating the need for bespoke adjustments. When the device connects to AWS IoT Core initially, it swaps its claim certificate for a unique X.509 certificate, authenticated by the AWS Certificate Authority (CA), and a corresponding private key. For added security, the device should send a unique identifier, like an embedded hardware secret, during provisioning. This token can be cross-checked against an approved list using a pre-provisioning Lambda function to affirm the device's authenticity.

Setup Requirements

Manufacturers opting for claim-based provisioning should

- Uphold and manage a fleet provisioning template and a corresponding AWS Lambda function equipped with extra validation logic
- Safeguard claim certificates and conduct periodic checks to avert potential abuse

Device Requirements

Devices are expected to

- Incorporate logic to interact with fleet provisioning MQTT topics, accept the permanent credentials, and securely store these credentials

When to Opt for Provisioning by Claim

This method is suitable when

- Unique credential provisioning on the device isn't feasible.
- Trusted user provisioning isn't an option.

However, devices passing through potentially insecure channels, such as third-party distribution, should avoid using claim-based provisioning. This is due to the inherent risk of exposing shared claim credentials, which are common to all devices before their maiden connection to AWS IoT Core.

MQTT in IoT Telemetry

MQTT Overview

MQTT, or Message Queuing Telemetry Transport, is a lightweight protocol tailored for efficient and dependable communication within IoT environments and similar low-resource networks. This protocol operates on a publish-subscribe model, where entities can either send (publish) or receive (subscribe) messages through specific channels called topics.

Key Features and Concepts

- **Efficiency**: Designed for low-power, limited-bandwidth devices, MQTT employs a concise binary protocol to cut down network overhead.
- **Publish-Subscribe Model:** Devices or applications (publishers) transmit messages to designated topics. In turn, other devices or applications (subscribers) receive messages from topics they've shown interest in, much like following a Twitter account to view its tweets.

- **MQTT Broker**: At the heart of MQTT communication lies the broker, a central hub (e.g., AWS IoT Core Message Broker) responsible for routing published messages to the appropriate subscribers based on their topic interests.
- **Asynchronous Communication**: MQTT promotes asynchronous interaction, meaning that publishers and subscribers operate independently of each other, ensuring flexibility and scalability in IoT setups.
- **Security**: MQTT integrates robust security measures, including Transport Layer Security (TLS) encryption and authentication protocols, safeguarding data integrity and privacy during transmission.

MQTT and AWS IoT Security

- **Transport Layer Security (TLS)**: This advanced encryption protocol ensures that data between MQTT clients and brokers remains confidential and tamper-proof.
- **Authentication**: Through TLS, MQTT enables mutual authentication, where both client and broker validate each other's digital certificates, ensuring genuine identities.
- **AWS IoT Standards**: AWS IoT enforces stringent security by requiring TLS for all connections. Devices must support TLS and offer valid certificates to establish a trustworthy link.
- **Certificate-Based Authentication**: AWS IoT uses X.509 digital certificates to authenticate devices, ensuring only genuine devices can interact with the platform.
- **System Reserved Topics**: AWS IoT designates topics starting with a dollar sign ($) for internal operations. While users can send or receive messages on these topics, creating new ones with this prefix is restricted.

Life Cycle Events: AWS IoT documents various device life cycle events, such as connection status or updates. These events can inform actions like notifications when a device disconnects.

For instance:

- Monitoring device statuses
- Action triggers based on specific events, like notifications for new device additions
- Analyzing trends in device behavior to enhance performance

MQTT with the RETAIN Flag

Using MQTT with the RETAIN flag during message publication ensures that the broker (here, AWS IoT Core) holds onto the message. This results in the broker storing the most recent message and its QoS for that specific topic. When a fresh client subscribes, it immediately receives the retained message from the broker, ensuring prompt access to the latest information without waiting for new messages.

Regarding AWS IoT Core's role:

- It holds the last message transmitted on a topic if the RETAIN flag is active.
- These messages are conserved within the AWS IoT Core's message broker.
- The detailed mechanics of AWS's internal storage aren't publicly shared. Direct querying or accessing these retained messages outside the MQTT framework isn't feasible. To obtain a retained message for a topic, one would need to subscribe to it.
- Any client subscribing to a topic on AWS IoT Core is sent the retained message unless a null payload message with the RETAIN flag clears it.

However, a few considerations are essential:

- Retained messages should be used discerningly, as excessive use may flood the broker with outdated data.
- An MQTT client can remove a retained message from a topic by sending a zero-length payload message with the RETAIN flag active.
- AWS may impose limits on the quantity or size of retained messages depending on your specific use case and requirements. For a clear understanding of these constraints, please consult the official AWS IoT Core documentation.

In Summary: MQTT, with its efficient publish-subscribe model, plays a pivotal role in numerous IoT applications, offering scalable communication between devices and cloud services with minimal resource usage. When combined with AWS IoT's rigorous security standards, it ensures safe and secure data transmissions across the IoT spectrum.

Simple Testing with AWS IoT Core MQTT Client

In upcoming chapters, we'll send messages using the device. But for clarity, let's first explore how publish/subscribe operates using the AWS IoT Core MQTT Client, as shown in Figure 2-1.

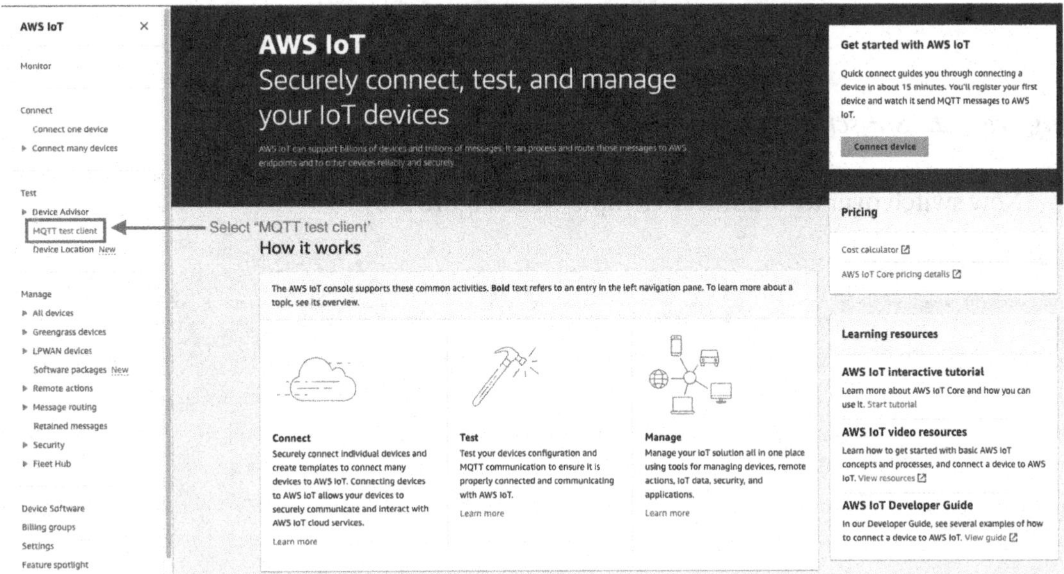

***Figure 2-1.** AWS IoT Core MQTT Test client*

Subscribe to a topic, that is, "*awsiotbook/myFirstSubTopic*" (see Figure 2-2).

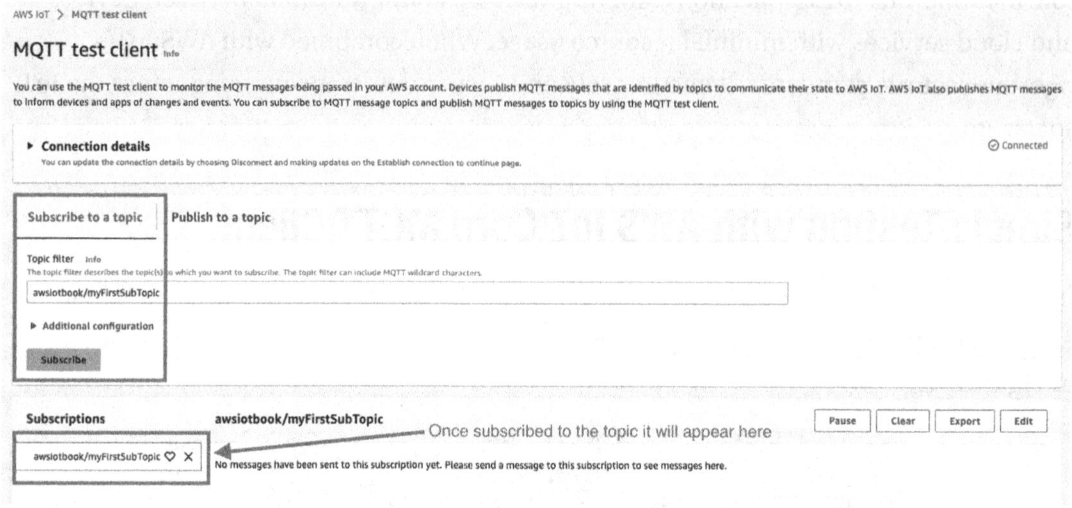

Figure 2-2. *Subscribing to an MQTT topic*

Now switch over to "Publish to a topic" (see Figure 2-3).

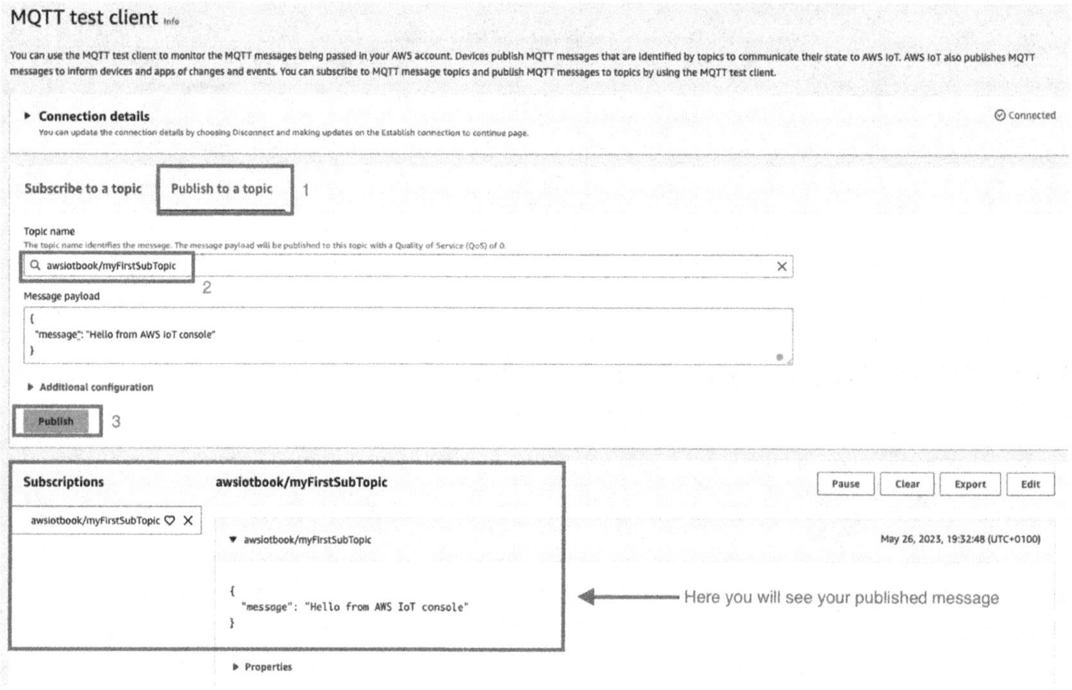

Figure 2-3. *Publishing to an MQTT topic.*

After publishing the message, you'll notice it appears on the topic to which you subscribed and published. This demonstration provides a clear understanding of the MQTT protocol, offering a solid foundation of the publish/subscribe mechanism.

What You Have Learned

AWS IoT Policies and Certificates: We underscored the criticality of AWS IoT policies in facilitating secure and structured communication within the IoT ecosystem. These policies meticulously define permissions, outlining the boundaries of what devices are permitted and prohibited from doing, thereby fine-tuning their interactions with IoT Core. Complementing this, security certificates (device and cloud) form the bedrock of reliable connections. Transport Layer Security (TLS) emerges as a key player, safeguarding data confidentiality and integrity throughout MQTT communications.

Understanding MQTT: MQTT, pivotal in the realm of IoT communications, embraces an agile publish-subscribe framework. Drawing parallels to social media interactions, it facilitates publishers in disseminating messages through designated topics, while subscribers aligned with those topics are recipients of the messages. The inherent scalability of this model fosters streamlined and precise communication within IoT infrastructures.

JITP, JITR, Manual Registration, and Fleet Provisioning: JITP offers an efficient pathway for devices to onboard, enabling them to retrieve distinct identities from AWS IoT Core during their initial connection. JITR enhances this process by automating device registration and seamlessly integrating devices with pertinent credentials and permissions as they connect. Further enriching our understanding, we navigated through other notable strategies, including manual registration without a CA and fleet provisioning, exploring both trusted user and claim-based approaches and appreciating their unique advantages.

Exploration of the AWS IoT Core MQTT Test Client: In the concluding segments, we acquainted you with the AWS IoT Core MQTT Test client, offering a hands-on experience with the MQTT publish and subscribe mechanism, laying a solid foundational grasp.

Summary

In this chapter, we embarked on a comprehensive journey through the vast landscape of AWS IoT. We began by demystifying the essential roles of AWS IoT policies and security certificates, emphasizing their crucial part in forging secure connections to IoT Core. The intricacies of MQTT were unraveled, illuminating its foundational publish-subscribe model crucial for streamlined IoT communications. Our exploration further extended to the innovative mechanisms of Just-in-Time Provisioning (JITP) and Just-in-Time Registration (JITR), showcasing their adaptability and significance in various device onboarding scenarios. Additionally, hands-on interactions with the AWS IoT Core MQTT Test client provided practical insights into MQTT dynamics. Through this chapter's holistic lens, we've been equipped with a profound understanding of AWS IoT, positioning us to harness its rich capabilities in crafting bespoke IoT solutions.

CHAPTER 3

Connecting and Publishing to AWS IoT

Welcome to the immersive world of AWS IoT Core, where the convergence of IoT devices and cloud services paves the way for seamless connectivity and transformative possibilities. In this chapter, we will delve deep into the intricacies of leveraging AWS IoT Core to connect IoT devices, specifically virtual devices and physical devices like the Raspberry Pi 4, and explore the power of MQTT protocol for efficient data transmission.

Central to AWS IoT Core is its powerful MQTT-driven messaging framework, fostering efficient and secure exchanges between devices and the cloud. Within the confines of AWS IoT Core, we'll demystify the implementation of this system. Leveraging MQTT's adaptability and scalability, you'll grasp the nuances of creating two-way communication pathways. This ensures devices can relay telemetry data to the cloud while simultaneously obtaining real-time commands or updates.

As we embark on this journey, our primary focus will be on the concept of virtual devices and the principles of bootstrapping. By employing virtual devices, you can emulate IoT devices connecting to the AWS IoT Core console, simulating real-world scenarios, and producing telemetry data. This approach is especially beneficial for those looking to bootstrap their way to a Minimum Viable Product (MVP).

Bootstrapping, by its nature, emphasizes lean operations and rapid prototyping, allowing you to test and refine your IoT solution without the overhead of physical hardware. This ensures a quicker time to market, with the agility to iterate designs efficiently, leading to significant reductions in both development time and expenses. By harnessing the capabilities of these virtual simulations and adopting a bootstrapping mindset, you'll be well equipped to swiftly build, test, and deploy effective IoT solutions.

Upon successfully channeling telemetry data into AWS IoT Core, we'll venture into the domain of IoT data ingestion and its effective management. With AWS IoT Core at the helm, there's a seamless synergy with other AWS services. Take Amazon S3, for

S. Rehan, *AWS IoT With Edge ML and Cybersecurity*, https://doi.org/10.1007/979-8-8688-0011-5_3

instance, which facilitates the storage and systematic arrangement of vast amounts of telemetry data. This chapter will shed light on the best practices for data ingestion, emphasizing data partitioning and compression and optimizing time-series data, which we will delve deeper into later in the book.

However, our exploration isn't restricted to just data storage. The formidable rules engine of AWS IoT Core stands as a testament to its capabilities, allowing you to shape, process, and direct telemetry data to diverse endpoints, AWS Lambda and Amazon Kinesis being notable examples. We'll dive deep into the potential of this rule's engine, guiding you on crafting rules that resonate with MQTT topics, the essence of messages, or device-specific attributes. These meticulously designed rules can catalyze actions like data transformation, enrichment, and even aggregation, enabling you to extract profound insights from your telemetry data.

Transitioning to the topic of data lakes, we will introduce the blueprint for sculpting an IoT data lake infrastructure, harmoniously integrating AWS IoT Core and Amazon S3. It's essential to recognize that Amazon S3 stands as a cornerstone for curating data lakes.

By the culmination of this chapter, you'll be well versed in the intricacies of AWS IoT Core, the nuances of telemetry data ingestion, the prowess of the rule's engine, and the seamless fusion with data lakes. Equipped with this enriched knowledge, you'll be poised to design and deploy state-of-the-art IoT solutions that not only foster secure device connections but also maximize the capabilities of MQTT, refining data processes and unveiling the latent insights within your IoT data lake.

Prepare to immerse yourself in this enlightening journey, witnessing the symbiosis of IoT, AWS IoT Core, MQTT, and data lakes. Together, let's tap into the boundless potential of your IoT devices, channeling the might of AWS to reshape your data-driven strategies. Let us embark on this exploration, bridging the realms of IoT devices, telemetry data, and data lakes, all under the umbrella of AWS IoT Core.

Connecting and Publishing to AWS IoT

Before connecting to AWS IoT Core and publishing data on specific topics, it is essential to establish a robust authentication and authorization mechanism. AWS IoT Core offers various methods to ensure secure device connections and control access to MQTT topics. Device authentication typically involves the use of X.509 certificates. This mechanism verifies the identity of devices, ensuring only authorized entities can connect to the IoT Core platform. Once authenticated, AWS IoT Core's fine-grained authorization policies allow you to define access permissions for specific MQTT topics. By granting or restricting access to topics, you can ensure that data is published only to the intended destinations, maintaining data privacy and security within your IoT ecosystem.

MQTT Topic Usage

In AWS IoT, MQTT topics play a crucial role in facilitating communication and data exchange between devices and the cloud. MQTT topics are strings that devices use to publish messages or subscribe to receive messages. They follow a hierarchical structure, allowing for organized and targeted message routing within an IoT system.

AWS IoT MQTT topics are organized in a topic namespace specific to each AWS account and region.

The topic structure is typically represented as topicPrefix/topicLevel1/topicLevel2/.../topicLevelN, where each topic level represents a specific category or attribute.

Here are some key aspects of AWS IoT MQTT topic usage:

- **Publishing**: Devices publish messages to specific topics using the MQTT PUBLISH command. Publishing a topic allows devices to send data, updates, or notifications to interested parties or other devices. For example, a temperature sensor may publish its readings to a topic like sensors/temperature.
- **Subscribing**: Devices can subscribe to one or more MQTT topics to receive messages published on those topics. Subscriptions can be specific to a single topic, use wildcards, or utilize topic filters to receive messages matching specific criteria. For instance, a display device in a smart home system might subscribe to the topic smartHome/livingRoom/# to receive updates from multiple sensors in the living room.
- **Topic Hierarchy**: AWS IoT allows you to organize topics hierarchically to provide structure and flexibility in message routing. You can define meaningful topic levels based on your system's needs, such as device types, locations, or specific application domains. This hierarchy enables fine-grained control over message distribution and access.

- **Wildcards**: AWS IoT supports two types of wildcards in MQTT topic subscriptions: + and #. The + wildcard represents a single level in the topic hierarchy and can match any string within that level. The # wildcard represents multiple levels and can match any number of levels within the topic hierarchy. Wildcards provide flexibility in subscribing to a range of topics efficiently.
- **Access Control**: AWS IoT Core uses fine-grained access control policies to authorize devices' actions on MQTT topics. Access control policies are associated with devices or device groups and specify which topics they can publish or subscribe to. This mechanism ensures that only authorized devices can access specific topics and helps maintain security and data privacy within an IoT system.

By leveraging MQTT topics effectively, you can establish a flexible and scalable communication infrastructure within your IoT solution. The hierarchical structure, along with wildcards, allows you to handle a variety of use cases, ranging from individual device interactions to system-wide data distribution and orchestration.

Create an AWS IoT Thing

In this section, we will create our "First" IoT thing, and download the certificates to connect. The same step applies whether you are using a virtual device or physical hardware such as "Raspberry Pi".

Go to the AWS IoT Core console (from the AWS Console) then Select "*Create Things*" (see Figure 3-1):

- Select Manage
    - Select All devices
    - Select Things
    - Select Create Things

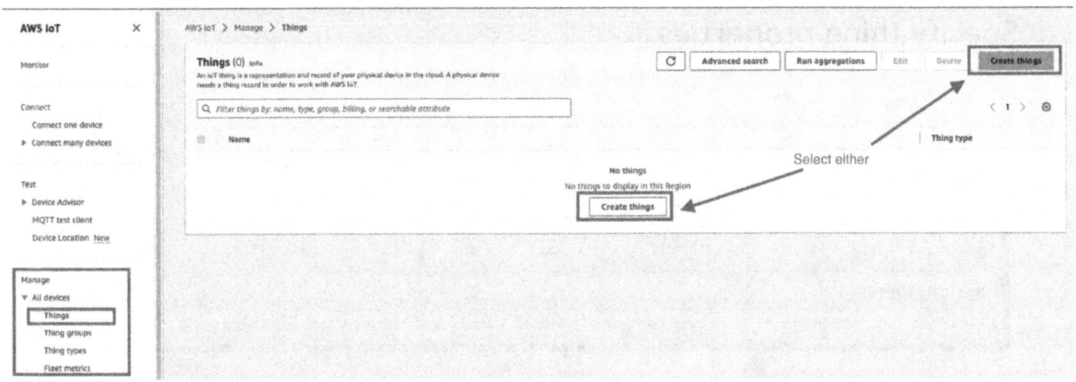

Figure 3-1. *Creating an AWS IoT thing (device)*

Select "*Create single thing*" and click Next.

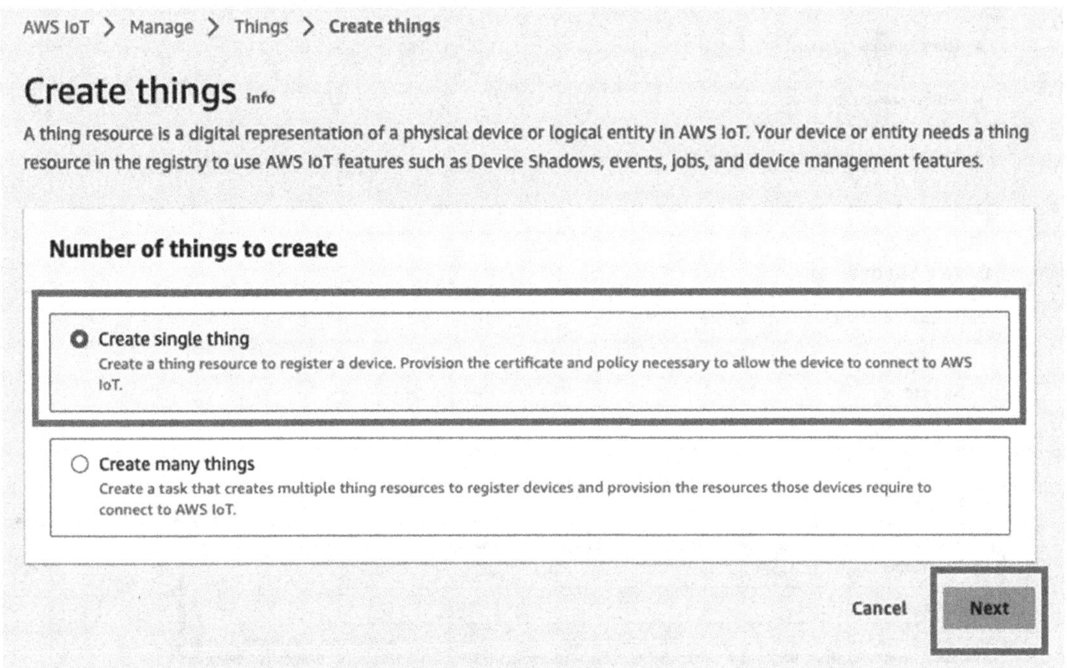

Figure 3-2. *Creating a single IoT device*

Now let's give IoT thing the name "*myFirstIoTDevice*" and select "*Named shadow*" and name it "*firstShadow*"; we will discuss shadow in depth in the next chapter; for now, let's click "*Next*" and continue (see Figure 3-3).

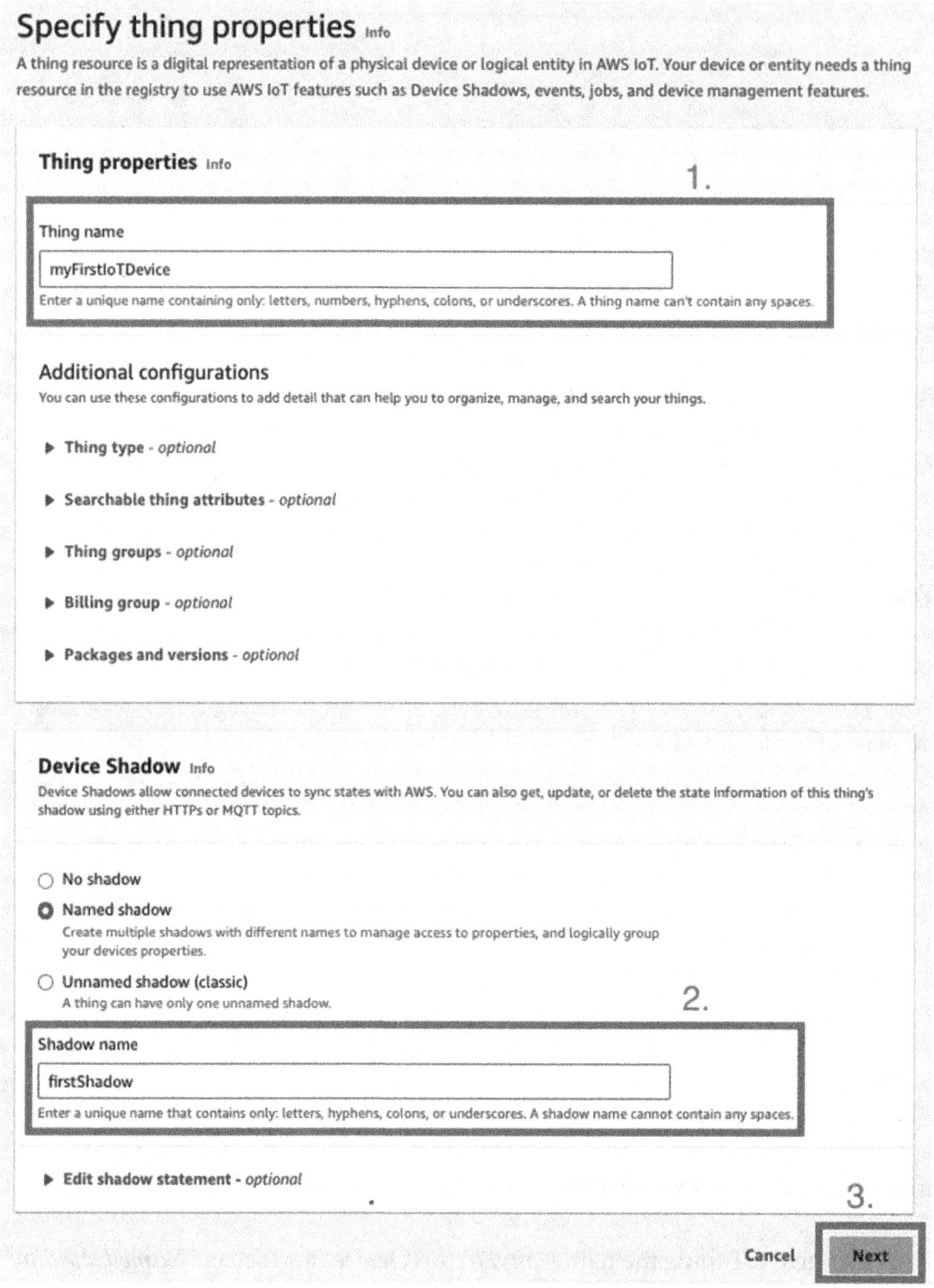

Specify thing properties Info

A thing resource is a digital representation of a physical device or logical entity in AWS IoT. Your device or entity needs a thing resource in the registry to use AWS IoT features such as Device Shadows, events, jobs, and device management features.

Thing properties Info

1.

Thing name

myFirstIoTDevice

Enter a unique name containing only: letters, numbers, hyphens, colons, or underscores. A thing name can't contain any spaces.

Additional configurations

You can use these configurations to add detail that can help you to organize, manage, and search your things.

▶ Thing type - *optional*

▶ Searchable thing attributes - *optional*

▶ Thing groups - *optional*

▶ Billing group - *optional*

▶ Packages and versions - *optional*

Device Shadow Info

Device Shadows allow connected devices to sync states with AWS. You can also get, update, or delete the state information of this thing's shadow using either HTTPs or MQTT topics.

○ No shadow

● Named shadow
Create multiple shadows with different names to manage access to properties, and logically group your devices properties.

○ Unnamed shadow (classic)
A thing can have only one unnamed shadow.

2.

Shadow name

firstShadow

Enter a unique name that contains only: letters, hyphens, colons, or underscores. A shadow name cannot contain any spaces.

▶ Edit shadow statement - *optional*

3.

Cancel Next

Figure 3-3. *Creating Device properties*

Let's create "*device certificates*"; select the "*Auto-generate option*" and click "*Next*" (see Figure 3-4).

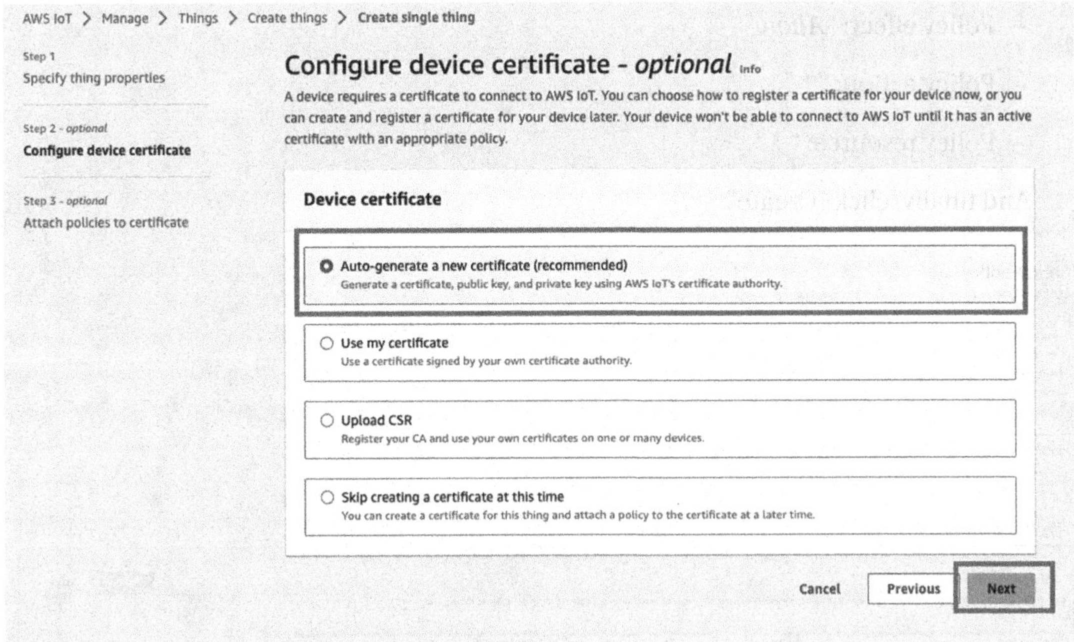

Figure 3-4. *Creating a device certificate*

Click "Create policy" (Figure 3-5).

AWS IoT > Manage > Things > Create things > Create single thing
Step 1
Specify thing properties
Step 2 - optional
Configure device certificate
Step 3 - optional
Attach policies to certificate
Attach policies to certificate - optional Info
AWS IoT policies grant or deny access to AWS IoT resources. Attaching policies to the device certificate applies this access to the device.
Policies (2)
Select up to 10 policies to attach to this certificate.
Create policy
Filter policies
1

Figure 3-5. *Create policy*

In the Create policy screen (since it's our first policy, we will keep it open/generic to make it easier for the reader to follow through the exercises; these open policies are only for testing purposes and not for the production environment).

Populate policy details as follows (see Figure 3-6):

– Policy name: "*myFirstDemoNonProductionPolicy*"

– Policy effect: "*Allow*"

– Policy action: " * "

– Policy resource: " * "

And finally, click "Create".

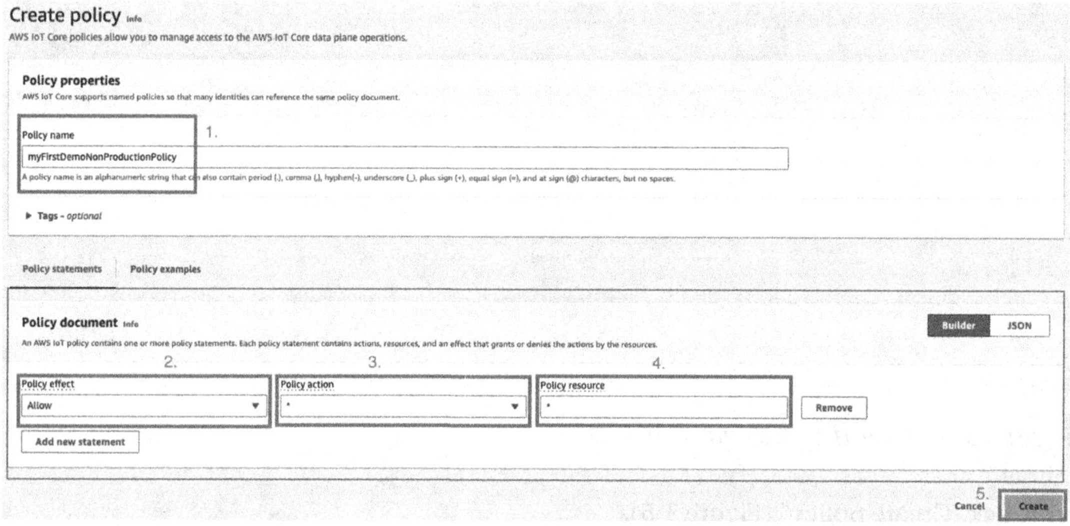

Figure 3-6. Policy details

Once the policy is created, we can select the policy and click "*Create thing*" (see Figure 3-7).

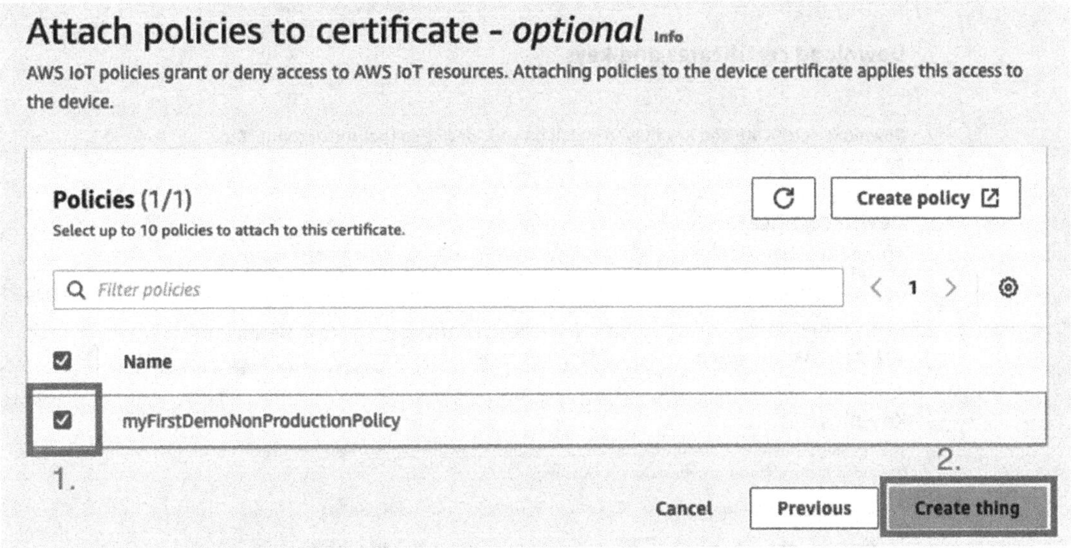

Figure 3-7. *Attaching a policy*

On the final screen, make sure to download the following certificates; this is the only time you can download the key files for this certificate.

Once you have downloaded "all" four files, only then click "*Done*".

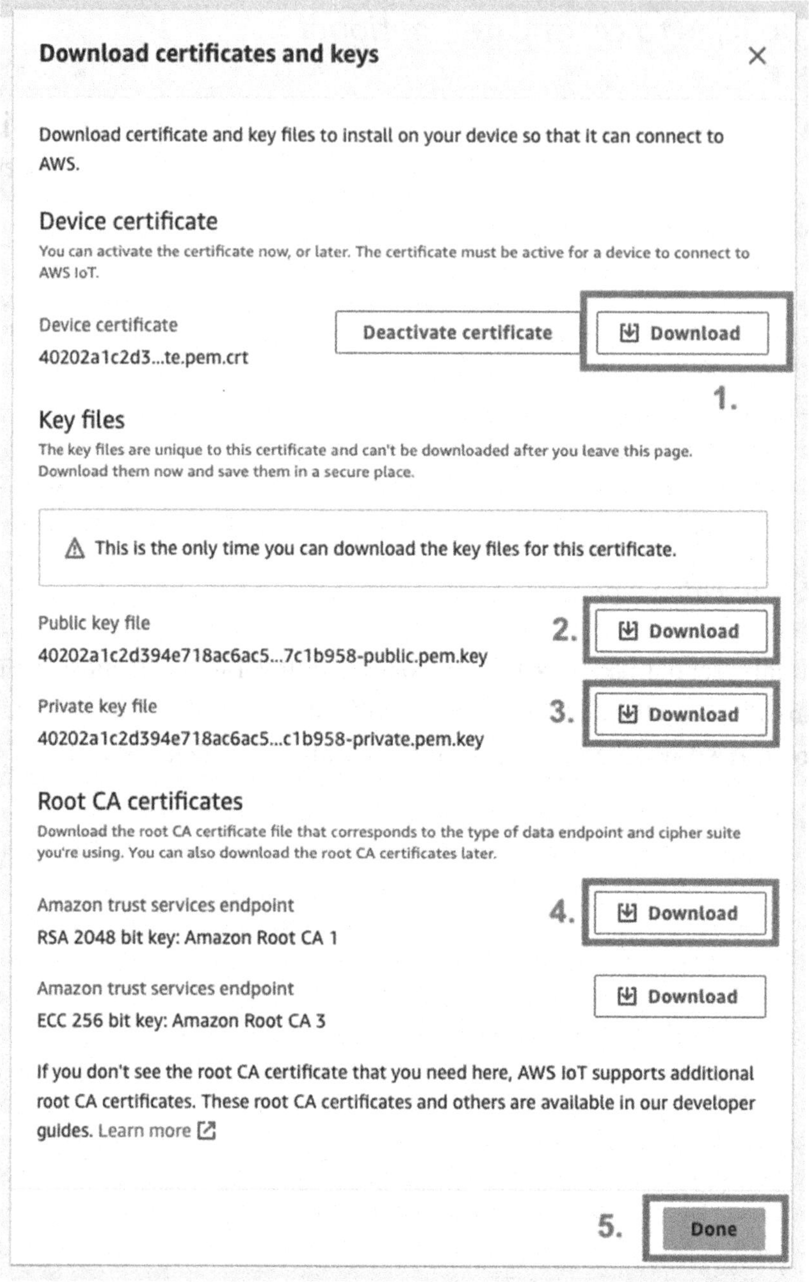

Download certificates and keys

Download certificate and key files to install on your device so that it can connect to AWS.

Device certificate

You can activate the certificate now, or later. The certificate must be active for a device to connect to AWS IoT.

Device certificate
40202a1c2d3...te.pem.crt

Deactivate certificate

Download

1.

Key files

The key files are unique to this certificate and can't be downloaded after you leave this page. Download them now and save them in a secure place.

This is the only time you can download the key files for this certificate.

Public key file
40202a1c2d394e718ac6ac5...7c1b958-public.pem.key

2. Download

Private key file
40202a1c2d394e718ac6ac5...c1b958-private.pem.key

3. Download

Root CA certificates

Download the root CA certificate file that corresponds to the type of data endpoint and cipher suite you're using. You can also download the root CA certificates later.

Amazon trust services endpoint
RSA 2048 bit key: Amazon Root CA 1

4. Download

Amazon trust services endpoint
ECC 256 bit key: Amazon Root CA 3

Download

If you don't see the root CA certificate that you need here, AWS IoT supports additional root CA certificates. These root CA certificates and others are available in our developer guides. Learn more

5. Done

Figure 3-8. *AWS IoT Core, Device Credentials*

Having established an AWS IoT thing within the AWS IoT Core Device registry, we're poised to configure its certificates. We can then proceed to connect to AWS IoT Core, either virtually using AWS Cloud9 or utilizing the Raspberry Pi as our physical device.

Obtain an AWS IoT Endpoint

Before we delve into connecting either virtual or physical devices, it's essential to note that both will utilize the same endpoint. To proceed, it's crucial to identify the endpoint address. To retrieve this, execute the following command either on the AWS Cloud9 "*terminal*" or the Raspberry Pi "*terminal.*" Ensure that your AWS CLI is configured appropriately, and upon successful execution, the endpoint address will be displayed as shown here:

```
aws iot describe-endpoint --endpoint-type "iot:Data-ATS"
```

You should see something similar to the one shown in Figure 3-9.

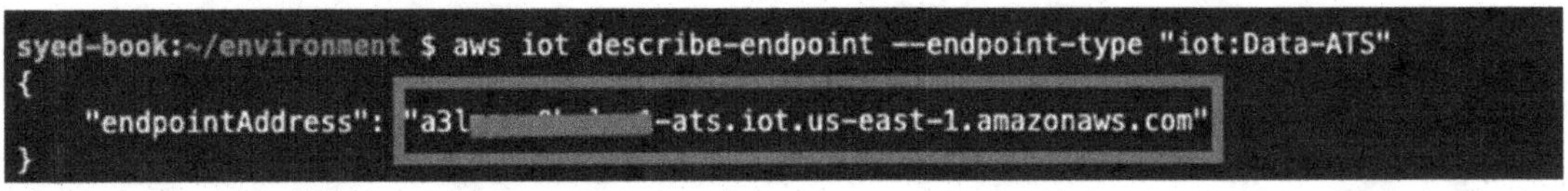

```
syed-book:~/environment $ aws iot describe-endpoint --endpoint-type "iot:Data-ATS"
{
    "endpointAddress": "a3l[illegible]-ats.iot.us-east-1.amazonaws.com"
}
```

Figure 3-9. *AWS IoT endpoint*

Make note of the address between speech marks, that is, *a3lxxxxxxxxxxxxx-ats.iot.us-east-1.amazonaws.com.*

You can also obtain this address using the AWS IoT Core console (Figure 3-10).

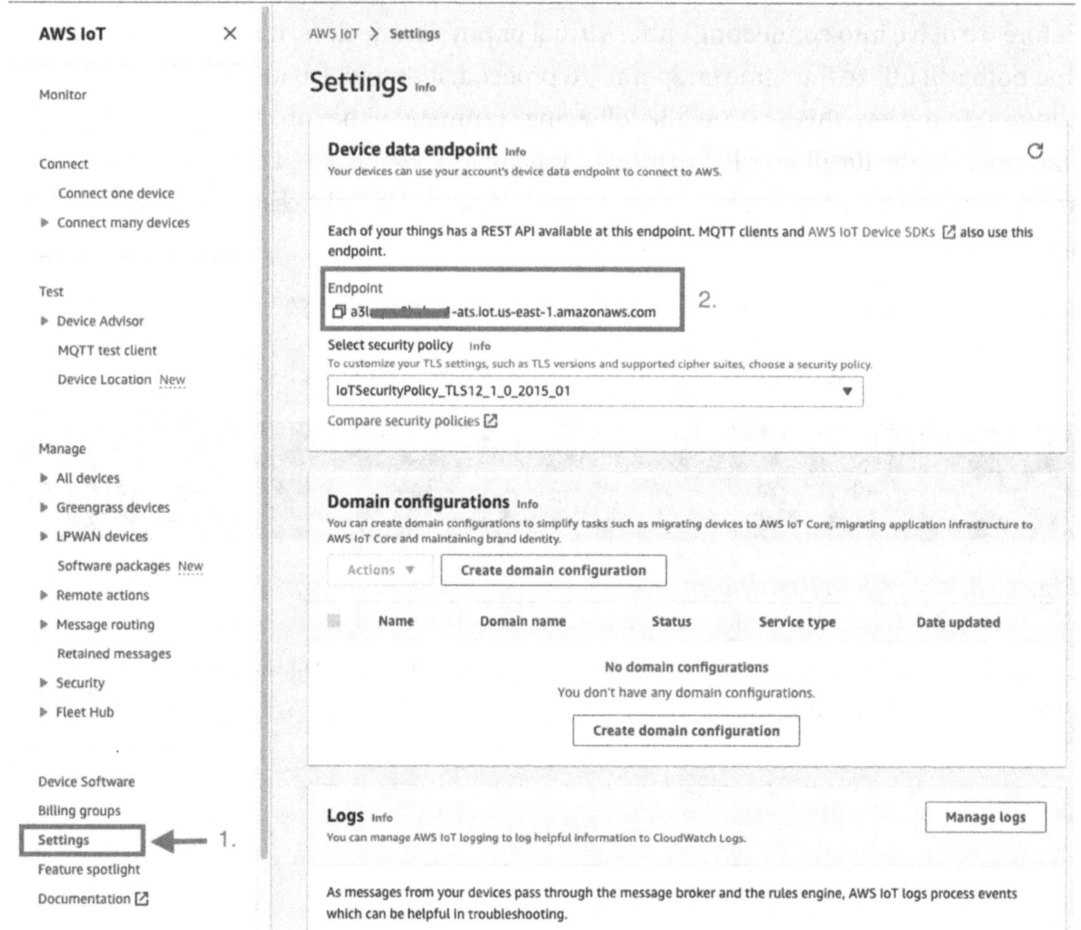

Figure 3-10. *AWS IoT endpoint from the AWS IoT Core console*

We will need this address to connect all our devices in the subsequent sections and chapters.

MQTT JSON Payload Using Virtual Hardware

Let's use the certificates we have created in the earlier section and connect our IoT thing (*virtual device*) to the AWS IoT Core MQTT Broker. Go to the AWS Cloud9 console and open the environment we created in an earlier chapter.

Then upload the certificates on the AWS Cloud9 environment by following the subsequent process.

First, let's create a folder to keep certificates and our Python code for the device to connect.

Run the following command to create folders:

```
mkdir -p $HOME/myFirstIoTDevice/certs
touch $HOME/myFirstIoTDevice/myFirstIoTDevice.py
```

Once we have done this, we can upload our certificates and then copy our Python code to create/connect the IoT thing.

Upload the Certificates

Select the "certs" folder in the AWS Cloud9 folder pane (Figure 3-11).

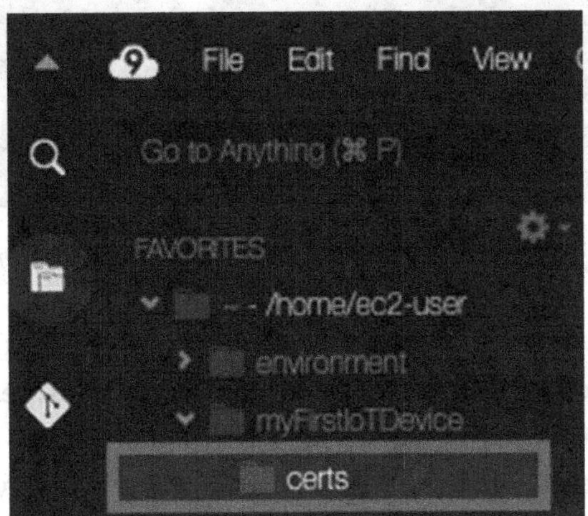

Figure 3-11. *Selecting folder to upload files*

Select "*File*", then select "*Upload Local Files*" (Figure 3-12).

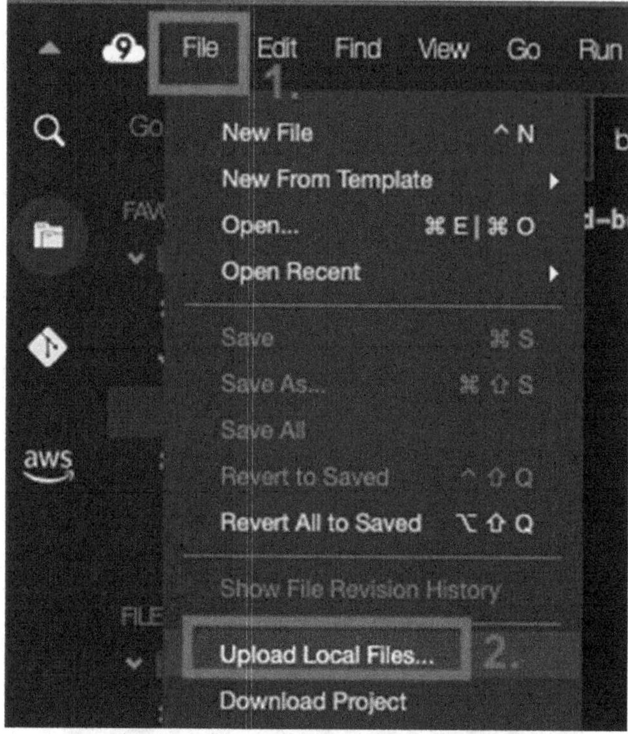

Figure 3-12. *Selecting and uploading files downloaded earlier*

Upload all four downloaded files (certificate and keys). Please make sure you have at "**minimum" uploaded the following three files** ending with **.pem.crt**, **-private.pem.key**, and **AmazonRootCA1.pem** specifically to the */home/ubuntu/myFirstIoTDevice/certs* directory before proceeding. We will use this location in the Python code to point the certificate location.

Navigate to the Correct Folder Path

For the terminal, you can use the procedure shown in Figure 3-13 to obtain a folder path.

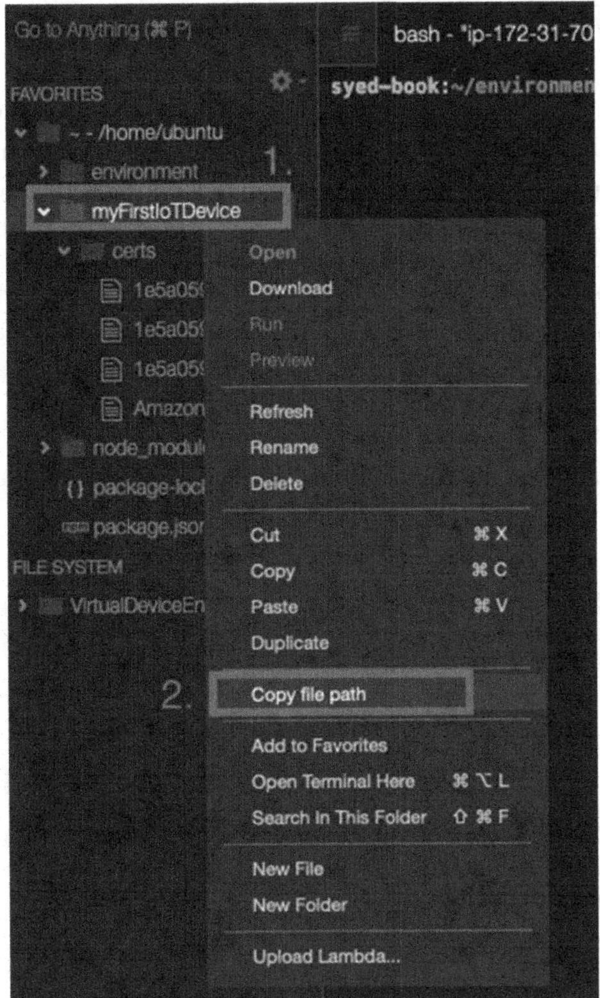

Figure 3-13. *Obtaining a folder path*

In the terminal, run the following command:

```
cd $HOME/myFirstIoTDevice
```

In the next step, we will place our Python code file and connect to AWS IoT Core.

Setting Up a Python IoT Device File

1. Start with the provided Python code, sourced either from the book's GitHub repository or copied from the content shown here. Ensure you adjust relevant settings to match your certificates and designated file paths.
2. If you've previously created "*myFirstIoTDevice.py*" in an earlier step, update it with the new content. Otherwise, create and save the script as "*myFirstIoTDevice.py*".
3. Place this file in the same directory as your certificates folder. Ideally, the file path should be ***/home/ubuntu/myFirstIoTDevice/myFirstIoTDevice.py.***

```
# fileName: myFirstIoTDeviceVirtual.py

import json
import random
import time


from AWSIoTPythonSDK.MQTTLib import AWSIoTMQTTClient

# AWS IoT Core configuration
# REPLACE settings details below per your settings

#### Replace start

endpoint = "REPLACE_HERE"  # Replace with your AWS IoT Core endpoint
root_ca_path = "REPLACE_HERE-path/to/root/ca.pem"  # Replace with the path
to your root CA certificate
private_key_path = "REPLACE_HERE-path/to/private/private-key.pem.key"  #
Replace with the path to your private key
certificate_path = "REPLACE_HERE-path/to/certificate.pem.crt"  # Replace
with the path to your device certificate
client_id = " myFirstIoTDevice "  # Replace if you used different
thing name
```

```
# Define the topic to publish to
topic = "awsiotbook/myTopic"  # Replace with the topic you want to
publish to
####Replace End

# Create an MQTT client
mqtt_client = AWSIoTMQTTClient(client_id)
mqtt_client.configureEndpoint(endpoint, 8883)
mqtt_client.configureCredentials(root_ca_path, private_key_path,
certificate_path)

# Connect to AWS IoT Core
mqtt_client.connect()

for _ in range(5):
    # Create a JSON payload with random temperature value
    payload = {
        "sensor": "temperature",
        "value": random.randint(20, 30),
        "timestamp": int(time.time()),
    }

    # Publish the JSON payload to the topic
    mqtt_client.publish(topic, json.dumps(payload), 1)

    # Wait for a short interval before the next iteration
    time.sleep(2)

# Disconnect from AWS IoT Core
mqtt_client.disconnect()
```

Before we run this, make sure to subscribe to the topic. Here, we are using *"awsiotbook/myTopic"*.

Subscribe to this topic in the AWS IoT Core MQTT Test client so we can see data coming in.

Once you have subscribed to this topic, let's run this code using the following command (make sure you are in the right folder as described previously):

```
python3 myFirstIoTDevice.py
```

You will see messages displaying on the terminal too (see Figure 3-14).

```
syed-book:~/myFirstIoTDevice $ python3 myFirstIoTDevice.py
Published message to topic awsiotbook/myTopic: {"sensor": "temperature", "value": 26, "timestamp": 1695381060}
Published message to topic awsiotbook/myTopic: {"sensor": "temperature", "value": 22, "timestamp": 1695381062}
Published message to topic awsiotbook/myTopic: {"sensor": "temperature", "value": 30, "timestamp": 1695381064}
Published message to topic awsiotbook/myTopic: {"sensor": "temperature", "value": 23, "timestamp": 1695381066}
Published message to topic awsiotbook/myTopic: {"sensor": "temperature", "value": 25, "timestamp": 1695381068}
```

Figure 3-14. *Message being posted to AWS IoT Core*

You will see the JSON payload showing a random "*temperature*" value five times before the Python script terminates (see Figure 3-15).

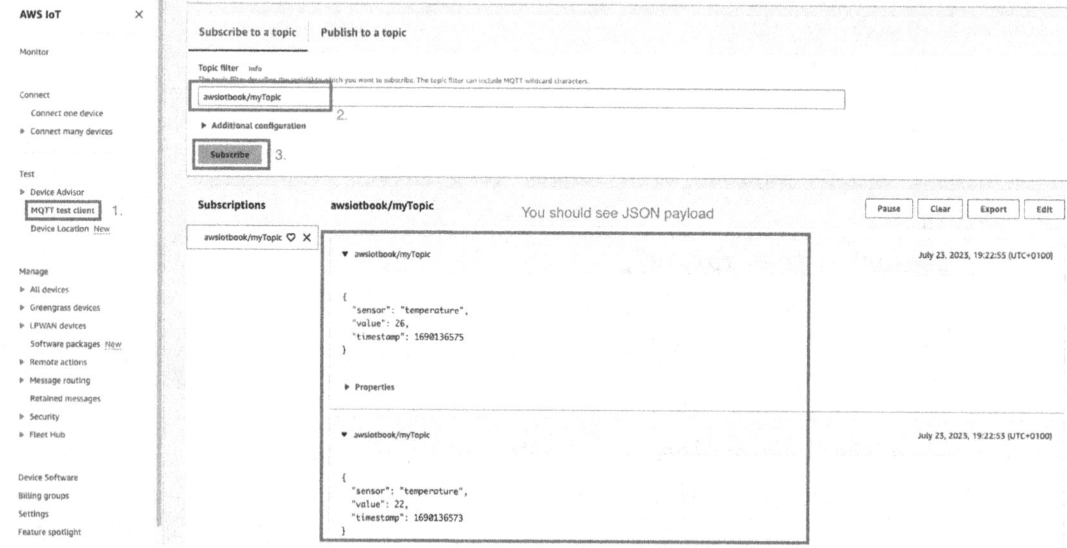

Figure 3-15. *JSON payload arriving from our IoT thing*

AWS IoT Rules Engine: Data Processing Simplified

Effortlessly streamline and automate your IoT data flow with AWS IoT rules engine.

Understanding AWS IoT Rules

The AWS IoT Rules feature, an integral component of AWS IoT Core, offers a robust mechanism for data processing and automation as telemetry data streams into AWS IoT Core from IoT devices. These rules empower users to delineate conditions and corresponding actions that determine the processing, filtering, transformation, and routing of incoming IoT data. Designed with SQL-like syntax, crafting intricate data manipulation logic becomes intuitive. If an incoming message aligns with a rule's conditions, AWS IoT Rules promptly executes the defined actions.

These could encompass storing the data in Amazon DynamoDB, relaying messages to other devices, invoking AWS Lambda for advanced processing, triggering Amazon SNS notifications, or even republishing the data as an MQTT message to IoT Core topics.

The capabilities of AWS IoT Rules allow developers to adeptly navigate and scrutinize vast IoT data reservoirs. They can derive valuable insights, respond to events in real time, and foster a harmonized and smart IoT ecosystem.

Setting Up an AWS IoT Rule

To harness the full potential of AWS IoT Rules, let's create a rule centered on the JSON MQTT messages received by the AWS IoT Core MQTT Broker.

From the AWS IoT Core console, navigate to the "*Manage*" section, then select (see Figure 3-16)

- Message routing
  - Rules
  - Click "*Create rule*".

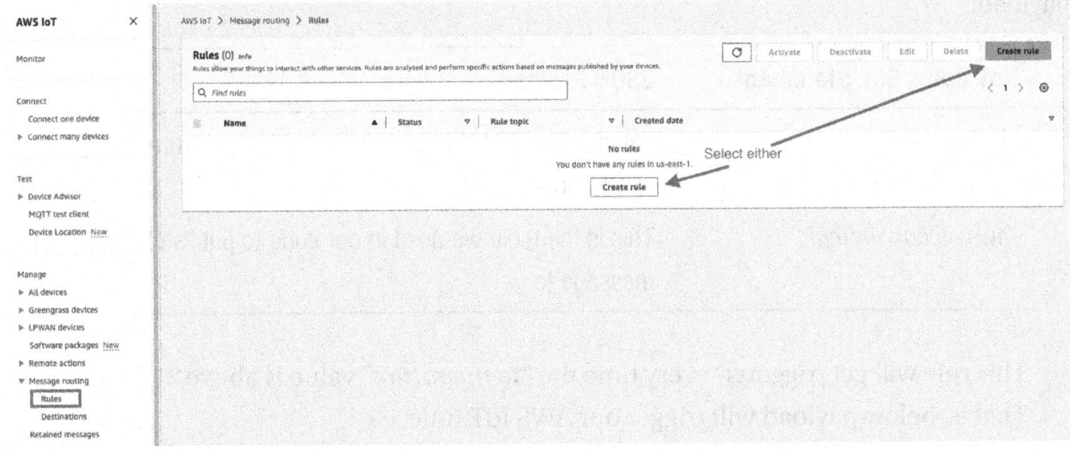

Figure 3-16. *Setting up an AWS IoT Rule*

Give the rule name such as "*myFirstIoTRule*" and description and click "*Next*" (see Figure 3-17).

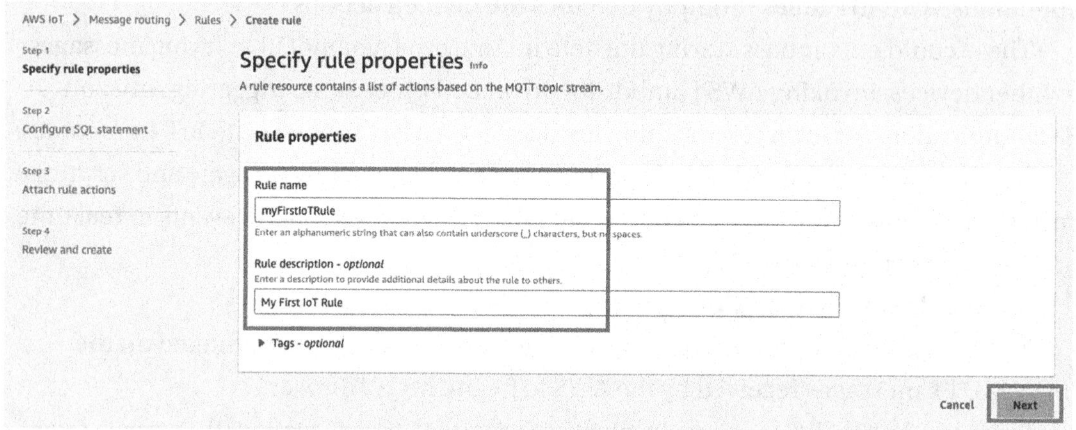

Figure 3-17. *Specifying rule properties*

Let's populate the SQL statement (see Figure 3-18):

```
SELECT value FROM 'awsiotbook/myTopic' Where value > 21
```

From the preceding statement, let's look at the corresponding section with our JSON payload.

IoT Rules SQL Statement	JSON Payload
value	Value from the JSON payload is the temperature value carrier
awsiotbook/myTopic	This is the topic we used in our code to publish the message to

This rule will get triggered every time the "*temperature*" value is above 21. That is, below payload will trigger our AWS IoT Rule.

```
{
  "sensor": "temperature",
  "value": 26.94,
  "timestamp": 1690149822
}
```

Populate and create the rule.

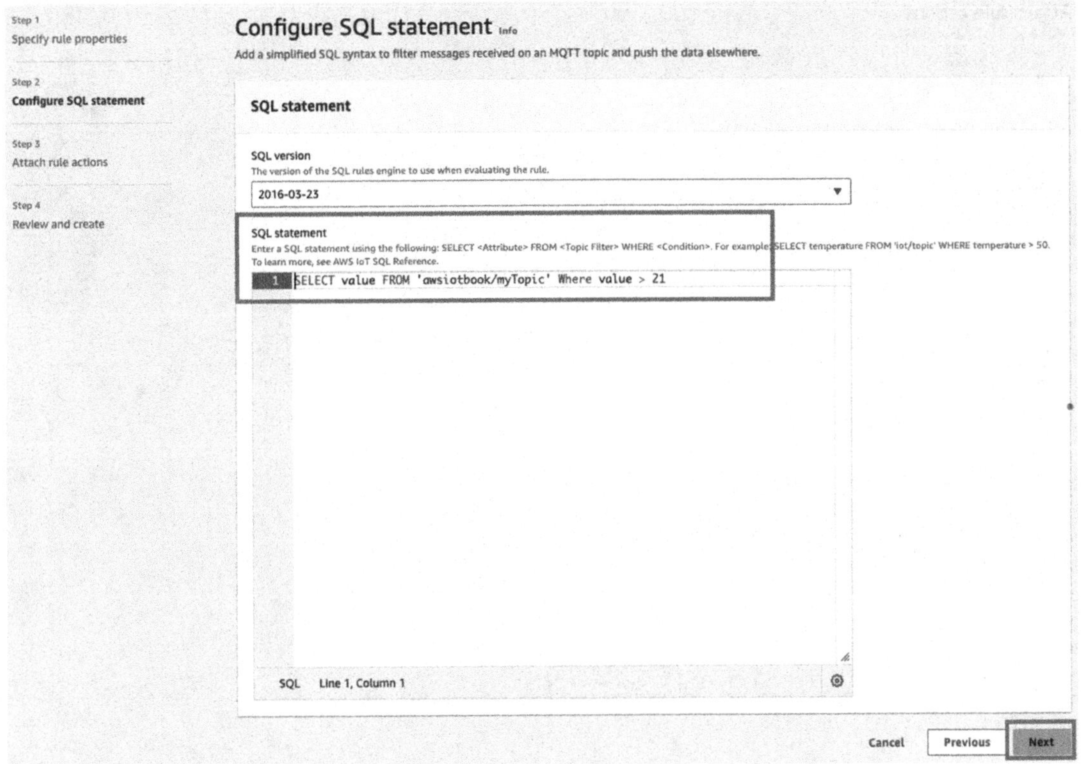

Figure 3-18. *SQL-like statement*

In the "*Attach rule actions*" screen (see Figure 3-19), populate as follows:

1. Select Action 1 to "*Republish to AWS IoT Topic*"
2. Select Topic to "*awsiotbook/republishTopic*"
3. Create a new role and name it as "*IOTRulesIAM*"
4. Click "*Next*"

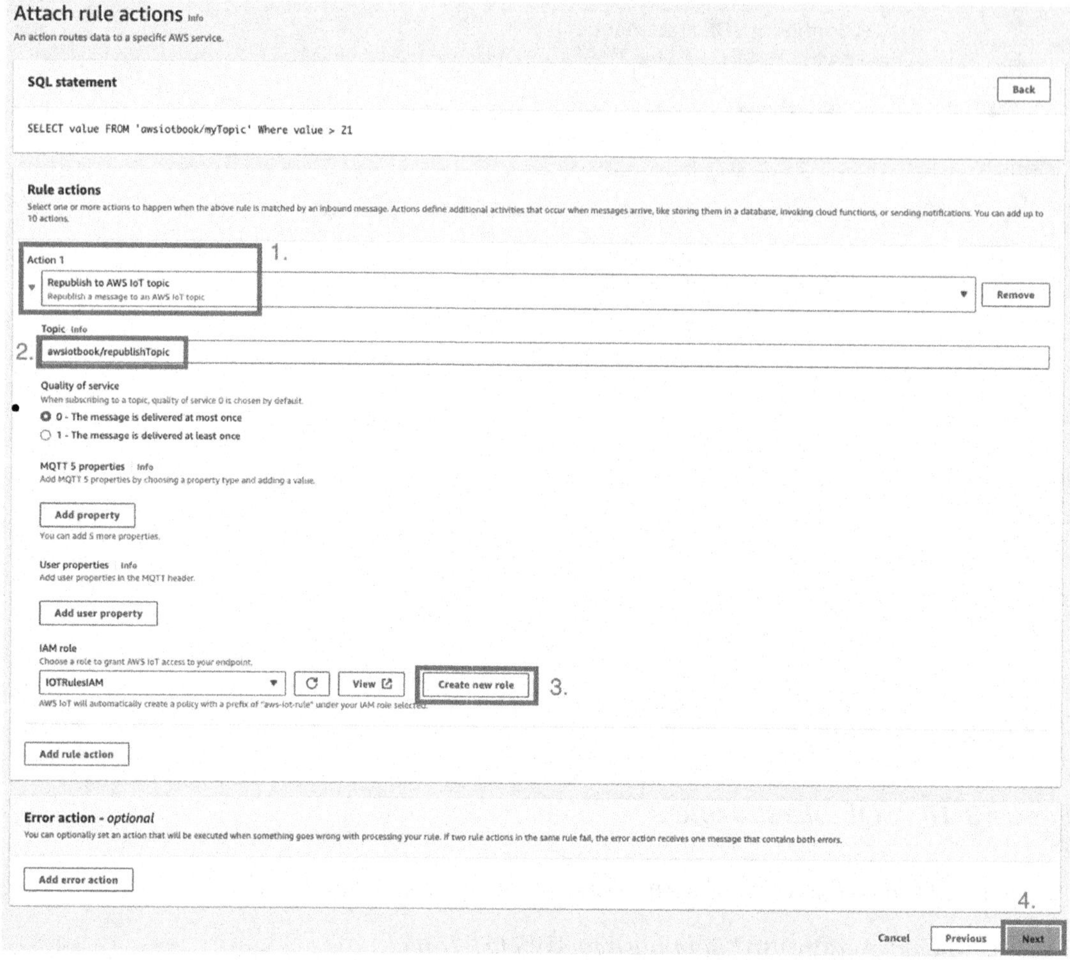

Figure 3-19. *Rule actions*

At the "*Review and Create*" screen, select "*Create*" and complete the creation of the rule.

Go Test section on the AWS IoT Core console and onto the "*MQTT Test client screen*" and subscribe to the topic "*awsiotbook/republishTopic*"

Run our Python code tested above (*either will work in Cloud9 environment or Raspberry Pi*)

Subscribe to a topic | Publish to a topic

Topic filter Info
The topic filter describes the topic(s) to which you want to subscribe. The topic filter can include MQTT wildcard characters.
awsiotbook/republishTopic
▶ Additional configuration
Subscribe

Subscriptions | awsiotbook/myTopic | Pause | Clear | Export | Edit
awsiotbook/myTopic
awsiotbook/republishTopic
▼ awsiotbook/myTopic — July 23, 2023, 23:36:59 (UTC+0100)

```
{
  "sensor": "temperature",
  "value": 28.56,
  "timestamp": 1690151819
}
```

▶ Properties

Figure 3-20. *Payload triggering rule*

We can see every MQTT payload arriving at AWS IoT Core which has a "*temperature*" value above 21c will trigger our AWS IoT Rule (see Figure 3-20), and we can see its republishing the extracted value into our topic "*awsiotbook/republishTopic*" (see Figure 3-21).

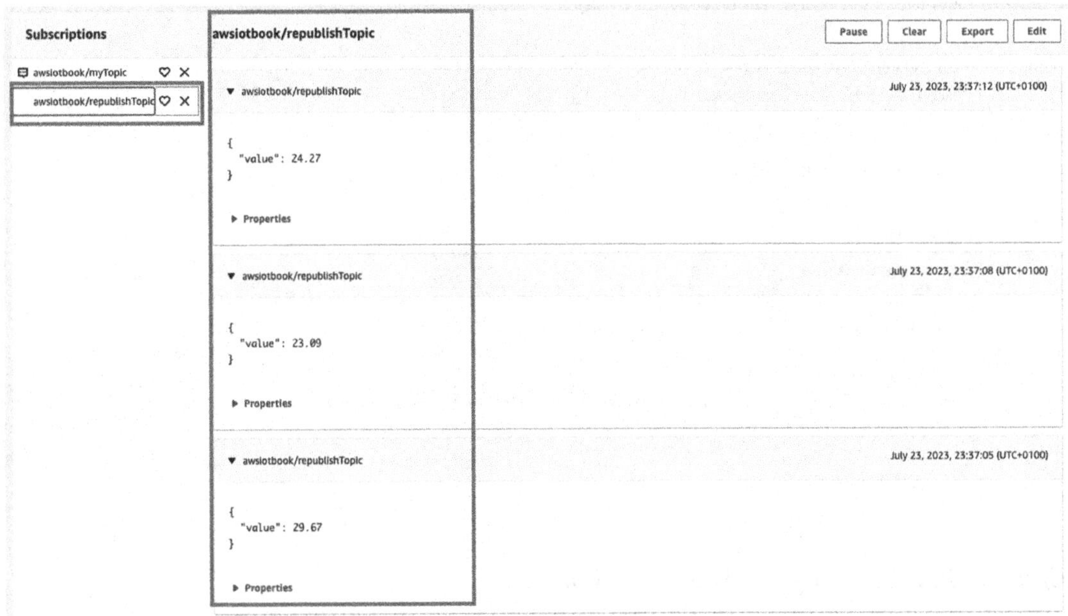

Figure 3-21. *Rule republishing the payload (confirming success)*

With this, we can carry out many other actions and fan out to many AWS services based on JSON payload arriving at AWS IoT Core.

AWS IoT Rules Actions for Data Lakes

Let's use our earlier created rule and modify it to send to the Amazon S3 bucket for data lake purposes.

Create an Amazon S3 Bucket

If you have an S3 bucket which is your data lake that you can use, you don't need to re-create a new bucket.

If you need to create, do the following:

From the AWS Console, go to the Amazon S3 console and create a bucket named "*myiotrulebucket*" and create it in the "*US East*" region by keeping everything as default. You will need to give a unique name as S3 buckets are globally unique names (one option is to use your date and time as suffix for bucket name) (see Figure 3-22).

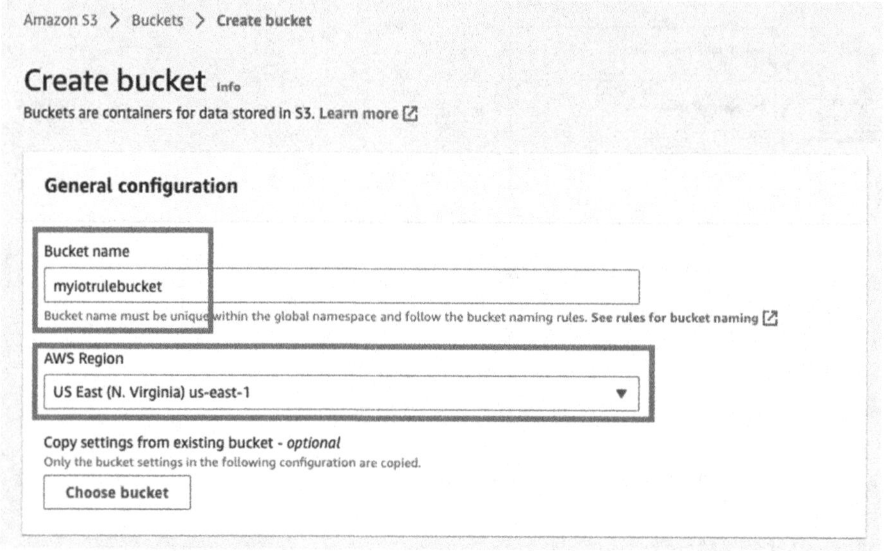

Figure 3-22. *Creating an Amazon S3 bucket*

Once created, go ahead and modify our existing *"myFirstIoTRule"* (see Figure 3-23).

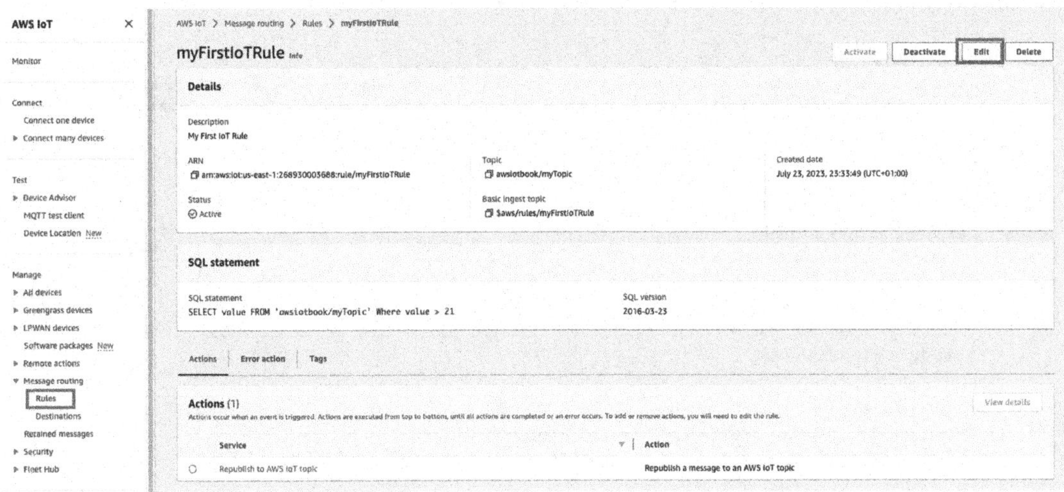

Figure 3-23. *Editing an existing rule*

Click "*Add rule action*" and "*Add error action*" (see Figure 3-24).

Rule actions

Select one or more actions to happen when the above rule is matched by an inbound message. Actions define additional activities that occur when messages arrive, like storing them in a database, invoking cloud functions, or sending notifications. You can add up to 10 actions.

Action 1

Republish to AWS IoT topic
Republish a message to an AWS IoT topic

Remove

Topic Info

awsiotbook/republishTopic

Quality of service
When subscribing to a topic, quality of service 0 is chosen by default.

0 - The message is delivered at most once

1 - The message is delivered at least once

MQTT 5 properties Info
Add MQTT 5 properties by choosing a property type and adding a value.

Add property
You can add 5 more properties.

User properties Info
Add user properties in the MQTT header.

Add user property

IAM role
Choose a role to grant AWS IoT access to your endpoint.

IOTRulesIAM

View

Create new role

AWS IoT will automatically create a policy with a prefix of "aws-iot-rule" under your IAM role selected.

Add rule action 1.

Error action - *optional*

You can optionally set an action that will be executed when something goes wrong with processing your rule. If two rule actions in the same rule fail, the error action receives one message that contains both errors.

Add error action 2.

3.

Cancel Update

Figure 3-24. *Adding more actions to an existing rule*

For Action 2, populate as follows:

1. Select *S3 bucket for Action*
2. Select our bucket "*myiotrulebucket*" by selecting "*Browse S3*"
3. In the Key section, use "*${topic(1)}/${topic(2)}/${timestamp()}.json*"
4. Select our earlier created IAM Rule "*IOTRulesIAM*"

By selecting Key as "*${topic(1)}/${topic(2)}/${timestamp()}.json*", we can auto-create an S3 folder structure and save our timestamped JSON files in there (see Figure 3-25).

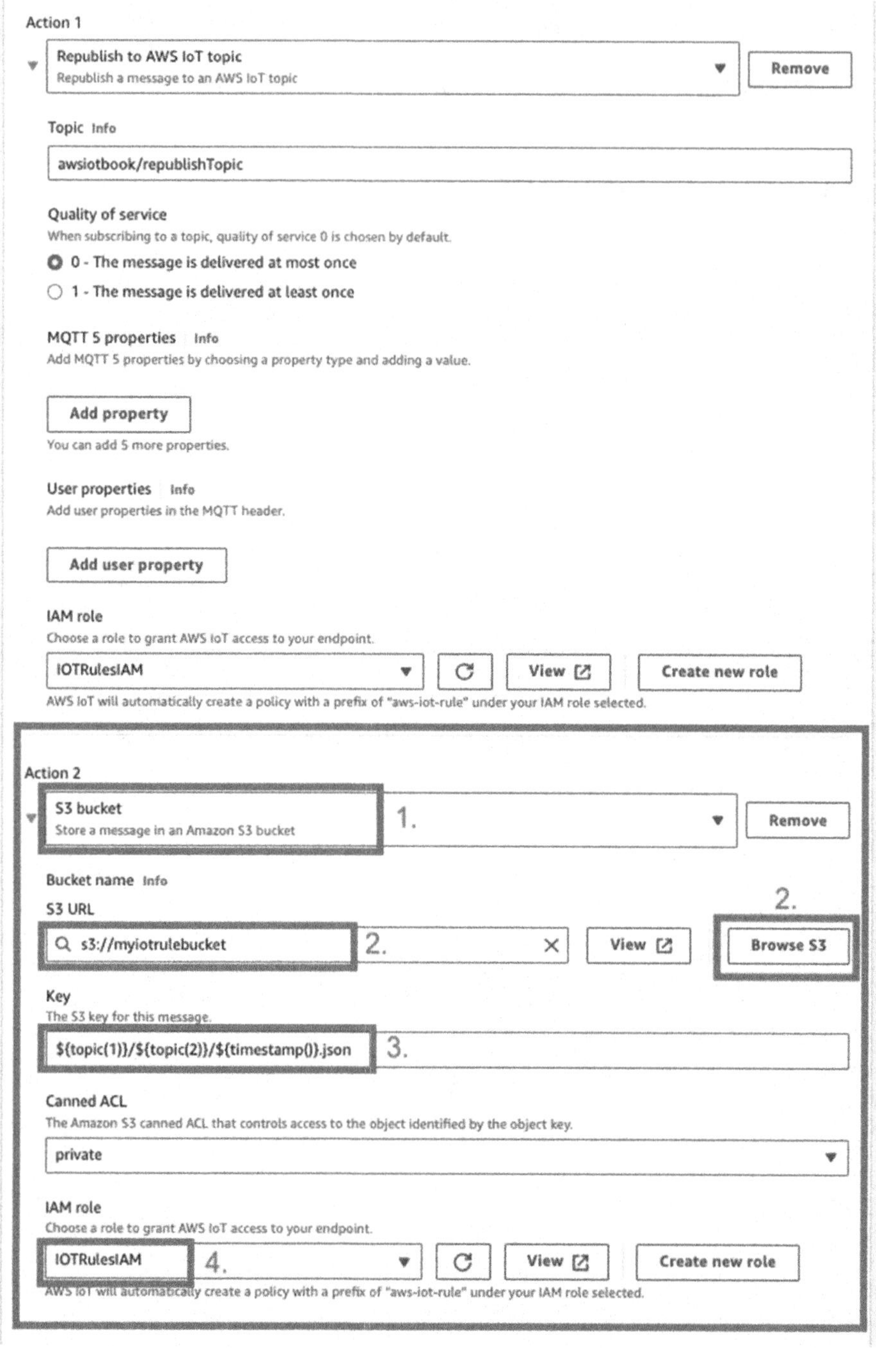

***Figure 3-25.** JSON file saving structure*

For Error action, let's set up as follows (see Figure 3-26):

1. For Action, select "*Republish to AWS IoT Topic*"
2. For Topic, use "*awsiotbook/failed*"
3. Select our earlier created IAM Rule "*IOTRulesIAM*"
4. Click "*Update*"

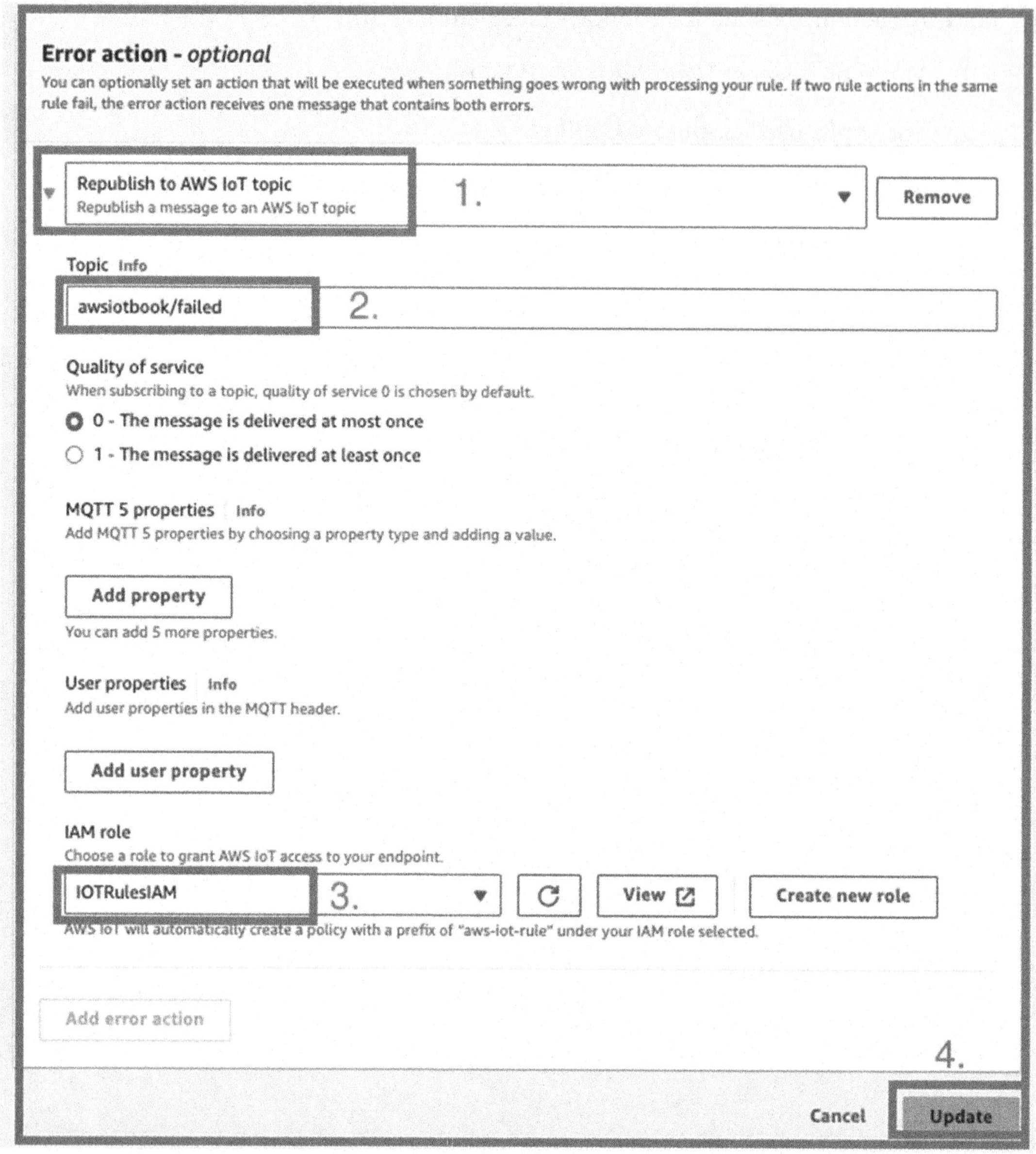

***Figure 3-26.** Adding error actions for fail safe*

Let's relaunch our Python script to trigger the actions:

```
python3 myFirstIoTDevice.py
```

Verifying Amazon S3 Bucket Content

To ensure that our setup is working as expected, navigate to the Amazon S3 console and inspect the "*myiotrulebucket*" (or the name you used). Examine the folder structure and verify that the files have been written correctly. If everything is set up correctly, you should see the desired folders and files reflecting the data sent from your IoT devices.

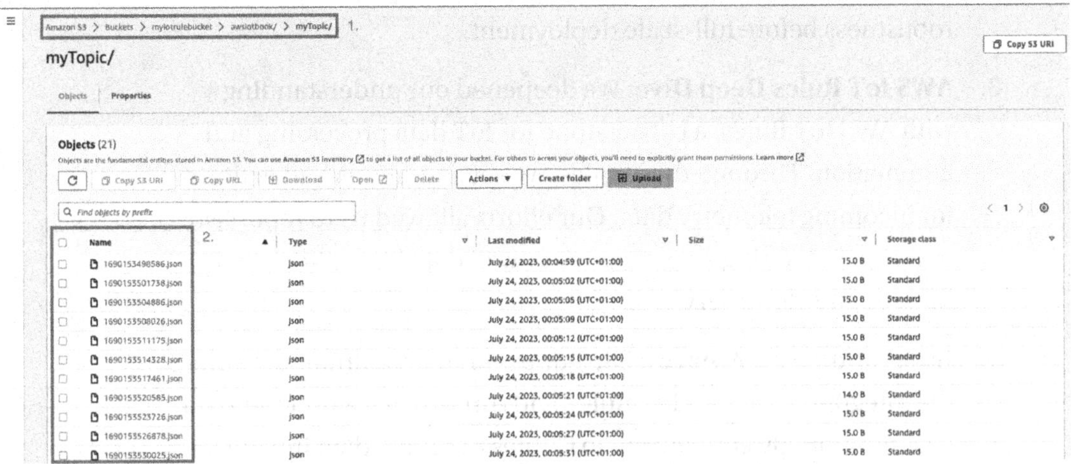

Figure 3-27. *Amazon S3 saving our JSON payload*

We can see from our Amazon S3 bucket that (1) folder structure is getting written as expected based on our topic "*awsiotbook/myTopic*" and (2) files are written with timestamped JSON extension as expected (see Figure 3-27).

What You Have Learned

1. **AWS IoT Thing Setup:** Our exploration began with the AWS IoT thing, where we grasped the nuances of registering, provisioning, and securely connecting IoT devices to AWS IoT Core. By provisioning devices with unique certificates and policies, we established a foundation for secure message publishing and streamlined communication.

2. **Virtual Environment Interactions:** Utilizing the AWS IoT Python SDK, we simulated IoT devices in a virtual environment. This enabled us to generate test data and publish messages to AWS IoT Core via MQTT. Such a simulation offers a versatile platform for testing and validating IoT application workflows, ensuring robustness before full-scale deployment.

3. **AWS IoT Rules Deep Dive:** We deepened our understanding with AWS IoT Rules, a cornerstone for IoT data processing and automation. Through these rules, we set conditions and actions for incoming telemetry data. Our efforts allowed us to republish messages, ensuring a continuous flow of data between virtual devices and cloud services.

4. **Integration with Amazon S3:** Our exploration culminated with the integration of AWS IoT Rules and Amazon S3, a premier data lake solution. By configuring IoT Rules to funnel data into an S3 bucket, we paved the way for advanced data storage and analytics, positioning ourselves for comprehensive data-driven initiatives.

Summary

Throughout our exploration of AWS IoT, we delved deeply into its vast array of features and functionalities. We learned the intricacies of registering and securely connecting IoT devices to AWS IoT Core, ensuring a foundation for secure and efficient communication. By harnessing the AWS IoT Python SDK, we simulated device interactions, providing a practical platform for building a Minimum Viable Product. Our focus then shifted to AWS IoT Rules, enabling us to set data processing conditions and ensuring seamless data flow from virtual simulated devices into AWS cloud services. The culmination of our journey was the seamless integration of AWS IoT with Amazon S3, ushering in opportunities for advanced data storage and analytics. As we concluded this chapter, we emerged with a comprehensive understanding of AWS IoT's offerings, ready to craft, deploy, and enhance IoT solutions within the AWS cloud ecosystem.

CHAPTER 4

Digital Twin with AWS IoT Device Shadow and Basic Ingest Routing

In the world of IoT, the concept of a "digital twin" has emerged as a revolutionary approach to virtually represent physical devices and assets. In this chapter, we delve into the fascinating realm of digital twin technology, exploring its practical implementation using AWS IoT Device Shadow. By leveraging AWS IoT Device Shadow, we can establish a bidirectional communication channel between the physical devices and their digital representations in the cloud, enabling seamless control and monitoring capabilities.

The essence of a digital twin lies in its ability to mirror physical devices in a virtual environment. At the heart of this concept is AWS IoT Device Shadow, a service that captures telemetry data from physical entities and replicates it onto their cloud-based digital counterparts. This virtual representation, or "shadow," retains crucial attributes, states, and configurations of the actual device, ensuring real-time synchronization between the two.

As previously discussed in Chapter 3, AWS IoT Rules are pivotal in routing data within the AWS IoT domain. They enable dynamic transfer of telemetry data from device shadows to AWS services, facilitating real-time analytics, storage, and processing. This equips businesses with the flexibility to extract deep insights into device dynamics and operations.

The state of a device, which could range from temperature readings to location data, offers a real-time snapshot of its status. Harnessing these states paves the way for enhanced device monitoring, operational optimization, and even preemptive issue detection.

S. Rehan, *AWS IoT With Edge ML and Cybersecurity*, https://doi.org/10.1007/979-8-8688-0011-5_4

In this exploration, we'll unravel the nuances of various device states - from the "*reported*" to the "*desired*" - and their roles in intertwining the tangible and virtual domains. Grasping these distinctions is pivotal in maximizing the advantages of digital twin technology.

Moreover, we'll touch upon AWS IoT Device Management's suite of features. This suite presents a robust toolkit to simplify IoT device handling at scale, covering facets from device onboarding to software updates and security.

This chapter's focus will be on the intricacies of digital twins, AWS IoT Device Shadow, and AWS IoT Device Management. It's worth noting that while digital twins offer a comprehensive visualization capability, this chapter won't delve into that aspect. Instead, our aim is to arm readers with insights into constructing efficient IoT solutions that seamlessly merge the physical and digital realms, unlocking avenues for innovation and operational excellence.

Harnessing Basic Ingest with AWS IoT Rules for Data Routing

In our last chapter, we delved into the realm of data ingestion, examining diverse strategies to effectively channel data into our environment. Central to our exploration was the use of Amazon S3 as a dynamic data lake. This powerful AWS service gave us a unified platform to store copious amounts of varied data in a scalable, economical fashion.

Now, as we progress, our attention turns to the utility of Basic Ingest within the AWS IoT services. The beauty of Basic Ingest lies in its straightforwardness and efficiency. In this chapter, we'll uncover how this approach not only enhances our data-handling prowess but also optimizes associated costs. By simplifying the data ingestion trajectory and tapping into AWS IoT's inherent capabilities, we position ourselves to manage and react to data streams more effectively.

Understanding Basic Ingest in AWS IoT

AWS IoT Basic Ingest is a specialized feature within AWS IoT Core, designed to transmit device data to various AWS services without the associated messaging costs. If you're considering leveraging Basic Ingest, it's essential to keep the following key aspects in mind:

- **Cost Efficiency:** With Basic Ingest, the costs are primarily tied to rule actions and the triggering of these rules. Notably, messages relayed to AWS IoT Core's reserved topics under Basic Ingest don't incur the standard messaging fees (as of the time of writing).
- **Subscription Limitations:** Devices and rules cannot subscribe to Basic Ingests reserved topics.
- **Broker Distribution:** When your setup necessitates a publish/subscribe broker to distribute messages to various endpoints (like dispatching to different devices or the rules engine), it's recommended to leverage AWS IoT's primary message broker. This involves publishing messages on custom topics, separate from the ones used by Basic Ingest.
- **Inactive Rule Handling:** Should you transmit a message to a Basic Ingest topic linked to a nonexistent or inactive rule, AWS will log a "*RuleNotFound*" metric in Amazon CloudWatch, aiding in troubleshooting.
- **Quality of Service (QoS) Level:** When publishing to a Basic Ingest topic with QoS level 1, a PUBACK acknowledgment confirms successful message delivery. However, this doesn't guarantee the successful execution of the associated rule - only that the message reaches its destination.
- **Policy Permissions:** Ensure that your device policy permits publishing actions.

For our hands-on example from the previous chapter involving the "*$aws/rules/myFirstIoTRule*" topic: if you've been following along, our IoT thing's policy (dubbed "*myFirstDemoNonProductionPolicy*") was set to allow all actions and resources, simplifying our learning process (not to be used in the production environment). However, in a live production environment, it's crucial to configure your policies to restrict publishing permissions, granting access exclusively to your designated AWS IoT Rule.

Let's modify our AWS IoT Rule which we created in Chapter 3 for Basic Ingest purposes (see Figure 4-1).

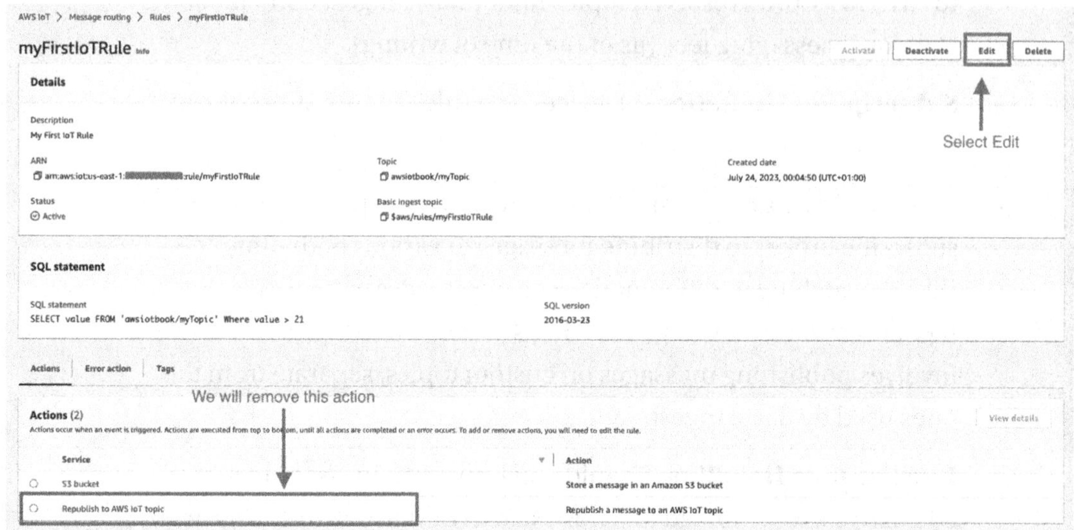

Figure 4-1. *Editing the AWS IoT Rule*

We will remove the republish action, and we will keep the Amazon S3 bucket publish action (see Figure 4-2).

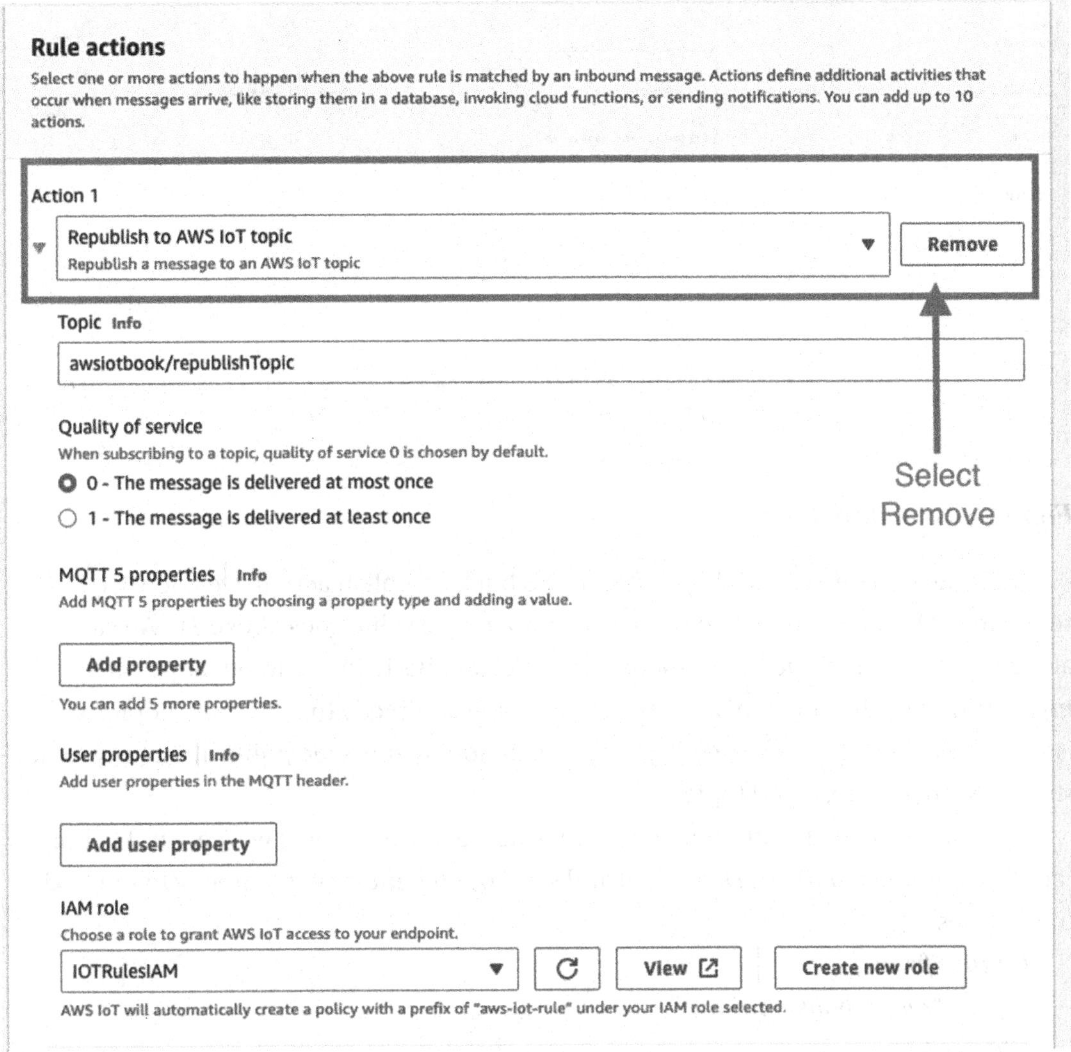

Figure 4-2. *Removing the republish action*

Once done, select "*Update*", leaving the rest of the options as before.

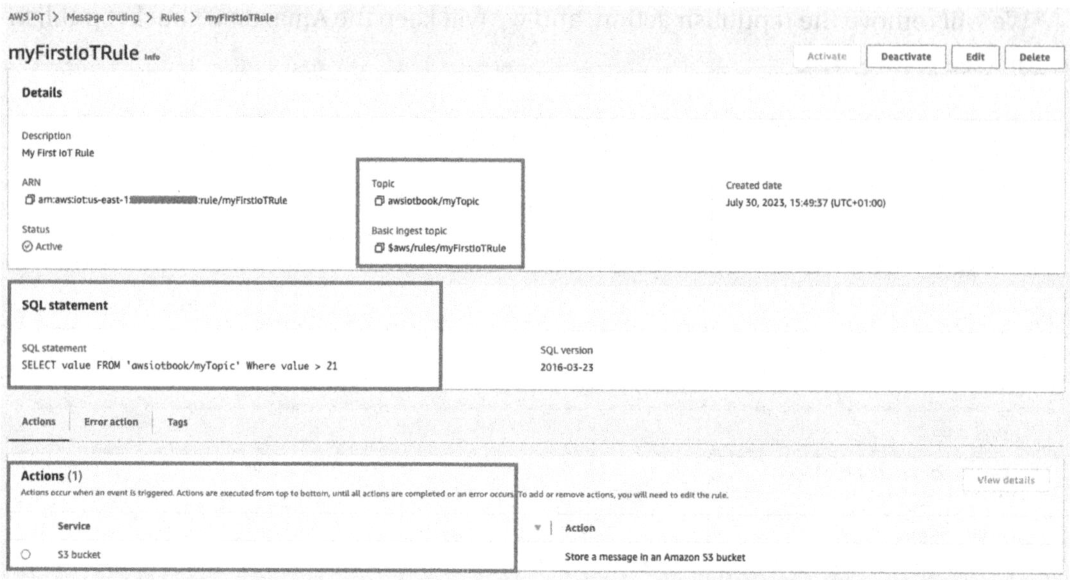

***Figure 4-3.** Rule details*

After the update, we should just see the S3 bucket publish action; we know we set up the SQL statement to run when the temperature value goes above 21. We can also see our custom topic (*awsiotbook/myTopic*) and Basic Ingest topic (*$aws/rules/myFirstIoTRule*). By doing this, we are able to publish directly to our "*rules*" topic, which is a reserved topic; this removes any cost association on message publication (any topic starting with *$* is a reserved topic).

We now just need to alter our code from Chapter 3 which topic we were publishing to (applies to both: *myFirstIoTDevice.py*) and send our telemetry data directly to the Basic Ingest rules topic.

*Change **from***

topic = "*awsiotbook/myTopic*"

*Change **to***

topic = "*$aws/rules/myFirstIoTRule/awsiotbook/myTopic*"

In this scenario, "*$aws/rules/myFirstIoTRule*" represents the Basic Ingest topic for the rule in question. However, to execute this rule, it's necessary to specify the complete topic name in conjunction with the Basic Ingest topic (see Figure 4-3). The reason we add the full topic name is primarily to determine the path in Amazon S3, but it's important to note that the rule's trigger is solely based on the Basic Ingest. When data is published to the modified reserved topic "*$aws/rules/myFirstIoTRule/awsiotbook/myTopic*", any instance where the temperature exceeds 21 will result in a payload being published to our Amazon S3 data lake in JSON format (as depicted in Figure 4-4).

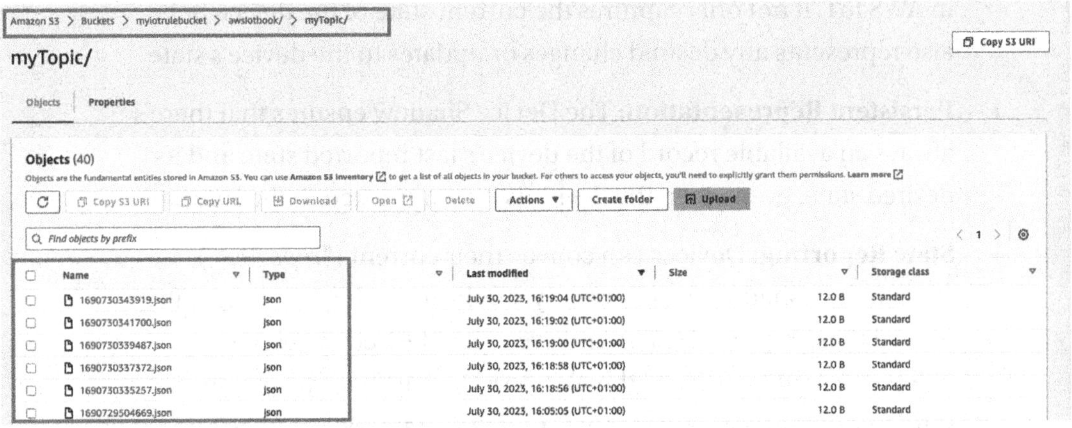

Figure 4-4. *JSON payload saving in Amazon S3 bucket*

By adopting this method, we bypass messaging costs when activating the rule without publishing to our custom topic. However, while we save on messaging costs, there are still nominal charges associated with the initiation and actions of the rule.

Digital Twin Using Device Shadow

Let's now explore AWS IoT Device Shadow to create digital twins. Bridging physical and virtual realms, this technology synchronizes real-world devices with cloud-based replicas. Unlocking remote monitoring, control, and predictive analytics, we delve into the power of device shadows for seamless communication and intelligent decision-making. Discover the transformative potential of digital twins with AWS IoT Device Shadow.

Understanding AWS IoT Device Shadow and Its States

AWS IoT Device Shadow, commonly referred to as "*Shadow*," is an integral feature of AWS IoT Core. This service facilitates the seamless and secure interaction of connected devices with cloud applications and other devices, regardless of the device's connectivity status.

Key components of AWS IoT Device Shadow

- **Shadow Document:** This JSON document serves as the repository for the current and desired state information of a device (or "thing") in AWS IoT. It not only captures the current state of the device but also represents any desired changes or updates to the device's state.
- **Persistent Representation:** The Device Shadow ensures that there's always an available record of the device's last reported state and its desired state, even when the device is not connected to the Internet.
- **State Reporting:** Devices can convey their current (*"reported"*) state to their shadow. Concurrently, applications have the capability to read these reported states and prescribe desired states. One of the standout features of the AWS IoT Device Shadow service is its automatic management of the *"delta"* state. When there's a discrepancy between the *"desired"* and *"reported"* states, AWS IoT determines the *"delta"* or difference.
- **State Synchronization:** The Device Shadow service can discern any mismatch between a device's *"desired"* and *"reported"* states. In situations where there's an inconsistency, AWS IoT can dispatch a message directing the device toward the desired state, provided the device is online. Alternatively, applications can monitor these state transitions and adapt accordingly.
- **Offline Functionality:** A cornerstone feature of the Device Shadow is its ability to function even during device connectivity lapses. Applications can still retrieve the device's last known state and propose state alterations. Upon re-establishing connectivity, the device can reconcile its state with that of its shadow.

Significance of AWS IoT Device Shadow

Device Shadow plays a pivotal role in enhancing the resilience, scalability, and reliability of IoT applications. It proves particularly invaluable when devices grapple with sporadic Internet connectivity, ensuring uninterrupted state tracking and management.

Let's create an AWS IoT thing and name it *"shadowUpdateThing"*.

From IoT Core Console (see Figure 4-5):

- Under the "*Manage*" section, select "*All devices*"
  - Things
    - Create things
      - Select Create single thing
        - Thing name: "*ShadowUpdateThing*"
      - Select Named shadow
        - Give a name: "*testShadow*"
- For the device certificate, use "*Auto-generate a new certificate (recommended)*". Select "*Next*". For policy, select "*myFirstDemoNonProductionPolicy*" and then select "*Create thing*". **Before** selecting "*Done*", make sure to download the device certificate, key files, and Amazon Root CA 1 as we did in an earlier chapter.

Edit the shadow statement with the following:

```
{
  "state": {
    "reported": {
      "temperature": 0
    },
    "desired": {
      "temperature": 21
    }
  }
}
```

This Device Shadow document contains the *reported, desired,* and *delta* values of the device's state. You can edit the state values here or programmatically. This is where our device (*thing*) will sync its state while it's connected to AWS IoT.

Once we have created/updated these, select *Next.*

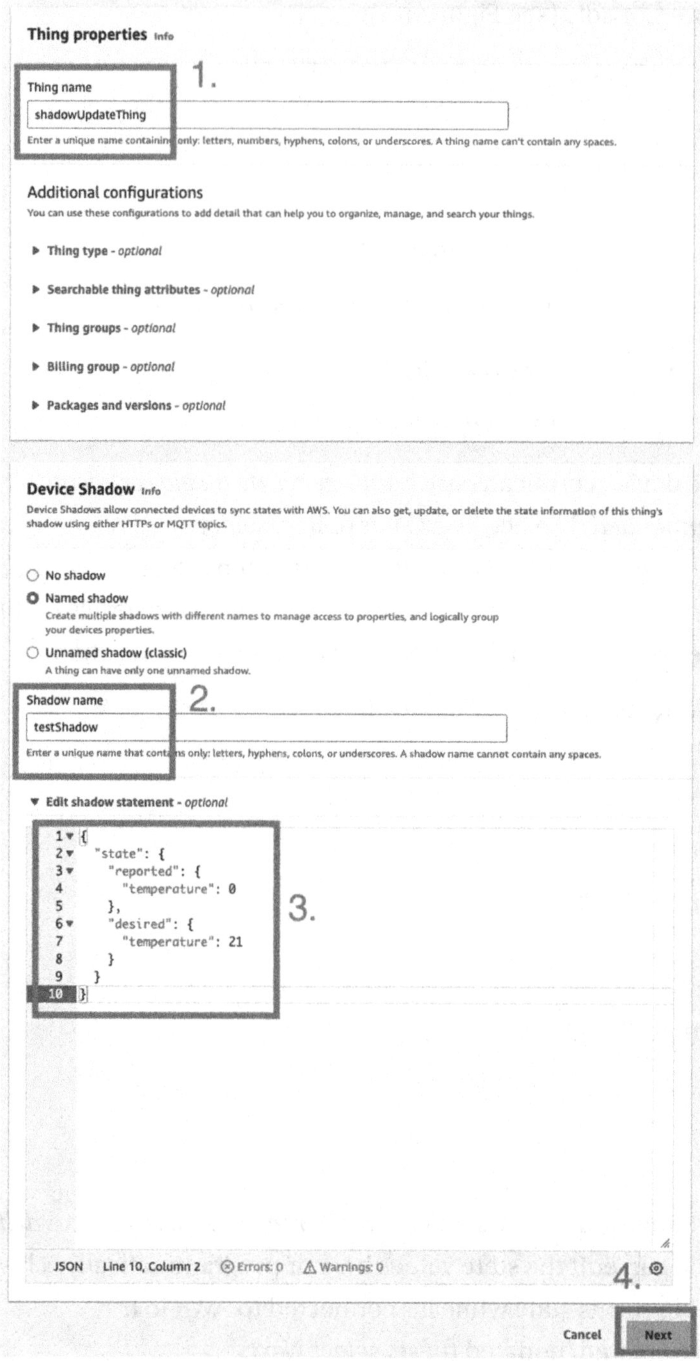

Figure 4-5. *Updating shadow statement*

After obtaining the necessary keys and certificates, we can proceed to place them in the appropriate directory (i.e., */home/ubuntu/shadowUpdateThing/certs/*). The process remains consistent regardless of whether you are using a virtual device or any other method, as described in the previous chapter.

Execute the following command to create the required folder and file:

```
mkdir -p /home/ubuntu/shadowUpdateThing/certs/
touch /home/ubuntu/shadowUpdateThing/shadowUpdate.py
```

If you've already executed the command earlier, simply populate the "*shadowUpdate.py*" file, located in "*/home/ubuntu/shadowUpdateThing/*", with the following content or obtained from the book's GitHub repository (*modify REPLACE_HERE with correct values*). The code for this file can be retrieved from the GitHub repository corresponding to Chapter 4 of the book.

```
# FileName: shadowUpdate.py

import asyncio
import json
import time

from awscrt import auth, http, io, mqtt
from awsiot import mqtt_connection_builder

# Callback when connection is accidentally lost.
Def on_connection_interrupted(connection, error, **kwargs):
    print(f"Connection interrupted. Error: {error}")

# Callback when an interrupted connection is re-established.
Def on_connection_resumed(connection, return_code, session_present,
**kwargs):
    print(
        f"Connection resumed. Return_code: {return_code} session_present:
        {session_present}"
    )

# Callback when the subscribed message is received.
Def on_message_received(topic, payload, dup, qos, retain, **kwargs):
    print(f"Received message from topic '{topic}': {payload}")
    print("--------------")
```

```
async def get_and_update_shadow():
    #### Replace start
    endpoint = "REPLACE_HERE"  # Replace with your AWS IoT Core endpoint
    cert_filepath = "REPLACE_HERE-path/to/certificate.pem.crt"  # Replace
    with the path to your device certificate
    pri_key_filepath = "REPLACE_HERE-path/to/private/private-key.pem.
    key"  # Replace with the path to your private key
    ca_filepath = "REPLACE_HERE-path/to/root/ca.pem"  # Replace with the
    path to your root CA certificate

    client_id = "shadowUpdateThing"  # Replace if different
    thing_name = "shadowUpdateThing"  # Replace if different
    shadow_name = "testShadow"  # Replace if different
    ####Replace End

    # Initiate MQTT connection
    event_loop_group = io.EventLoopGroup(1)
    host_resolver = io.DefaultHostResolver(event_loop_group)
    client_bootstrap = io.ClientBootstrap(event_loop_group, host_resolver)

    mqtt_connection = mqtt_connection_builder.mtls_from_path(
        endpoint=endpoint,
        cert_filepath=cert_filepath,
        pri_key_filepath=pri_key_filepath,
        client_bootstrap=client_bootstrap,
        ca_filepath=ca_filepath,
        on_connection_interrupted=on_connection_interrupted,
        on_connection_resumed=on_connection_resumed,
        client_id=client_id,
        clean_session=False,
        keep_alive_secs=6,
    )

    print(f"Connecting to {endpoint} with client ID '{client_id}'…")
    connect_future = mqtt_connection.connect()
    while not connect_future.done():
        time.sleep(0.1)
    print("Connected!")
```

```
# First, let's get the current shadow state.
Print(

    f"Subscribing to topic $aws/things/{thing_name}/shadow/name/
    {shadow_name}/get/accepted..."
)
subscribe_future, packet_id = mqtt_connection.subscribe(
    topic=f"$aws/things/{thing_name}/shadow/name/{shadow_name}/get/
    accepted",
    qos=mqtt.QoS.AT_LEAST_ONCE,
    callback=on_message_received,
)

while not subscribe_future.done():
    time.sleep(0.1)
print("Subscribed.")

# Now that we're subscribed, let's send a get request.
Print(
    f"Publishing get request to $aws/things/{thing_name}/shadow/name/
    {shadow_name}/get..."
)
mqtt_connection.publish(
    topic=f"$aws/things/{thing_name}/shadow/name/{shadow_name}/get",
    payload=json.dumps({}),
    qos=mqtt.QoS.AT_LEAST_ONCE,
)

# Wait for a few seconds to receive the response
await asyncio.sleep(3)

# Now let's update the shadow
message = {
    "state": {"desired": {"temperature": 22}}  # Replace this for
    your testing
}
print(
```

```
            f"Publishing update to $aws/things/{thing_name}/shadow/name/
            {shadow_name}/update..."
        )
        mqtt_connection.publish(
            topic=f"$aws/things/{thing_name}/shadow/name/{shadow_name}/update",
            payload=json.dumps(message),
            qos=mqtt.QoS.AT_LEAST_ONCE,
        )

        # Disconnect
        print("Disconnecting...")
        disconnect_future = mqtt_connection.disconnect()
        while not disconnect_future.done():
            time.sleep(0.1)
        print("Disconnected")

# Run the script
loop = asyncio.get_event_loop()
loop.run_until_complete(get_and_update_shadow())
```

Let's see what is the preceding code actually doing.

The script "*shadowUpdate.py*" is designed to interact with the AWS IoT Device Shadow service for our "*shadowUpdateThing*" IoT device.

1. **Establishing Connection:** The script initiates a connection to the AWS IoT Core using MQTT with provided credentials, which include the endpoint, certificate, private key, and root CA.

2. **Fetching the Current Shadow State:** Once connected, the script subscribes to a topic that provides the current state of the device's shadow. It then sends a request to retrieve this state.

3. **Updating the Desired State:** After retrieving the current shadow state, the script updates the "desired" state for the device's temperature to 22°C.

4. **Simulating the Reported State:** After a brief pause (simulating some delay like the device processing time), the script updates the "reported" state of the device to match the previously set desired temperature (22°C in this case).

5. **Disconnection:** Finally, the script disconnects from the AWS IoT Core.

Throughout this process, any incoming messages related to the Device Shadow are printed to the console, providing feedback on the script's actions.

Before we run this code, let's get our self-setup on the AWS IoT Core console and see reserved topics where Shadow states can be viewed.

From the AWS IoT Core console, under "*Manage*", select "*All devices*" and then

- Select "*Things*"
    - Select "*shadowUpdateThing*"
        - Select the "*Device Shadows*" tab
            - Lastly select our "*testShadow*" (see Figure 4-6)

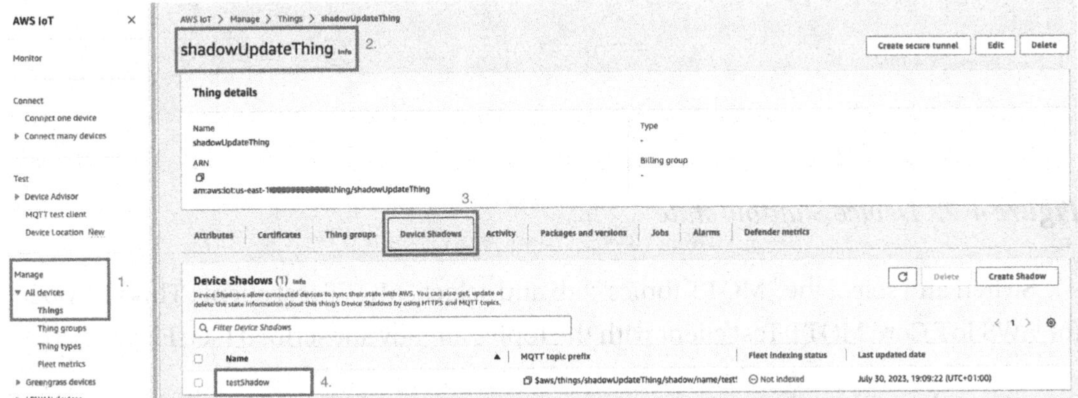

***Figure 4-6.** Device shadow*

In our "*testShadow*", let's have a look at the Device Shadow state; when we run our code shown previously, we should have these values updated (see Figure 4-7).

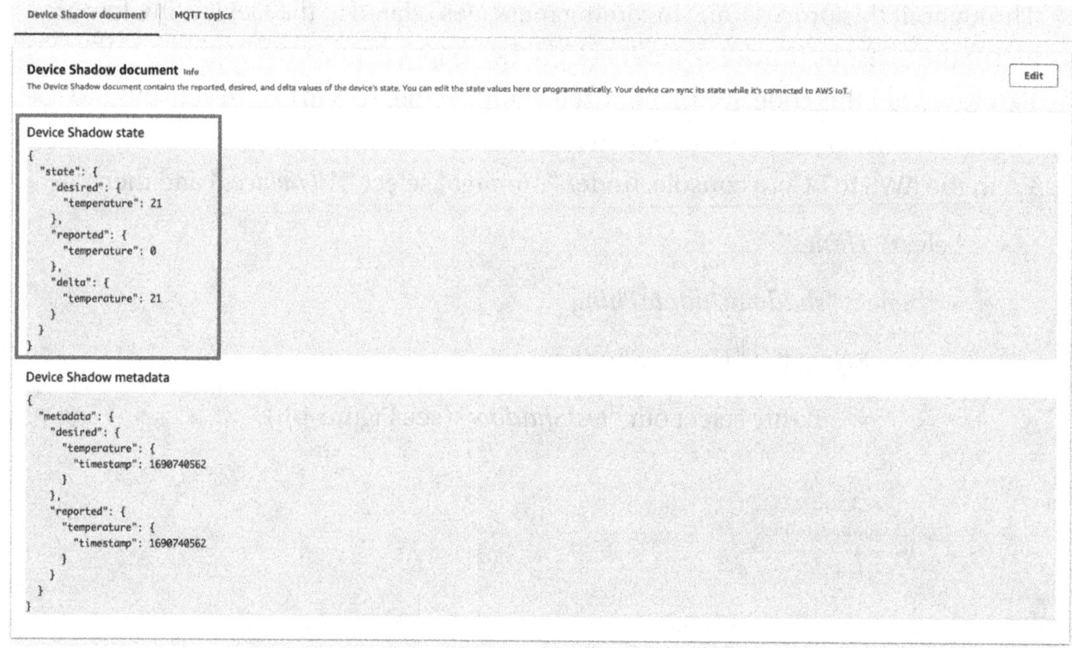

Figure 4-7. *Device Shadow state*

Switch and select the "MQTT topics" tab and select "MQTT test client". This will open the AWS IoT Core MQTT Test client with the topics already subscribed (see Figure 4-8).

Device Shadow document | MQTT topics 1.

MQTT topics Info

MQTT topics for this Device Shadow allow applications to publish and subscribe to MQTT messages that interact with this thing's Device Shadow.

2. MQTT test client

Name	Action	MQTT topic
/get	Publish	$aws/things/shadowUpdateThing/shadow/name/testShadow/get
/get/accepted	Subscribe	$aws/things/shadowUpdateThing/shadow/name/testShadow/get/accepted
/get/rejected	Subscribe	$aws/things/shadowUpdateThing/shadow/name/testShadow/get/rejected
/update	Publish	$aws/things/shadowUpdateThing/shadow/name/testShadow/update
/update/delta	Subscribe	$aws/things/shadowUpdateThing/shadow/name/testShadow/update/delta
/update/accepted	Subscribe	$aws/things/shadowUpdateThing/shadow/name/testShadow/update/accepted
/update/documents	Subscribe	$aws/things/shadowUpdateThing/shadow/name/testShadow/update/documents
/update/rejected	Subscribe	$aws/things/shadowUpdateThing/shadow/name/testShadow/update/rejected
/delete	Publish	$aws/things/shadowUpdateThing/shadow/name/testShadow/delete
/delete/accepted	Subscribe	$aws/things/shadowUpdateThing/shadow/name/testShadow/accepted
/delete/rejected	Subscribe	$aws/things/shadowUpdateThing/shadow/name/testShadow/rejected

Figure 4-8. *MQTT topics related to this shadow*

Here, we can see all our topics subscribed relevant to our shadow (see Figure 4-9).

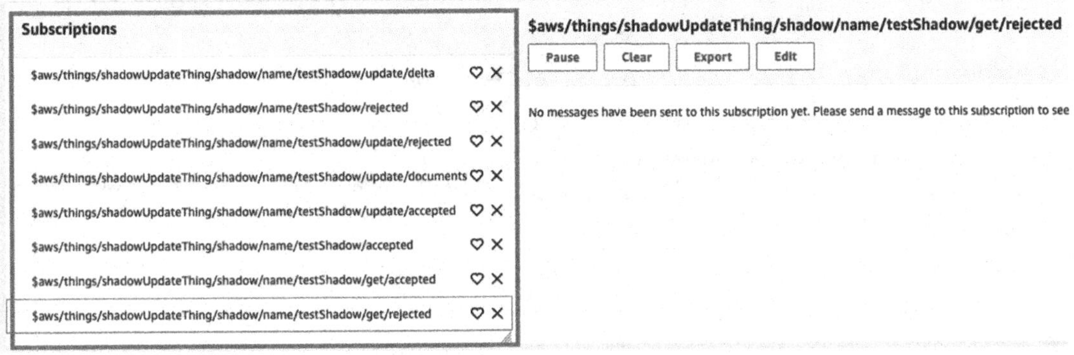

Subscriptions

$aws/things/shadowUpdateThing/shadow/name/testShadow/update/delta
$aws/things/shadowUpdateThing/shadow/name/testShadow/rejected
$aws/things/shadowUpdateThing/shadow/name/testShadow/update/rejected
$aws/things/shadowUpdateThing/shadow/name/testShadow/update/documents
$aws/things/shadowUpdateThing/shadow/name/testShadow/update/accepted
$aws/things/shadowUpdateThing/shadow/name/testShadow/accepted
$aws/things/shadowUpdateThing/shadow/name/testShadow/get/accepted
$aws/things/shadowUpdateThing/shadow/name/testShadow/get/rejected

$aws/things/shadowUpdateThing/shadow/name/testShadow/get/rejected

Pause Clear Export Edit

No messages have been sent to this subscription yet. Please send a message to this subscription to see

Figure 4-9. *Shadow topics subscribed*

Let's run our code using the following command:

```
cd /home/ubuntu/shadowUpdateThing/
python3 shadowUpdate.py
```

In the terminal window, we will see as following, status retrieved from AWS IoT Core and we sending the update.

```
Connected!
Subscribing to topic $aws/things/shadowUpdateThing/shadow/name/testShadow/get/accepted...
Subscribed.
Publishing get request to $aws/things/shadowUpdateThing/shadow/name/testShadow/get...
Received message from topic '$aws/things/shadowUpdateThing/shadow/name/testShadow/get/accepted':
":21}},"metadata":{"desired":{"temperature":{"timestamp":1690740562}},"reported":{"temperature":
---------------
Publishing update to $aws/things/shadowUpdateThing/shadow/name/testShadow/update...
Disconnecting...
Disconnected
```

Figure 4-10. *Shadow updates*

In our MQTT test client, we can see our reserved topics being updated as updates come through; first one, we can see when the shadow is "*accepted*" (see Figure 4-11).

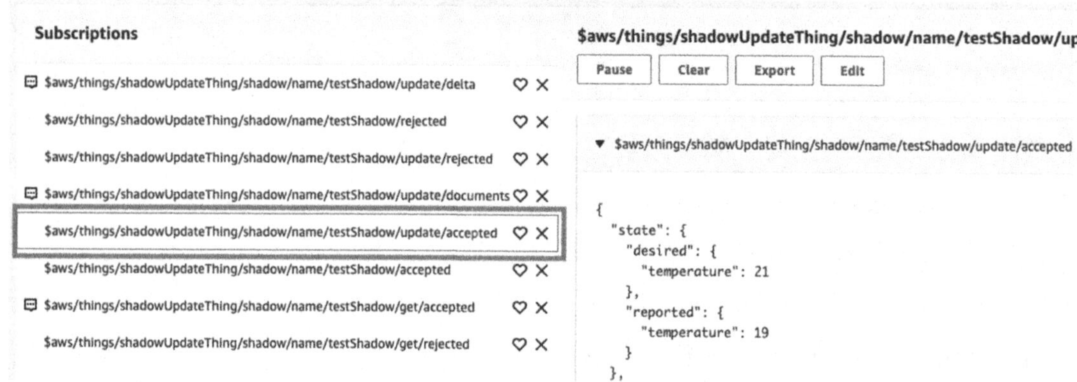

Figure 4-11. *Accepted state*

Subsequently, we can also see "*delta*" as there is a difference between the "*reported*" and the "*desired*" state (see Figure 4-12).

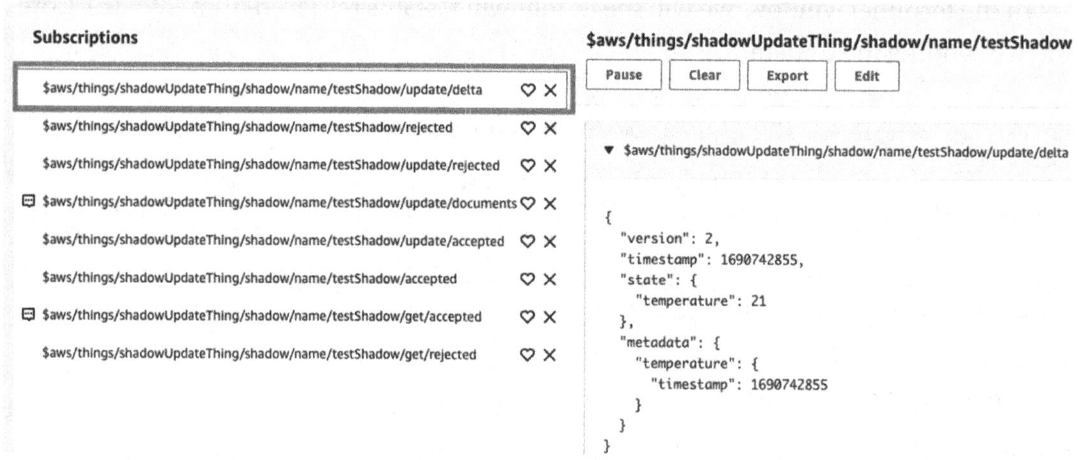

Figure 4-12. *Delta update*

If we go back to AWS IoT ➤ *Manage* ➤ *Things* ➤ *shadowUpdateThing* ➤ *DeviceShadows* and then select "*testShadow*", we can also see the reported value updated with what our virtual device sent (see Figure 4-13).

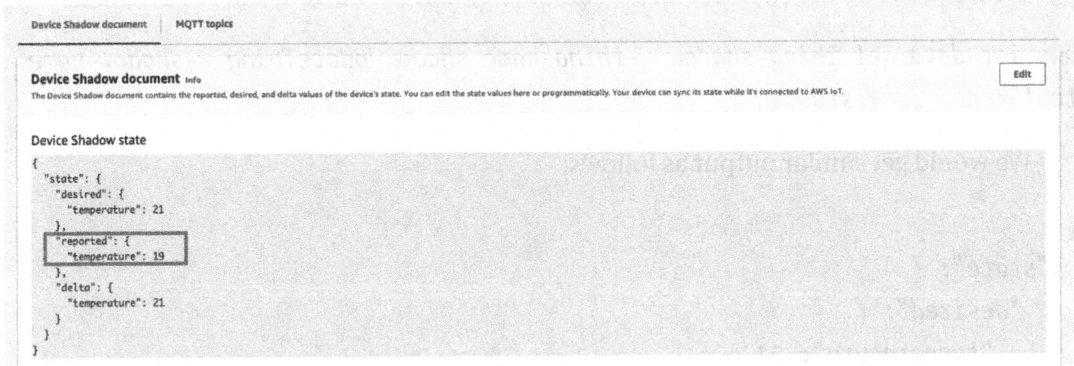

Figure 4-13. *Reported state*

Switch to the "*Activity*" tab and we can see what activity was carried out when we connected our virtual device (see Figure 4-14).

Attributes | Certificates | Thing groups | Device Shadows | Activity | Packages and versions | Jobs | Alarms | Defender metrics

Activity (4) Info

Lists the most recent MQTT messages related to Device Shadow activity since you opened the thing details page. To see more messages related to this activity, choose the **MQTT test client** button.

Clear | MQTT test client

▸ **Shadow updated - testShadow** July 30, 2023, 19:51:39 (UTC+01:00) Accepted
$aws/things/shadowUpdateThing/shadow/name/testShadow/update/accepted

▸ **Disconnected** July 30, 2023, 19:51:39 (UTC+01:00)
$aws/events/presence/disconnected/shadowUpdateThing

▸ **Subscribed** July 30, 2023, 19:51:36 (UTC+01:00)
$aws/events/subscriptions/subscribed/shadowUpdateThing

▸ **Connected** July 30, 2023, 19:51:36 (UTC+01:00)
$aws/events/presence/connected/shadowUpdateThing

Figure 4-14. *Shadow activity*

By thoroughly exploring this section, we have uncovered the remarkable capabilities of Device Shadow in effectively embodying the concept of a "*digital twin*." Imagine a scenario where a thermostat is controlled remotely through a dedicated app, enabling us to set the desired temperature (*desired* state). Simultaneously, the thermostat communicates its current temperature readings (*reported* state) based on the room conditions. This powerful representation of the digital twin concept showcases how Device Shadow can truly work wonders in bridging the physical and digital realms seamlessly.

We can also run the AWS CLI command and obtain the current state of the shadow:

```
aws iot-data get-thing-shadow --thing-name shadowUpdateThing --shadow-name
testShadow /dev/stdout
```

We would get similar output as follows:


```
{
  "state": {
    "desired": {
      "temperature": 21
    },
    "reported": {
      "temperature": 19
    },
    "delta": {
      "temperature": 21
    }
  },
  "metadata": {
    "desired": {
      "temperature": {
        "timestamp": 1690743099
      }
    },
    "reported": {
      "temperature": {
        "timestamp": 1690743099
      }
    }
  },
  "version": 3,
  "timestamp": 1690746435
}
```

which will give us the *reported* state as well as the *desired* state set in our shadow document.

Architect Our Solution

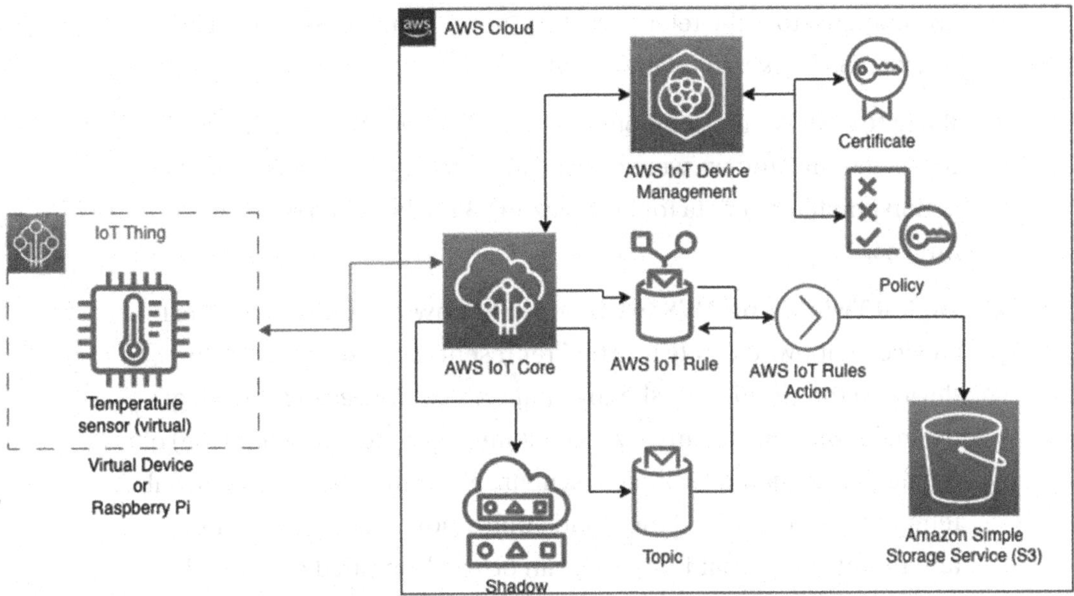

Figure 4-15. *Solution Architecture we built in this chapter*

Here is the architecture we built in our virtual device simulation, which illustrates an IoT solution implemented using AWS services. Let's break down the components and the flow of data:

- **AWS IoT Device Management:** We used device management features by utilizing the IoT device registry (registering our thing) and device security by allocating unique certificates and policies attached to this certificate.
- **Temperature Sensor (Virtual)**: This represented our virtual temperature sensor running on a cloud-based development environment like AWS Cloud9 or on a physical device like a Raspberry Pi or if you used MCU, then it can be that too. The sensor generated random simulated temperature readings.

- **AWS IoT Rules**: We configured AWS IoT Rules to listen to the temperature data from the virtual sensor, which we set up to trigger an action whenever the temperature exceeds a threshold (e.g., above 21 degrees Celsius).
- **Amazon S3 Bucket**: When the AWS IoT Rules detected that the temperature has gone above 21 degrees Celsius, then we initiated an action to store the telemetry data (temperature readings) in an Amazon S3 bucket in JSON format.
- **Basic Ingest**: We replaced our custom topic with the AWS IoT Basic Ingest feature, and we were directly able to trigger our AWS IoT Rules action and fan out data to the Amazon S3 bucket, thus reducing our cost.
- **Digital Twin Using AWS IoT Device Shadow**: We utilized AWS IoT Device Shadow to create a virtual representation (shadow) of the device in the cloud. This shadow maintained the *desired* state (e.g., desired temperature) and *reported* state (e.g., actual temperature) of the device. It enabled seamless synchronization between the virtual temperature sensor and the cloud application, enhancing control and monitoring capabilities that can be easily applied in our real-world use case.

What You Have Learned

- AWS IoT Basic Ingest
- Digital twin via AWS IoT Device Shadow

Our exploration commenced with understanding the intricacies of the IoT device registry, where we successfully registered our "Thing" and activated it, ensuring it was primed for operations.

Prioritizing security, we allocated a unique certificate to each device and linked it with a pertinent policy. These certificates, acting as digital passports, equipped devices to establish secure connections with AWS IoT Core, ensuring data remained confidential and unaltered during transmissions.

Simulating real-world scenarios, we deployed a virtual temperature sensor. Versatile in nature, this sensor was adaptable to various environments, from cloud platforms like AWS Cloud9 to tangible devices such as Raspberry Pi or MCUs. The sensor's role was pivotal: generating simulated temperature readings, closely replicating readings one would expect from actual sensors in the field.

Our journey also illuminated the benefits of AWS IoT Basic Ingest. By integrating this feature, we streamlined data flow, doing away with custom topics. This integration not only simplified our architecture but also facilitated triggering AWS IoT Rules actions, efficiently directing data to Amazon S3. The result was a leaner, more agile data ingestion and processing mechanism.

The standout feature of our exploration of the "digital twin" through AWS IoT Device Shadow. This didn't involve creating a virtual model but rather mapping the device's states, specifically the desired state set by users, the reported state from the device, and the calculated delta between them. This foundational understanding of the device's states, and the synchronization between them, enables enhanced control and user interactions within the IoT ecosystem.

Summary

In this chapter, we explored AWS IoT's expansive capabilities, starting with the registration and activation of our "Thing" in the IoT device registry. Emphasizing security, we implemented unique device certificates, ensuring data integrity and confidentiality with AWS IoT Core.

We introduced a versatile virtual temperature sensor, adaptable across platforms like AWS Cloud9 and devices like Raspberry Pi, simulating real-world temperature readings. Integrating AWS IoT Basic Ingest streamlined our data flow, enabling efficient data transfer to Amazon S3 without custom topics.

A notable focus was the "digital twin" concept through AWS IoT Device Shadow. Rather than creating a visual 3D model replica, we captured the device's state, enhancing device control and user interactions.

By the end, our grasp of AWS IoT Device Management deepened, preparing us to manage devices securely, process data effectively, and harness digital twin insights. With this foundation, we're ready to innovate and navigate the IoT landscape.

Further Learning: Delving Deeper into AWS IoT Digital Twin (Visual 3D Model)

Two noteworthy resources for those interested in AWS IoT Digital Twin (visual representation):

1. **AWS IoT TwinMaker:** An advanced tool designed to further enhance the capabilities of your digital twin implementations (3D representation)

   Learn more here: `https://github.com/aws-samples/aws-iot-twinmaker-samples`

2. **Smart Territory Framework:** A comprehensive guide and framework for deploying and managing large-scale IoT territories, providing valuable insights for expansive projects

   Learn more here: `https://github.com/aws-samples/aws-stf`

CHAPTER 5

Remote Actions Using AWS IoT

In an increasingly interconnected world, the significance of IoT devices in our daily lives continues to escalate. These devices, integrated into various sectors like manufacturing, transportation, healthcare, and domestic environments, generate vast quantities of data that must be effectively managed, updated, and debugged to ensure optimal performance. With the growing scale and complexity of IoT ecosystems, there is an urgent need for robust, secure, and scalable solutions to manage these devices seamlessly and remotely.

Amazon Web Services (AWS) offers a comprehensive IoT service suite, AWS IoT, that has revolutionized the way we handle IoT devices and data. It not only provides extensive functionalities for device connectivity and management but also enables remote updating and debugging, which is the focus of this chapter.

The ability to perform remote updates ensures that IoT devices can be equipped with the latest software patches and updates without the need for on-site human intervention. This translates into operational efficiency and increased device security as vulnerabilities can be patched promptly. Debugging, on the other hand, is crucial for maintaining the health and efficiency of IoT devices. Remote debugging allows developers to identify and fix issues from a distance, again negating the need for physical presence.

This chapter is designed to instruct on the implementation of remote updates and debugging using AWS IoT. By taking advantage of AWS IoT's robust services and offerings, organizations can ascertain that their devices are consistently updated, secure, and functioning at peak efficiency, thereby improving overall business performance.

S. Rehan, *AWS IoT With Edge ML and Cybersecurity*, https://doi.org/10.1007/979-8-8688-0011-5_5

Device Firmware: The Hardware-Centric Perspective in the IoT Ecosystem

In the world of IoT, device firmware is an integral piece of software that forms the very backbone of an IoT device's functionality. It is this embedded software that commands the device's hardware, translating high-level systemic instructions into low-level hardware operations. From a silicon perspective, firmware bridges the gap between the tangible hardware and the abstract software, sitting closer to the device's silicon and controlling the behavior of hardware components and peripherals, such as microprocessors, sensors, and connectivity modules.

The firmware, stored in nonvolatile memory chips, persists even when power is switched off. It's intricately linked to the device's hardware, directly influencing the way data is processed, power is managed, and communication protocols are executed. In the context of IoT devices, firmware may govern tasks ranging from basic operations like LED blinking to complex functionalities such as managing sensor data and enabling network connectivity.

The necessity to maintain the firmware's efficiency and security underpins the importance of AWS IoT Jobs. AWS IoT Jobs is a service that enables the remote management of IoT devices, including the deployment of firmware updates on a large scale. This service allows developers to define a set of remote operations that are sent across and executed on one or multiple IoT devices.

The relationship between AWS IoT Jobs, firmware, and device hardware is synergistic. AWS IoT Jobs can be used to roll out firmware updates to fix bugs, patch vulnerabilities, and introduce new features, improving the functionality and security of the hardware. From a silicon perspective, these updates enable better performance, higher efficiency, and improved reliability of the device's hardware components, strengthening the overall IoT ecosystem.

Let's explore the interplay between AWS IoT Jobs, device firmware, and hardware from a silicon-based perspective. By understanding this relationship, one can appreciate the importance of services like AWS IoT Jobs in managing firmware updates and maintaining a robust and secure IoT infrastructure.

What Are AWS IoT Jobs

AWS IoT Jobs is a feature of AWS IoT Core that allows you to define, execute, and manage tasks, or "jobs," on connected devices remotely. Use AWS IoT Jobs to define a set of remote operations that can be sent to and run on one or more devices connected to AWS IoT.

Jobs can include anything from firmware updates, rebooting or resetting devices, deploying security patches, configuring settings, and running maintenance routines.

Here are a few strategies to effectively use AWS IoT Jobs for your IoT devices.

Firmware and Software Updates

AWS IoT Jobs is primarily designed for the remote management of firmware and software updates. You can use it to schedule and deploy updates to your IoT devices in a secure and scalable manner. For instance, you could use AWS IoT Jobs to deploy a new version of your device software, patch security vulnerabilities, or roll out new features.

Configuration Management

You can use AWS IoT Jobs to change the configuration settings of your devices remotely. This can be useful if you need to update network settings, adjust sensor parameters, or modify any other configurable aspects of your device's operation.

Scheduled Tasks and Maintenance

AWS IoT Jobs can be used to perform regular maintenance tasks on your devices, such as clearing logs, resetting connections, or recalibrating sensors. These tasks can be scheduled and managed from the AWS IoT console, providing a centralized solution for device maintenance.

Error Handling and Monitoring

AWS IoT Jobs offers features to monitor the status of job executions and handle errors. Jobs can be tracked as they progress, and notifications can be set up to alert when jobs fail, are rejected, or complete successfully. This makes it easier to track issues and ensure devices are operating as expected.

Batch Operations

If you have a fleet of IoT devices, you can use AWS IoT Jobs to perform operations across multiple devices simultaneously. This is beneficial when you want to push updates, and configurations, or perform actions across all of your devices.

Security

AWS IoT Jobs integrates with AWS IoT Core's security features to ensure that operations are performed securely. You can leverage AWS IoT Core's authentication and authorization mechanisms to control which devices can perform which operations.

Using AWS IoT Jobs

Let's look at AWS IoT Jobs functions and their terminology.

A **job**, in the context of AWS IoT, represents a remote procedure or operation that's dispatched to and executed on one or more devices connected to AWS IoT. This operation could range from commanding a group of devices to download and implement an application, executing firmware upgrades, restarting, replacing security certificates, to undertaking remote diagnostic actions.

A **job document** is a file that details the set of instructions that AWS IoT Jobs will execute on a remote device. The document is defined in JSON (UTF-8 encoded) and can include standard fields provided by AWS or custom data defined by the user. The job document is downloaded by the device and used to carry out the job.

Targets are the devices (things or thing groups in AWS IoT Core parlance) that the job will be executed on. You specify these when you create a job. Jobs can be sent to a single device or can be deployed across an entire fleet of devices.

Deployment: A job begins with the creation of a job document and the identification of your target devices. After this, the job document is sent to the specified remote target devices to kickstart the update process. For "*snapshot jobs*," the job concludes once it's deployed to the designated devices. However, with "*continuous jobs*," the job is relayed to devices continually as they are added to the group.

The **rollout configuration** defines how many devices will receive the job document every minute. This is used to stagger the deployment of a job across multiple devices to manage load and prevent all devices from becoming busy at once.

Abort Configuration: If a certain number of devices fail to execute the job successfully, you can set the job to automatically cancel to prevent a potentially faulty update from affecting the entire fleet.

Timeout Configuration: You can define a timeout for a job to automatically fail if it does not receive a response from a device within a certain duration.

Retry Configuration: If a job fails or times out, AWS IoT Jobs can be set to automatically resend the job document to the device.

Scheduling: You can schedule jobs for a future date and time and can even set up recurring jobs that execute at predefined intervals. This is useful for routine maintenance tasks.

Job Life Cycle: AWS IoT Jobs sends a message to a device when a job is available. The device starts executing the job by downloading the job document, carrying out the instructions it specifies, and reporting its progress to AWS IoT. You can track the progress of a job across all targets or for a specific target using AWS IoT Jobs' tracking features.

Jobs have various statuses indicating their progress, such as "in progress," "succeeded," "failed," or "timed out." Devices report their status to AWS IoT Jobs as they execute the job.

A **job execution** symbolizes an instance or occurrence of a job on a targeted device. The target device kickstarts an execution of a job by fetching the job document. Post that, it carries out the operations outlined in the document and communicates its progress back to AWS IoT. Each job execution on a specific target is given a unique identifier known as an execution number. The AWS IoT Jobs service offers commands to keep tabs on the progress of a job execution on a specific target and monitor the progress of the job across all the targets.

Job Execution States

Table 5-1 provides a brief overview of each possible state that a job execution can be in, along with a description of what each state signifies.

Table 5-1. *Job execution states explained*

Job execution state	Description
QUEUED	*The job has been dispatched to the device but has not begun yet.*
IN_ PROGRESS	*The device has accepted the job and has started execution.*
FAILED	*The job execution failed on the device.*
SUCCEEDED	*The job execution was successful on the device.*
CANCELED	*The job execution was cancelled by the device or the service before it was completed. This can be due to an update to the job or abort criteria being met.*

(continued)

Table 9-1. (*continued*)

Job execution state	Description
REJECTED	*The job execution was rejected by the device. Possible reasons could include: the device is not in a state where it can execute the job, or the job document has a syntax error.*
REMOVED	*The job execution was deleted from the device by an external action, like using the API call such as DeleteJobExecution.*
TIMED_OUT	*The job execution was not completed within the execution window and was terminated by the service. This could be due to the job not being accepted within a certain timeframe or not being completed within the expected completion time after acceptance.*

Handling Timeouts

Job timeouts ensure you're alerted if a job execution lingers in the IN_PROGRESS state beyond the expected duration.

The following are descriptions of the various types of timers available in AWS IoT Jobs.

In-Progress Timers

When creating a job, you can define an "*inProgressTimeoutInMinutes*" value within the optional "*TimeoutConfig*" object. This timer is immutable once set and applies uniformly to all job executions pertaining to that job. If any job execution stays in the **IN_PROGRESS** state beyond this time, it is considered a failure and transitions to the final **TIMED_OUT** status. This event also triggers an MQTT notification by AWS IoT.

Step Timers

For a specific job execution, you can introduce a step timer by allocating a value to "*stepTimeoutInMinutes*" during an "*UpdateJobExecution*" call. This timer is exclusive to the particular job execution being updated and can be redefined with each update. Additionally, a step timer can be established during a "*StartNextPendingJobExecution*" invocation. If a job execution does not progress past the **IN_PROGRESS** state within the duration defined by the step timer, it's deemed unsuccessful and moves to the **TIMED_OUT** status. Notably, the step timer operates independently and does not influence the in-progress timer set during job creation.

Remote Action Using AWS IoT Jobs

In this section, we will utilize AWS IoT Jobs in conjunction with Amazon S3 to perform remote tasks, including downloading files from Amazon S3 and saving them on our IoT device.

Assuming your device, termed as an "*IoT thing*," needs an application update while deployed in the field, this section will guide you on downloading the most recent application file from Amazon S3. We will then replace the device-side application configuration with the latest version available on Amazon S3. This IoT Jobs action is illustrated in Figure 5-1.

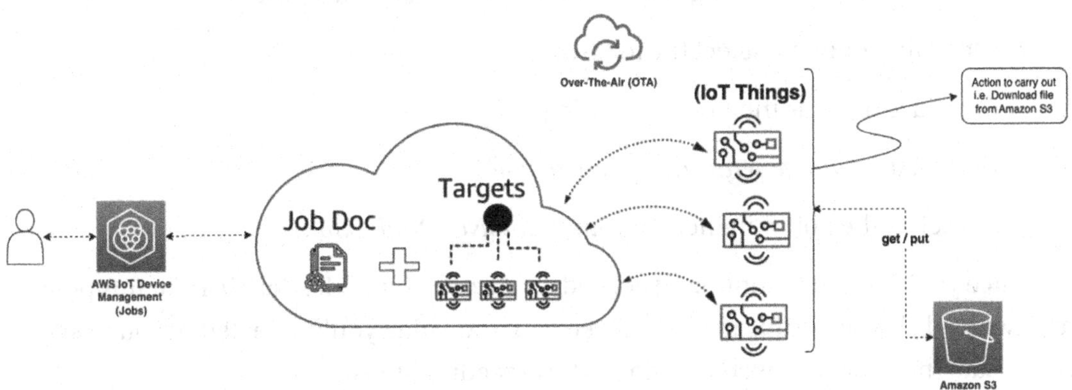

Figure 5-1. *AWS IoT Jobs action flow*

Using Open Source AWS IoT Device Client

The AWS IoT Device Client, written in C++, is a free and open-source modular software tailored for embedded Linux-based IoT devices. It offers out-of-the-box integration with AWS IoT Core, AWS IoT Device Management, and AWS IoT Device Defender. Designed as a reference blueprint, it incorporates operational best practices, streamlining the development of proof of concept (PoC) for IoT ventures. The added benefit of its Apache 2.0 license ensures broad permissions in terms of modification and use, allowing for bespoke alterations to cater to business specifics. Furthermore, this adaptability proves instrumental when transitioning from a PoC stage to full-scale production.

In the subsequent sections of this chapter, we will employ the AWS IoT Device Client to execute AWS IoT Jobs tasks and conduct remote debugging through Secure Tunneling.

Establishing the AWS IoT Device Client

To integrate with AWS IoT, start by creating an AWS IoT thing within the AWS IoT Device Management, commonly known as the device registry. This device will be designated as "*IoTDeviceClientThing*".

From the AWS IoT Core console, under the "Manage" section, select the following:

- Expand "*All Devices*"
    - Then, select *Things*
        - Click on *Create things*
        - Choose to *Create single thing*
        - For the "*Thing name*", enter "*IoTDeviceClientThing*"

For the other options, select the following:

- Leave them as their default settings
- Opt to "*Auto-generate device certificate*"
- Select the policy named "*myFirstDemoNonProductionPolicy*"

Once you've set these options, proceed to "*Create Thing*". It's "**critical**" at this point to download all four certificates associated with the Thing you've created (if you miss download, then you will need to redo all the preceding steps):

1. Download the device certificate (the file ending with .pem.crt)
2. Download the public key file (the file ending with public.pem.key)
3. Download the private key file (the file ending with private.pem.key)
4. Lastly, download the Amazon Root CA 1

Having successfully created our AWS IoT thing for the AWS IoT Device Client, it's time to set up the Device Client in our environment. This setup procedure is consistent for both the virtual device environment using Cloud9 as well as Raspberry Pi (hardware).

Set Up AWS IoT Device Client

We will utilize the AWS IoT Device Client available on GitHub at `https://github.com/awslabs/aws-iot-device-client`. The "*setupDeviceClient.sh*" script (book provided, GitHub repository - Chapter 5) will handle the setup for you.

Execute the Setup Process

1. Retrieve the "*setupDeviceClient.sh*" script from the GitHub book (Chapter 5) repository
2. Ensure it has executable permissions
3. Run the following command:

```
chmod 755 setupDeviceClient.sh #set permission to execute
./setupDeviceClient.sh
```

Using this script, we'll retrieve and configure all prerequisites required for the AWS IoT Device Client and subsequently establish the appropriate folder structure for it.

Obtain AWS IoT Endpoint

You'll require an endpoint address. You can retrieve it using the command provided here. Please store it safely, as we'll need it for the subsequent setup:

```
aws iot describe-endpoint --endpoint-type iot:Data-ATS
```

Navigate to the Directory and Configure

After a successful build, execute the following command. If you wish to install it as a service, run the "*setup.sh*" with *sudo* privileges.

```
cd ~/aws-iot-device-client/
./setup.sh
```

At this stage, you'll be asked to supply specific information to create configuration file for Device Client. This will encompass the file paths to your thing certificates, notably for your device titled "*IoTDeviceClientThing*". Make sure you've prepared and can access the paths to these certificates to respond appropriately.

The sample configuration settings I've provided are tailored for Ubuntu. Please note that they may vary depending on your operating system:

```
Do you want to interactively generate a configuration file for the AWS IoT
Device Client? y/n
y
Specify AWS IoT endpoint to use:
xxxxxxxxxxxxxxxxxx-ats.iot.us-east-1.amazonaws.com
Specify path to public PEM certificate:
/home/ubuntu/IoTDeviceClientThing/xxxxxxxxxxxxxxxxxx50dbdb49ff6f1b3601
6b72812ba6d11df4b83eb0d34c9e-certificate.pem.crt
```

```
Specify path to private key:
/home/ubuntu/IoTDeviceClientThing/ xxxxxxxxxxxxxxxxxx50dbdb49ff6f1b3601
6b72812ba6d11df4b83eb0d34c9e-private.pem.key
Specify path to ROOT CA certificate:
/home/ubuntu/IoTDeviceClientThing/AmazonRootCA1.pem
Specify thing name (Also used as Client ID):
IoTDeviceClientThing
Would you like to configure the logger? y/n
y
Specify desired log level: DEBUG/INFO/WARN/ERROR
DEBUG
Specify log type: STDOUT for standard output, FILE for file
FILE
Specify path to desired log file (if no path is provided, will default to /
var/log/aws-iot-device-client/aws-iot-device-client.log:

Creating default log directory...
Would you like to configure the SDK logging? y/n
n
Enable Jobs feature? y/n
y
Specify absolute path to Job handler directory (if no path is provided,
will default to /home/ubuntu/.aws-iot-device-client/jobs):

Enable Secure Tunneling feature? y/n
y
Enable Device Defender feature? y/n
y
Specify an interval for Device Defender in seconds (default is 300):

Enable Fleet Provisioning feature? y/n
n
Enable Pub Sub sample feature? y/n
y
Specify a topic for the feature to publish to:
/awsiotbook/dc/publish
```

```
Specify the path of a file for the feature to publish (if no path is
provided, will default to /home/ubuntu/.aws-iot-device-client/pubsub/
publish-file.txt):

Specify a topic for the feature to subscribe to:
/awsiotbook/dc/subscribe
Specify the path of a file for the feature to write to (if no path is
provided, will default to /home/ubuntu/.aws-iot-device-client/pubsub/
subscribe-file.txt):
/home/ubuntu/device-client/subscribe-file.txt
Enable Config Shadow feature? y/n
n
Enable Sample Shadow feature? y/n
n
```

Before saving the settings to the file, please confirm the JSON config as presented in Figure 5-2 is correct for your OS (pay attention to file paths).

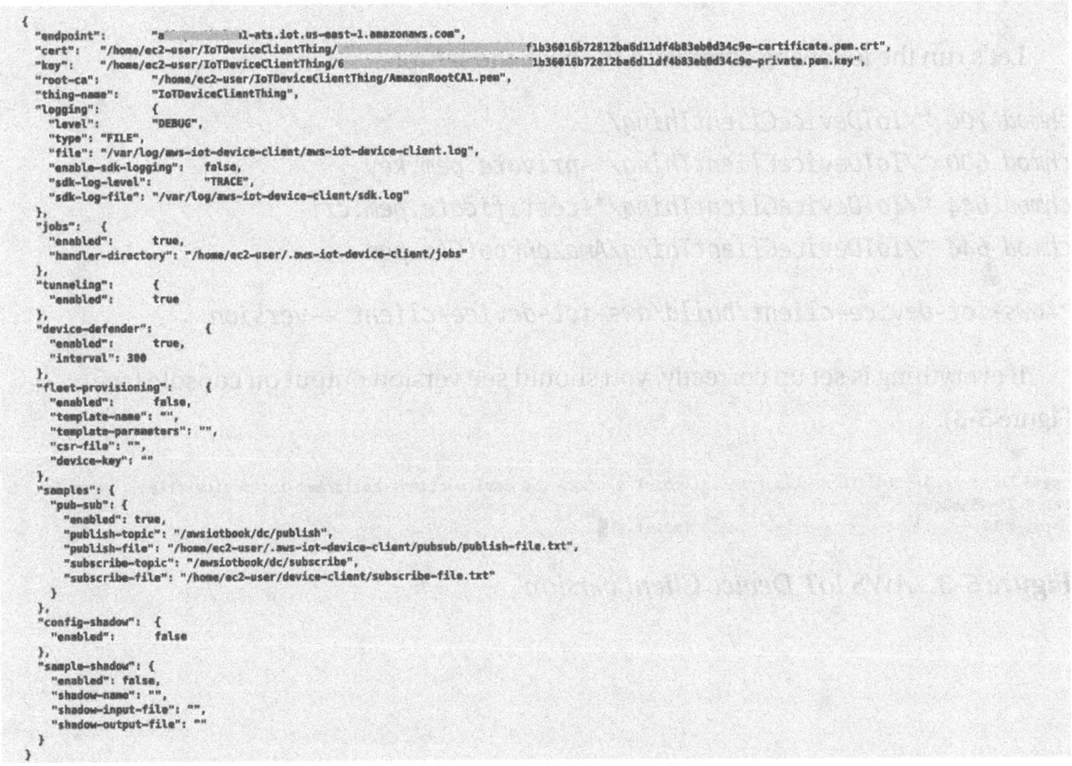

```
{
  "endpoint":       "a[illegible]l-ats.iot.us-east-1.amazonaws.com",
  "cert":   "/home/ec2-user/IoTDeviceClientThing/[illegible]f1b36016b72812ba6d11df4b83eb0d34c9e-certificate.pem.crt",
  "key":    "/home/ec2-user/IoTDeviceClientThing/6[illegible]1b36016b72812ba6d11df4b83eb0d34c9e-private.pem.key",
  "root-ca":        "/home/ec2-user/IoTDeviceClientThing/AmazonRootCA1.pem",
  "thing-name":     "IoTDeviceClientThing",
  "logging":        {
    "level":        "DEBUG",
    "type": "FILE",
    "file": "/var/log/aws-iot-device-client/aws-iot-device-client.log",
    "enable-sdk-logging":   false,
    "sdk-log-level":        "TRACE",
    "sdk-log-file": "/var/log/aws-iot-device-client/sdk.log"
  },
  "jobs":   {
    "enabled":      true,
    "handler-directory": "/home/ec2-user/.aws-iot-device-client/jobs"
  },
  "tunneling":      {
    "enabled":      true
  },
  "device-defender":        {
    "enabled":      true,
    "interval": 300
  },
  "fleet-provisioning":     {
    "enabled":      false,
    "template-name": "",
    "template-parameters": "",
    "csr-file": "",
    "device-key": ""
  },
  "samples": {
    "pub-sub": {
      "enabled": true,
      "publish-topic": "/awsiotbook/dc/publish",
      "publish-file": "/home/ec2-user/.aws-iot-device-client/pubsub/publish-file.txt",
      "subscribe-topic": "/awsiotbook/dc/subscribe",
      "subscribe-file": "/home/ec2-user/device-client/subscribe-file.txt"
    }
  },
  "config-shadow":  {
    "enabled":      false
  },
  "sample-shadow": {
    "enabled": false,
    "shadow-name": "",
    "shadow-input-file": "",
    "shadow-output-file": ""
  }
}
```


Figure 5-2. *AWS IoT Device Client config (JSON)*

Once the configuration is complete, you can find the file written here (the default path for Ubuntu might differ based on other Linux OS used):

```
/home/ubuntu/.aws-iot-device-client/aws-iot-device-client.conf
```

For the rest of the settings, select as follows:

```
Does the following configuration appear correct? If yes, configuration will
be written to /home/ubuntu/.aws-iot-device-client/aws-iot-device-client.
conf: y/n
y
Configuration has been successfully written to /home/ubuntu/.aws-iot-
device-client/aws-iot-device-client.conf
Creating default pubsub directory...
Do you want to copy the sample job handlers to the specified handler
directory (/home/ubuntu/.aws-iot-device-client/jobs)? y/n
y
Do you want to install AWS IoT Device Client as a service? y/n
n
```

Let's run the following command to check the setup:

```
chmod 700 ~/IoTDeviceClientThing/
chmod 600 ~/IoTDeviceClientThing/*-private.pem.key
chmod 644 ~/IoTDeviceClientThing/*-certificate.pem.crt
chmod 644 ~/IoTDeviceClientThing/AmazonRootCA1.pem

~/aws-iot-device-client/build/aws-iot-device-client --version
```

If everything is set up correctly, you should see version output on console (see Figure 5-3).

```
syed-book:~/aws-iot-device-client/build (main) $ ~/aws-iot-device-client/build/aws-iot-device-client —version
v1.8.28-95db8c9
syed-book:~/aws-iot-device-client/build (main) $
```

Figure 5-3. *AWS IoT Device Client version*

Let's perform another check by publishing data to AWS IoT Core using the AWS IoT Device Client. First, subscribe to the topic "*/awsiotbook/dc/publish*" using the "*AWS IoT Core MQTT Test client*" (see Figure 5-4). Then, execute the following command at this stage; let's leave our Device Client running (you can exit by using *CTRL+C, unless set up as service*):

```
~/aws-iot-device-client/build/aws-iot-device-client
```

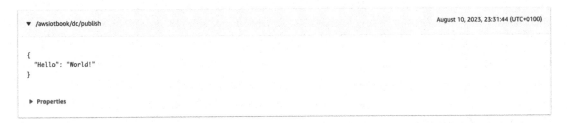

Figure 5-4. *Message on MQTT topic*

The data originates from the following location (unless you've modified the default settings for publish file): ~/**.aws-iot-device-client/pubsub/publish-file.txt**.

Before proceeding to the next step, let's also watch logs using the following command:

```
tail -F /var/log/aws-iot-device-client/aws-iot-device-client.log
```

Make sure you have AWS IoT Device Client running at this stage; if not, start using the following command:

```
~/aws-iot-device-client/build/aws-iot-device-client
```

Using AWS IoT Jobs to Retrieve the Application from an External URL

In this section, we will simulate an action where you can download a file or script from a trusted external URL to your IoT thing (device) by defining its action using AWS IoT Jobs.

From the AWS IoT Core console, under the "*Manage*" section" (see Figure 5-5):

- Select "*Remote actions*"
    - Select "*Jobs*"
        - Click "*Create job*"

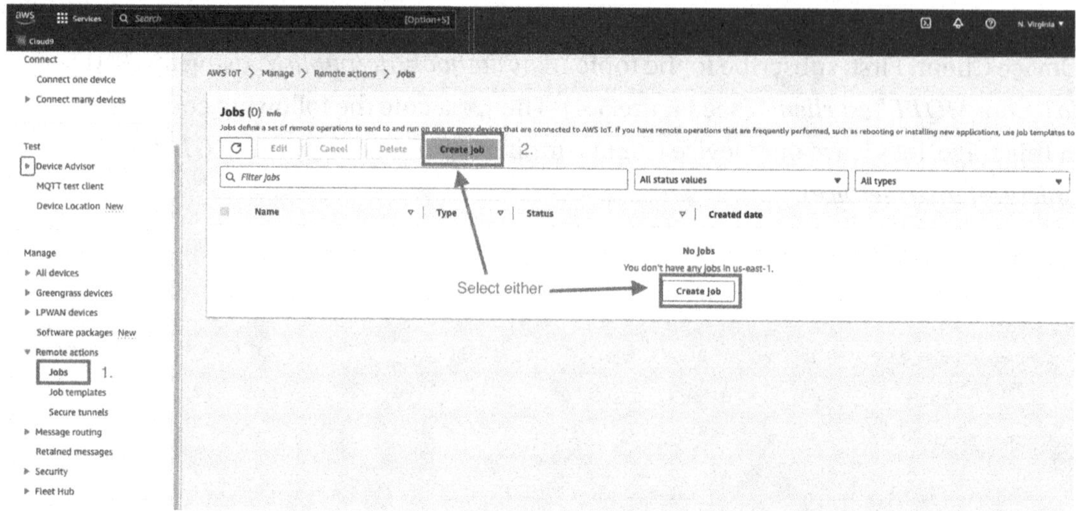

Figure 5-5. *Creating a job*

In the Create job screen, select "*Create custom job*" and click "*Next*" (see Figure 5-6).

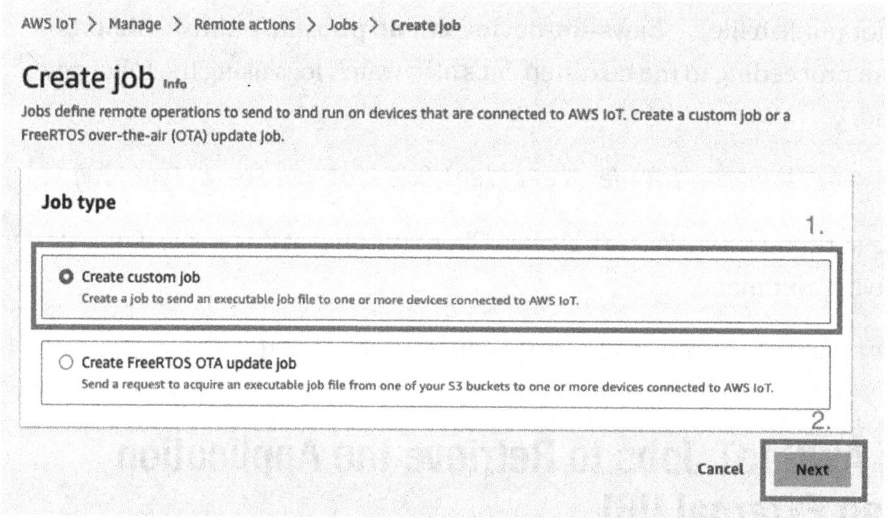

Figure 5-6. *Creating a custom job*

Give a job name such as "*myFirstJob*" and give a description and click "*Next*" (see Figure 5-7).

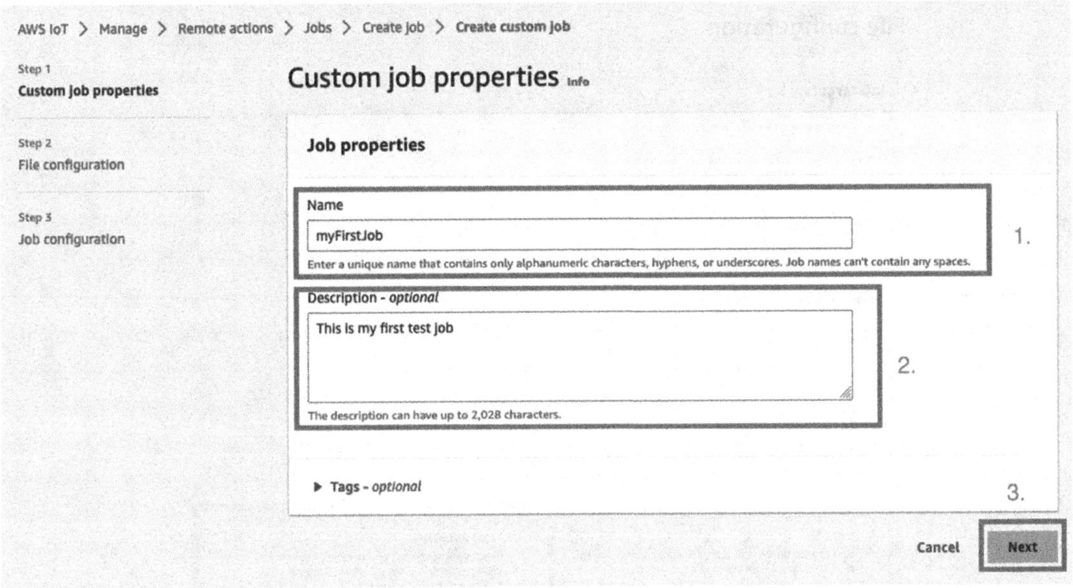

Figure 5-7. *Custom job properties*

The File configuration screen is the most important section, and we will populate it as follows:

Select our thing: "*IoTDeviceClientThing*"

For job document (see Figure 5-8):

- Select From template
- For Template type: Select *AWS managed templates*
- For Template: Select *AWS-Download-File*
- For downloadUrl: Use book GitHub (Chapter 5) URL for script:

  `https://github.com/syed-awsbook/aws_iot_with_ml_book_code/blob/73fecb5ed52f8795a08dd6f8a0a7226477dc9842/Chapter%205/aws_iot_jobs_test_program.sh` <***This is example path (use your own path, you can use Amazon S3 with pre-signed URL)***>
- For filePath (Ubuntu): */home/ubuntu/device-client/*
- For filePath (Raspberry Pi – replace admin with your username): */home/admin/device-client/*

Leave runAsUser and pathToHandler empty and click "*Next*".

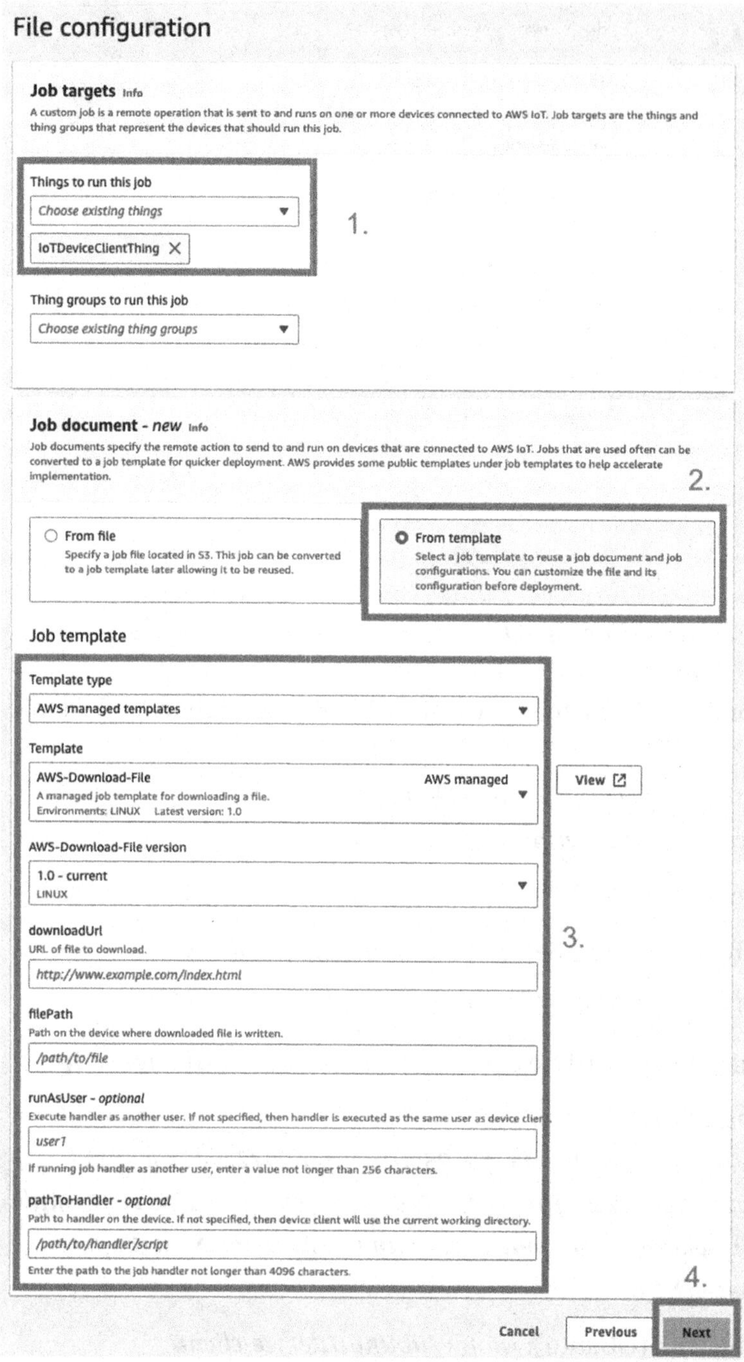

Figure 5-8. *Job configuration*

Select "*Snapshot*" and click "*Submit*" (see Figure 5-9).

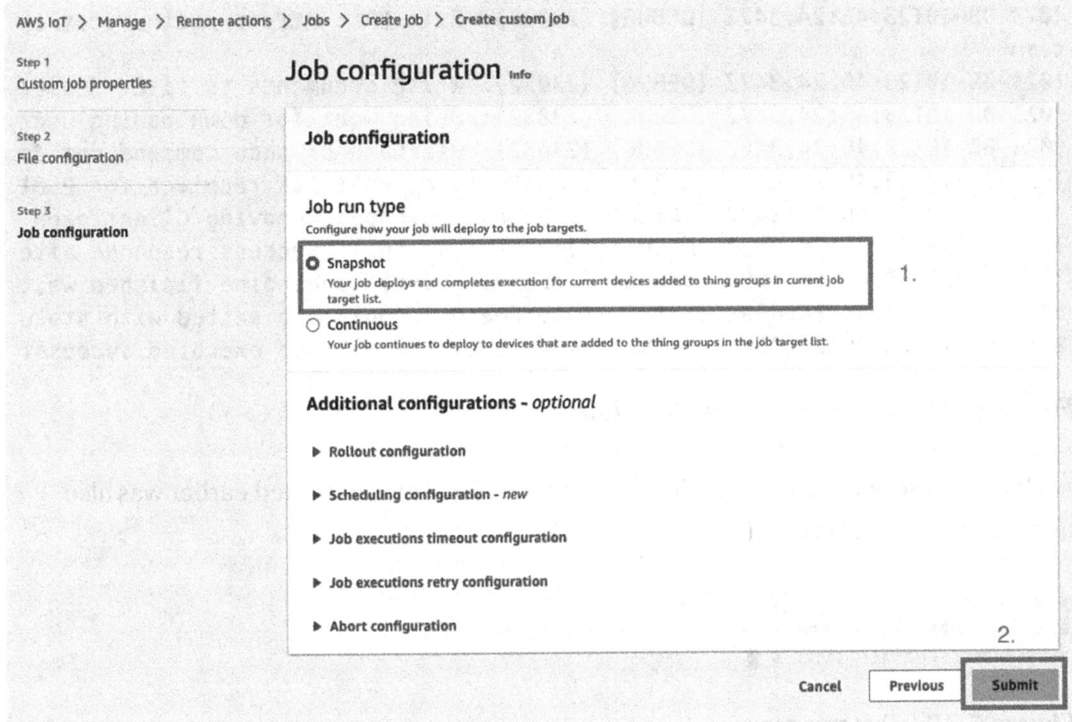

Figure 5-9. *Selecting Snapshot*

We can see our First Job created, and in the Rollout phase, it should complete quickly if you refresh it and should show status as "*Completed*".

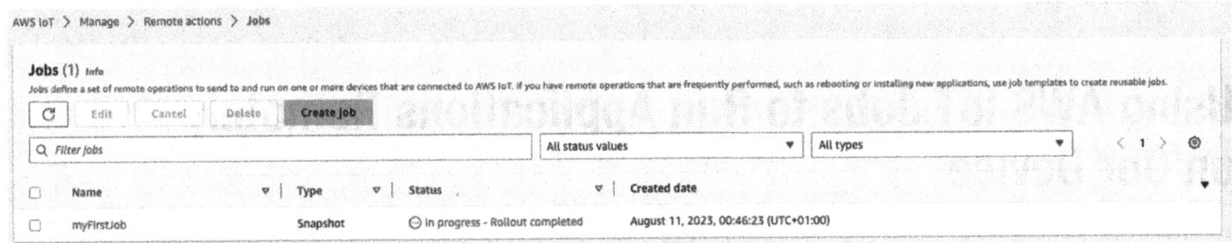

Figure 5-10. *Job status update*

We can also see when we were monitoring (tail logs) on our IoT device, the job was executed and completed "successfully" by saving the file we asked for on the designated directory (see Figure 5-11).

```
2023-08-10T23:46:24.347Z [DEBUG] {23032}: Running download-file.sh
2023-08-10T23:46:24.347Z [DEBUG] {23032}: Username:
2023-08-10T23:46:24.347Z [DEBUG] {23032}: File URL: https://github.com/sy
n.sh
2023-08-10T23:46:24.347Z [DEBUG] {23032}: Write documents to file: /home/
2023-08-10T23:46:24.347Z [DEBUG] {23032}: Using wget for downloading user
2023-08-10T23:46:24.348Z [DEBUG] {23032}: username or sudo command not fo
2023-08-10T23:46:24.363Z [DEBUG] {JobsFeature.cpp}: Ack received for Publ
2023-08-10T23:46:24.363Z [DEBUG] {JobsFeature.cpp}: Removing ClientToken
2023-08-10T23:46:24.363Z [DEBUG] {JobsFeature.cpp}: Success response afte
2023-08-10T23:46:24.459Z [DEBUG] {JobEngine.cpp}: JobEngine finished wait
2023-08-10T23:46:24.459Z [INFO]  {JobsFeature.cpp}: Job exited with statu
2023-08-10T23:46:24.459Z [INFO]  {JobsFeature.cpp}: Job executed successf
```

Figure 5-11. *Job status on the terminal*

We can also see the remote file which our AWS IoT Jobs executed earlier was also saved in the right directory (see Figure 5-12).

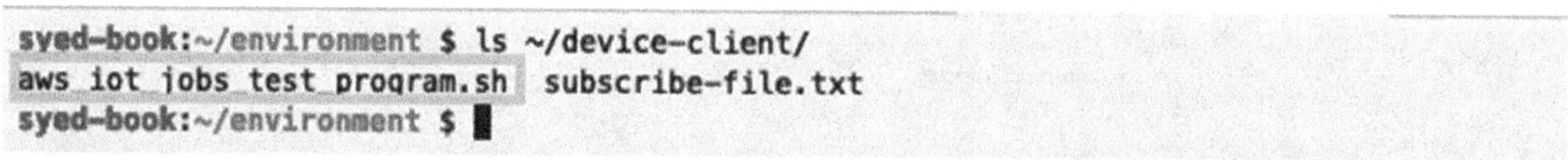

```
syed-book:~/environment $ ls ~/device-client/
aws_iot_jobs_test_program.sh  subscribe-file.txt
syed-book:~/environment $ 
```

Figure 5-12. *Test program*

This section demonstrates how to use AWS IoT Jobs to remotely download and update applications, application configurations, or firmware on your IoT device. It guides you through preparing the file in the designated location on the device using remote actions.

Using AWS IoT Jobs to Run Applications Remotely on Our Device

In the previous section, we downloaded the "*aws_iot_jobs_test_program.sh*" file using AWS IoT Jobs to our remote device; now we will use this file to execute using our AWS IoT Jobs remote action.

What does this file do? Let's look into this code:

```
#!/bin/bash

# Define the output file path
OUTPUT_FILE="/var/log/AWSIoTJobs-test-program-output.txt"

# Check if the user has permission to write to the file or create a new one
in /var/log/
if [ ! -w "$OUTPUT_FILE" ] && [ ! -w "/var/log/" ]; then
    echo "Permission denied to write to $OUTPUT_FILE. Try running the
script with sudo."
    exit 1
fi

# Write a message to the output file
echo "Test data from the AWS IoT Jobs test program: $(date)" >> $OUTPUT_FILE

echo "Data written to $OUTPUT_FILE"
```

It will write Text into this file: "*/var/log/AWSIoTJobs-test-program-output.txt*".

In the production environment, this can easily be a remote application update, configuration update, or firmware update of your IoT device.

From AWS IoT Core's "*MQTT test client*", subscribe to the system topics presented in Table 5-2.

Table 5-2. *Topics for AWS IoT Jobs*

Topic	Description
$aws/things/IoTDeviceClientThing/jobs/get	Devices publish a message to this topic to check for any pending job executions
$aws/things/IoTDeviceClientThing/jobs/notify	Devices subscribe to this topic to receive notifications when a job execution is added to or removed from the list of pending executions for a thing
$aws/things/IoTDeviceClientThing/jobs/get/accepted	Devices subscribe to this topic to acknowledge successful responses from AWS IoT Core, indicating a successful request for pending job executions

Let's look at the AWS IoT Job on executing this (we will create two jobs: one to set up the permission and carry out executable settings on the file and another to execute the script).

From the AWS IoT Core console, navigate to

- *"Manage"*
    - Then "*Remote actions*"
    - Select "*Jobs*" and then "*Create job*"
- Select "*Create custom job*"
    - Name: "*executeRemoteScriptJob1*"
    - Give a description
    - Select "*Next*"
- For job targets:
    - Select "*IoTDeviceClientThing*"
- For job document (see Figure 5-13):
    - Select "*From template*"
        - Template type: *All templates*
        - Template: *AWS-Run-Command*
        - In the command box (it's space sensitive so use a comma after chmod and after 755):
            - *chmod,755,/home/ubuntu/device-client/aws_iot_jobs_test_program.sh*
        - Leave the rest of the settings as default
        - Select "*Next*"
        - Select job run type: "*Snapshot*"
        - Leave the rest as default; select "*Submit*"

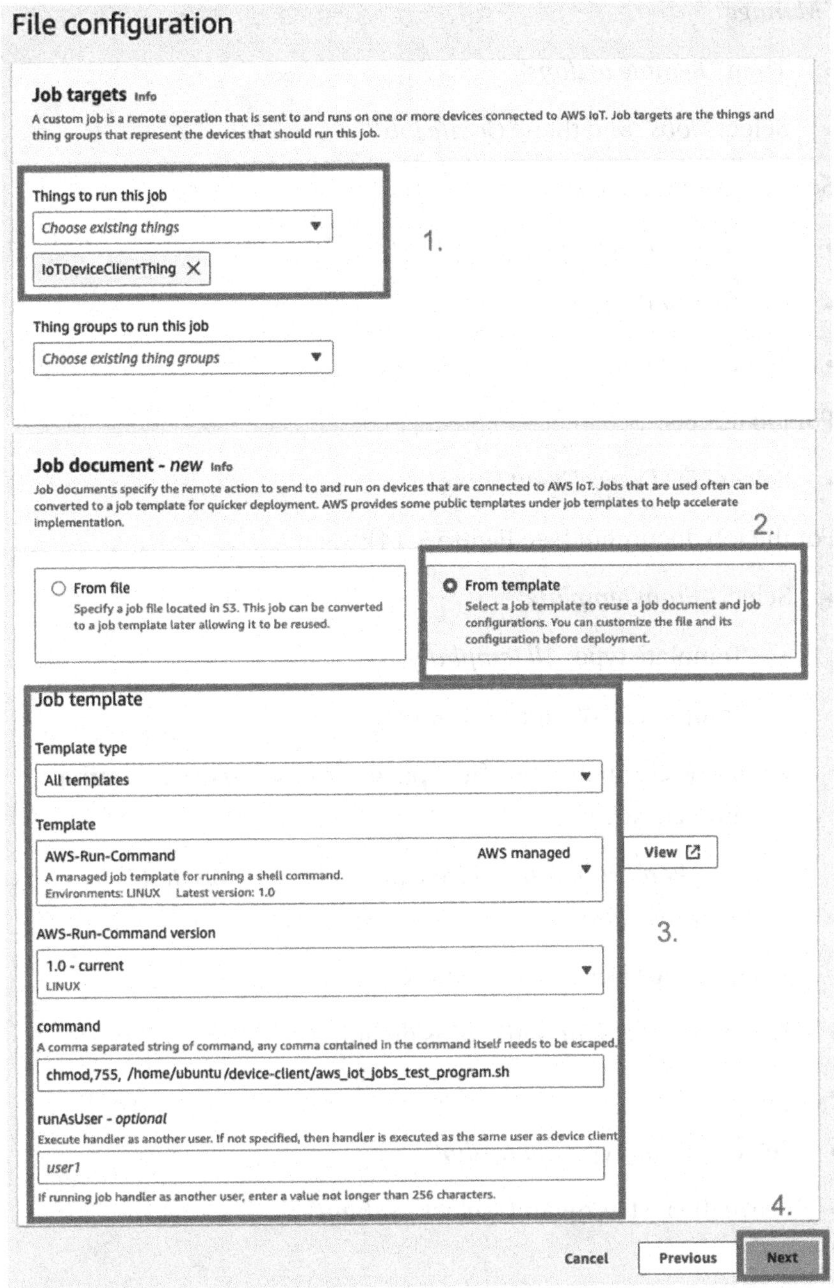

File configuration

Job targets Info

A custom job is a remote operation that is sent to and runs on one or more devices connected to AWS IoT. Job targets are the things and thing groups that represent the devices that should run this job.

Things to run this job

Choose existing things

IoTDeviceClientThing

1.

Thing groups to run this job

Choose existing thing groups

Job document - new Info

Job documents specify the remote action to send to and run on devices that are connected to AWS IoT. Jobs that are used often can be converted to a job template for quicker deployment. AWS provides some public templates under job templates to help accelerate implementation.

2.

From file

Specify a job file located in S3. This job can be converted to a job template later allowing it to be reused.

From template

Select a job template to reuse a job document and job configurations. You can customize the file and its configuration before deployment.

Job template

Template type

All templates

Template

AWS-Run-Command

AWS managed

A managed job template for running a shell command.

Environments: LINUX Latest version: 1.0

View

3.

AWS-Run-Command version

1.0 - current

LINUX

command

A comma separated string of command, any comma contained in the command itself needs to be escaped.

chmod,755, /home/ubuntu /device-client/aws_iot_jobs_test_program.sh

runAsUser - optional

Execute handler as another user. If not specified, then handler is executed as the same user as device client

user1

If running job handler as another user, enter a value not longer than 256 characters.

4.

Cancel Previous Next

Figure 5-13. *chmod execution job configuration*

Now let's create our second job:

From the AWS IoT Core console, navigate to

- *"Manage"*
    - Then *"Remote actions"*
    - Select *"Jobs"* and then *"Create job"*
- Select *"Create custom job"*
    - Name: *"executeRemoteScriptJob2"*
    - Give a description
    - Select *"Next"*
- For job targets:
    - Select *"IoTDeviceClientThing"*
- For the job document (see Figure 5-14):
    - Select *"From template"*
        - Template type: *All templates*
        - Template: *AWS-Run-Command*
        - In the command box (it's space sensitive so use a comma after chmod):
            - */home/ubuntu/device-client/aws_iot_jobs_test_program.sh*
        - In runAsUser box type: sudo
    - Leave the rest of the settings as default
    - Select *"Next"*
    - Select job run type: *"Snapshot"*
    - Leave the rest as default; select *"Submit"*

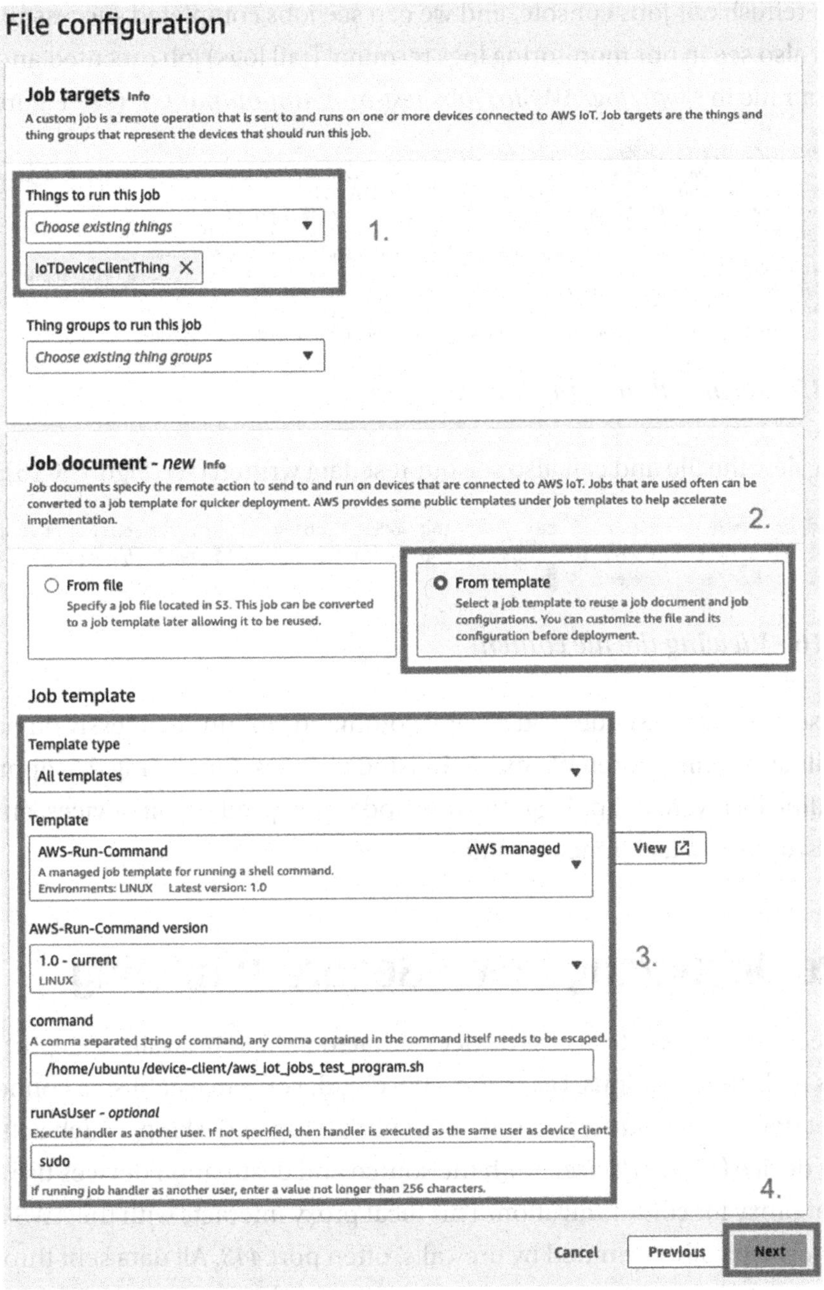

File configuration

Job targets Info

A custom job is a remote operation that is sent to and runs on one or more devices connected to AWS IoT. Job targets are the things and thing groups that represent the devices that should run this job.

Things to run this job

Choose existing things

IoTDeviceClientThing

1.

Thing groups to run this job

Choose existing thing groups

Job document - *new* Info

Job documents specify the remote action to send to and run on devices that are connected to AWS IoT. Jobs that are used often can be converted to a job template for quicker deployment. AWS provides some public templates under job templates to help accelerate implementation.

2.

From file

Specify a job file located in S3. This job can be converted to a job template later allowing it to be reused.

From template

Select a job template to reuse a job document and job configurations. You can customize the file and its configuration before deployment.

Job template

Template type

All templates

Template

AWS-Run-Command AWS managed

A managed job template for running a shell command.

Environments: LINUX Latest version: 1.0

View

AWS-Run-Command version

1.0 - current

LINUX

3.

command

A comma separated string of command, any comma contained in the command itself needs to be escaped.

/home/ubuntu /device-client/aws_iot_jobs_test_program.sh

runAsUser - *optional*

Execute handler as another user. If not specified, then handler is executed as the same user as device client.

sudo

If running job handler as another user, enter a value not longer than 256 characters.

4.

Cancel Previous Next

Figure 5-14. *Job execution of our script*

We can refresh our jobs console, and we can see jobs completed successfully.

We can also see in our monitoring logs terminal (tail logs) job executed and data got written to our file in "*/var/log/AWSIoTJobs-test-program-output.txt*" (see Figure 5-15).

```
2023-08-11T00:29:57.050Z [DEBUG] {JobEngine.cpp}: argv[0]: sudo
2023-08-11T00:29:57.050Z [DEBUG] {JobEngine.cpp}: argv[1]:   /home/ubuntu/device-client/aws_iot_jobs_test_program.sh
2023-08-11T00:29:57.050Z [DEBUG] {JobEngine.cpp}: Child process now running
2023-08-11T00:29:57.050Z [DEBUG] {JobEngine.cpp}: Child process about to call execvp
2023-08-11T00:29:57.050Z [DEBUG] {JobEngine.cpp}: Parent process now running, child PID is 14134
2023-08-11T00:29:57.061Z [DEBUG] {14134}: Data written to /var/log/AWSIoTJobs-test-program-output.txt
2023-08-11T00:29:57.062Z [DEBUG] {JobEngine.cpp}: JobEngine finished waiting for child process, returning 0
2023-08-11T00:29:57.062Z [INFO]  {JobsFeature.cpp}: Job exited with status: 0
2023-08-11T00:29:57.062Z [INFO]  {JobsFeature.cpp}: Job executed successfully!
2023-08-11T00:29:57.062Z [DEBUG] {JobsFeature.cpp}: Attempting to update job execution status!
```

Figure 5-15. *Terminal showing job executed*

We can view the file and can also see our test data written (see Figure 5-16).

```
syed-book:~/environment $ cat /var/log/AWSIoTJobs-test-program-output.txt
Test data from the AWS IoT Jobs test program: Fri Aug 11 00:29:57 UTC 2023
syed-book:~/environment $
```

Figure 5-16. *Viewing the file content*

In this section, we've sequenced several commands to run seamlessly on our remote device, facilitating efficient remote execution and updates. Employing this approach can streamline firmware or application code updates in production devices, ensuring minimal disruption to user functionalities.

Remote Debugging Using Secure Tunneling

Leverage secure tunneling to access devices situated behind firewalls with port restrictions at distant locations. Using the AWS cloud, you can establish a connection to the target device (*destination device*) from your laptop or desktop, which acts as the originating device (*source device*). Both the source and destination devices use an open source local proxy for communication. This local proxy interacts with the AWS cloud through a port typically permitted by firewalls, often port *443*. All data sent through this tunnel is encrypted using Transport Layer Security (*TLS*). Since we installed the *AWS IoT Device Client*, this feature is baked in so we don't need to install local proxy separately. On the Operator device (*source device*), unless we are using browser-based secure tunneling using SSH, we would need a local proxy for terminal connection.

Terminology

- **Destination Device**: Remote end device (our IoT device - which we are connecting to)
- **Source Device**: Operator device (device where we are connecting from)

Destination Device Setup

In this step, we will set the destination device (remote device), which is our Cloud9 or Raspberry Pi:

- SSH private and public keys.
- Add a public key to the authorized_keys file so we are allowed to connect from an SSH perspective.
- Set permission to the SSH folder correctly.

We've provided a script to streamline this step. However, if you already possess a private key and its corresponding public key is added to the "authorized_keys" file, you can use your existing key.

Run the Script

1. Retrieve the *"generate_authorise_ssh_keys.sh"* script from the GitHub book (Chapter 5) repository
2. Ensure it has executable permissions (*chmod +x generate_authorise_ssh_keys.sh*)
3. Run the following command:

```
chmod +x generate_authorise_ssh_keys.sh
./generate_authorise_ssh_keys.sh
```

```
syed-book:~/environment $ chmod +x generate_authorise_ssh_keys.sh
syed-book:~/environment $ ./generate_authorise_ssh_keys.sh
Generating public/private rsa key pair.
Your identification has been saved in  /home/ubuntu/.ssh/id_rsa.
Your public key has been saved in  /home/ubuntu/.ssh/id_rsa.pub.
The key fingerprint is:
SHA256:7                                  Ts ec2-user@ip-         162.ec2.internal
The key's randomart image is:
+---[RSA 4096]----+
|        o..      |
|        o. .     |
|          .      |
|          .      |
|         +       |
|          .      |
|                 |
|                 |
|                 |
+----[SHA256]-----+
SSH key generated at  /home/ubuntu/.ssh/id_rsa
Public key added to ~/.ssh/authorized_keys
Please securely copy the 'private key' from:  /home/ubuntu/.ssh/id_rsa
```

Figure 5-17. *Generation of SSH keys*

Make sure to download the private key (*id_rsa*) (see Figure 5-18), which we will use later to connect from the browser in the next step (see Figure 5-17).

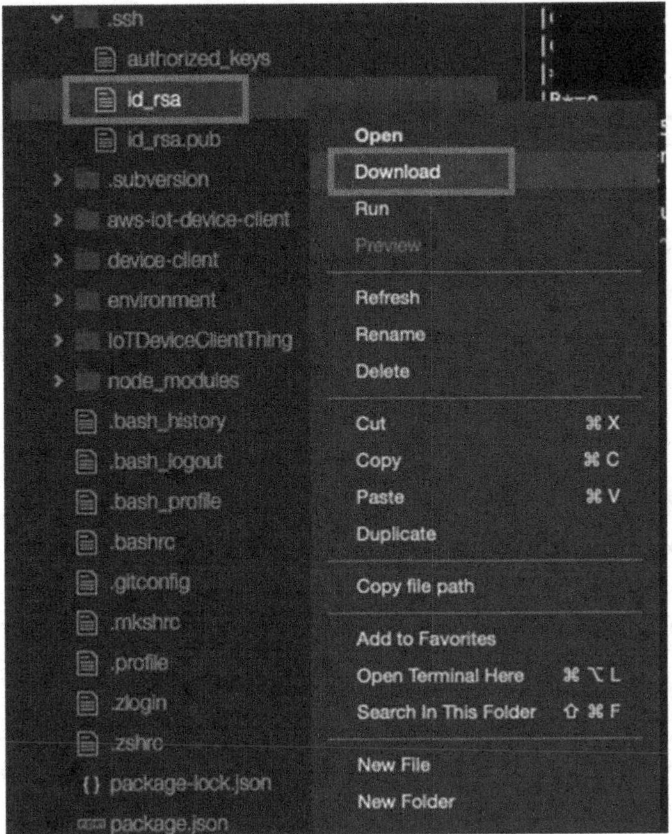

Figure 5-18. *Downloading the private key*

Operator Device (Source Device)

Let's set up a Secure tunnel using **browser-based** SSH with the AWS IoT Secure tunnel feature.

From the AWS IoT Core console, under the "*Manage*" section (see Figure 5-19):

- Select Remote actions
  - Select Secure tunnels
    - Click Create tunnel

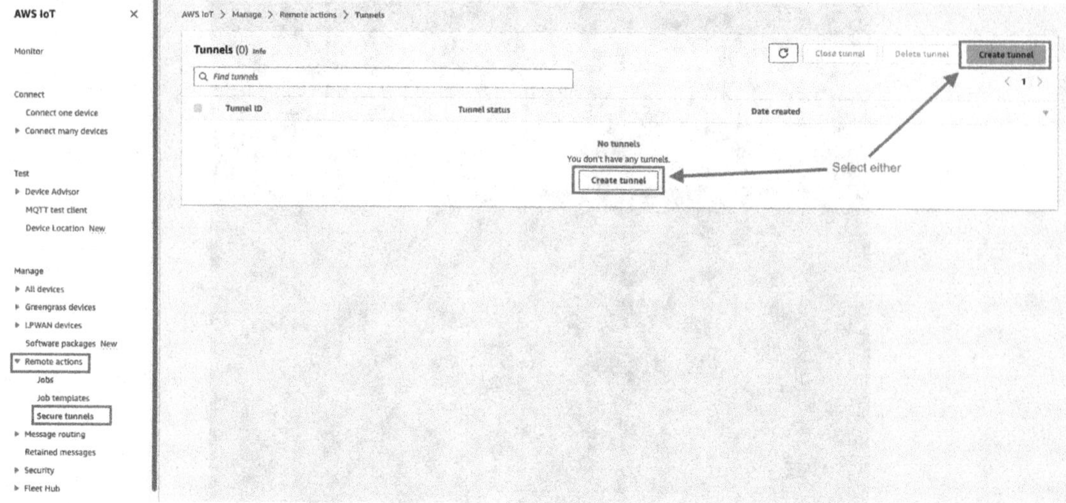

Figure 5-19. *Creating the tunnel*

On the tunnel creation screen, select "*Manual Setup*" and click "*Next*" (see Figure 5-20).

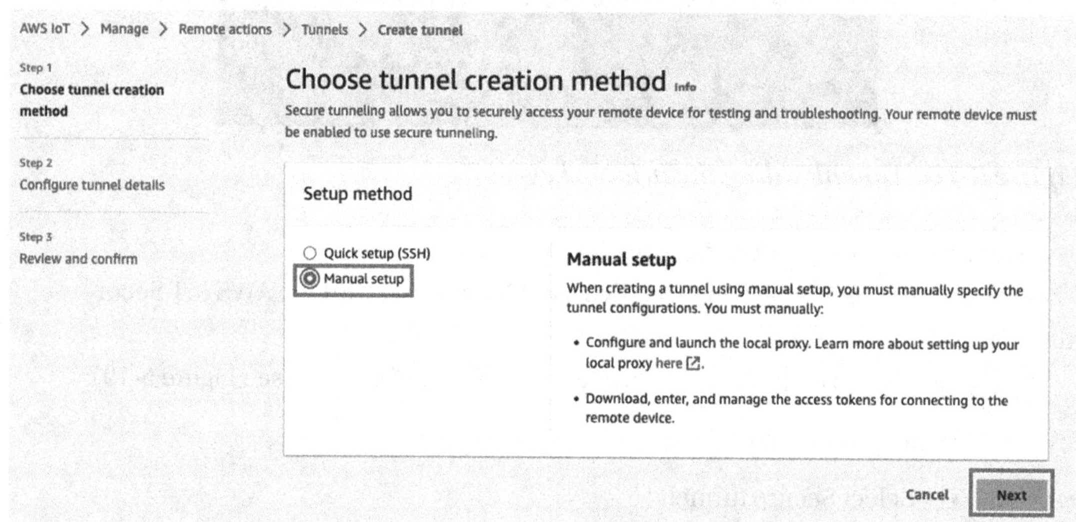

Figure 5-20. *Tunnel setup (manual)*

In Manual selection screen, populate details as follows (see Figure 5-21):

- Tunnel description (give meaningful details): *AWSIoTBookTunnel*
- Select "*Add new service*" and enter "SSH"

- For Thing name, select "*IoTDeviceClientThing*"
- Click "*Next*"
- Select "*Confirm and create*"

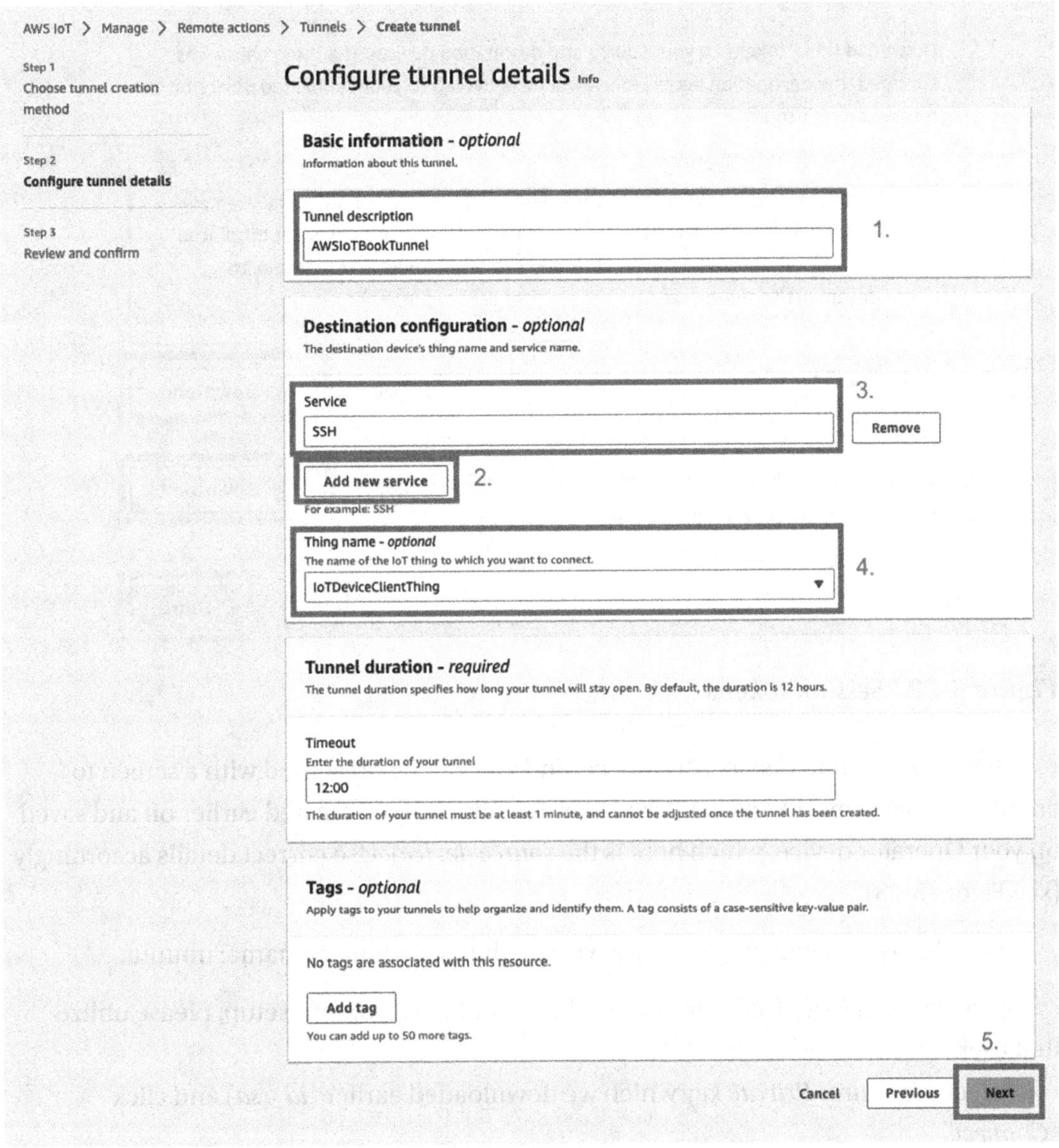

Figure 5-21. *Tunnel configuration*

Once the tunnel is created, you will be presented with source and destination tokens; download and save both (see Figure 5-22).

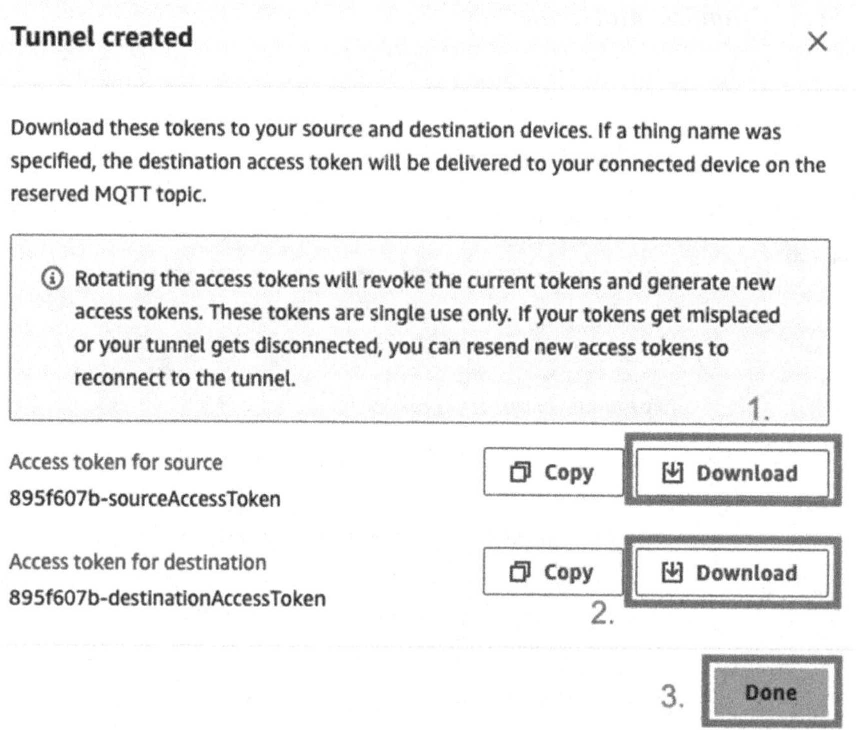

Figure 5-22. *Session tokens*

Once "*downloaded*", select "*Connect*" and you will be presented with a screen to enter your username and select Private key (use the one we created earlier on and saved on your Operator device, which here is the *source device*). Use correct details accordingly (see Figure 5-23).

- For our Cloud9 instance, we will use the following username: ubuntu.

If you've established a different user during our environment setup, please utilize that user.

Select the *Source Private key* which we downloaded earlier (*id_rsa*) and click "*Connect*".

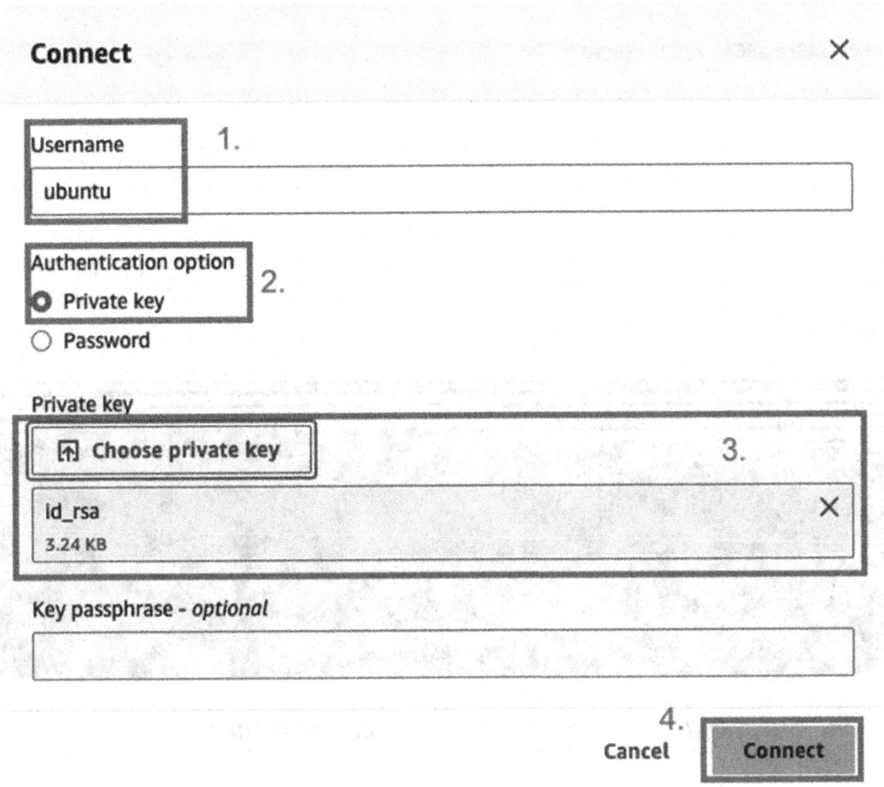

Connect

Username 1.

ubuntu

Authentication option 2.

Private key

Password

Private key

Choose private key 3.

id_rsa

3.24 KB

Key passphrase - *optional*

4.

Cancel Connect

Figure 5-23. *SSH connection setup screen*

Once we are connected, we can see the SSH terminal connected to our end device (*destination device*) (see Figure 5-24).

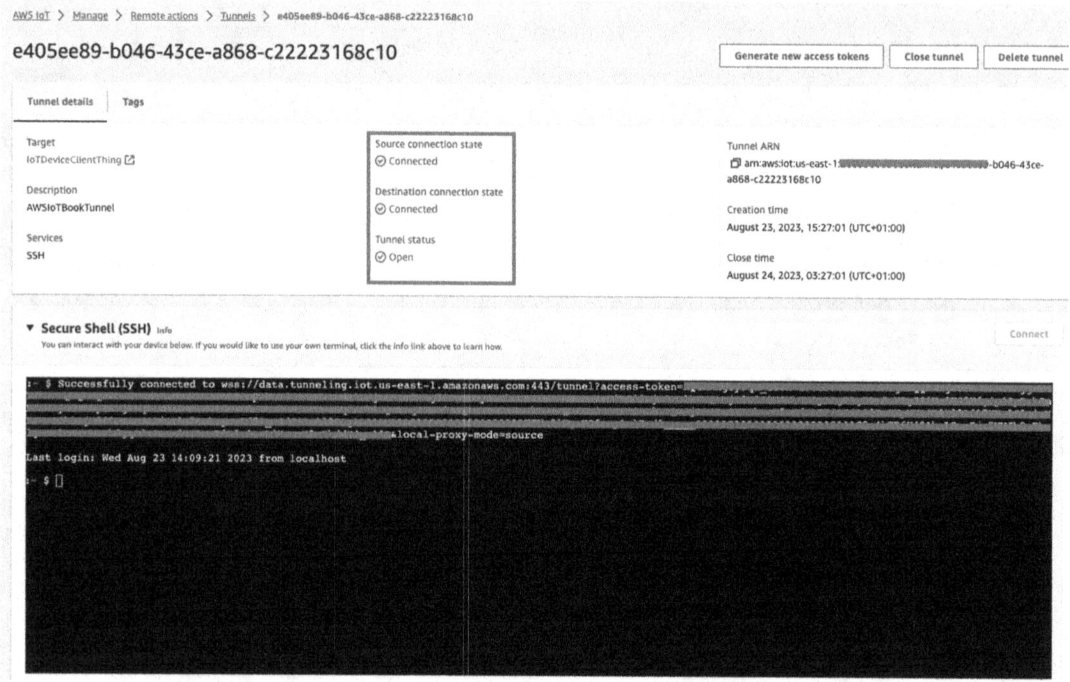

Figure 5-24. *Successfully connected SSH through the browser*

If we were monitoring our device client logs (*tail -F /var/log/aws-iot-device-client/aws-iot-device-client.log*), we would see MQTT tunnel notification and connection status (see Figure 5-25).

```
2023-08-23T14:37:22.741Z [DEBUG] {SecureTunnelingContext.cpp}: SecureTunnelingContext::OnSendDataComplete
2023-08-23T14:37:22.742Z [DEBUG] {TcpForward.cpp}: TcpForward::OnReadable error_code=0
2023-08-23T14:37:22.742Z [DEBUG] {SecureTunnelingContext.cpp}: SecureTunnelingContext::OnTcpForwardDataReceive data.len=96
2023-08-23T14:37:22.742Z [DEBUG] {SecureTunnelingContext.cpp}: SecureTunnelingContext::OnSendDataComplete
2023-08-23T14:37:51.004Z [DEBUG] {SecureTunnelingContext.cpp}: SecureTunnelingContext::OnDataReceive data.len=48
2023-08-23T14:37:51.992Z [DEBUG] {SecureTunnelingContext.cpp}: SecureTunnelingContext::OnDataReceive data.len=48
2023-08-23T14:38:21.008Z [DEBUG] {SecureTunnelingContext.cpp}: SecureTunnelingContext::OnDataReceive data.len=48
2023-08-23T14:38:21.994Z [DEBUG] {SecureTunnelingContext.cpp}: SecureTunnelingContext::OnDataReceive data.len=48
2023-08-23T14:38:51.018Z [DEBUG] {SecureTunnelingContext.cpp}: SecureTunnelingContext::OnDataReceive data.len=48
2023-08-23T14:38:51.998Z [DEBUG] {SecureTunnelingContext.cpp}: SecureTunnelingContext::OnDataReceive data.len=48
2023-08-23T14:39:21.019Z [DEBUG] {SecureTunnelingContext.cpp}: SecureTunnelingContext::OnDataReceive data.len=48
2023-08-23T14:39:21.995Z [DEBUG] {SecureTunnelingContext.cpp}: SecureTunnelingContext::OnDataReceive data.len=48
2023-08-23T14:39:51.020Z [DEBUG] {SecureTunnelingContext.cpp}: SecureTunnelingContext::OnDataReceive data.len=48
2023-08-23T14:39:51.995Z [DEBUG] {SecureTunnelingContext.cpp}: SecureTunnelingContext::OnDataReceive data.len=48
2023-08-23T14:40:21.016Z [DEBUG] {SecureTunnelingContext.cpp}: SecureTunnelingContext::OnDataReceive data.len=48
2023-08-23T14:40:21.988Z [DEBUG] {SecureTunnelingContext.cpp}: SecureTunnelingContext::OnDataReceive data.len=48
2023-08-23T14:40:51.019Z [DEBUG] {SecureTunnelingContext.cpp}: SecureTunnelingContext::OnDataReceive data.len=48
2023-08-23T14:40:51.999Z [DEBUG] {SecureTunnelingContext.cpp}: SecureTunnelingContext::OnDataReceive data.len=48
2023-08-23T14:41:01.929Z [DEBUG] {DeviceDefender.cpp}: Recv: Topic:($aws/things/IoTDeviceClientThing/defender/metrics/json/accepted),
":"ACCEPTED","timestamp":1692801661791}
```

Figure 5-25. *Log output showing SSH success*

Once we have tested this feature, you should always (***good security practice***) *close and delete* the tunnel.

This wraps up the section on remote tunneling and executing tasks for our IoT devices.

What You Have Learned

Key Takeaways: Understanding device firmware, deep dive into AWS IoT Jobs, execution states and their utilization, handling timeouts in AWS IoT Jobs, executing remote actions via AWS IoT Jobs, and employing AWS IoT Secure Tunneling for remote device access.

Throughout this chapter, we navigated the complex landscape of device firmware, emphasizing its relevance from a hardware lens. Our central focus was AWS IoT Jobs, an integral tool for remote device management and operation. We unpacked the layers of AWS IoT Jobs, deciphering its various execution states and their practical implications.

AWS IoT Jobs, in essence, provides a robust and adaptable framework for governing remote operations on IoT devices. It offers granular control over task execution, deployment, and scheduling, ensuring precision and efficiency in device interactions.

Our exploration also touched upon the strategies AWS IoT Jobs employs to handle timeouts, a vital aspect that underpins consistent and uninterrupted device operations. Moreover, we delved into the capability of AWS IoT Jobs to execute remote actions. This includes tasks like downloading and implementing application updates, showcasing the system's versatility in remote device management.

A notable highlight was our introduction to AWS Secure Tunneling. This feature facilitates the creation of a secure remote tunnel to our IoT device. It underscores the immense value and potential of cloud-based tools in amplifying device accessibility and streamlined management.

Summary

In this chapter, we delved into the intricate world of device firmware and its significance in the broader IoT landscape. Central to our exploration was AWS IoT Jobs, an essential tool that stands out in managing and orchestrating remote device operations. This robust framework not only ensures precise task execution and deployment but also adeptly handles timeouts, a cornerstone for seamless device operations.

Our journey provided insights into the multifaceted capabilities of AWS IoT Jobs, especially its ability to conduct diverse remote actions ranging from application updates to intricate management tasks. A standout discovery was the transformative potential of AWS Secure Tunneling, which offers a gateway for secure remote access to IoT devices.

As we concluded the chapter, it became evident that the hardware, firmware, and cloud-centric services like AWS IoT Jobs exist in a synergistic relationship. Their collaborative interplay is instrumental in forging a cohesive and vibrant IoT ecosystem. The knowledge and insights garnered from this chapter serve as a robust foundation, preparing us for the ever-evolving challenges and innovations within the vast domain of IoT.

CHAPTER 6

Edge Development Using AWS IoT Greengrass

The modern technology landscape is witnessing a dramatic shift, from centralized cloud-only architectures to more decentralized, edge-driven solutions. The term "edge" in edge computing specifically denotes the practice of processing data near the source of that data, which, in the case of IoT, means the myriad smart devices that have seamlessly integrated into our daily lives.

Take, for instance, our homes. Smart thermostats can adjust the temperature of a room based on our preferences, while IoT-enabled refrigerators can monitor their contents, sending notifications when milk is running low or when a vegetable is close to its expiry. Smart speakers, like Amazon Echo, not only play our favorite tunes but also control other smart devices in the house, set reminders, or even offer weather updates.

Then, there's the world of wearables. Smartwatches and fitness trackers monitor our daily steps, heart rates, and sleep patterns. They not only provide us with health metrics but can also notify us of calls, messages, or reminders.

Processing data directly on these devices – at the edge – enables more immediate response times, enhances user experiences, and alleviates strain on centralized servers or cloud infrastructures. Rather than funneling all data back to a central data center, devices can discerningly choose what to retain, process, or discard. This approach not only curtails costs but also ensures users receive pertinent information efficiently.

Delving into the details, AWS IoT Greengrass stands out as pivotal in amplifying the benefits of edge computing. Recognizing the revolutionary potential of edge computing, Amazon Web Services (AWS), known for its trailblazing cloud solutions, introduced AWS IoT Greengrass V2 as an open source service. This innovation seamlessly connects AWS cloud to edge devices, allowing devices to process data locally. This means they can execute code, synchronize data, and manage local computations without continuously depending on the cloud.

S. Rehan, *AWS IoT With Edge ML and Cybersecurity*, https://doi.org/10.1007/979-8-8688-0011-5_6

In this chapter, we will delve deep into the nuances of edge development using AWS IoT Greengrass. We will cover the various types of edge development that businesses can leverage, elaborate on the importance of compute at the edge, and discuss the vital role of Interprocess Communication (IPC) within AWS IoT Greengrass. By the end of this chapter, you will also learn how to simulate and harness local edge data using this robust AWS service, ensuring that your edge solutions are not only scalable but also reliable and resilient.

Let's delve into how AWS IoT Greengrass is sculpting the edge development horizon. Whether you're a business aiming to refine your processes or a developer keen on tapping into edge computing's merits, this chapter offers insights that will equip you to excel. Moreover, it will guide you in constructing a Minimum Viable Product (MVP), laying the groundwork for your production-level IoT device endeavors.

What's AWS IoT Greengrass

AWS IoT Greengrass is an open source edge runtime that facilitates the development, deployment, and management of device software.

Some of the key features of AWS IoT Greengrass entail the following:

Components: AWS IoT Greengrass offers ready-made (AWS publicly provided) components for typical scenarios, enabling you to seamlessly discover, import, set up, and deploy applications and services at the edge. This negates the need for diving into varied device protocols, handling credentials, or interacting with external APIs. Additionally, you have the flexibility to design custom components or replicate shared business logic across multiple AWS IoT Greengrass devices. Being modular, AWS IoT Greengrass allows you to tailor its components based on your IoT needs and the device's CPU and memory constraints. For instance, you might opt for AWS IoT Greengrass components such as stream manager, edge ML inference components only when your application demands data stream processing or integrate machine learning components exclusively when local machine learning inference is required on your devices.

- **Local Processing:** AWS IoT Greengrass allows you to run code and applications on edge devices, even when they are offline or have intermittent connectivity to the cloud. This means that your devices can react to events and make decisions without having to wait for the cloud, which can improve performance and responsiveness.

- **Local Support for AWS IoT Device Shadows:** AWS IoT Greengrass extends the features of AWS IoT Device Shadows. This Device Shadow acts as a cache, preserving the device's status, functioning like a digital twin or digital *"shadow"* of each device (as we learnt in a prior chapter). It monitors the disparity between the device's present and intended state, and when a connection is accessible, it synchronizes that state with the cloud.
- **Local Development:** AWS IoT Greengrass enables quick code development and debugging on a test device, prior to deploying it to your operational devices via the cloud. The AWS IoT Greengrass command-line interface (CLI) facilitates local application development and debugging on your device. Additionally, the local debug console provides a visual aid for troubleshooting applications.
- **Local Compute Using AWS Lambda:** AWS IoT Greengrass incorporates AWS Lambda support. This enables you to execute AWS Lambda functions directly on the device, allowing for rapid responses to local events, engagement with on-device resources, and efficient data processing to reduce the expenses associated with transferring data to the cloud.
- **Local Resource Access:** Denotes buses and peripherals physically situated on the AWS IoT Greengrass host, as well as a file system volume present on the host OS of AWS IoT Greengrass. For instance, to interact with devices linked through Modbus/CAN bus, an AWS IoT Greengrass Lambda function would require access to the device's serial port. Such local resources are established within the scope of an AWS IoT Greengrass group, allowing all Lambdas within that group to utilize the designated local resources.
- **Local Messaging:** AWS IoT Greengrass provides a secure and reliable messaging system for devices to communicate with each other and with the cloud. This allows you to build applications that are more scalable and resilient (we will learn in this chapter by building smart home simulation).

- **Data Management:** AWS IoT Greengrass provides tools for managing data on edge devices, including storing, filtering, and aggregating data. This can help you to reduce the amount of data that needs to be sent to the cloud, which can save bandwidth and improve performance.
- **Machine Learning Inference:** AWS IoT Greengrass allows you to run machine learning models on edge devices. This can be useful for applications that need to make predictions or classifications in real time, without having to send data to the cloud (we will learn this in the subsequent chapter).
- **Secure Connectivity:** AWS IoT Greengrass ensures robust connectivity between devices, the cloud, and third-party services. It not only supports secure credentials through its Secrets Manager but also integrates with TPM (Trusted Platform Module) for enhanced security.
    - **AWS IoT Greengrass Secrets Manager:** This tool provides secure storage, management, and rotation of essential secrets, including credentials, keys, and configurations, at the device's edge. When a Greengrass component needs authentication, the required secrets are deployed directly to the Greengrass core. An example use case is the configuration of private Docker registry credentials.
    - **Hardware Security Integration:** With AWS IoT Greengrass, devices can store their private keys in a secure hardware module (TPM). This capability, combined with the Secrets Manager, guarantees that sensitive data remains encrypted and protected at the edge, cementing a foundation of security and trust.
- **Docker Support:** AWS IoT Greengrass supports Docker containers, which makes it easy to deploy and manage your applications.
- **Stream Manager:** AWS IoT Greengrass allows you to gather, process, and export data streams from IoT devices, also overseeing the data's life cycle on the device to reduce development duration. It offers

a consistent methodology for data stream processing, local data retention policy management, and data transmission to AWS cloud services, including Amazon S3, Amazon Kinesis, AWS IoT Core, and AWS IoT Analytics.

- **Community Component Catalog:** The Greengrass Software Catalog is a compilation of AWS IoT Greengrass components curated by the Greengrass community. Instead of crafting individual device components for each necessary function, you now have the advantage of quickly installing, utilizing, and adapting components from a curated list of pre-established software modules available on GitHub. This streamlines the initiation of your IoT edge projects. Take, for instance, a security monitoring system. With the Amazon Kinesis Video Streams (KVS) component, you can ingest video and audio feeds from RTSP cameras linked to an AWS IoT Greengrass core device. This data can be relayed to a local monitoring setup or uploaded to the cloud. Alternatively, if your focus is on immediate analytics and on-site operations tracking, the InfluxDB and Grafana modules are at your disposal to process and graphically represent data from IoT sensors and edge devices on the spot. These modules serve as illustrative examples of frequently employed patterns.
- **OTA (Over-the-Air) Updates:** AWS IoT Greengrass allows for software updates on its devices. Through the AWS IoT Greengrass console, APIs, or command-line interface, you can upgrade the version of the Greengrass cores or components on your devices.

Types of Edge Development

Edge development has garnered significant attention as various industries realize the benefits of processing data closer to its origin. This proximity offers advantages like decreased latency, bandwidth conservation, and more prompt data-driven actions. As edge computing continues to evolve, we see the emergence of distinct development categories. Here's a concise outline of these main avenues:

1. **Device Edge Development**
    - **Smart Consumer Devices**: Examples encompass smart thermostats and refrigerators. These appliances process data locally for instant actions such as temperature adjustments or user notifications.
    - **Wearable Tech**: Devices like smartwatches and AR glasses offer real-time processing to deliver immediate user feedback or visual outputs.
2. **Constrained Edge Development**
    - **Sensor Nodes**: Common in sectors like agriculture and industry, these nodes gather data points (e.g., temperature or vibration) and might process them locally before transmitting aggregated or critical data to a central hub.
    - **IoT Gateways**: These facilitate data collection from multiple sensors and devices. They can preprocess this data before relaying it, serving as a nexus between the device and the cloud.
3. **Industrial Edge Development**
    - **Manufacturing Equipment**: Factory machinery with edge functionality processes data instantly to enhance operations, foresee maintenance needs, or boost safety measures.
    - **Energy Grid Devices**: Instruments like smart grids employ edge processing to adapt in real time to fluctuations in demand or to identify potential challenges.
4. **Infrastructure Edge Development**
    - **Content Delivery Networks (CDNs)**: Beyond their traditional caching roles, contemporary CDNs function as computation hubs, executing code near users for diminished latency.
    - **Telco Edge**: With 5G's advent, telecom entities are moving computations closer to their network's edge, catering to applications requiring low latency.

5. **Ruggedized Edge Development**
    - **Vehicular Systems**: Edge computing plays a pivotal role in vehicles, especially autonomous ones, analyzing copious data volumes in real time for instantaneous decision-making.
    - **Remote Environments**: In areas like offshore oil platforms or ships, where stable connectivity is sporadic, rugged edge systems operate on-site, transmitting essential data when a connection is established.
6. **Specialized Edge Development**
    - **Medical IoT (MIoT)**: Medical equipment, such as patient monitors, necessitates rapid and reliable data processing, particularly in emergent scenarios.
    - **Aviation Systems**: In-flight real-time data processing is essential for navigation and maintaining passenger well-being.

Selecting the appropriate edge development trajectory largely hinges on the distinct needs of an application, factoring in aspects like latency, connectivity range, energy usage, and computational demands.

Compute at the Edge Using AWS IoT Greengrass

Let's delve into the inner workings of Greengrass by examining the core device, understanding the Greengrass component, exploring the concepts of recipes, artifacts, and dependencies, and learning how component deployment functions.

Overview of AWS IoT Greengrass V2 Components

AWS IoT Greengrass V2 components are pivotal, laying the foundation for diverse workflows such as machine learning inference, local data processing, messaging, and data management. These components streamline the intricate process, allowing for a more intuitive and efficient workflow.

Key Highlights

- **Preconfigured Components**: AWS IoT Greengrass V2 offers preconfigured components like the Stream Manager and Log Manager, simplifying the data export process to both local and cloud-based platforms.
- **Efficient Application Creation**: These components allow developers to expedite the application creation process, eliminating the need to navigate complex device protocols or handle credentials and external APIs. This efficiency enhances the development process, allowing for a more focused approach.
- **Seamless Interaction**: Ensure seamless interaction with AWS services and third-party applications without the need for manual coding. This seamless integration facilitates smoother operations and interactions, enhancing overall efficiency and productivity.
- **Custom Component Creation**: Developers have the liberty to create custom components within the AWS IoT Greengrass platform. This flexibility allows for a more tailored approach to component creation and implementation.
- **Consistent Business Logic**: Ensure consistent business logic across multiple AWS IoT Greengrass devices, promoting uniformity and consistency across various devices and platforms.
- **Streamlined Processes**: AWS IoT Greengrass V2 components streamline the discovery, configuration, and deployment process for components at the edge, enhancing efficiency and effectiveness in the deployment process.

Greengrass "Core Device"

A Greengrass core device is an edge computing device equipped with AWS IoT Greengrass Core software. It's recognized within the AWS ecosystem as an IoT "thing" and can be grouped with other core devices within AWS IoT thing groups, forming a cohesive, manageable cluster of Greengrass core devices.

Greengrass Component Details

A Greengrass Component is a software module designed to operate exclusively on a Greengrass core device. Any software component developed and/or deployed on AWS IoT Greengrass automatically adopts the component model, ensuring seamless integration and operation within the Greengrass ecosystem. AWS IoT Greengrass enhances functionality by offering a variety of pre-built components, ready for immediate deployment to your devices.

- **Nucleus Component**

  The Nucleus Component, termed as "*aws.greengrass.Nucleus*", is a crucial element in the Greengrass structure. It stands as the foundational component for operating the AWS IoT Greengrass Core software on any device. This component facilitates remote customization and updates, allowing you to modify various settings, including proxy and device role configurations. Since most AWS-provided components are dependent on specific versions of the Greengrass nucleus, timely updates are essential to ensure seamless operation and integration of all components within the Greengrass ecosystem.

- **Plug-In Component**

  The Greengrass nucleus seamlessly manages plug-in components within its own Java Virtual Machine (JVM) environment. In the event of a version update of any plug-in component on the core device, the nucleus is restarted to ensure optimal functionality. To guarantee the efficient installation and operation of these plug-in components, it's crucial to configure the Greengrass nucleus to operate as a system service (by default, using standard installation will do that).

  Numerous components provided by AWS fall under the category of plug-in components, thereby enabling them to interface directly with the essential Greengrass nucleus. It's worth noting that these plug-in components and the Greengrass nucleus utilize a common log file, ensuring streamlined logging activities.

- **Generic Component**

  The Greengrass nucleus is adept at executing the life cycle scripts of a generic component, assuming the component possesses a defined life cycle (refer to Figure 6-1). In the case of custom components, the type is automatically designated as generic, ensuring smooth integration and operation within the Greengrass ecosystem.

- **Lambda Component**

  In terms of Lambda function components, the Greengrass nucleus functions through the Lambda launcher component. Any component derived from a Lambda function naturally assumes this type, ensuring consistency and reliability in operation.

Component Life Cycle

The component life cycle outlines the diverse stages that the AWS IoT Greengrass Core software navigates to successfully deploy and operate components. Each phase is characterized by specific configured script actions (if defined for each state) and related data that guide the component's operations. For example, during the installation phase, the Greengrass Core software activates the "*Install*" life cycle script for the respective component, ensuring a smooth transition through the subsequent life cycle states (this could include installing prerequisite software needed for this component) (refer to Figure 6-1).

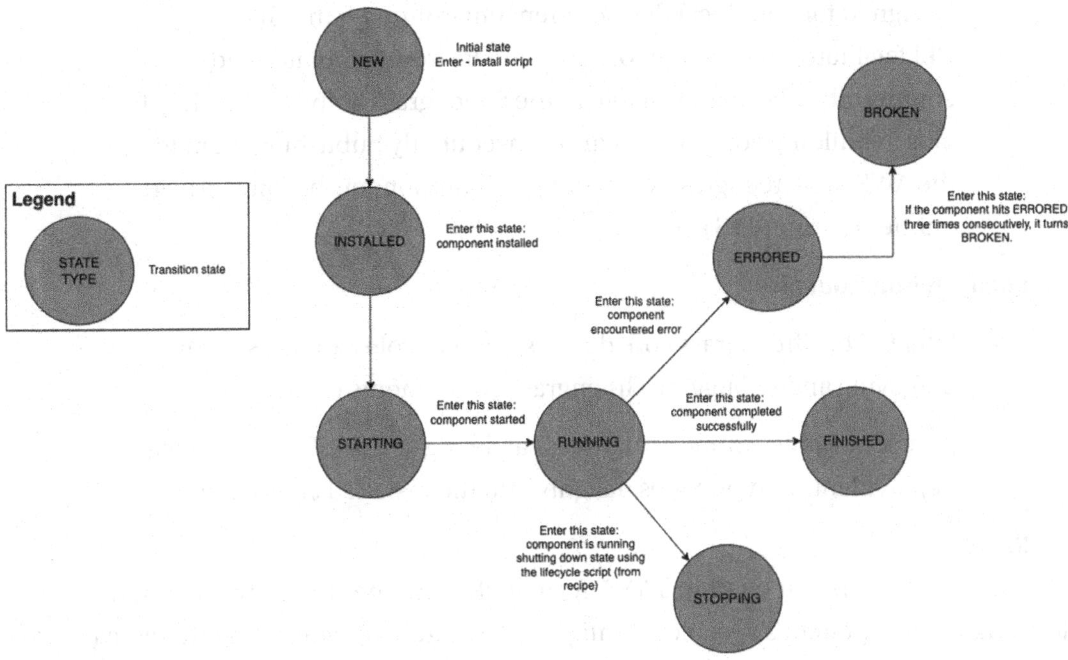

Figure 6-1. *AWS IoT* ***Greengrass Component life cycle*** *"states"*

Greengrass Development Tools

AWS IoT Greengrass equips developers with an array of tools specifically crafted for the various stages of Greengrass component development (utilizing AWS CLI). These tools aid in creating, testing, building, publishing, and deploying custom Greengrass components, ensuring a comprehensive development experience.

- **Greengrass Command-Line Interface (Greengrass CLI)** - *most popular*

  This interface is tailored for Greengrass core devices, assisting in the deployment and debugging of Greengrass components. As a deployable component itself, the Greengrass CLI empowers your core devices to initiate local deployments, inspect details about the incorporated components, and access log files.

- **Greengrass Development Kit CLI (GDK CLI)** - *relatively new*

Designed for your local development environment, the GDK CLI facilitates the creation of components from templates and community offerings available in the Greengrass Software Catalog. It aids in building components and subsequently publishing them to the AWS IoT Greengrass service. These components become private entities in your AWS account.

Local Debug Console

- Situated on Greengrass core devices, this console can be used for deploying and debugging Greengrass components locally.
- As a deployable component, the local debug console facilitates local deployments and provides insights into the installed components.

Recipe

This is a file, either in JSON or YAML format, that outlines the software module, detailing the component's specifics, configuration, and parameters. It's advisable not to define the component type in a recipe. AWS IoT Greengrass automatically determines and sets the type for you upon component creation.

Artifact

Artifacts comprise the source code, binaries, or scripts that manifest as the software running on the device. They can be fashioned from scratch, or developers can generate a component leveraging Lambda functions, Docker containers, or bespoke runtimes.

Dependency

This refers to the interrelation between components, allowing for the automation of updates or restarts in reliant components. For instance, if a message processing component relies on an encryption component, any updates to the latter will trigger automatic updates and restarts of the message processing component.

Greengrass Service Role (GreengrassV2TokenExchangeRole)

The *GreengrassV2TokenExchangeRole* is a role that AWS IoT Greengrass creates in your AWS account. It's specifically created by the Greengrass service, not manually by users. This role is used to grant permissions for core devices to assume roles and interact with AWS services. When a core device needs to interact with an AWS service, it assumes this role to get temporary credentials. As we know, Greengrass nucleus is the runtime component of AWS IoT Greengrass V2. It doesn't "create" the role, but it uses the role (or more specifically, uses the temporary credentials obtained by assuming the role) to interact with AWS services. In summary, the GreengrassV2TokenExchangeRole is created by the AWS IoT Greengrass service, not the Greengrass nucleus component, although the nucleus does utilize it, it is a data plane role.

What Is Interprocess Communication?

Component-to-Component Communication (IPC)

Components active on your core device can employ the AWS IoT Greengrass Core Interprocess communication (IPC) library, part of the AWS IoT Device SDK, to interface with the AWS IoT Greengrass nucleus and other related components. For the creation and execution of custom components leveraging IPC, it's imperative to utilize the AWS IoT Device SDK. This SDK ensures proper connectivity to the AWS IoT Greengrass Core IPC service and facilitates efficient IPC tasks.

The IPC interface provides two primary operational modalities:

Request/Response

- Components forward a request to the IPC service.
- In return, they receive a response encapsulating the outcome of their initial request.

Subscription

- Components dispatch a subscription appeal to the IPC service, anticipating a continual flow of event messages (stream).
- For this, components are equipped with a subscription handler responsible for managing event messages, potential errors, and the eventual termination of the stream.
- Furthermore, the AWS IoT Device SDK is enriched with a handler interface, ensuring appropriate response and event categorizations for every IPC activity.

Key Aspects of AWS IoT Greengrass IPC

Connectors and Lambda Functions: AWS IoT Greengrass uses connectors (pre-built integrations) and Lambda functions (custom code) to perform tasks. IPC allows these components to communicate with each other and with the Greengrass core system.

IPC SDK: AWS provides SDKs (Software Development Kits) for developers. These SDKs include features for IPC, allowing developers to make their software components interoperable within the Greengrass environment.

IPC Mechanisms: The actual IPC can happen in various ways, like shared memory, message queues, or sockets, depending on the requirements and the nature of the communication.

Security: IPC within Greengrass respects the same security boundaries and principles that AWS IoT Greengrass enforces. For example, for two Lambda functions to communicate, they both need to have the appropriate permissions.

Use Cases: A common use case for IPC is when one Lambda function wants to publish a message to the local MQTT broker, but it doesn't have the permission to do so directly. In this scenario, the function can communicate with another function (or connector) that does have the required permissions.

Decoupling: IPC also allows for a decoupled architecture, where different functions or components are responsible for different tasks. They can work independently and only communicate when necessary, making the system more modular and easier to manage.

In summary, AWS IoT Greengrass IPC is a means of facilitating communication between different software components within the Greengrass environment. This allows for a flexible, secure, and modular system where components can interact and collaborate on various tasks.

Set Up and Test AWS IoT Greengrass

Before we can install AWS IoT Greengrass, we need to set up an IAM service role (the service role is used by services to interact with other AWS services depending on the permissions granted in the policy attached to the role). This role enables AWS IoT Greengrass to authenticate client devices and oversee their connectivity details (*Control plane role*).

Prerequisite

From the AWS Console, go to the IAM console and select "*Roles*" and then "*Create role*" (see Figure 6-2).

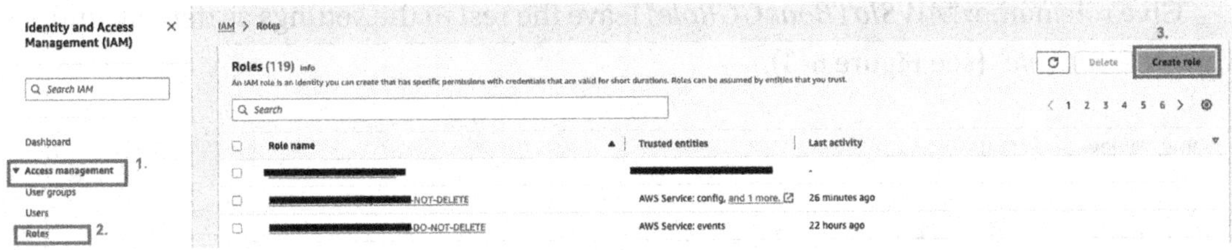

Figure 6-2. *IAM console, Create role*

From the *Trusted entity type*, select "*AWS service*", and from *Use cases for other AWS services,* select *Greengrass* and then click "*Next*" (see Figure 6-3).

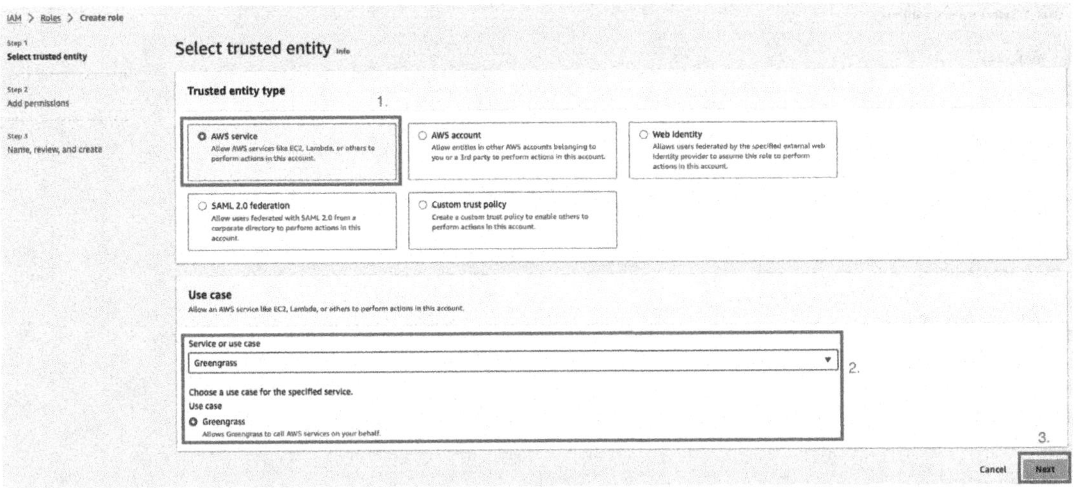

Figure 6-3. *Setting up a role for Greengrass service*

In the Add permissions screen, "*search*" for an existing policy, "*AWSGreengrassResourceAccessRolePolicy*", and select it and click "*Next*" (see Figure 6-4).

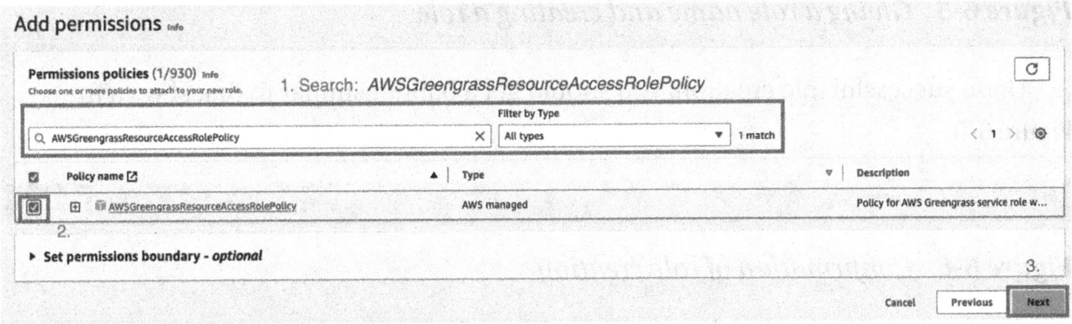

Figure 6-4. *Attaching a policy*

Give role name: "*AWSIoTBookGGRole*", leave the rest of the settings as default, and click "*Create role*" (see Figure 6-5).

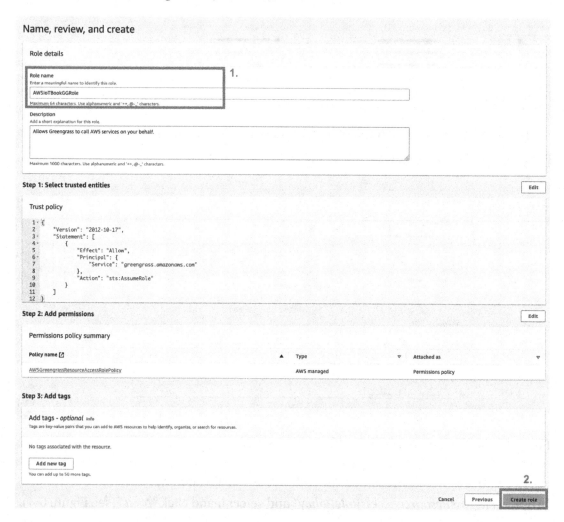

Figure 6-5. *Giving a role name and creating a role*

Upon successful role creation, you should get a banner similar to that shown in Figure 6-6.

Figure 6-6. *Confirmation of role creation*

Let's switch to the AWS IoT Core console, select "*Settings*", and in the Greengrass service role section, click "*Attach role*" (see Figure 6-7).

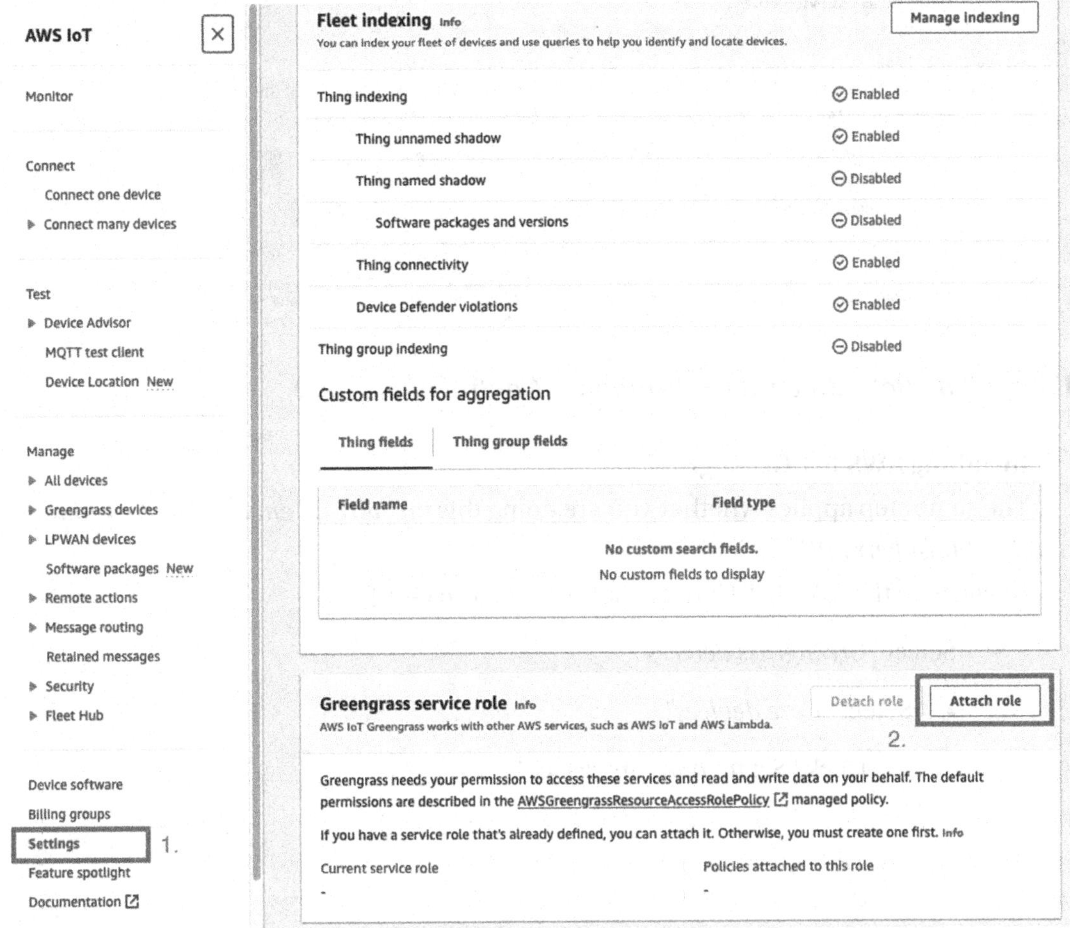

Figure 6-7. *Attaching a newly created role in settings*

Select our recently created role, "*AWSIoTBookGGRole*", and click "*Attach role*" (see Figure 6-8).

Figure 6-8. *Selecting AWSIoTBookGGRole*

Once created, we should get success notification and role as shown in Figure 6-9.

Greengrass service role Info
AWS IoT Greengrass works with other AWS services, such as AWS IoT and AWS Lambda.
Detach role
Change role
Greengrass needs your permission to access these services and read and write data on your behalf. The default permissions are described in the AWSGreengrassResourceAccessRolePolicy managed policy.
If you have a service role that's already defined, you can attach it. Otherwise, you must create one first. Info
Greengrass service role has been updated successfully.
Current service role
arn:aws:iam::████████:role AWSIoTBookGGRole
Policies attached to this role
AWSGreengrassResourceAccessRolePolicy

Figure 6-9. *Role attached confirmation (Control plane role)*

Installing AWS IoT Greengrass

The same step applies whether you are doing this on "*virtual environment - Cloud9*" or using "*Raspberry Pi*".

Navigate to the AWS IoT Core console (see Figure 6-10).

- Select "*Greengrass devices*".
    - Select "*Core devices*".
        - Click "*Set up one core device*".

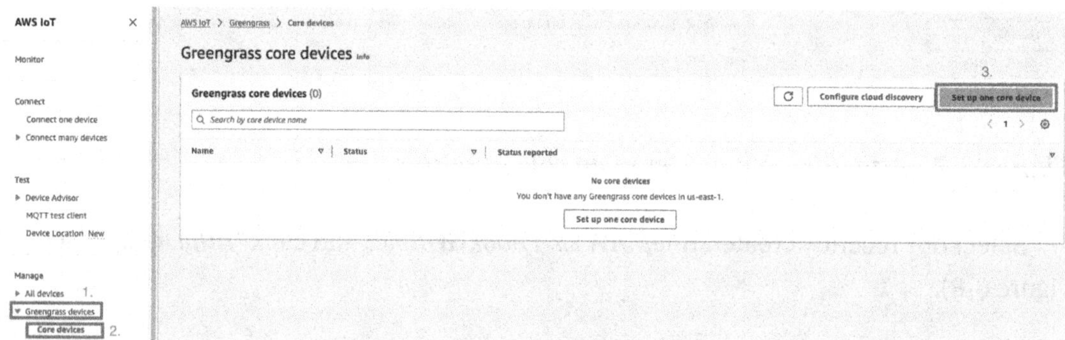

Figure 6-10. *Creating a Greengrass core device*

When setting up a core device, select settings as shown in Figure 6-11:

- Core device name: *UbuntuGGv2.*
- Thing group name: *UbuntuGGv2Group.*
- Operating system: *Linux.*
- Copy the command from the "*Download the installer*" box.
    - Copy and paste it in your terminal window (Cloud9 or RPi terminal).
- From the "*Run the installer*" box.
    - Copy the command and paste it in the terminal window too.

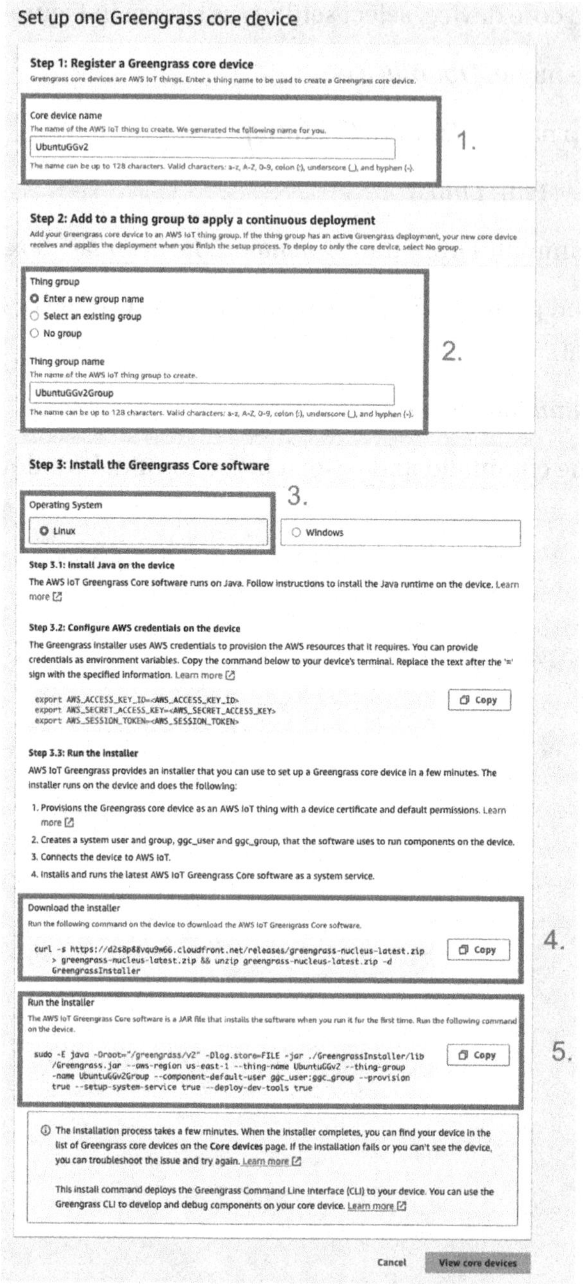

Figure 6-11. *Setting up Greengrass core on the edge device*

Upon successful completion, select "*View core devices*", and in our terminal window, we should see the output as shown in Figure 6-12.

```
syed-book:~/environment $ sudo -E java -Droot="/greengrass/v2" -Dlog.store=FILE -jar ./GreengrassInstaller/lib/Greengrass.jar
omponent-default-user ggc_user:ggc_group --provision true --setup-system-service true --deploy-dev-tools true
Provisioning AWS IoT resources for the device with IoT Thing Name: [UbuntuGGv2]...
Found IoT policy "GreengrassV2IoTThingPolicy", reusing it
Creating keys and certificate...
Attaching policy to certificate...
Creating IoT Thing "UbuntuGGv2"...
Attaching certificate to IoT thing...
Successfully provisioned AWS IoT resources for the device with IoT Thing Name: [UbuntuGGv2]!
Adding IoT Thing [UbuntuGGv2] into Thing Group: [UbuntuGGv2Group]...
Successfully added Thing into Thing Group: [UbuntuGGv2Group]
Setting up resources for aws.greengrass.TokenExchangeService ...
Attaching TES role policy to IoT thing...
No managed IAM policy found, looking for user defined policy...
IAM policy named "GreengrassV2TokenExchangeRoleAccess" already exists. Please attach it to the IAM role if not already
Configuring Nucleus with provisioned resource details...
Downloading Root CA from "https://www.amazontrust.com/repository/AmazonRootCA1.pem"
Created device configuration
Successfully configured Nucleus with provisioned resource details!
Creating a deployment for Greengrass first party components to the thing group
Configured Nucleus to deploy aws.greengrass.Cli component
Creating user ggc_user
ggc_user created
Creating group ggc_group
ggc_group created
Added ggc_user to ggc_group
Successfully set up Nucleus as a system service
```

Figure 6-12. *Successful setup of the Greengrass core device (edge device)*

We can also run the following command in the terminal screen to obtain the status of the AWS IoT Greengrass service:

```
sudo systemctl status greengrass.service
```

We can see our core device status as "*Healthy*" (see Figure 6-13) and select our core device to review components installed (see Figure 6-14).

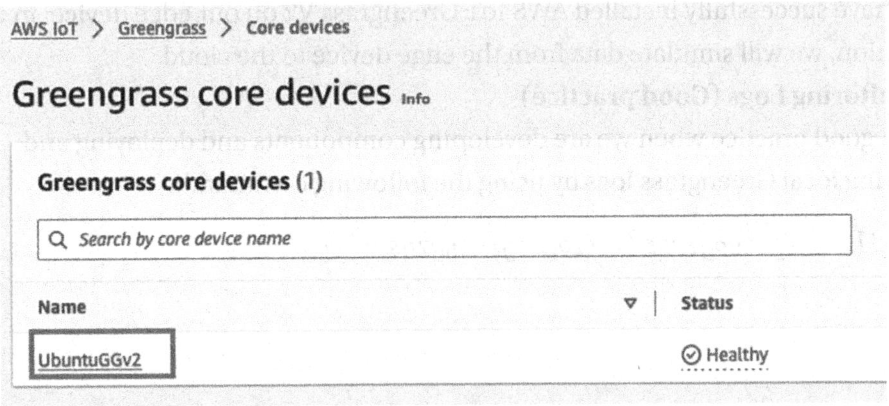

Figure 6-13. *Core device showing the status healthy*

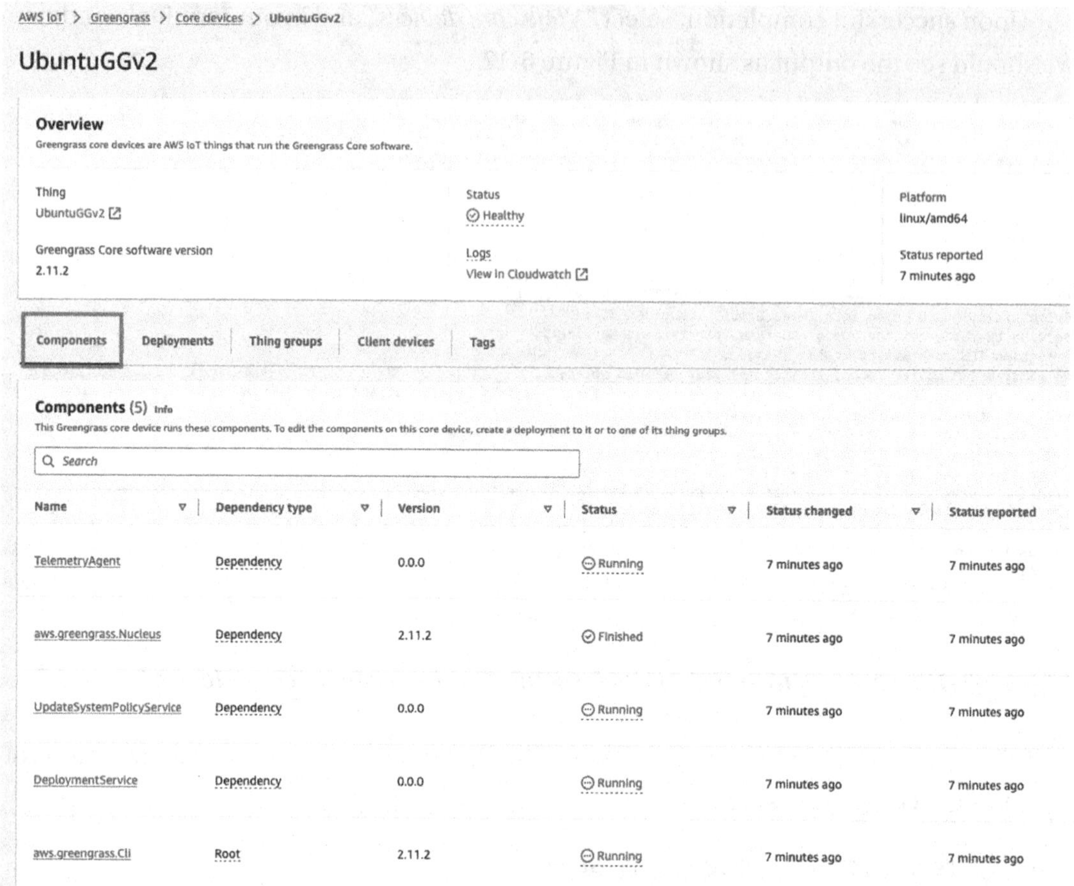

Figure 6-14. *We can review installed components by default*

We have successfully installed AWS IoT Greengrass V2 on our edge device; in the next section, we will simulate data from the edge device to the cloud.

Monitoring Logs (Good practice)

It's a good practice when we are developing components and deploying and monitoring local Greengrass logs by using the following command:

```
sudo tail -F /greengrass/v2/logs/greengrass.log
```

Simulate/Harness Local Edge Data Using AWS IoT Greengrass

We'll explore a scenario where an IoT device, like a smart home appliance, doesn't directly connect to the Greengrass core device, for instance, a home hub equipped with AWS IoT Greengrass. By utilizing AWS's MQTT Bridge, the Greengrass device evolves into a Local MQTT Gateway. This setup is optimal for architectures focusing on local communication and processing, especially in smart home environments. Through this gateway, IoT device data is channeled to IoT Core for further processing.

In our simulation, we'll employ the edge gateway we previously set up, named AWS IoT Greengrass (UbuntuGGv2). Running the Greengrass core, this gateway collects data from an external IoT device. Typically, in an edge environment, this device might send metrics like humidity, temperature, and air quality, similar to those from a home thermostat. The "Local MQTT Bridge" then relays this information to AWS IoT Core. Additionally, we will delve into how to monitor these devices using Amazon CloudWatch (see Figure 6-15).

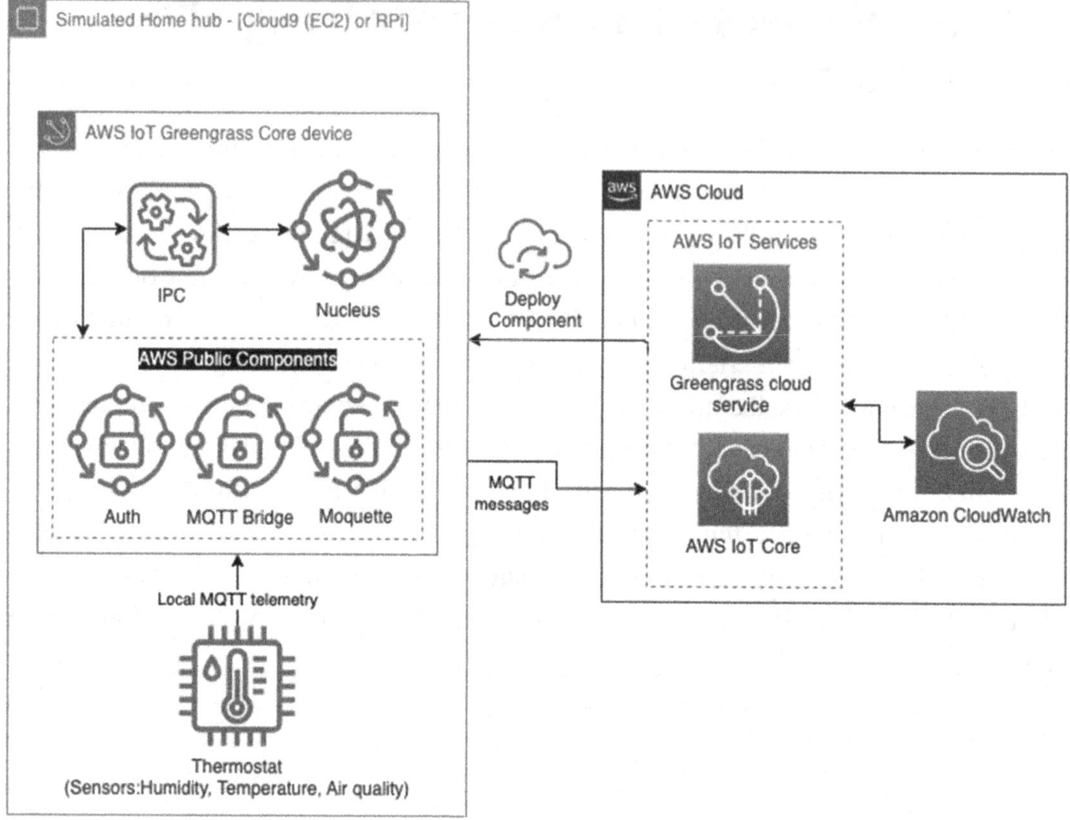

Figure 6-15. *Simulated environment architecture*

IAM Policy for GreengrassV2TokenExchangeRole (Mandatory Permission)

The token exchange role permits device access to non-IoT services (such as Amazon S3). The Greengrass core device recognizes only the token exchange role alias, as defined in the nucleus configuration. To adjust device permissions, modify the IAM policies linked to this role (as we will do here), and the device will inherit the permissions specified in those updated policies.

In this section, we will guide you through creating an IAM policy tailored for ***educational purposes***, allowing our role (*GreengrassV2TokenExchangeRole*) to access various AWS services. Here's a breakdown:

- **Amazon S3**
    - **Permissions:** Create, list, upload, and download within all S3 buckets.
- **AWS IoT**
    - **Permissions:** Perform any actions across all IoT resources.
- **AWS Greengrass**
    - **Permissions:** Execute all actions within the Greengrass service.

This comprehensive policy ensures smooth interaction and management within these pivotal AWS services, providing a practical, hands-on "***learning experience***".

Note It's crucial to remember that this policy is not designed for production use. It grants extensive permissions and is intended solely for learning and exploration. Ensure to delete this policy once your educational endeavors are completed to maintain robust security standards within your AWS environment.

From the IAM console (see Figure 6-16):

- Select Policies.
    - Create policy.

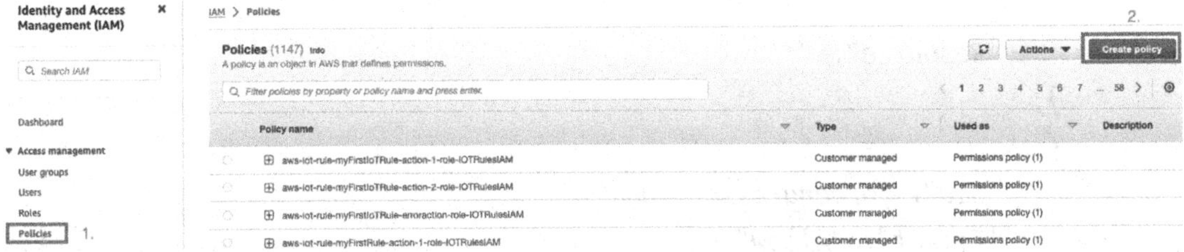

Figure 6-16. *Creating an IAM policy*

On the "*Specify Permissions*" page, choose the JSON option. Ensure you remove any existing JSON, then copy and paste the following JSON:

Note You must not use this policy in production; it's only for educational purposes and should be deleted after you have completed your learning.

```
{
    "Version": "2012-10-17",
    "Statement": [
        {
            "Sid": "S3BucketActions",
            "Effect": "Allow",
            "Action": [
                "s3:CreateBucket",
                "s3:ListAllMyBuckets",
                "s3:GetBucketLocation",
                "s3:PutObject",
                "s3:GetObject",
                "s3:ListBucket"
            ],
            "Resource": [
                "arn:aws:s3:::*"
            ]
        },
        {
            "Effect": "Allow",
            "Action": [
                "iot:*"
            ],
            "Resource": "*"
        },
        {
            "Sid": "GreengrassActions",
            "Effect": "Allow",
            "Action": [
                "greengrass:*"
            ],
            "Resource": "*"
        }
    ]
}
```

Navigate to the "*Next: Review and create*" screen.

- Give the policy the following name: "*awsiotbook_gg_policy*".
- Provide a description: "*Greengrass non-production testing usage policy only.*"
- Select "*Create policy*".

After successful creation, we will see a success notification banner (see Figure 6-17).

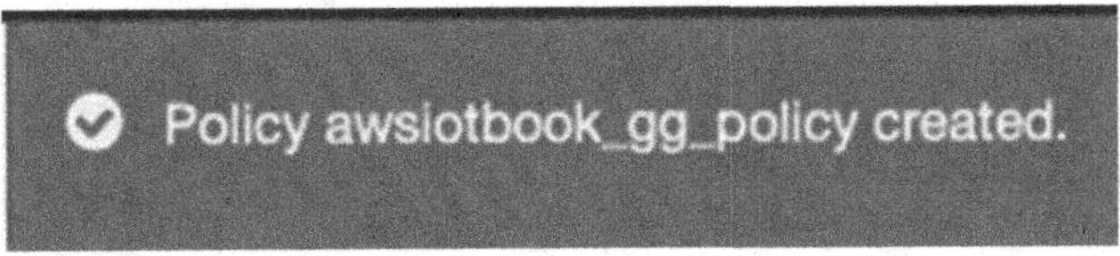

Figure 6-17. *Success banner upon IAM policy creation*

Finally, we need to attach this policy to our *GreengrassV2TokenExchangeRole*. In the IAM console, please navigate to *Roles* and search the following *Role: GreengrassV2TokenExchangeRole* (see Figure 6-18).

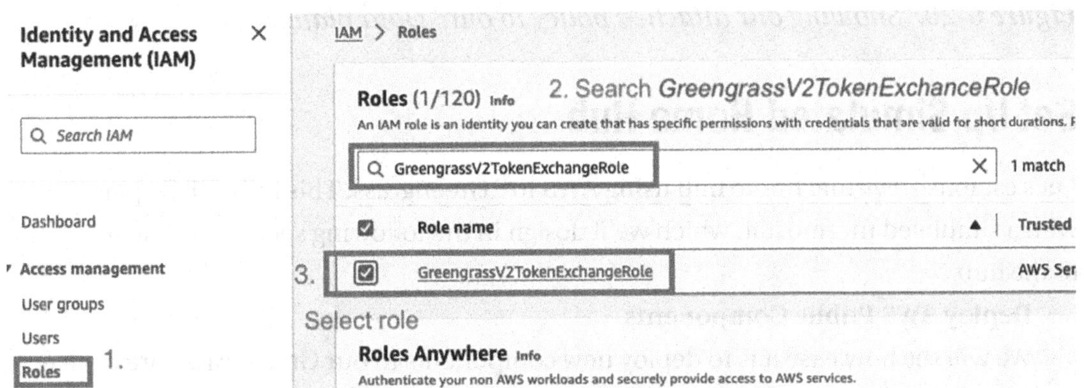

Figure 6-18. *Search for the role "GreengrassV2TokenExchangeRole"*

Under "*Add Permissions*", click "*Attach Policies*" (see Figure 6-19) and then search for and select the "*awsiotbook_gg_policy*" you created earlier, and finally select "*Add permissions*".

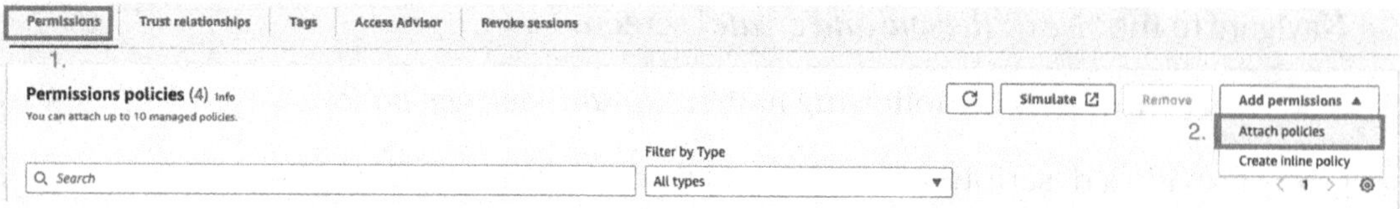

Figure 6-19. Attaching a policy

Once done, we will be able to see our policy attached to our role (*GreengrassV2TokenExchangeRole*) (see Figure 6-20).

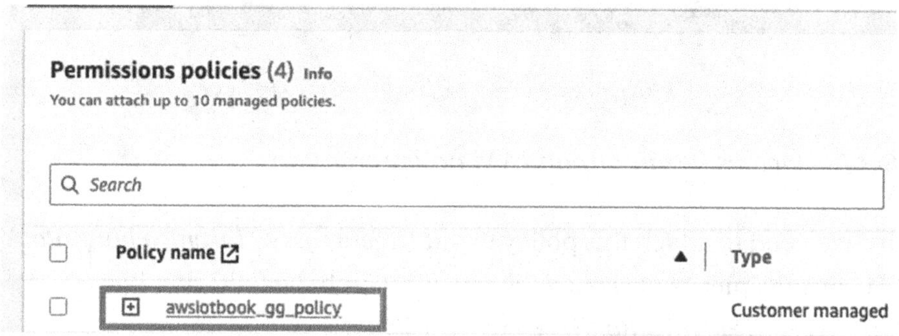

Figure 6-20. Showing our attached policy to our "Data plane role"

Set Up Simulated Home Hub

Let's establish a virtual home hub using AWS IoT Greengrass. This hub will be paired with a simulated thermostat, which we'll design in the following section, to transmit data to the hub.

Deploy AWS Public Components

We will see how easy it is to deploy new components to our Greengrass core device; let's deploy it publicly available AWS IoT Greengrass following components:

- *aws.greengrass.clientdevices.Auth*
- *aws.greengrass.clientdevices.mqtt.Bridge*
- *aws.greengrass.clientdevices.mqtt.Moquette*

Auth Component

The "client device auth" component ensures the authentication of client devices and grants authorization for their actions, enabling them to connect to the Greengrass core device. This component generates the certificate provided by the local MQTT broker.

Bridge Component

The "MQTT bridge" component facilitates the exchange of MQTT messages among client devices, Greengrass components, and AWS IoT Core.

Moquette Component

The "Moquette MQTT broker" component offers an MQTT broker, derived from Moquette, allowing client devices to connect to your Greengrass core device.

Before we deploy these components, let's run the following command on our edge device (*UbuntuGGv2*) terminal:

```
sudo /greengrass/v2/bin/greengrass-cli component list
```

This will give us default components installed thus far (see Figure 6-21).

```
syed-book:~/environment $ sudo /greengrass/v2/bin/greengrass-cli component list
Components currently running in Greengrass:
Component Name: aws.greengrass.Nucleus
    Version: 2.11.2
    State: FINISHED
    Configuration: {"awsRegion":"us-east-1","componentStoreMaxSizeBytes":"1000000
ervalSeconds":86400.0},"greengrassDataPlaneEndpoint":"","greengrassDataPlanePort"
taEndpoint":"a3lmpss0bulsm1-ats.iot.us-east-1.amazonaws.com","iotRoleAlias":"Gree
rkProxy":{"proxy":{}},"platformOverride":{},"runWithDefault":{"posixShell":"sh","
Component Name: FleetStatusService
    Version: 0.0.0
    State: RUNNING
    Configuration: null
Component Name: DeploymentService
    Version: 0.0.0
    State: RUNNING
    Configuration: null
Component Name: aws.greengrass.Cli
    Version: 2.11.2
    State: RUNNING
    Configuration: {"AuthorizedPosixGroups":null,"AuthorizedWindowsGroups":null}
Component Name: UpdateSystemPolicyService
    Version: 0.0.0
    State: RUNNING
    Configuration: null
Component Name: TelemetryAgent
    Version: 0.0.0
    State: RUNNING
    Configuration: null
```

***Figure 6-21.** Running components installed by default*

Monitoring Edge Device Log

We can monitor logs on our edge device running Greengrass core by using following command:

```
sudo tail -F /greengrass/v2/logs/greengrass.log
```

Revise Deployment and Install a Public Component

Navigate to the AWS IoT Core console (see Figure 6-22).

- Select *Greengrass devices*
  - *Deployments*
    - *Find by deployment name or target name: UbuntuGGv2Group*
  - Select the check box for
    - *Target name: UbuntuGGv2Group*
  - Select *Revise*
    - *Select "Revise deployment" on pop-up*

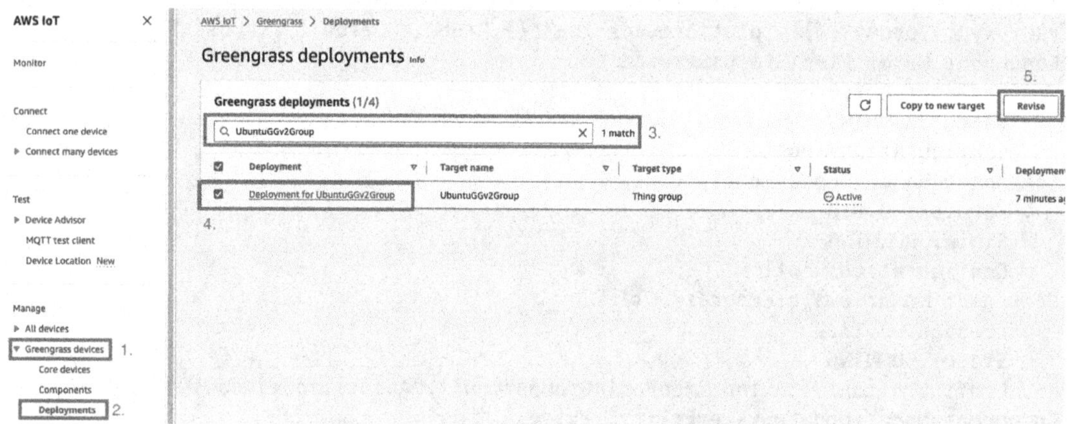

Figure 6-22. *Selecting a deployment to revise*

In this screen, give a name; it can be anything (or reuse the previous deployment name, i.e., *Deployment for UbuntuGGv2Group 2*), and click *"Next"* (see Figure 6-23).

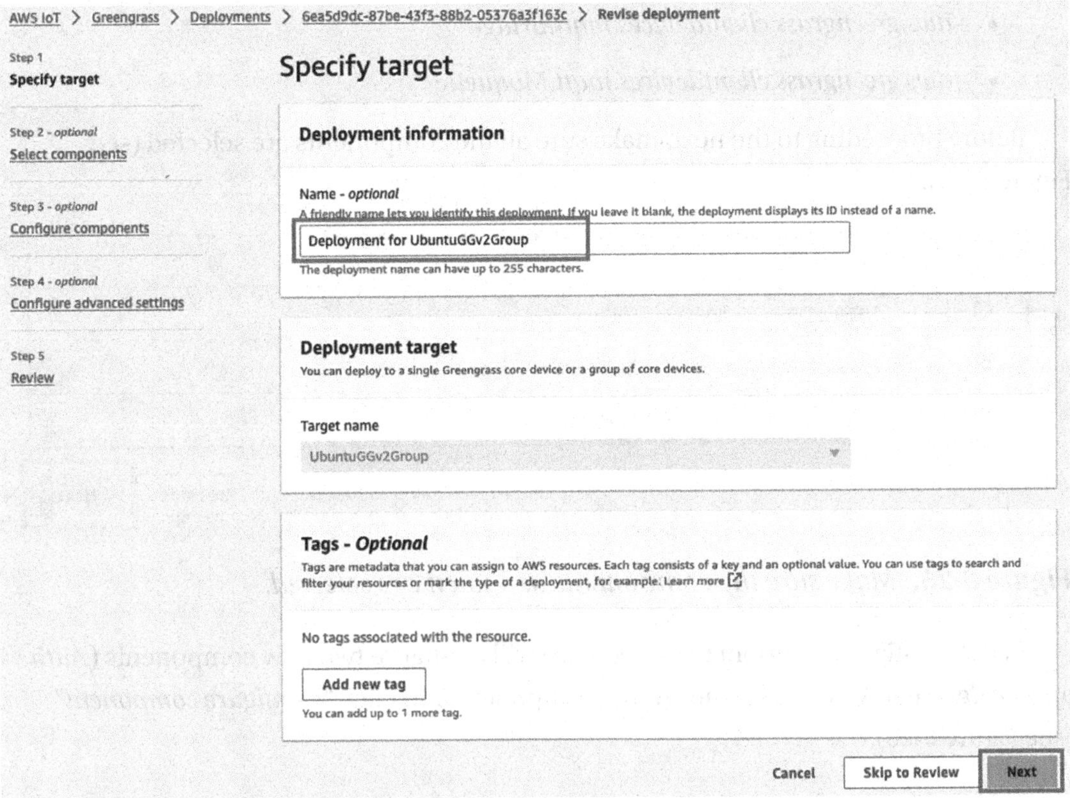

Figure 6-23. *Specifying target name selection*

In the Select Components screen under "Public components" (toggle off: *Show only selected components*) (see Figure 6-24).

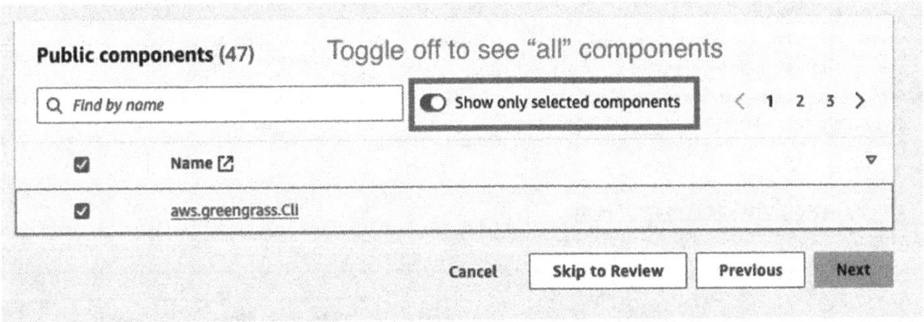

Figure 6-24. *Toggle off to see "all" public components.*

In Find by name – select following components:

- *aws.greengrass.clientdevices.Auth*
- *aws.greengrass.clientdevices.mqtt.Bridge*
- *aws.greengrass.clientdevices.mqtt.Moquette*

Before proceeding to the next, make sure all the components are selected (see Figure 6-25).

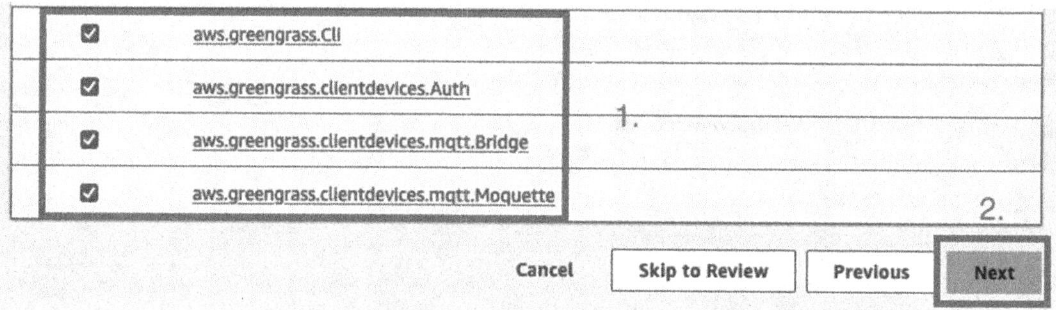

***Figure 6-25.** Make sure the components as shown are selected.*

In the Configure components screen, we will configure two new components (*Auth* and *Bridge*). For Auth, select the "*Auth*" component and click "*Configure component*" (see Figure 6-26).

Selected components (4)　2. Configure component

Find by name　< 1 >

Name	Version	Modified?
aws.greengrass.Cli	2.11.2	-
aws.greengrass.clientdevices.Auth　1.	2.4.3	-
aws.greengrass.clientdevices.mqtt.Bridge	2.2.6	-
aws.greengrass.clientdevices.mqtt.Moquette	2.3.3	-

Cancel　Skip to Review　Previous　Next

***Figure 6-26.** Selecting and configuring a component*

In the Configuration update section, in *Configuration to merge (aws.greengrass.clientdevices.Auth)*, delete curly braces and use the content shown here (*Content file can also be downloaded from Chapter 6 of the book's GitHub location – file name: Auth-Configuration to merge.json*) (see Figure 6-27).

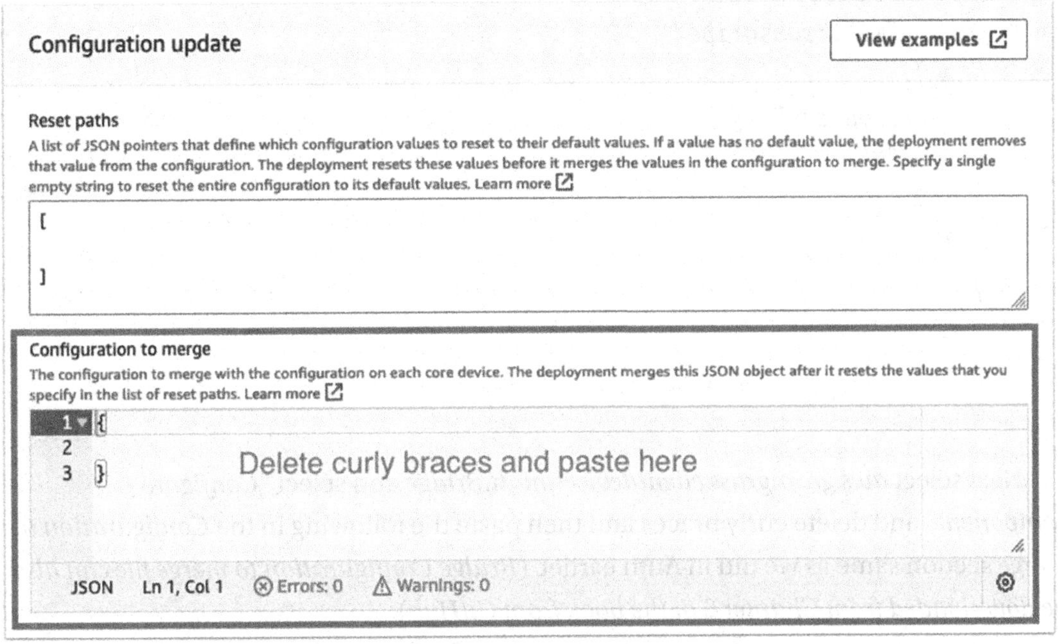

Configuration update

View examples

Reset paths

A list of JSON pointers that define which configuration values to reset to their default values. If a value has no default value, the deployment removes that value from the configuration. The deployment resets these values before it merges the values in the configuration to merge. Specify a single empty string to reset the entire configuration to its default values. Learn more

[

]

Configuration to merge

The configuration to merge with the configuration on each core device. The deployment merges this JSON object after it resets the values that you specify in the list of reset paths. Learn more

1 {
2
3 }

Delete curly braces and paste here

JSON Ln 1, Col 1 Errors: 0 Warnings: 0

Figure 6-27. *Pasting the content in Configuration to merge*

Use the following content for *Auth - Configuration to merge* and then select "*Confirm*":

```
{
  "deviceGroups": {
    "formatVersion": "2021-03-05",
    "definitions": {
      "MyDeviceGroup": {
        "selectionRule": "thingName: Thermostat* OR thingName: Doorlock*",
        "policyName": "EdgeClientDevicePolicy"
      }
    },
    "policies": {
      "EdgeClientDevicePolicy": {
```

```
        "AllowAll": {
          "statementDescription": "Allow client devices.",
          "operations": [
            "mqtt:connect",
            "mqtt:publish",
            "mqtt:subscribe"
          ],
          "resources": [
            "*"
          ]
        }
      }
    }
  }
}
```

Next select *aws.greengrass.clientdevices.mqtt.Bridge* and select "*Configure component*" and delete curly braces and then paste the following in the *Configuration to merge* section same as we did in Auth earlier. (*Bridge Configuration to merge file can also be downloaded from Chapter* 6 *of the book from GitHub*).

```
{
    "mqttTopicMapping": {
        "AWSIoTBookIotCoreMapping": {
            "topic": "devices/+/data/value",
            "source": "LocalMqtt",
            "target": "IotCore"
        }
    }
}
```

After pasting, select "*Confirm*". Once we have done "***both***" configuration for Auth and Bridge, click "*Next*" (see Figure 6-28).

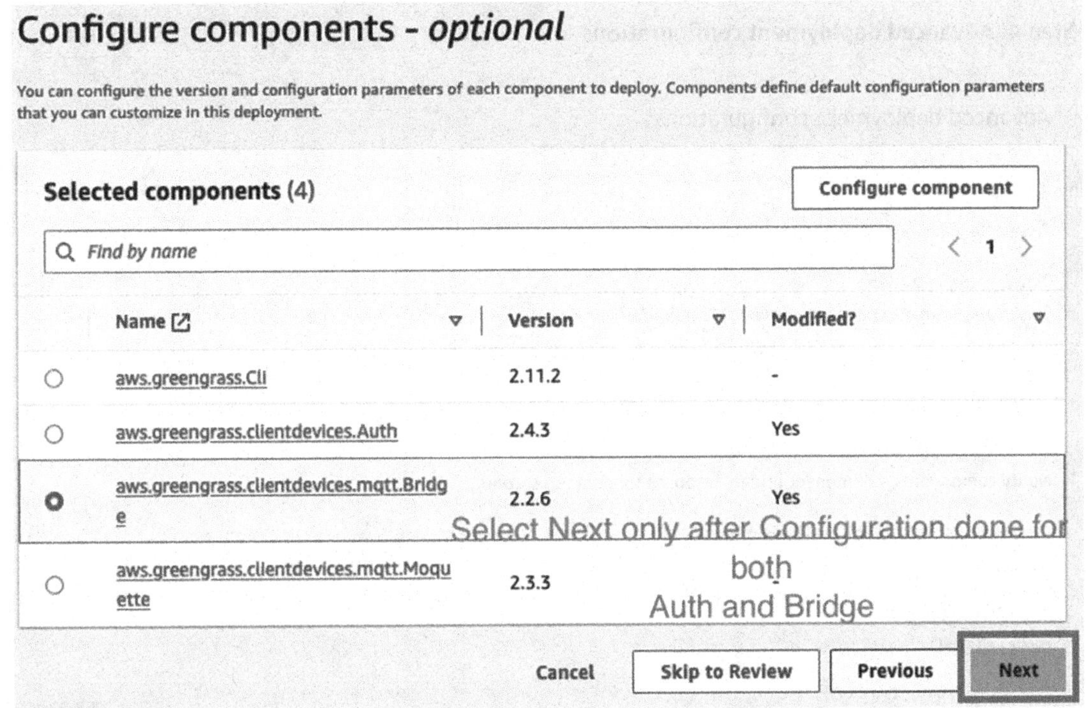

Figure 6-28. *Click Next once you have configured both Auth and Bridge*

For the "*Configure advanced settings - optional*" screen, click "*Next*". In the final "*Review*" screen, click "*Deploy*" (see Figure 6-29).

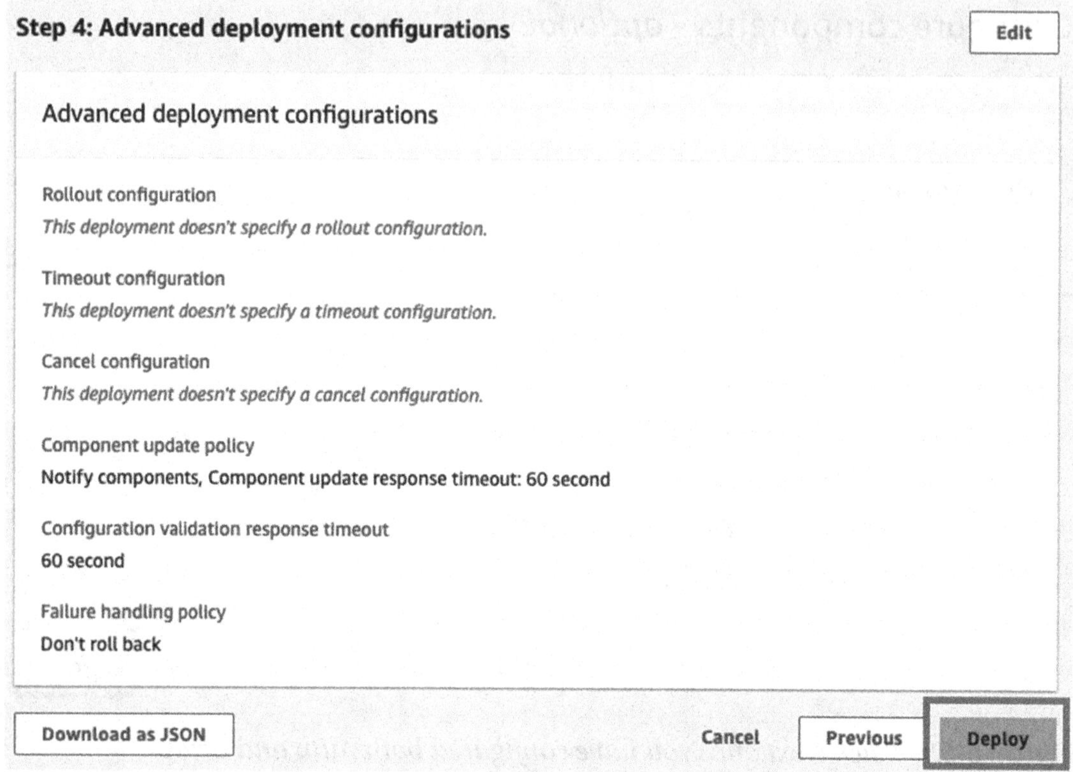

Figure 6-29. *In the Review screen, we can just go ahead and deploy*

We can see deployment successfully created (see Figure 6-30).

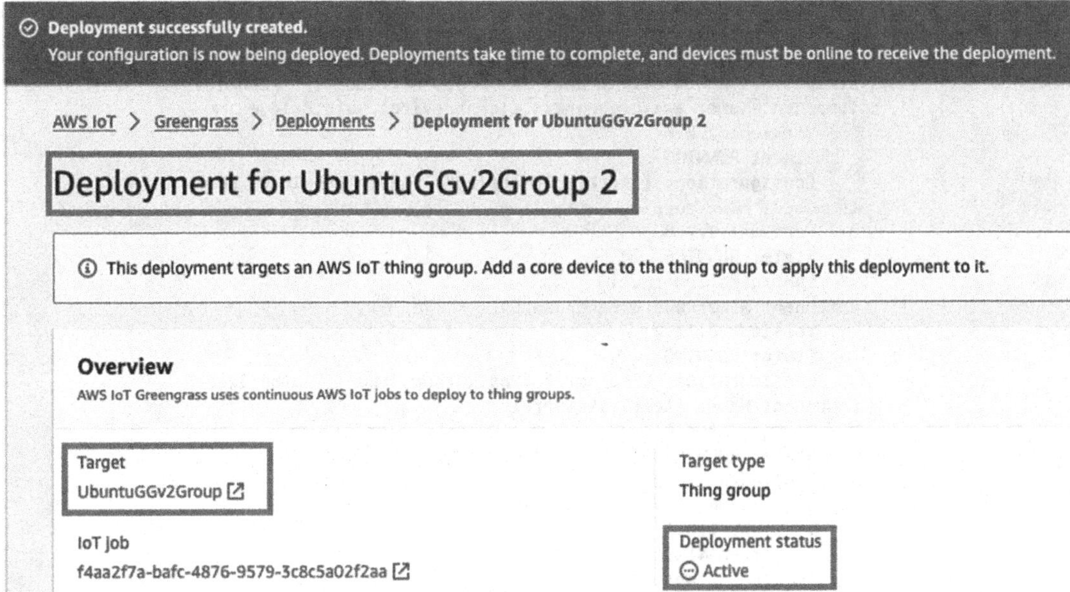

Figure 6-30. *Successful deployment done*

After deployment is successfully finished, we can also run the component list command (in the terminal window) and see new components deployed (see Figure 6-31):

```
sudo /greengrass/v2/bin/greengrass-cli component list
```

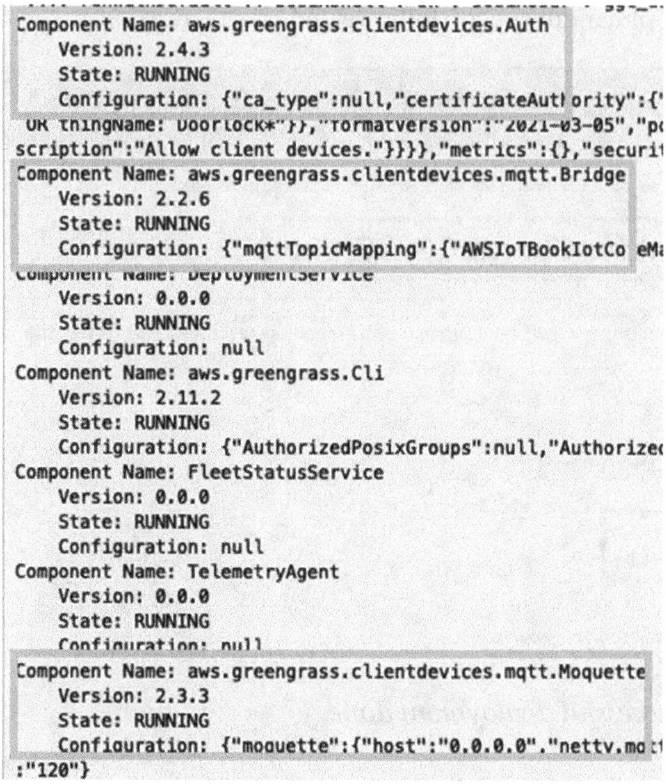

```
Component Name: aws.greengrass.clientdevices.Auth
    Version: 2.4.3
    State: RUNNING
    Configuration: {"ca_type":null,"certificateAuthority":{"
 OR thingName: DoorLock*"}},"formatVersion":"2021-03-05","p
scription":"Allow client devices."}}}},"metrics":{},"securi
Component Name: aws.greengrass.clientdevices.mqtt.Bridge
    Version: 2.2.6
    State: RUNNING
    Configuration: {"mqttTopicMapping":{"AWSIoTBookIotCo eM
Component Name: DeploymentService
    Version: 0.0.0
    State: RUNNING
    Configuration: null
Component Name: aws.greengrass.Cli
    Version: 2.11.2
    State: RUNNING
    Configuration: {"AuthorizedPosixGroups":null,"Authorize
Component Name: FleetStatusService
    Version: 0.0.0
    State: RUNNING
    Configuration: null
Component Name: TelemetryAgent
    Version: 0.0.0
    State: RUNNING
    Configuration: null
Component Name: aws.greengrass.clientdevices.mqtt.Moquette
    Version: 2.3.3
    State: RUNNING
    Configuration: {"moquette":{"host":"0.0.0.0","netty.mqt
:"120"}
```

Figure 6-31. *We can see newly installed components deployed and running*

Our simulated hub is now primed to accept local device connections and relay telemetry messages to AWS IoT Core.

Create Thermostat IoT Thing (Simulated)

Let's retrieve the *createThermostat.sh* script from Chapter 6 of the book's GitHub repository and run it to set up our IoT thing.

Run the following command where you have placed your file to make sure our script is executable (in the terminal window):

```
chmod +x createThermostat.sh
./createThermostat.sh
```

What Does This Script Do?

In this script, the following steps are executed in sequence to set up an IoT thing locally as a client:

1. **Check for Curl Utility:**
   - Verify if the *"curl"* utility is installed on the system.
   - If not, the script will install it.
2. **Install Paho-MQTT:**
   - Utilize *"pip3"* to install *"paho-mqtt."*
   - This library is crucial for setting up the IoT thing as a local client.
3. **Create IoT Thing:**
   - Use the *"aws cli"* to establish an IoT thing named *"Thermostat."*
4. **Generate Certificates:**
   - Generate corresponding certificates for the created IoT thing, *"Thermostat."*
5. **Download Amazon Root CA1.pem:**
   - Download the *"Amazon Root CA1.pem"* file for secure communication.
6. **Attach Policy to Certificate:**
   - Associate the *"myFirstDemoNonProductionPolicy"* with the certificate generated in step 4.
7. **Create a Python File:**
   - Generate a Python file named *"thermostatThing.py"*.
   - The file is created in the directory (*$HOME/environment/devices/thermostat/thermostatThing.py*).

Each of these steps contributes to ensuring that the IoT thing, "Thermostat," is properly set up and configured for further operations and interactions within the AWS IoT environment.

On successful execution, a confirmation message is showcased, as depicted in Figure 6-32.

```
syed-book:~/environment $ ./createThermostat.sh
  % Total    % Received % Xferd  Average Speed   Time    Time     Time  Current
                                 Dload  Upload   Total   Spent    Left  Speed
100  1188  100  1188    0     0  12345      0 --:--:-- --:--:-- --:--:-- 12247
{
    "thingName": "Thermostat",
    "thingArn": "arn:aws:iot:us-east-1:            :thing/Thermostat",
    "thingId": "40574004-dac3-4b9d-8d5b-801b1d8a1798"
}
Device Thermostat created, Amazon Root CA 1 downloaded, and policy setup completed successfully!
```

Figure 6-32. *IoT thing thermostat successfully created*

We can also check in the *AWS IoT Core* console (*"Thermostat"* – thing created):

- Manage
  - All devices
    - Things
      - Thermostat

Open the newly created file *"thermostatThing.py"* (see Figure 6-33).

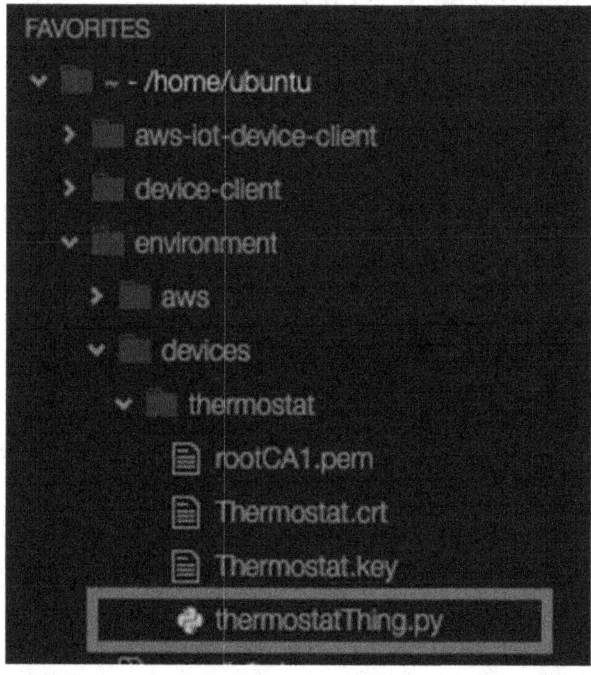

Figure 6-33. *Open thermostatThing.py.*

Use the following content for this file; you can download the code from Chapter 6 of the book's GitHub location.

```
import paho.mqtt.client as mqtt
import time
import random
import ssl

# Configuration
BROKER_HOST = "localhost"
BROKER_PORT = 8883
TOPIC = "devices/thermostat/data/value"
CLIENT_ID = "Thermostat"

def on_connect(client, userdata, flags, rc):
    if rc == 0:
        print("Connected to broker")
    else:
        print(f"Connection failed with code {rc}")

# Set up the MQTT client
client = mqtt.Client(client_id=CLIENT_ID)
client.on_connect = on_connect
client.tls_set(ca_certs="ca.pem", certfile="Thermostat.crt",
keyfile="Thermostat.key")

# Connect to the broker
client.connect(BROKER_HOST, BROKER_PORT, 60)
client.loop_start()  # Start the loop to handle background tasks

def simulate_thermostat():
    time.sleep(2)  # Give some time for the connection to establish
    for _ in range(3):  # Simulate 3 times
        # Generate random temperature data
        temperature = round(20 + (random.random() * 5), 2)
        humidity = round(40 + (random.random() * 20), 2)
        aqi = round(random.random() * 300)
```

```
        # Construct the payload
        payload = f"Temperature: {temperature}°C, Humidity: {humidity}%,
        AQI: {aqi}"

        # Publish the payload
        result = client.publish(TOPIC, payload, qos=0)
        if result.rc == mqtt.MQTT_ERR_SUCCESS:
            print(f"Published: {payload}")
        else:
            print(f"Failed to publish. Reason code: {result.rc}")

        time.sleep(3)  # Pause between simulations

if __name__ == "__main__":
    try:
        simulate_thermostat()
        time.sleep(4)  # Give some time for the last publish operation to
        complete
    except KeyboardInterrupt:
        print("\nSimulation stopped.")
    finally:
        client.loop_stop()  # Stop the loop

        client.disconnect()  # Disconnect from the broker
```

What This Code Is Doing

We start by importing the necessary modules needed for our Thermostat client simulation. Following this, we set up the MQTT client configuration to connect to a broker. The client is then initialized with the necessary SSL/TLS settings for secure communication. Subsequently, the *simulate_thermostat* function is defined and executed. This function simulates a thermostat's behavior by generating random values for temperature, humidity, and AQI (Air Quality Index). It then publishes these values to the MQTT topic (*devices/thermostat/data/value*). The function runs this simulation three times consecutively without any interval and terminates the simulation.

Note Before we run our code, subscribe to the topic *devices/thermostat/#* in the AWS IoT Core console using *MQTT test client*.

Now let's run our code:

```
cd ~/environment/devices/thermostat/
python3 thermostatThing.py
```

Upon successful execution, we will see output in the terminal (see Figure 6-34) as well as AWS IoT Core MQTT test client (see Figure 6-35).

```
syed-book:~/environment/devices/thermostat $ python3 thermostatThing.py
Connected to broker
Published: Temperature: 20.93°C, Humidity: 44.32%, AQI: 147
Published: Temperature: 24.64°C, Humidity: 47.56%, AQI: 276
Published: Temperature: 20.21°C, Humidity: 59.4%, AQI: 195
```

Figure 6-34. *Terminal output of our "simulated thermostat"*

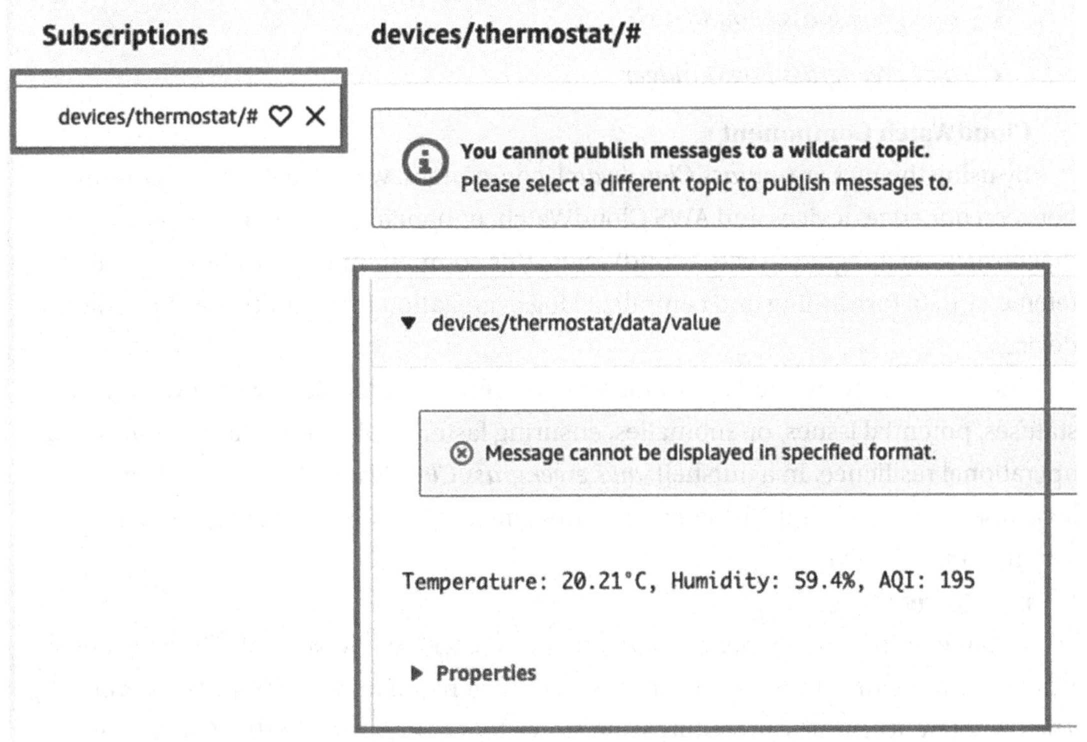

Figure 6-35. *AWS IoT Core – MQTT test client showing messages received*

In this section, we successfully simulated the following:

- A home hub powered by AWS IoT Greengrass
- A connected IoT device, specifically a thermostat, to the home hub

This example serves as an efficient foundation for creating a Minimum Viable Product (MVP). It allows us to emulate a similar setup before deploying it on actual hardware.

Monitoring and Maintenance

Log Manager and CloudWatch

It's good practice to have Log Manager and CloudWatch components installed in a Greengrass core device like we did earlier; you should install the following two components:

- *aws.greengrass.Cloudwatch*
- *aws.greengrass.LogManager*

CloudWatch Component

By using the *aws.greengrass.Cloudwatch* component, we can get a direct conduit between our edge devices and AWS CloudWatch, enhancing real-time monitoring and diagnostics. By integrating with CloudWatch, this component will allow for immediate telemetry data forwarding and centralized log aggregation from multiple Greengrass devices.

The result is streamlined operations, as you gain an immediate overview of device statuses, potential issues, or anomalies, ensuring faster troubleshooting and improved operational resilience. In a nutshell, *aws.greengrass.Cloudwatch* bridges the gap between local operations and cloud-based monitoring, making IoT device management more intuitive and effective.

LogManager

Installing the "*aws.greengrass.LogManager*" component in your AWS IoT Greengrass V2 environment offers invaluable benefits for efficient log management and monitoring. The component seamlessly captures and stores logs generated by other Greengrass components on your device, ensuring you have centralized access to critical system and application insights.

Its capabilities extend beyond mere collection; with built-in log rotation and retention policies, LogManager prevents the local storage from being overwhelmed, ensuring efficient usage of device resources. Furthermore, the integration with AWS CloudWatch Logs means that logs can be automatically uploaded for centralized monitoring, enabling easier debugging, analytics, and compliance tracking.

This becomes especially vital in large-scale deployments, where consolidating logs from multiple Greengrass devices in a unified platform, like CloudWatch, simplifies operations and reduces the time to issue resolution. In essence, "*aws.greengrass.LogManager*" acts as a bridge between edge devices and the AWS ecosystem, enhancing visibility and control over your IoT landscape.

Let's go through the setup process for the "*aws.greengrass.LogManager*" component in your AWS IoT Greengrass V2 environment for efficient log management and monitoring:

Overview

- **Purpose:** The LogManager component captures, stores, and manages logs from other Greengrass components on your device.
- Key Features
  - Centralized access to system and application logs
  - Built-in log rotation and retention policies
  - Integration with AWS CloudWatch for centralized monitoring
- **Benefits**
  - Prevents local storage overload
  - Enhances visibility and control over your IoT landscape
  - Facilitates easier debugging, analytics, and compliance tracking

Steps to enable LogManager

1. **Attach New Policy to Greengrass IAM Role:**
   - **Role Name**: *GreengrassV2TokenExchangeRole*
   - **Purpose**: Allows the Greengrass core to send logs to CloudWatch Logs

2. **Deploy the LogManager Component:**
   - **Configuration**: Merge settings to define log upload mode and details.

Detailed Setup

1. **IAM Policy Setup:**
   - **Policy Name**: *LogManagerGGv2Policy*
   - **File**: *IAM-PolicyLogManager-GGv2Policy.json* (you can download the JSON from Chapter 6 of the book's GitHub location)
   - **Content**: Allows actions like creating log groups and streams and putting log events
2. **Configuration Merge for Component Deployment:**
   - **Modes:**
     - **CONTINUOUS**: Continuous log uploads
     - **ON_DEMAND**: Uploads logs on the trigger
     - **PERIODIC**: Uploads logs at set intervals

Sample Configuration

Use the following content for this file (*file: IAM-PolicyLogManager-GGv2Policy.json*); you can download the code from Chapter 6 of the book's GitHub location.

```
{
  "Version": "2012-10-17",
  "Statement": [
    {
      "Effect": "Allow",
      "Action": [
        "logs:CreateLogGroup",
        "logs:CreateLogStream",
        "logs:PutLogEvents",
        "logs:DescribeLogStreams"
      ],
```

```
      "Resource": "*"
    }
  ]
}
```

Outcome:

- Efficient log management with LogManager
- Centralized log visibility in Amazon CloudWatch

By following these streamlined steps, you ensure efficient log management, enhancing the robustness and transparency of your IoT setup in the AWS environment.

Real-Life Edge Development Using AWS IoT Greengrass

Explore three diverse edge scenarios and discover how AWS IoT Greengrass enhances and streamlines development in each context. Witness firsthand the multifaceted applications of Greengrass in various fields and how it tailors its functionality to meet specific demands.

1. **Consumer Devices**

   Scenario:

   Imagine a unified network of smart home devices: *thermostats, leak detectors, smart locks, bulbs, security cameras, and alarm systems*. Beyond individual functions, these devices collaborate to simplify and enhance daily life.

- **Role of AWS IoT Greengrass**

  Here, AWS IoT Greengrass supercharges this ecosystem with its advanced ML inference capabilities, seamlessly integrated within a home hub, ensuring optimal performance even on limited hardware. It silently boosts device efficiency and enriches the user experience, making smart living more intuitive and reliable.

- **Architecture Insight**

  For a comprehensive understanding of this integrated system, refer to the "*Consumer IoT*" reference architecture diagram (see Architecture diagram 6A).

2. **Medical Devices (Risk-Averse)**

   Scenario:

   The realm of Medical IoT (**MIoT**) is marked by its unwavering adherence to stringent standards. Devices here bear the crucial role of influencing health outcomes, demanding utmost accuracy and robust data security in every design facet.

   - **Role of AWS IoT Greengrass**

     In this critical environment, AWS IoT Greengrass stands out as a trusted partner, enhancing system capabilities and simplifying processes, all while ensuring compliance with restricted local network-bound devices.

   - **Architecture Insight**

     Explore the specific MIoT architecture with the reference architecture diagram designed for this domain (see Architecture diagram 6B).

3. **Aviation Systems (Risk-Averse)**

   Scenario:

   In aviation, the emphasis is on real-time data processing and unwavering reliability, given the direct impact on passenger safety. Envision real-time computations taking place mid-flight, ensuring safety and functionality 35,000 feet above ground.

   - **Role of AWS IoT Greengrass**

     AWS IoT Greengrass seamlessly integrates into this high-stakes environment, offering reliable, efficient, and timely data processing, crucial for making real-time decisions and ensuring passenger safety.

- **Architecture Insight**

  To understand the integration of AWS IoT Greengrass in aviation, examine the tailored reference architecture diagram related to Flight Systems IoT (see Architecture diagram 6C).

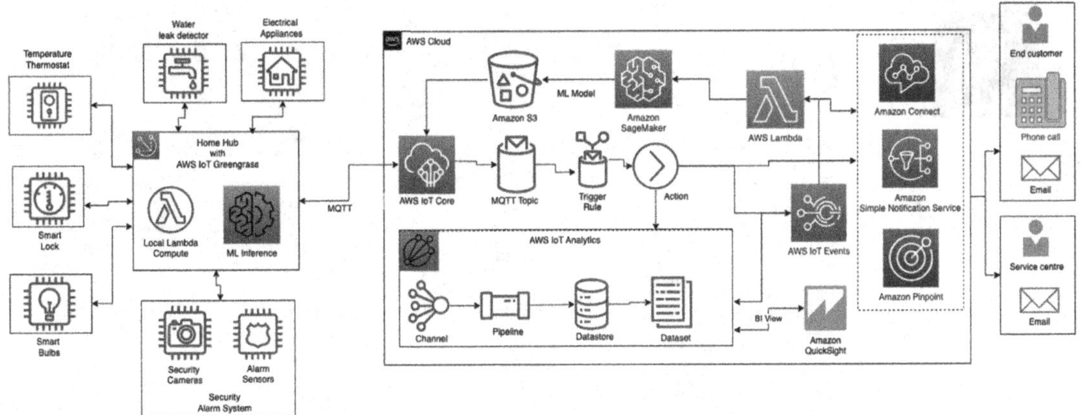

Architecture diagram 6A: Consumer IoT reference architecture

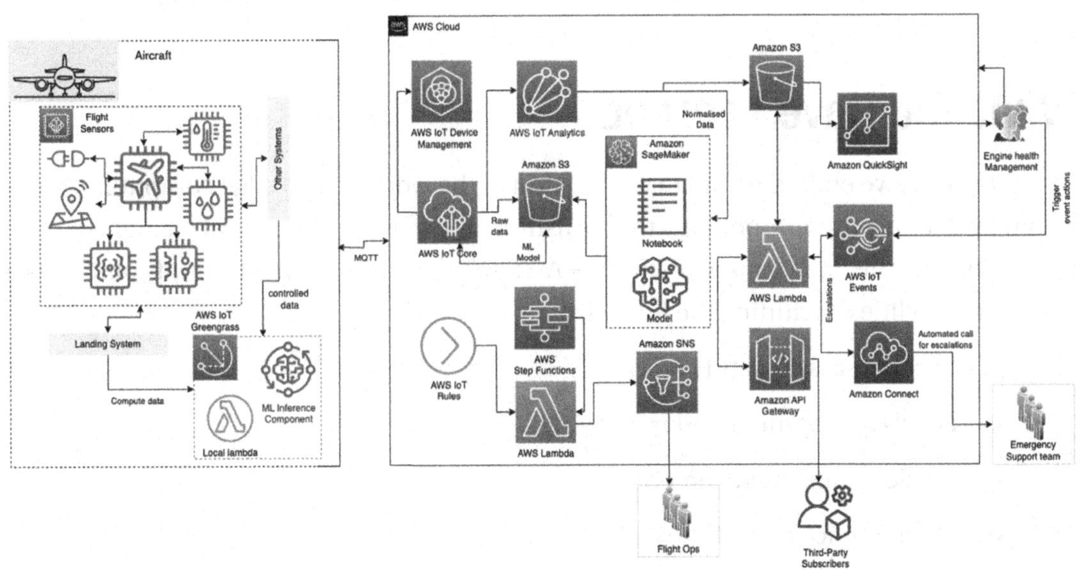

Architecture diagram 6B: Medical IoT reference architecture

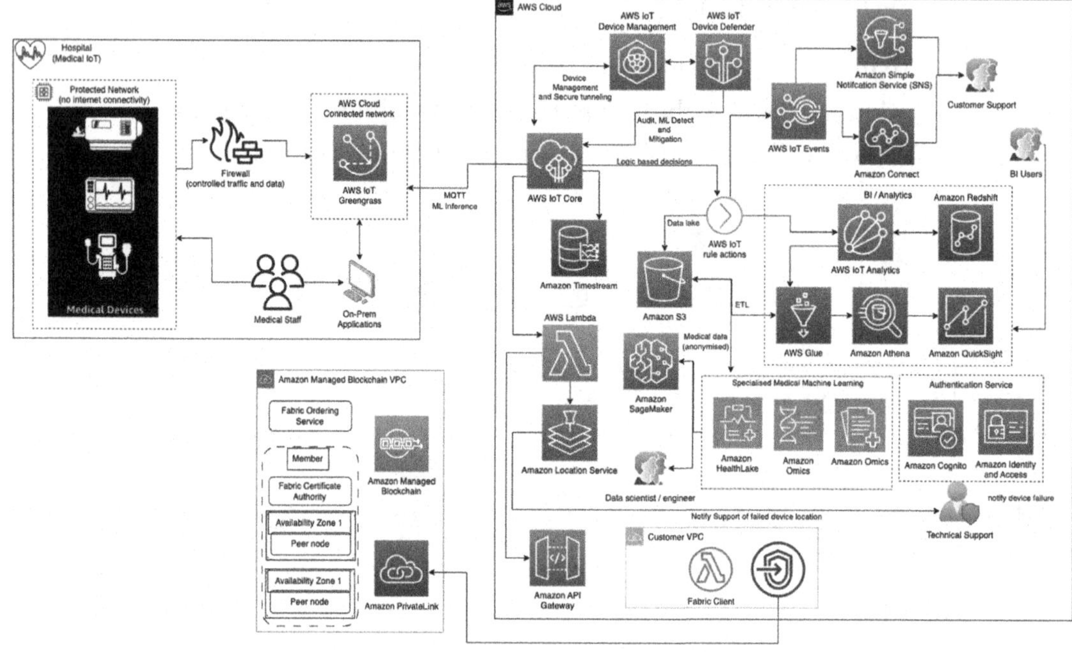

Architecture diagram 6C: Aviation-based reference architecture using AWS IoT Greengrass

What You Have Learned

In this chapter, we embarked on an exploration of the world of IoT edge computing. We began by defining the components that constitute the IoT edge. A central element of our discussion was the open source platform – AWS IoT Greengrass, which stands out for its suite of capabilities, including the following:

- Local processing and compute
- Local development and messaging
- Efficient data management
- ML inference capabilities
- Secure connectivity features
- Support for Docker
- Stream management capabilities
- The ability to design custom components

The subsequent sections peeled back the layers of Greengrass components. We explored both AWS-provided components and custom-made ones, understanding their life cycle states. Key concepts like "recipes" and "artifacts" were elucidated, emphasizing their dependencies during component development. An integral part of this conversation was the interaction dynamics between these components and the AWS IoT Greengrass core component, known as the nucleus.

Toward the end of this chapter, we ventured into practical applications by simulating a smart home use case. Here, we developed a simulated home hub powered by AWS IoT Greengrass and a simulated thermostat that communicated with the hub via MQTT messages. This simulation underscored the ease and efficiency with which such setups can be employed to rapidly develop a Minimum Viable Product (MVP). It paves the way for innovators to transition seamlessly from these simulations to actual physical implementations, harnessing the power of AWS IoT Greengrass to develop sophisticated connected systems.

Finally, we delved into the various types of edge development, highlighting areas such as smart consumer devices, industrial edge technologies, and infrastructure edge development. Three illustrative use cases, accompanied by their respective reference architecture diagrams, further solidified our understanding. These were

1. Consumer IoT systems
2. Risk-averse domains like Medical IoT and aviation systems

Summary

In this chapter, we journeyed through the intricate world of IoT edge computing, beginning with an understanding of the components that make up the AWS IoT edge. The focal point of our exploration was the comprehensive open source platform, AWS IoT Greengrass, renowned for its multifaceted capabilities ranging from local processing to support for Docker and custom component design.

We delved deeply into the various Greengrass components, gaining insights into both AWS-provided and custom-made components and their life cycle states. The chapter illuminated essential concepts such as "recipes" and "artifacts," highlighting their significant roles in component development. The interaction between these components and the AWS IoT Greengrass core component, known as the nucleus, was comprehensively analyzed.

As we progressed, we explored a practical smart home use case simulation, creating a home hub and thermostat using AWS IoT Greengrass. This example underscored the practicality, ease, and efficiency of employing AWS IoT Greengrass, showcasing its potential in fast-tracking the development of a Minimum Viable Product (MVP) for IoT solutions.

In the concluding sections, the chapter provided an in-depth look into various types of edge development, including consumer IoT systems, industrial edge technologies, and other risk-averse domains like Medical IoT and aviation systems. Detailed use cases, complemented by reference architecture diagrams, further enriched our understanding, offering a solid foundation for leveraging AWS IoT Greengrass in developing sophisticated and connected systems in various domains.

By the end of this chapter, you've gotten a solid grip on AWS IoT Greengrass! You now understand everything from the basic parts to its real-world uses, setting you up perfectly to create some awesome and innovative IoT edge computing solutions. Ready to get started? The world of IoT is at your fingertips!

CHAPTER 7

Industrial IoT with AWS IoT

At the dawn of the Fourth Industrial Revolution, the integration of digital technologies with traditional manufacturing processes has birthed an ecosystem that transcends the limitations of both domains. The Industrial Internet of Things (IIoT) is at the epicenter of this convergence, leveraging sensors, actuators, and embedded systems to impart intelligence and responsiveness to everyday industrial equipment. While the promise of IIoT is alluring, harnessing its full potential requires a robust, scalable, and secure platform. Enter AWS IoT: Amazon Web Service's dedicated suite designed to transform the way industries interact with the digital realm.

One standout service in AWS IoT's vast arsenal is AWS IoT SiteWise. This managed service seamlessly gathers, stores, and analyzes data from industrial equipment at scale. SiteWise's magic lies in its ability to make sense of the raw data flowing in from sensors, presenting it in user-friendly visualizations and offering invaluable insights into operational health, performance, and anomalies. For industries wading through the complexities of modernizing their operational insights, IoT SiteWise offers a beacon of clarity. This book will delve deep into the intricacies of this tool, guiding you step-by-step on how to architect, deploy, and optimize your industrial data streams using AWS IoT SiteWise.

What Is IIoT

Think of IIoT, or the Industrial Internet of Things, as the secret sauce that elevates traditional industrial setups into super-efficient, smart ecosystems. To understand it better, we'll dissect it:

S. Rehan, *AWS IoT With Edge ML and Cybersecurity*, https://doi.org/10.1007/979-8-8688-0011-5_7

1. **Industrial**: This isn't just about massive operations like manufacturing plants, factories, and power plants. It also encompasses the intricate dance of conveyor belts in distribution centers, the meticulous processes on farms, and even the water treatment facilities ensuring our tap water is clean.
2. **Internet of Things (IoT)**: Picture the transformation from a regular phone to a smartphone. It's the difference between a static object and one that's connected, responsive, and smart. IoT is what allows your smart fridge to send shopping reminders or lets your wearable fitness device celebrate when you hit 10,000 steps.

Combine these two, and the magic of IIoT comes alive:

- **Machines Talking to Each Other**: It's like having an orchestra where each instrument knows when to chime in perfectly. The conveyor belt at a biscuit manufacturing plant could adjust its speed based on the cooling rate of the biscuits, ensuring a seamless packaging process.
- **Predictive Maintenance**: Rather than the abrupt inconvenience of your car breaking down in the middle of a journey, imagine if it alerted you a week prior that it needed a specific part replacement. In industries, this predictive alert system can save millions by preventing downtime.
- **Energy Efficiency**: It's not just about saving on electricity bills. In a world grappling with climate change, systems that optimize energy use make industries more sustainable. Think of a textile factory where steam machines lower their energy consumption based on the moisture level in the air.
- **Safety and Monitoring**: In industries, stakes are high. A small error in a chemical plant could lead to significant hazards. Sensors can detect irregularities faster than humans. Picture sensors in a dairy plant detect a slight rise in bacteria levels, ensuring milk supplies remain safe for consumption.

- **Data Collection and Analysis**: In our everyday lives, we're used to recommendations. Be it movie suggestions on streaming platforms or shopping recommendations online. Similarly, IIoT's extensive data collection capabilities enable industries to glean insights they'd never have thought possible. A factory producing car parts, for example, can analyze which batches have the highest quality and during what conditions they were produced, thereby refining their processes.
- **Remote Monitoring**: Think about the convenience of checking your home's security cameras while you're on vacation. In the same way, IIoT allows managers and technicians to keep tabs on large-scale industrial operations from anywhere. This means a technician in New York could troubleshoot a machine issue in a Tokyo factory without boarding a plane.
- **Supply Chain Integration**: Imagine if your kitchen pantry could communicate directly with your local grocery store to restock items you're running low on. On a grander scale, IIoT helps industries maintain inventory levels, ensuring raw materials are ordered and processed just in time, preventing stock shortages or overstock issues.
- **Sustainability and Compliance**: Just as modern vehicles come equipped with systems to minimize emissions and meet environmental standards, IIoT can help industries become greener. By monitoring emissions, waste, and resource usage in real time, companies can ensure they're within regulatory limits and even reduce their carbon footprint.
- **Human-Machine Collaboration**: Similar to how voice assistants in our homes help with tasks by just listening to our commands, in an industrial setting, IIoT enables a harmonious collaboration between workers and machines. Robotic arms in assembly lines can adjust their movements based on a worker's position, ensuring safety and increasing efficiency.

To frame IIoT in a familiar context, it's the intricate web of connections and smart responses behind the scenes that make the magic happen. It's the stage crew ensuring every spotlight, sound cue, and set change in a theater performance is executed flawlessly. In the grand play of modern industry, IIoT is the director, choreographer, and backstage crew, all rolled into one, ensuring not just a successful show, but an evolving and adapting masterpiece.

In essence, IIoT isn't just a fancy tech term. It's the bridge between the raw strength of our industrial past and the digital finesse of the future. Imagine if the steadfast reliability of an old grandfather clock met the connectivity of a modern smartwatch. IIoT ensures our industries don't just work but thrive, adapt, and lead in this digital age.

IIoT Development Using AWS IoT

For IIoT, AWS IoT offers specialized services tailored specifically for industrial scenarios. These services can effectively collect, organize, and analyze data from industrial equipment on a vast scale. Complementing this, AWS IoT's edge components allow for local data collection and processing, enabling the creation of hybrid industrial applications that operate cohesively across both edge and cloud. Additionally, AWS provides a monitoring solution via AWS IoT SiteWise Monitor, which can be deployed at the edge to oversee production assets.

What's AWS IoT SiteWise

AWS IoT SiteWise is a managed service from Amazon Web Services that simplifies the process of gathering, storing, organizing, and monitoring data from industrial equipment on a large scale. Within the AWS IoT SiteWise ecosystem:

1. **AWS IoT SiteWise Edge:** This feature allows users to collect and process equipment data on-site, or "on-premises." It is especially beneficial for applications that require low latency or need to function even when cloud connectivity is lost.

2. **AWS IoT SiteWise Monitor:** This tool, available both in the cloud and on the edge, provides monitoring capabilities, enabling users to keep a watchful eye on their equipment and operations.

These tools and features make industrial data management more streamlined and efficient, catering to various scenarios and requirements.

Data Input in AWS IoT SiteWise

AWS IoT SiteWise processes data and links it to assets that mirror your industrial operations.

You can transmit industrial data to AWS IoT SiteWise via several methods:

1. **AWS IoT SiteWise Gateway**: Connect your data servers through this gateway, acting as a bridge between them and AWS IoT SiteWise. You can deploy AWS IoT Greengrass connectors on any compatible platform with AWS IoT Greengrass to establish this gateway. Supported server protocols include OPC UA, Modbus TCP, and Ethernet/IP.
2. **AWS IoT Core Rules**: Transfer data through MQTT messages that are either published by an AWS IoT device or another AWS service (similar to what we learnt in earlier chapters).
3. **AWS IoT Events Actions**: Upload data triggered by specific events (related to AWS IoT SiteWise) in AWS IoT Events.
4. **AWS IoT Greengrass Stream Manager**: Integrate data from local sources using edge devices.
5. **AWS IoT SiteWise API**: This API allows for data uploads from any other external sources.

During my time at AWS, I've consistently observed that when working with IIoT customers - particularly those with manufacturing setups or machinery that predates the widespread adoption of the Internet - the following three methods have consistently stood out:

- **AWS IoT Core Rules**
- **AWS IoT SiteWise API** (PUT Operation)
- **AWS IoT SiteWise Gateway** (especially beneficial for those using legacy protocols like OPC UA)

These methods have not only proven their efficiency but have also deeply resonated with customers steeped in legacy operations. You've already familiarized yourself with the first method in prior chapters.

Now, it's time to shift our focus to the remaining two and configure our monitoring portal to track these real-time data streams. For AWS IoT SiteWise API, we will build a "*conveyor belt*" model, and for OPC UA, we will use a simulated demo component (for AWS IoT Greengrass) provided by AWS IoT SiteWise.

Simulate a "Conveyor Belt" Using AWS IoT SiteWise API

With AWS IoT SiteWise, you can craft virtual representations of your industrial operations through SiteWise assets. An asset symbolizes entities like devices, equipment, or processes that transmit one or more data streams to AWS IoT SiteWise. Every data stream has a distinct property measurement. The data hierarchy is set as follows: Asset model ➤ Asset ➤ Asset property (measurement).

To illustrate, consider the measurement *"/Conveyor Belt Model/Conveyor Belt 01/ Motor Temperature"*. This refers to the current operating temperature of the conveyor belt. Among the values a conveyor might report are its belt speed, vibration, emergency stops, and operational hours. Utilizing these measurements, you can establish monitoring metrics in AWS IoT SiteWise Monitor, allowing you to assess real-time data input.

Before detailing an asset, it's essential to first design an asset model. Within this model, you'll also earmark properties for your assets. These properties act as repositories for asset data. They come in various types, including Attributes, Measurements, Transforms, and Metrics.

Sign in to the AWS Management Console and make your way to the *"AWS IoT SiteWise console."* Ensure you're operating in the US East: N. Virginia region for this exercise (see Figure 7-1).

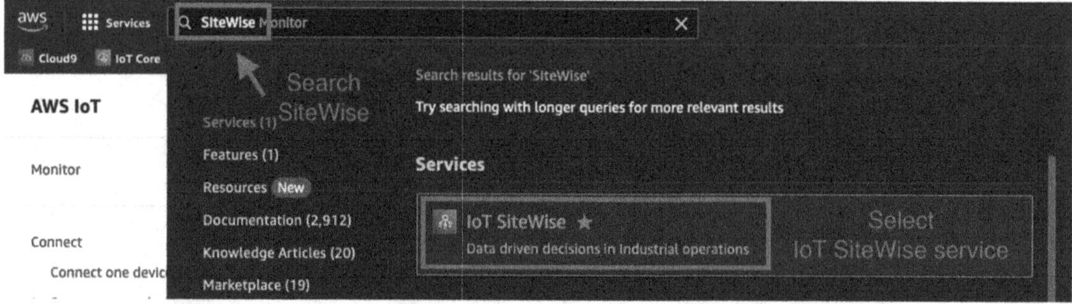

Figure 7-1. *Searching and navigating to the IoT SiteWise service*

Create a Model

We need to first create a **model** for the *"conveyor belt"* and select *"Models"* under *Build* (see Figure 7-2).

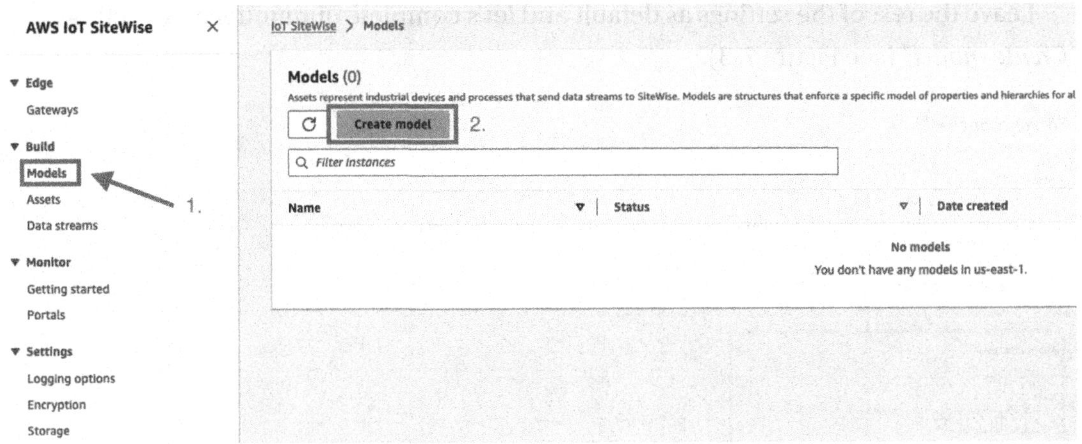

***Figure 7-2.** Creating an Industrial asset model*

For "*Model details*", populate data as follows:

Model Name: Conveyor Belt Model

Description: My first IIoT Model

For "*Measurement definitions*", populate data as follows:

Add five measurements by using the "*Add new measurement*" button.

Define measurements:

- **Name:** Motor Temperature, **Unit**: C, **Data type**: Double
- **Name:** Belt Speed, **Unit**: m/s, **Data type**: Double
- **Name:** Vibration, **Unit**: g-force, **Data type**: Double
- **Name:** Operational Hours, **Unit**: hours, **Data type**: Double
- **Name:** Emergency Stops, **Unit**: count, **Data type**: Integer

Leave the rest of the settings as default and let's complete our model by selecting "*Create model*" (see Figure 7-3).

Create model

Assets and models

Assets represent industrial devices and processes that send data streams to SiteWise. Models are structures that enforce a specific model of properties and hierarchies for all instances of each asset. You must create every asset from a model.

On this page, you can create a model with attributes, measurements, transforms, metrics, and hierarchies. Then, you can create assets from your models and populate each asset with asset-specific information. Learn more about modeling assets

Model details

Name
A friendly name lets you and others easily find and understand the model.
Conveyor Belt Model
Must be unique and less than 256 characters.
Description - *optional*
A description for the asset model.
My first IIoT Model
Must be less than 2048 characters.

Attribute definitions

Attributes are values for your asset that rarely change, such as a device serial number or part number. Learn more about defining attributes

Name	Default value	Data type	
Serial_number	Serial BLT123	String	Delete

Add new attribute

Measurement definitions

Measurements are timestamped raw data streams from devices and equipment. Learn more about defining measurements

Name	Unit	Data type	
Motor Temperature	C	Double	Delete
Belt Speed	m/s	Double	Delete
Vibration	g-force	Double	Delete
Operational Hours	hours	Double	Delete
Emergency Stops	count	Integer	Delete

Add new measurement

***Figure 7-3.** Creating a model with illustrated measurements*

Now that our *"conveyor belt"* model has been created we can go ahead and create *"Assets."* Select *"Assets"* under *"Build"* (see Figure 7-4).

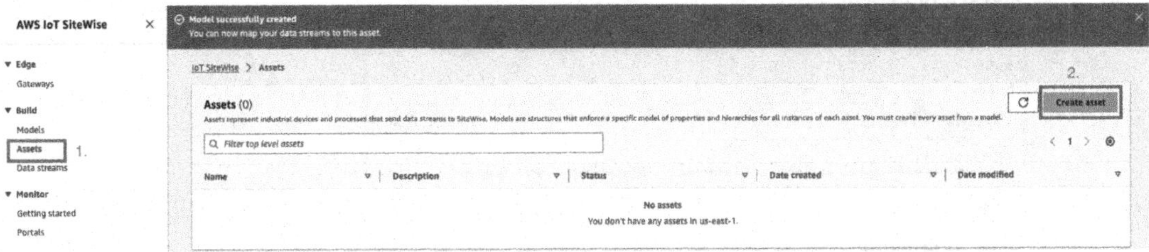

Figure 7-4. *Creating an asset*

Populate details as follows for the *"asset"* (see Figure 7-5):

Model: From the drop-down, select *Conveyor Belt Model.*

Asset Name: *Conveyor Belt 01*

Description: *First Conveyor Belt Asset*

Finally, complete by selecting *"Create asset".*

Create a new asset
Model information
Model
The asset inherits the properties defined in its model.
Conveyor Belt Model
Model is required.
1.
Asset information
Name
A friendly name lets you and others easily find and understand the asset.
Conveyor Belt 01
Must be unique under the same parent asset and less than 256 characters.
2.
Description - optional
A description for the asset.
First Conveyor Belt Asset
Must be less than 2048 characters.
3.
Tags
This resource doesn't have any tags.
Add tag
You can add up to 50 more tags.
4.
Cancel
Create asset

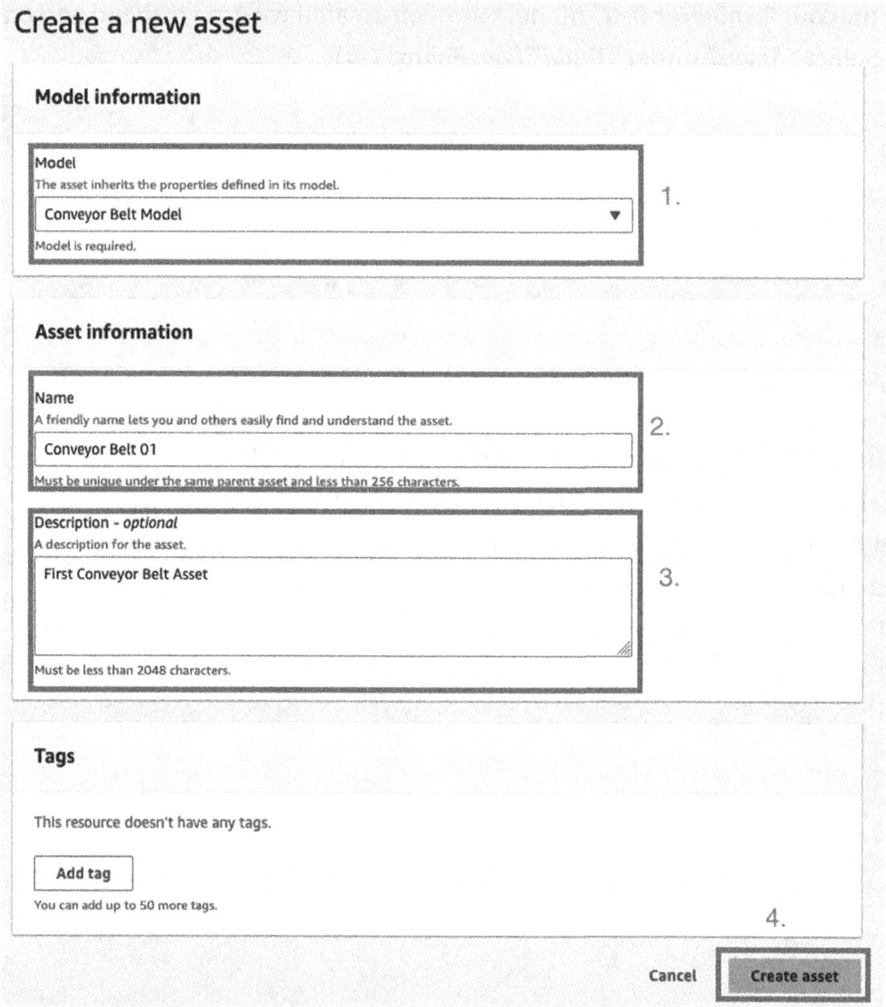

***Figure 7-5.** Creating an asset*

Before diving into the Python script simulation for the "conveyor belt," it's **crucial** to note the following "**measurement IDs**". Ensure you embed these IDs into the script. This will facilitate the accurate placement of data when it's dispatched to the AWS IoT SiteWise PUT API call.

- Asset ID
    - Measurement IDs
        - Belt Speed
        - Emergency Stops

- Motor Temperature
- Operational Hours
- Vibration

Navigate to the AWS IoT SiteWise console, and under the "*Build*" section, choose "*Assets*". Select "*Conveyor Belt 01*" from the list, where you will find the necessary "*Asset ID*" and "*Measurement IDs*" (see Figure 7-6). It's crucial to record these IDs as they will be used in the coding steps that follow.

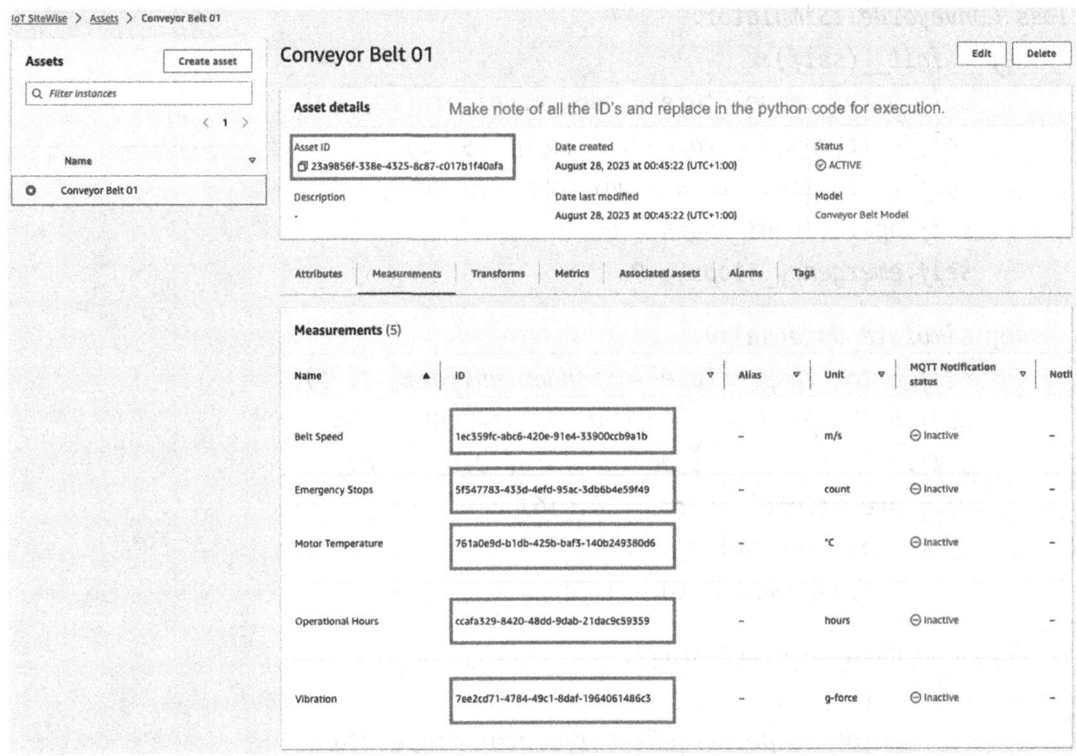

Figure 7-6. *Make note of the IDs and replace in Python code*

Run the following command to create our "*simulating*" Python script (*the script can also be downloaded from Chapter 7 of the book's GitHub location*):

```
touch conveyorBeltSimulation.py
```

After creating the file, insert the provided code. Ensure you replace the six placeholders labeled "*REPLACE_HERE*" with the respective measurement ID values you obtained earlier.

Use the following content for this file (*file: conveyorBeltSimulation.py*); you can download the code from Chapter 7 of the book's GitHub location.

```
import random
import sys
import time
import uuid

import boto3

class ConveyorBeltSimulator:
    def __init__(self):
        self.motor_temperature = random.uniform(20, 50)
        self.belt_speed = random.uniform(0.5, 2)
        self.vibration = random.uniform(0.05, 0.2)
        self.operational_hours = 0
        self.emergency_stops = 0

    def simulate_data(self):
        self.motor_temperature += random.uniform(-1, 1)
        self.belt_speed += random.uniform(-0.05, 0.05)
        self.vibration += random.uniform(-0.01, 0.01)
        self.operational_hours += 0.0167
        if random.random() < 0.20:
            self.emergency_stops += 1

    def send_data_to_cloud(self):
        data = {
            "motor_temperature": self.motor_temperature,
            "belt_speed": self.belt_speed,
            "vibration": self.vibration,
            "operational_hours": self.operational_hours,
            "emergency_stops": self.emergency_stops,
        }

        client = boto3.client("iotsitewise")
        asset_id = "REPLACE_HERE"  # OBTAIN FROM IoTSiteWise > Assets >
        Asset ID
```

```
    # Creating batch entries for each property value

    entries = []
    #  OBTAIN FROM IoTSiteWise > Assets > Measurements > ID for
    each metric.
    property_mapping = {
        "motor_temperature": "REPLACE_HERE",
        "belt_speed": "REPLACE_HERE",
        "vibration": "REPLACE_HERE",
        "operational_hours": "REPLACE_HERE",
        "emergency_stops": "REPLACE_HERE",
    }

    for prop, value in data.items():
        entries.append(
            {
                "entryId": str(uuid.uuid4()),
                "assetId": asset_id,
                "propertyId": property_mapping[prop],
                "propertyValues": [
                    {
                        "value": {"doubleValue": value},
                        "timestamp": {"timeInSeconds": int(time.
                        time())},
                    }
                ],
            }
        )

    try:
        client.batch_put_asset_property_value(entries=entries)
    except boto3.exceptions.Boto3Error as e:
        print(f"An error occurred: {e}")
        sys.exit(1)

def run_simulation(self, duration_minutes):
    for _ in range(duration_minutes):
```

```
            self.simulate_data()
            self.send_data_to_cloud()
            time.sleep(60)

if __name__ == "__main__":
    simulator = ConveyorBeltSimulator()
    simulator.run_simulation(10)
```

After correctly substituting the placeholders with the appropriate IDs for the *"Asset"* and its associated *"Measurement IDs"* six places in total, save the changes. Next, execute the script using the command provided.

```
python3 conveyorBeltSimulation.py
```

Back in AWS IoT SiteWise, in the Asset screen, we can see data arriving mapped to our ID's directly and refreshed using our *simulated* script; next let's set up the *Monitoring* portal for our Asset (see Figure 7-7).

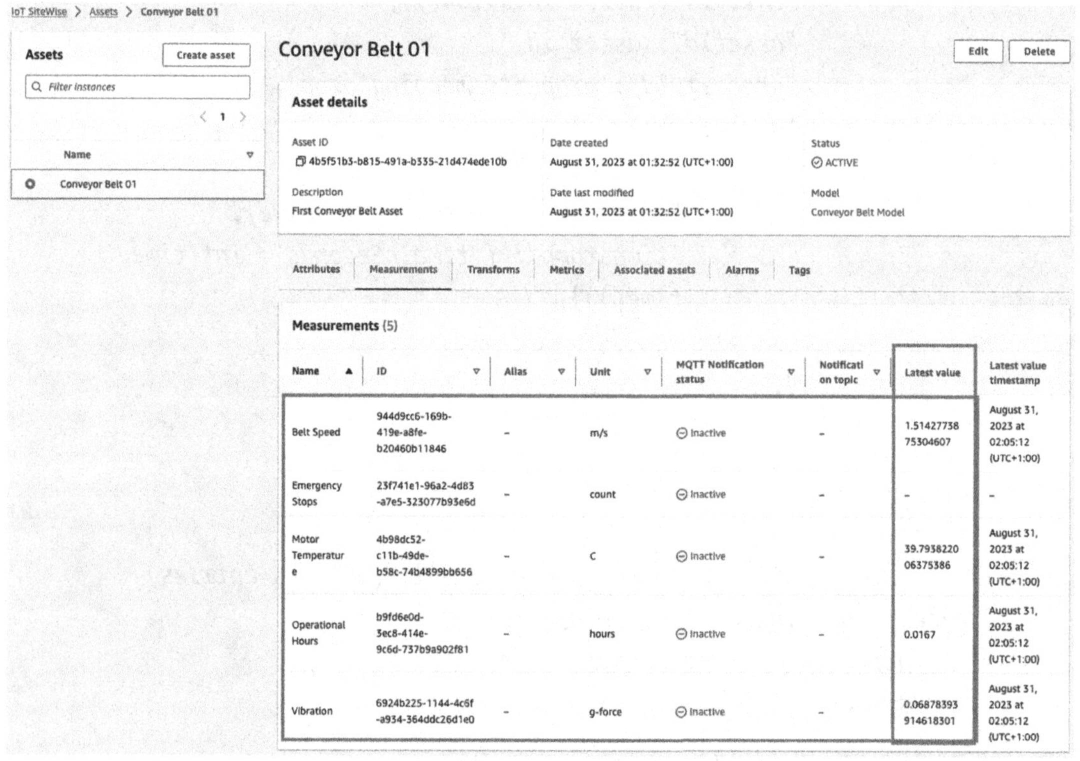

***Figure 7-7.** Real-time data arriving to our Asset measurements*

Monitoring Portal (AWS IoT SiteWise Monitor)

From the AWS IoT SiteWise console, under the "*Monitor*" section, select "*Portals*" (see Figure 7-8).

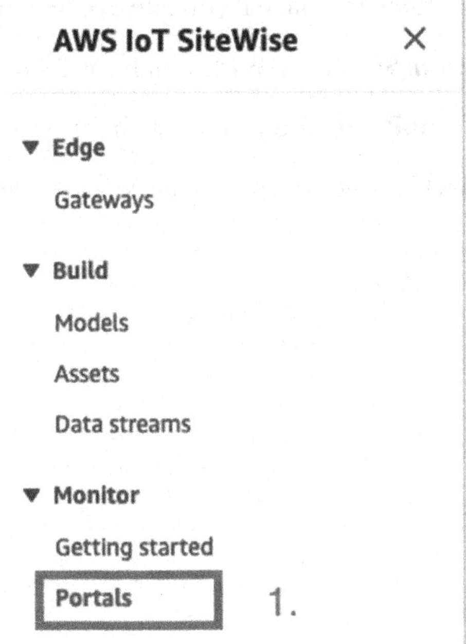

Figure 7-8. *Navigating to Portals*

Then click "*Create portal*" (see Figure 7-9).

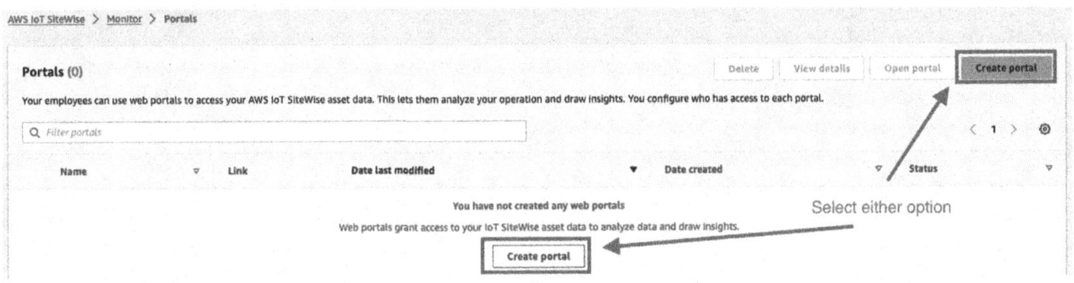

Figure 7-9. *Create a monitoring portal*

In the Portal configuration page, populate details as follows (see Figure 7-10):

- **Portal name**: *MyFirstPortal*
- **Description**: *My First Portal for Conveyor Belt*
- **Portal branding**: Select an image if you like to use that for logo
- **User authentication**: Select "*AWS IAM Identity Center*"
- **Support contact email:** Provide your email here
- **Permissions:** Select "*Create and use a new service role*"

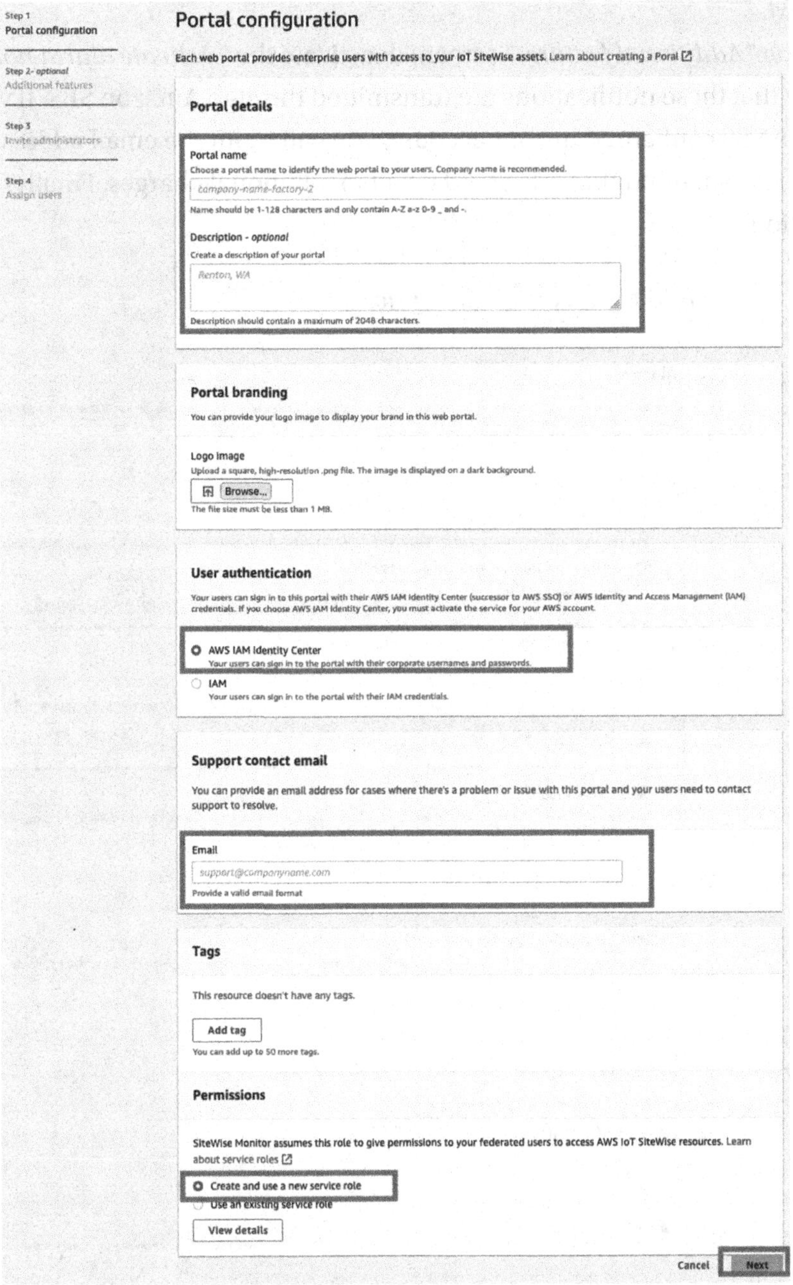

***Figure 7-10.** Creating an AWS IoT SiteWise monitoring portal*

Click *Next*.

Within the "*Additional features*" screen, deactivate the "*Activate alarm notifications*" option. Note that these notifications are transmitted through Amazon SES. If you have Amazon SES configured in your account, you can input the email address and configure it. Keep in mind that this could result in additional charges. Finally, click the "*Create*" option.

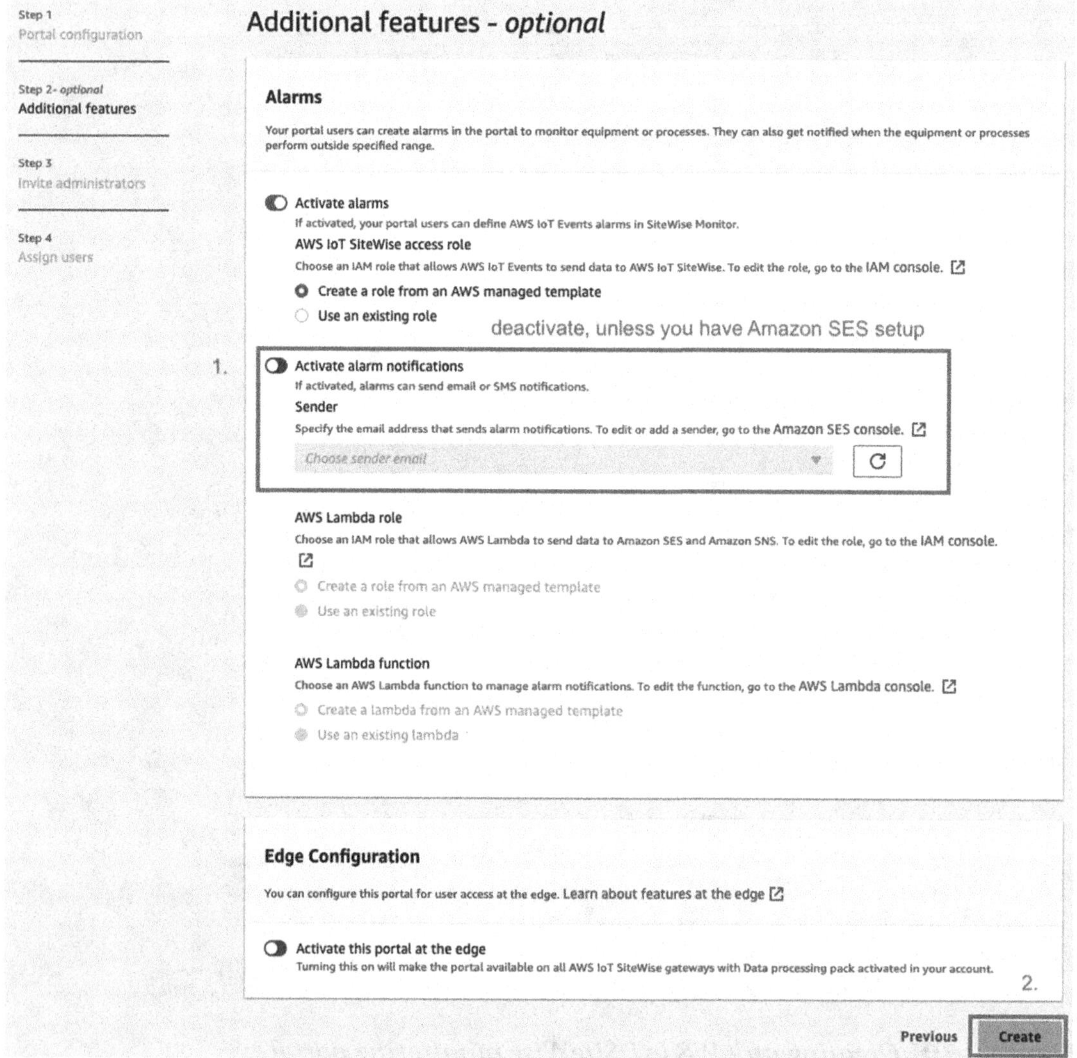

***Figure 7-11.** Select deactivate "Activate alarm notifications" and finally click Create.*

Navigate to the "Invite Administrators" screen and click "Create user". Enter the email address of the person you wish to assign as a user (see Figure 7-12). This individual will receive an invitation to activate their account. They must set a new password before they can log in.

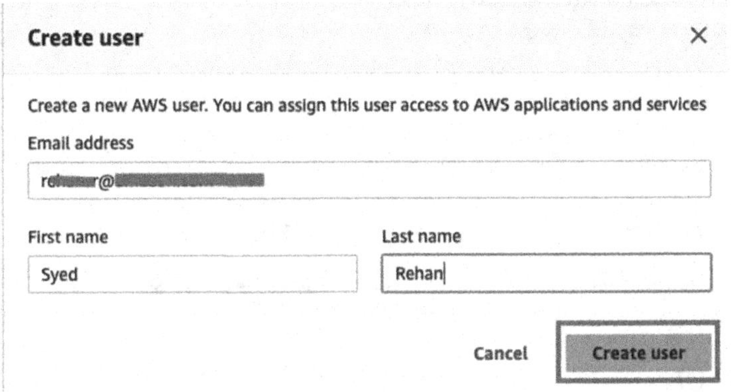

Figure 7-12. *Creating a user for the portal*

Once the user has been created, you can assign the relevant roles to this newly created user (see Figure 7-13).

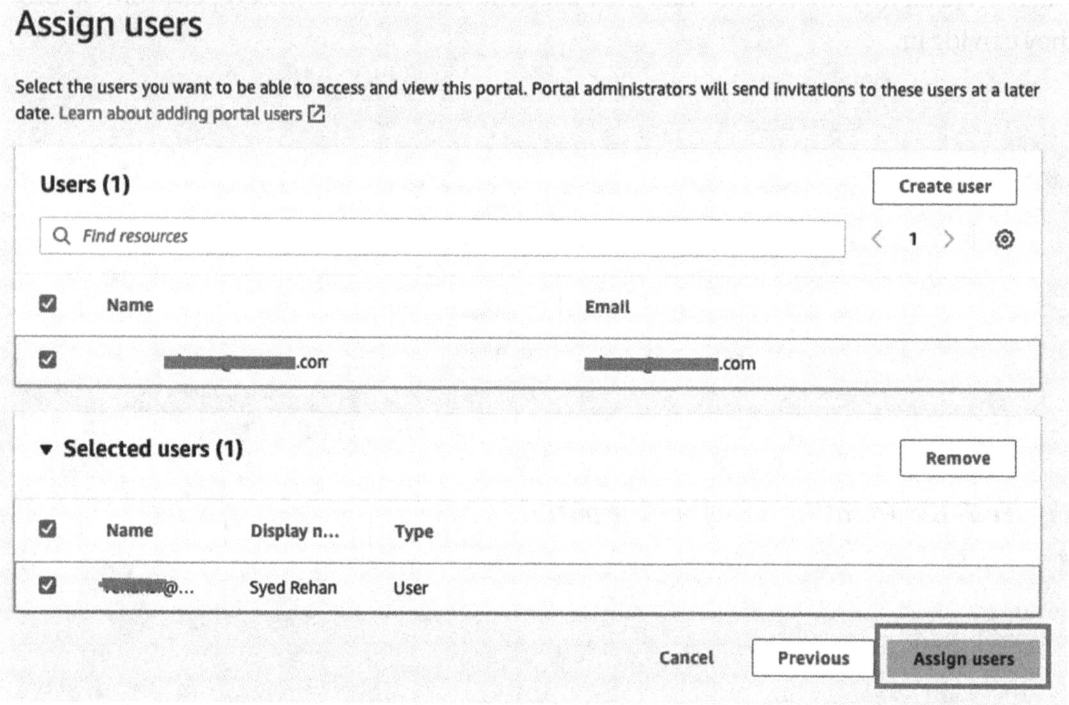

Figure 7-13. *Assigning users*

After the portal is set up and the user account activation is complete (via email activation and password setup), you can access and log into the portal (refer to Figure 7-14).

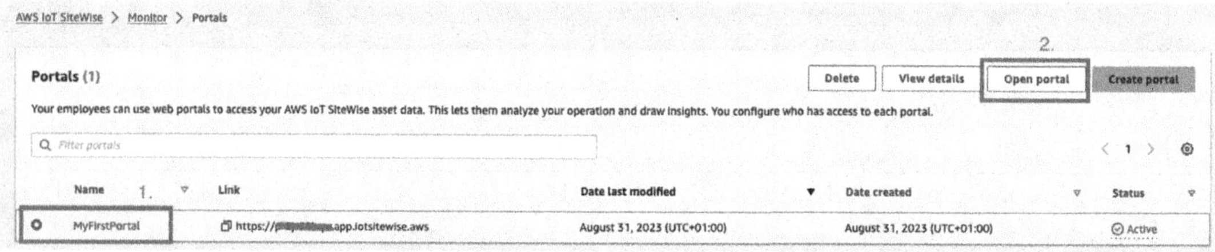

Figure 7-14. *Open the newly created portal*

Log in using your created "*username*" and "*password*" and let's create our dashboard and see data in near real-time visualization (see Figure 7-15).

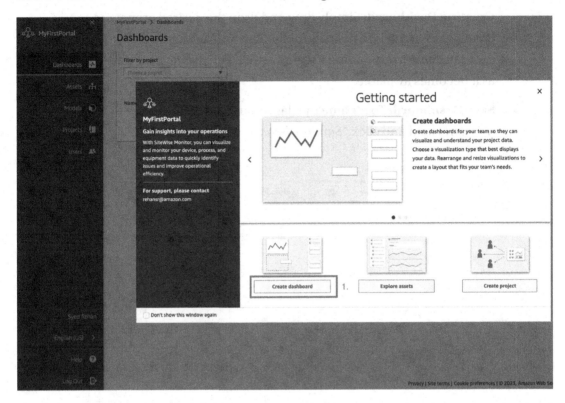

Figure 7-15. Select "Create dashboard"

Use the given option to go ahead and use the "*Model and Assets*" we already have created in the AWS IoT SiteWise console (see Figure 7-16) by selecting "*Create project and dashboard*".

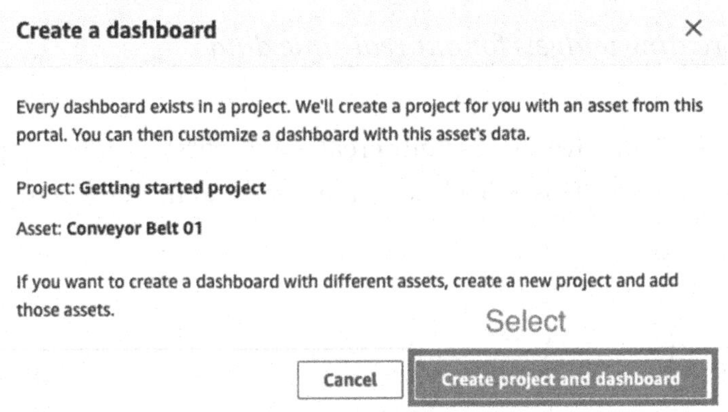

Figure 7-16. Select "Create project and dashboard"

Creating Dashboard with Widgets

- **Creating Dashboard:** Simply drag and drop the desired properties (data parameters) into the page pane. This will automatically generate the corresponding widgets, which will display real-time data as it becomes available.
- **Save Dashboard:** To rename the dashboard, enter "*Conveyor Belt*" in the name field and click "*Save dashboard*" (see Figure 7-17).

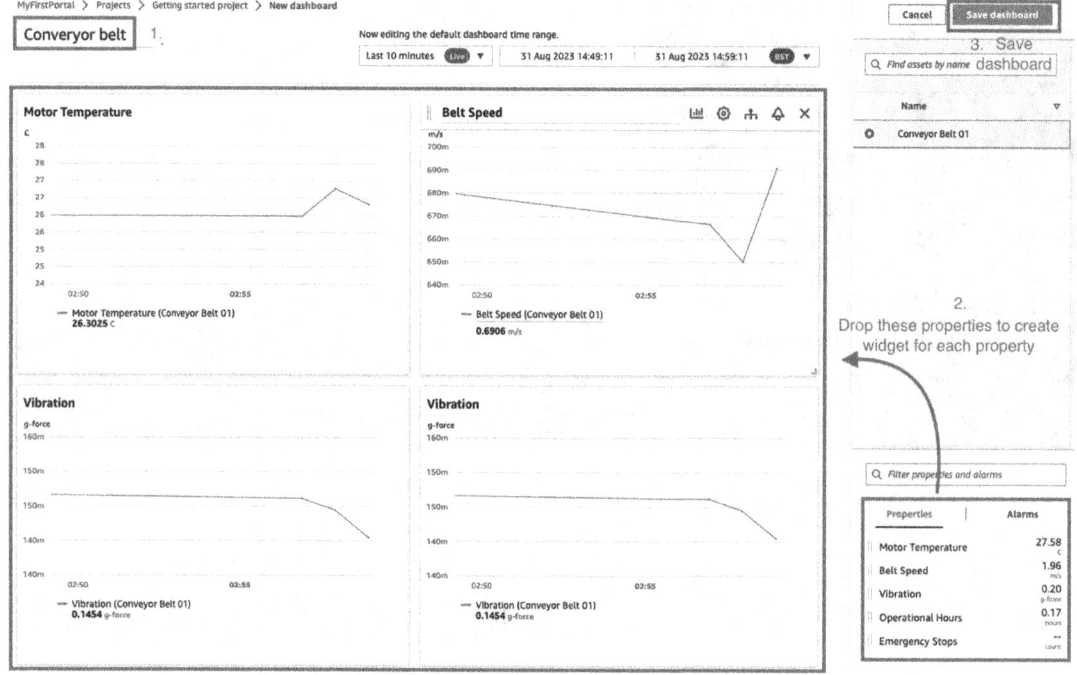

***Figure 7-17.** Creating widgets for our real-time data*

Congratulations! You have successfully created your first monitoring portal using *AWS IoT SiteWise Monitor*. This will allow you to track and monitor your assets in real time.

Using AWS IoT SiteWise Gateway with an OPC UA Data Simulator

In this section, we'll delve into using OPC UA data to simulate IIoT (Industrial IoT) interactions with the AWS SiteWise gateway, facilitating data ingestion into the AWS IoT SiteWise console. But first, let's discuss what OPC UA entails.

What Is OPC UA?

OPC UA, which stands for "OPC Unified Architecture," is a sophisticated machine-to-machine communication protocol developed by the OPC Foundation to enhance industrial interoperability. Evolving from previous OPC standards, OPC UA is platform agnostic, operating effortlessly across varied operating systems. It emphasizes stringent security, meticulous information modelling, and broad scalability. Engineered for reliable data transmission, it serves a wide array of devices, from small embedded systems to large-scale enterprise platforms. Given its adaptability, OPC UA is pivotal in industrial automation, manufacturing, and numerous IIoT devices. In our context, we'll harness this protocol to facilitate data ingestion into AWS IoT SiteWise via the edge gateway using the OPC UA protocol.

IAM Policy for GreengrassV2TokenExchangeRole (Mandatory Permission)

The token exchange role permits device access to other AWS services. The Greengrass core device recognizes only the token exchange role alias, as defined in the nucleus configuration. To adjust device permissions, modify the IAM policies linked to this role similar to what we did before in Chapter 6, and the device will inherit the permissions specified in those updated policies.

Create an IAM Policy

In the AWS IAM Console, navigate to policies:

- In the left navigation pane, click "*Policies*"
    - Click on the "Create policy" button (see Figure 7-18)

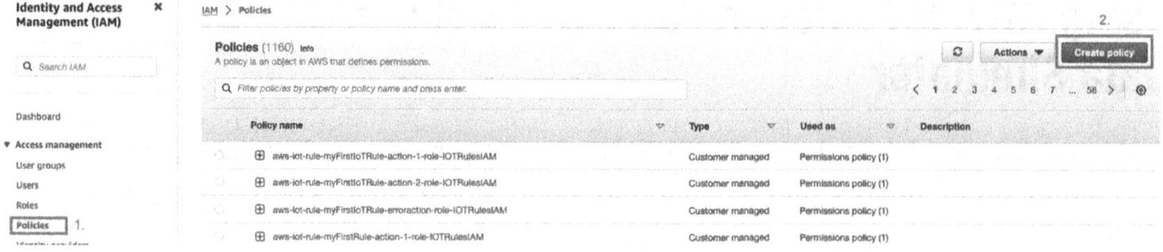

Figure 7-18. Creating a policy for SiteWise

- **Define the Policy:**
  - Select the JSON tab, and enter the policy document as follows (see Figure 7-19)

Note You must not use this policy in production; it is only for educational purposes and should be deleted after you have completed your learning.

Use the following content for this file (*file: awsiotbook_sitewise_policy_test.json*); you can download the code from Chapter 7 of the book's GitHub location.

```
{
    "Version": "2012-10-17",
    "Statement": [
        {
            "Sid": "SiteWiseActions",
            "Effect": "Allow",
            "Action": "iotsitewise:*",
            "Resource": "*"
        }
    ]
}
```

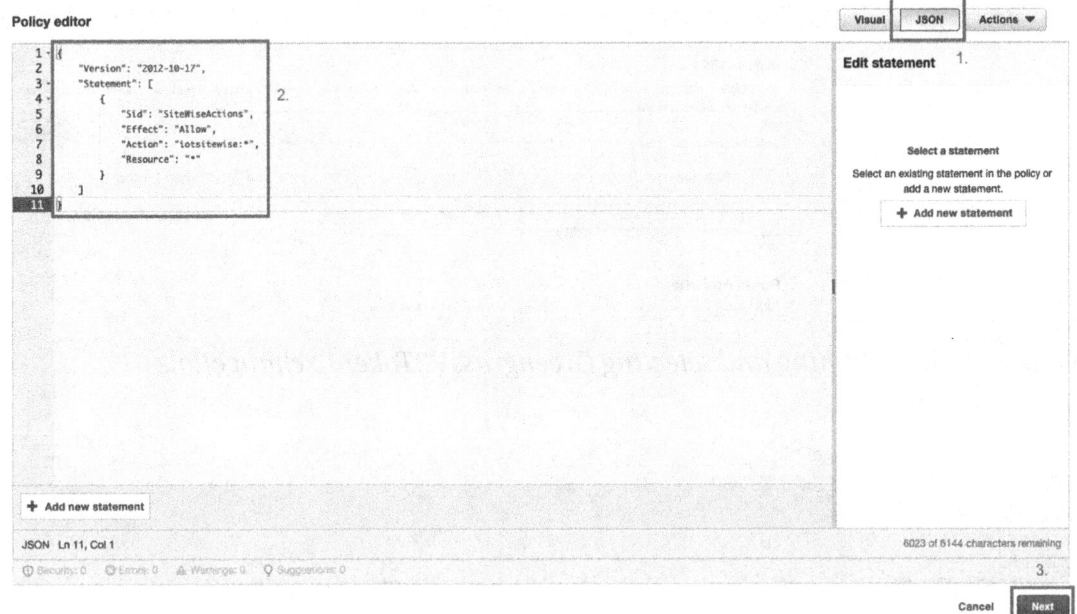

Figure 7-19. *Creating a policy*

- **Review and Name the Policy:** *"awsiotbook_sitewise_policy_test"* and finally *"Create policy"*

Attach to the Role

As we highlighted in Chapter 6, one AWS service requires permission to interact with another. In this context, we're ensuring that AWS IoT Greengrass, which operates AWS IoT SiteWise components, has the necessary permissions to transmit data to the AWS IoT SiteWise cloud.

Staying in the AWS IAM Console, navigate to

- Access management
  - Roles
    - Search for *GreengrassV2TokenExchangeRole* (see Figure 7-20)
    - Select and attach our policy *"awsiotbook_sitewise_policy_test"* (see Figure 7-21)

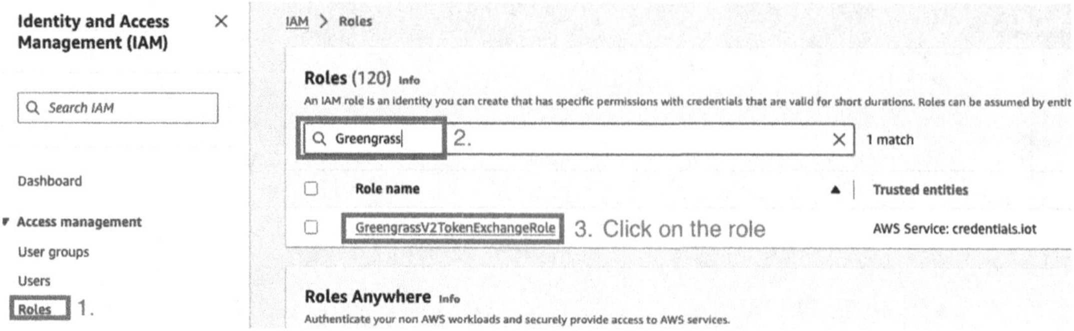

Figure 7-20. *Searching and selecting GreengrassV2TokenExchangeRole*

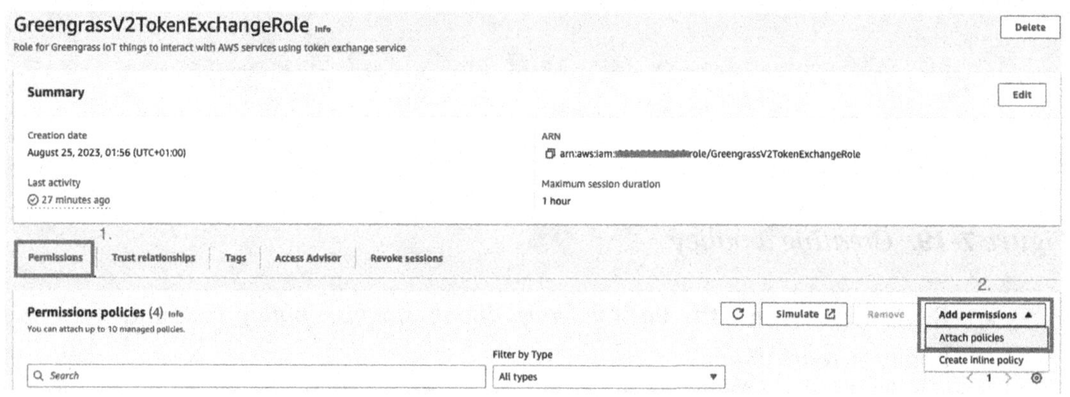

Figure 7-21. *Attaching our newly created test policy (name: "awsiotbook_sitewise_policy_test")*

- Search the policy with the following name: *awsiotbook_sitewise_policy_test*
- Select the policy and then "*Add permissions*" (see Figure 7-22)

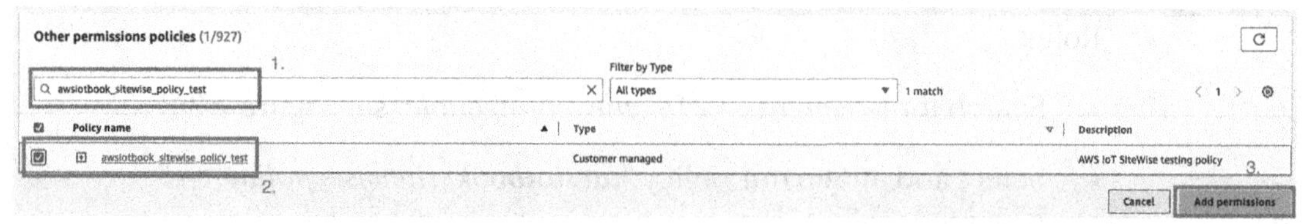

Figure 7-22. *Searching awsiotbook_sitewise_policy_test, selecting and adding permissions*

Now that we have the IAM policy and role set up, we can go ahead and set up the AWS IoT SiteWise Gateway.

Set Up OPC UA Data Simulator with AWS IoT SiteWise Gateway

To set up our AWS IoT SiteWise Edge gateway, navigate to the AWS IoT SiteWise console. Under the "*Edge*" section, choose "*Gateways*" and then click "*Create gateway*". Opt for "*Greengrass v2 (Recommended)*" (see Figure 7-23).

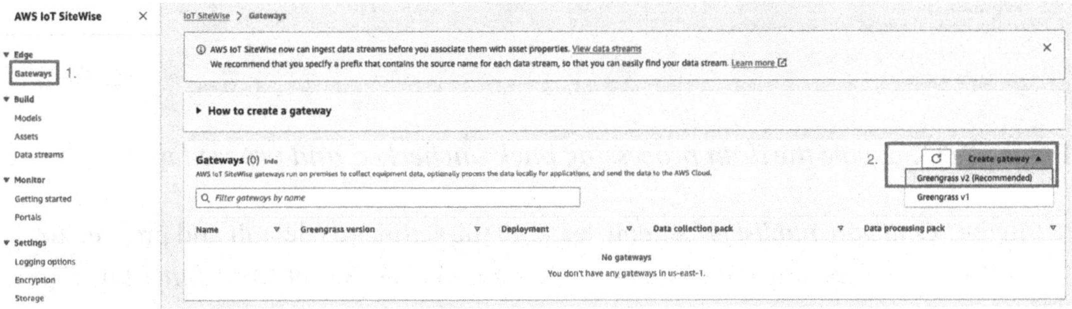

Figure 7-23. *Creating a gateway*

In the Configure a gateway screen, let's select our previously installed Greengrass core device (as AWS IoT SiteWise uses Greengrass core as its edge software and installs SiteWise components).

Define the following details:

Gateway name: *Gateway-Ubuntu*

Greengrass core device: Select *Advanced setup*.

From the Add Greengrass core device drop-down: Select *UbuntuGGv2*.

Then click "*Next*" (see Figure 7-24).

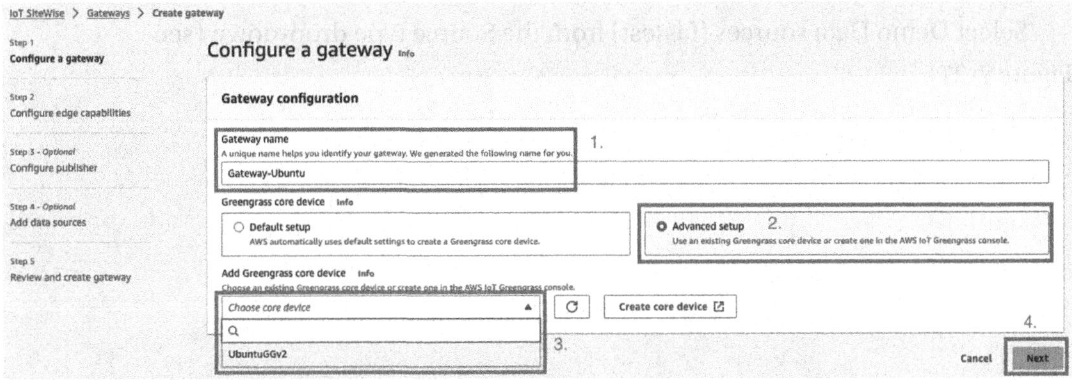

Figure 7-24. *Configuring the SiteWise gateway using an existing Greengrass core device*

During the "*Configure edge capabilities*" step, ensure "*Data processing pack*" is *not* selected and then click "*Next*" (see Figure 7-25).

Configure edge capabilities Info
Edge capabilities
Select packs to activate edge capabilities for your gateway. AWS IoT SiteWise activates the data collection pack by default when you add a data source.
Data processing pack
You can use asset models to compute metrics and transforms at the edge.
1.
Cancel Previous Next

Figure 7-25. *Leave the data processing pack unchecked and proceed to the next*

In the "*Configure publisher*" screen, leave all the settings as default and proceed to "*Next*". Now this is the important step in "*Add data sources*". Select "*Add data source*" (see Figure 7-26).

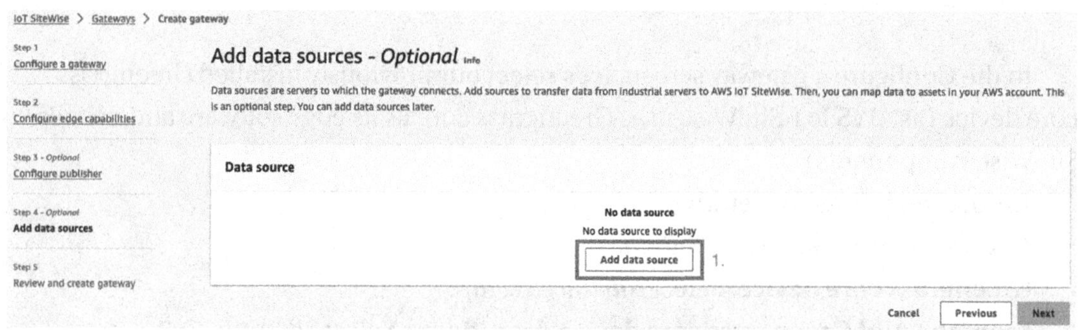

Figure 7-26. *Select to add our OPC UA Demo Data source.*

Select Demo Data sources (fastest) from the Source type drop-down (see Figure 7-27).

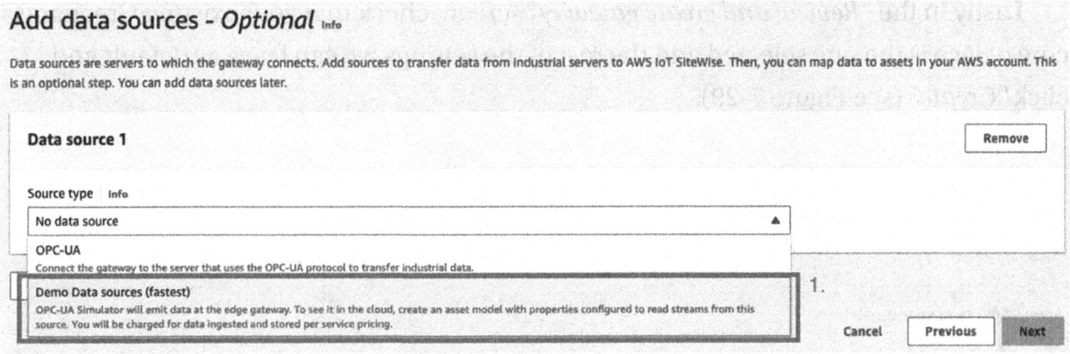

***Figure 7-27.** Adding a Demo Data source*

In the "*Data source 1*" screen, leave the settings as default and make sure "*AWS IoT SiteWise*" is selected and then select "*Add data source*" and click "*Next*" (see Figure 7-28).

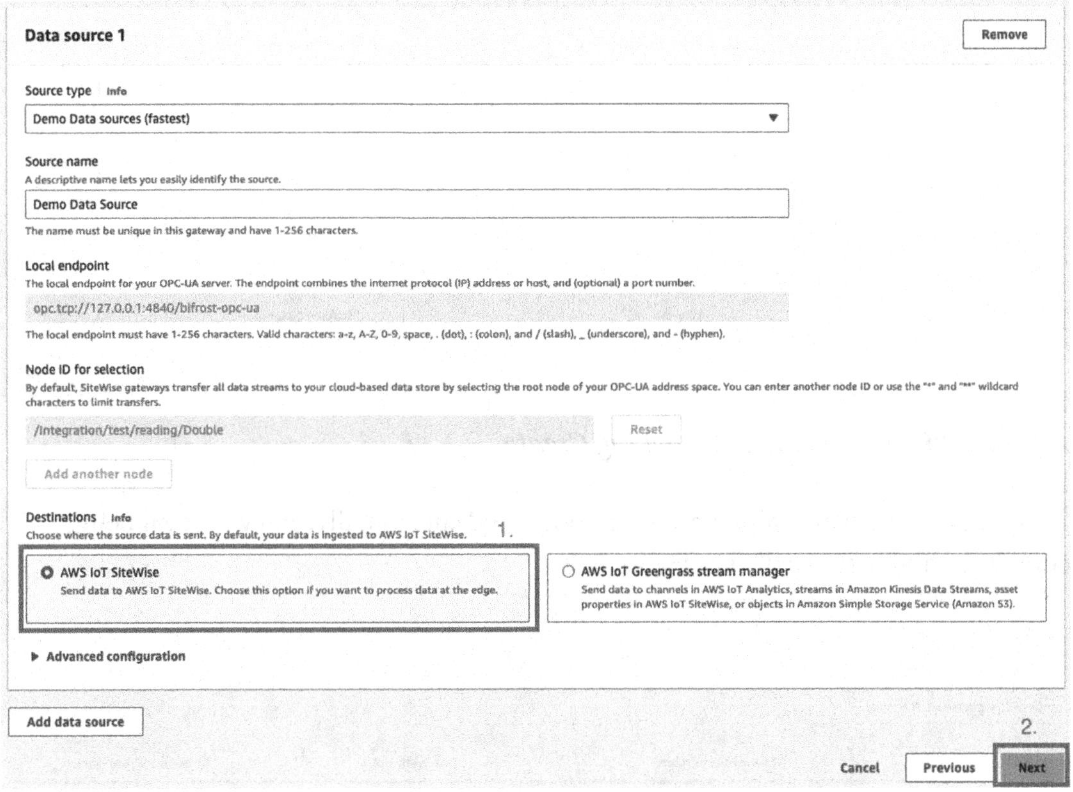

***Figure 7-28.** Selecting AWS IoT SiteWise as the destination and selecting Add data source*

Lastly in the "*Review and create gateway*" screen, check that your existing Greengrass core device is the one selected and the rest of the settings we can leave as default and click "*Create*" (see Figure 7-29).

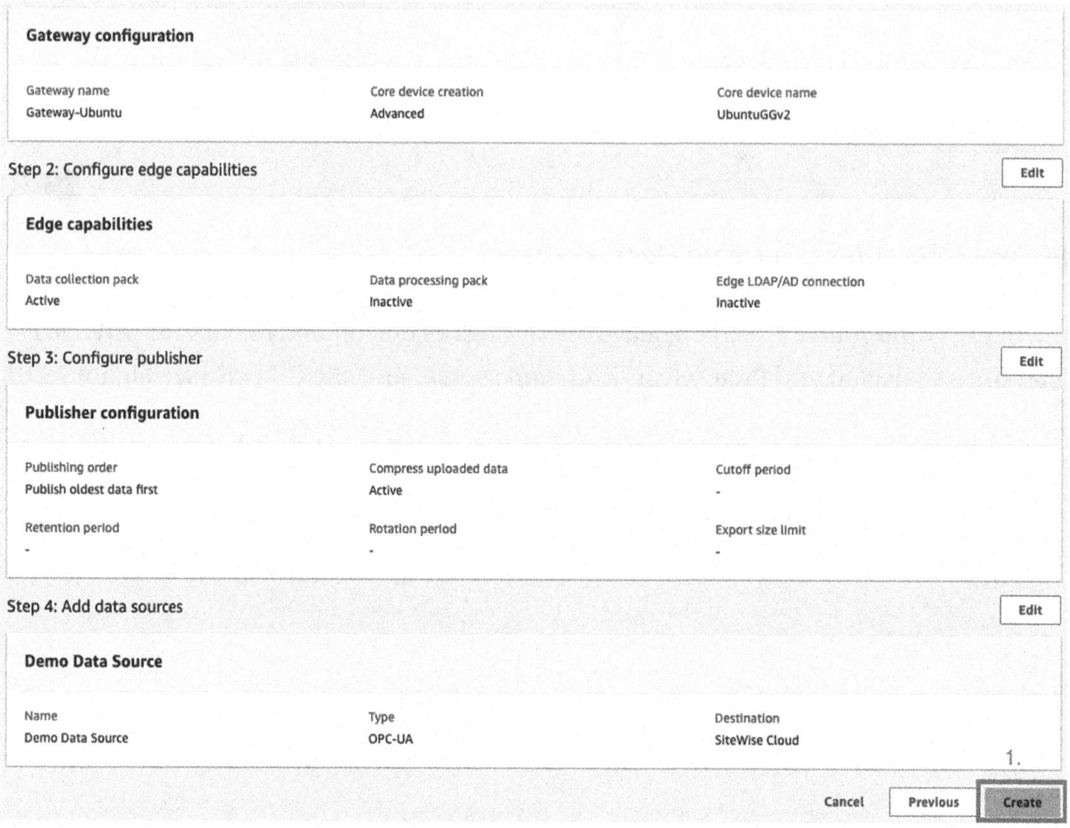

***Figure 7-29.** Reviewing and clicking Create*

Once our gateway "Deployment" is completed successfully, you will see it being completed and "activated" (see Figure 7-30).

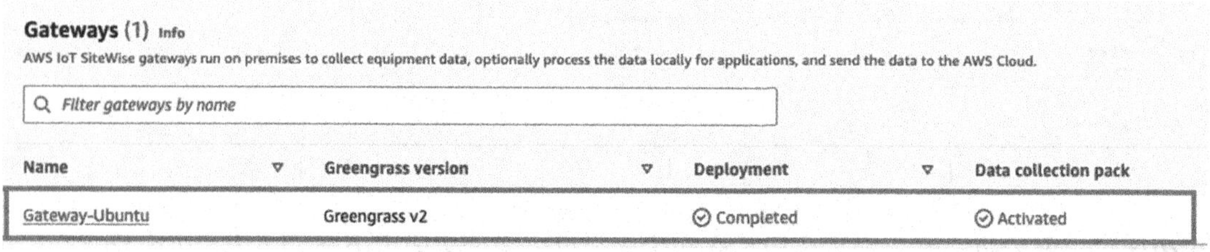

***Figure 7-30.** Deployed successfully with green ticks showing*

Let's see models created by our OPC UA data simulator automatically; select "*Models*" under "*Build*" and we will see the two new models showing up as "*Active*" (see Figure 7-31).

Models (3)

Assets represent industrial devices and processes that send data streams to SiteWise. Models are structures that enforce a specific

Create model

Filter instances

Name	Status
Conveyor Belt Model	ACTIVE
Simulator Wind Farm Asset Model	ACTIVE
Simulator Turbine Asset Model	ACTIVE

Figure 7-31. *Newly created model by our OPC UA demo data source*

To see data for our demo, under "*Build*", select "*Assets*" and expand "*Simulator Wind Farm Asset*" and finally click "*Simulator Turbine Asset for Demo*" (see Figure 7-32).

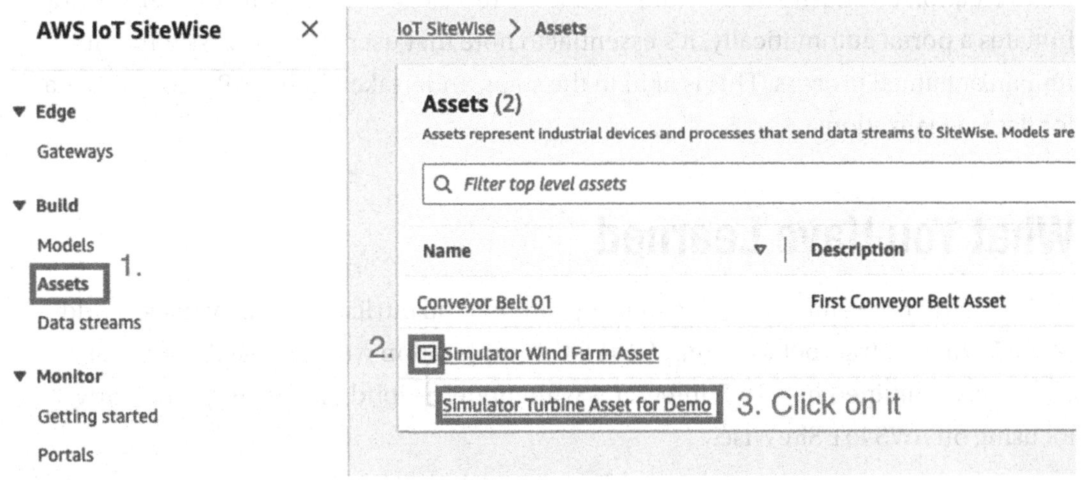

Figure 7-32. *Selecting our newly created demo data stream*

After selecting our "*Simulator Turbine Asset for Demo*", we can see data streams arriving for our "*Attributes*" (see Figure 7-33).

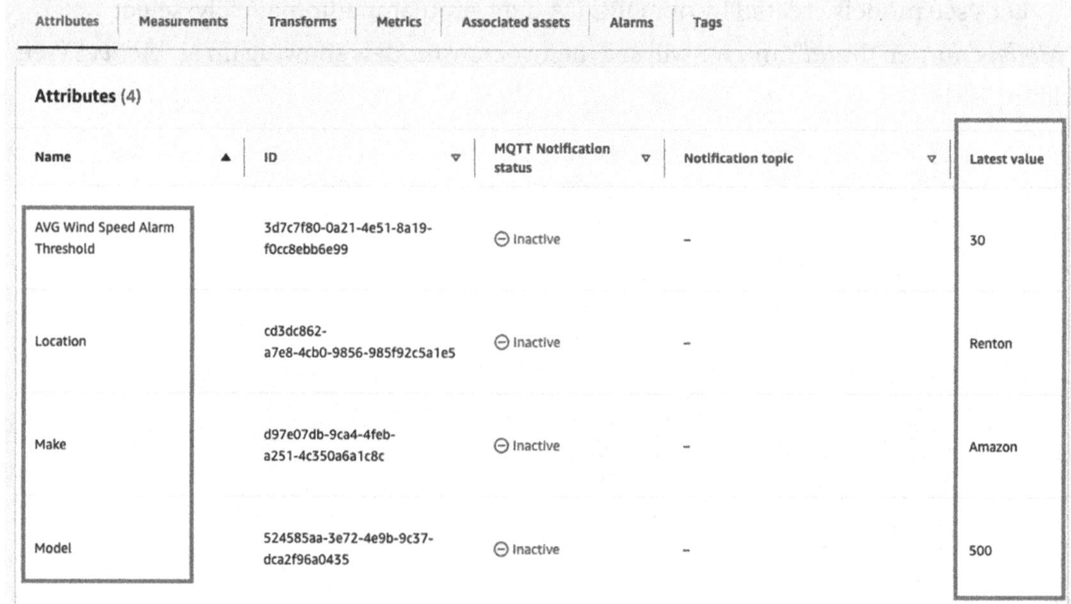

Figure 7-33. *Simulator demo sending data to AWS IoT SiteWise*

Using simulated data opens a wide array of opportunities. One notable application is the creation of a dashboard within AWS IoT SiteWise Monitor. While the demo setup initiates a portal automatically, it's essential to note that user roles and assignments remain a manual process. This is akin to the steps undertaken in the API scenario, vital for data visualization.

What You Have Learned

In this chapter, we embarked on a journey through the intricate and expansive world of the Industrial Internet of Things (IIoT). Our exploration was not just theoretical; we closely examined how IIoT integrates with modern cloud platforms, particularly focusing on AWS IoT SiteWise.

- **Introduction to IIoT**: IIoT stands at the convergence of industrial machinery (Industry 4.0) and smart digital technologies. It's a testament to how traditional industries are evolving in the age of the Internet, bringing with it a surge of possibilities.

- **AWS IoT SiteWise**: AWS has carved a niche in the IIoT realm with its SiteWise service. We explored its practical applications, understanding how it fits within the broader context of industrial operations and how it can revolutionize data-driven decision-making in these settings.
- **Three Key Methods in AWS IoT**
    - **AWS IoT Core Rules**: Suited best for the newer generation of IIoT devices, this method is dominant when devices come equipped with networking capabilities, allowing them to seamlessly interface with cloud services.
    - **AWS IoT SiteWise API (PUT Operation)**: This method has garnered significant attention from the IIoT community. We set up a simulated conveyor belt model to showcase its potential, emphasizing how real-time data can be mapped and utilized within the AWS IoT SiteWise monitor portal. This real-world example highlighted the tangible benefits, from data collection to in-depth visualization.
    - **AWS IoT SiteWise Gateway**: While new technologies continue to emerge, many industries still rely on legacy systems. The SiteWise Gateway is a bridge for such systems, especially those using the OPC UA protocol. This integration means that even older, tried-and-true machinery can benefit from the latest in IoT advancements.
- **Bridging the Old with the New**: Legacy devices have decades of reliability and functionality behind them, but they often lack modern connectivity. We delved into how these devices, especially those using the OPC UA protocols, can be brought into the fold of the modern IoT world. AWS provides tools that ensure these devices aren't left behind but incorporated into new data-driven ecosystems. Our exploration was enhanced by a hands-on demo setup from AWS, showcasing the seamless integration of these older systems with cutting-edge IoT platforms.

Summary

This chapter guided us through the extensive domain of the Industrial Internet of Things (IIoT), combining a thorough theoretical exploration with practical insight into IIoT's synergy with modern cloud platforms, especially AWS IoT SiteWise.

We began by introducing IIoT, highlighting its role as the intersection of industrial machinery and smart digital technologies. This convergence symbolizes the transformation of traditional industries in the Internet era, opening up a myriad of opportunities and possibilities.

Delving deeper, we discussed AWS IoT SiteWise, emphasizing its significant role in revolutionizing industrial operations. The service stands out in the IIoT landscape, offering practical solutions and contributing substantially to data-driven decision-making in industrial settings.

The chapter further explored three pivotal methods within AWS IoT:

1. **AWS IoT Core Rules**
2. **AWS IoT SiteWise API (PUT Operation)**
3. **AWS IoT SiteWise Gateway**

In essence, the chapter successfully bridged the gap between the old and new, ensuring a harmonious integration of legacy devices with modern IoT platforms, backed by a practical demonstration of the seamless integration capabilities offered by AWS. This comprehensive exploration provides a robust foundation for understanding and leveraging the extensive capabilities of IIoT, particularly within the AWS ecosystem.

CHAPTER 8

Machine Learning (ML) at Edge with AWS IoT

Up to this point in our exploration, we've delved deep into the realm of the Internet of Things (IoT) with AWS. Our journey has been comprehensive from the basics of setting up an IoT "thing" to the more intricate processes of configuring devices to transmit MQTT telemetry data to the IoT Core. We've ventured into edge development using AWS IoT Greengrass and also delved into the specialized arena of the Industrial Internet of Things (IIoT). We leveraged AWS's IoT offerings, specifically AWS IoT SiteWise, to create models for our industrial assets. This enabled us to stream data in real time, creating a virtual representation of the asset in the cloud that acts as its digital twin.

As we embark on the eighth chapter of our exploration, we shift our focus toward integrating machine learning (ML) at the edge with AWS IoT by utilizing Greengrass at the edge ML inference capabilities. The combination of IoT and ML opens a plethora of possibilities, enhancing not just the amount but also the quality and intelligence of our data interpretation. Given that IoT devices can generate vast quantities of telemetry data and images, imagine the potential if we could intelligently analyze this data, making it a gold mine for business insights or augmenting customer experiences or even enhancement of the world around it such as specifying and identifying endangered species.

We'll begin with the basics before delving into practical applications and integrations. What is machine learning, and where does machine learning inference stand within the wider context of ML and IoT? Let's explore these ideas together.

S. Rehan, *AWS IoT With Edge ML and Cybersecurity*, https://doi.org/10.1007/979-8-8688-0011-5_8

What Is Machine Learning and ML Inference

Machine learning and ML inference are crucial components of modern artificial intelligence systems, offering the capability to automatically learn from data and make predictions or decisions based on that learned knowledge. Let's delve deeper into understanding machine learning and the process of ML inference.

Machine Learning (ML)

At its core, machine learning (ML) is a subset of artificial intelligence that empowers intelligent computer systems to learn and make decisions from data without being explicitly programmed. Rather than being preconfigured with specific decision-making rules, machine learning models "**learn**" from the data they're exposed to, gradually refining their understanding and improving their predictions or classifications.

The process begins by inputting a substantial dataset into a machine learning model, termed the training dataset. This dataset consists of examples paired with their respective labels or outcomes. Take, for instance, an image classification task aimed at differentiating between images of cats, dogs, and other animals. The training dataset would comprise a multitude of images, each labeled accordingly as "cat," "dog," or the respective animal. Once trained, this model can then be integrated into applications to identify the content of newly introduced images.

Machine Learning Algorithm

An ML (machine learning) algorithm is a set of procedures or rules that a machine follows to achieve a specific goal using data. In the context of machine learning, this goal typically involves learning patterns from data. At a high level, ML algorithms learn from data, make predictions, or categorize information based on input.

Different ML algorithms are designed to address different types of tasks and are based on varied mathematical and statistical principles. Here are a few broad categories of ML algorithms:

- **Supervised Learning Algorithms**: These algorithms learn from labeled training data and make predictions based on that learning. For example, in "**image classification**," each image in the training dataset is labeled with a category (e.g., "cat," "dog," "tiger"). The algorithm learns to recognize and classify new images based on these labels.

- Examples of these algorithms are as follows:
    - Linear regression
    - Decision trees
    - Support vector machines
    - Neural networks
- **Deep Learning**: This field is a subset of machine learning and primarily employs artificial neural networks, which are algorithms inspired by the structure and function of the brain. Deep learning models, especially deep neural networks, possess multiple layers through which data is transformed. This structure allows them to automatically extract hierarchical features, making them particularly effective for dynamic tasks like *image* and *speech* recognition.
- **Deep Neural Networks**: These are a specific subset of neural networks and are a cornerstone of deep learning. While they typically operate within a supervised ML context, they are characterized by their multilayered architecture that is optimized for complex tasks.
    - Examples of deep neural networks include the following:
        - **Convolutional Neural Networks (CNNs)**: Primarily tailored for image classification and processing
        - **Recurrent Neural Networks (RNNs)**: Specialized for sequential data analysis

  It's essential to understand that while deep learning falls under the broader umbrella of machine learning, the most widely recognized applications of deep neural networks are within the context of supervised learning algorithms, specifically as advanced structures of neural networks.
- **Unsupervised Learning Algorithms**: These algorithms find hidden patterns or data groupings without the need for labels, for example, "**Customer Segmentation**" where retail stores analyze purchase histories and customer behavior. Using an unsupervised learning

algorithm (K-means clustering), they can identify distinct customer groups (e.g., "High Spenders," "Bargain Hunters," and "Loyal Regulars") without any prior labels, aiding in targeted marketing strategies.

- Examples of these algorithms are as follows:
    - K-means clustering
    - Hierarchical clustering
    - Principal component analysis

- **Reinforcement Learning Algorithms**: In this approach, an agent (the learning algorithm) interacts with an environment by performing actions and, based on these actions, receives rewards or penalties. A classic example is "**Game Play Optimization**" in chess. Here, the agent (the reinforcement learning algorithm) attempts to discover the best moves and strategies. It does so by playing the game, getting feedback on its moves, and iteratively adjusting its strategies for better outcomes.
    - Examples of these algorithms are as follows:
        - Q-learning
        - Deep adversarial networks

- **Semi-supervised and Transfer Learning**: These techniques utilize both labeled and unlabeled data or transfer knowledge from one domain or task to another.
    - **Semi-supervised Learning**: Consider the scenario of "**Handwriting Recognition.**" Envision a system developed to recognize handwritten digits. This system is trained using a modest amount of labeled data (drawings specifically labeled as "1", "2", "3", etc.) complemented by a more extensive set of unlabeled drawings. Initially, the algorithm leverages the labeled data to form a basic understanding. Subsequently, it refines its learning by using the copious unlabeled data, enhancing its proficiency in identifying diverse handwriting styles.

- **Transfer Learning**: Take "**image classification**" as an example. Assume a model has already been trained on a comprehensive dataset to identify 1000 distinct animals. Later, there arises a need to recognize particular dog breeds. Instead of constructing a model from ground zero, the previously trained model (imbued with features learned from the 1000 animals) is repurposed. This model is then retrained on a smaller dataset dedicated to dog breeds. By doing so, it capitalizes on the foundational learning from the extensive animal dataset and becomes more specialized in pinpointing different dog breeds.

- **Ensemble Methods**: Algorithms that combine the predictions from multiple other algorithms to improve accuracy and model robustness, for example, "**Stock Market Prediction**" where predicting stock market movements is notoriously complex due to the multitude of influencing factors. Ensemble method enhances the prediction's accuracy by amalgamating insights from distinct models. For instance, one model might analyze historical stock prices, another could focus on news sentiment, while a third examines macroeconomic indicators. By employing methods like "**Bagging or Stacking**," these individual forecasts are integrated to produce a more robust and accurate consensus prediction, minimizing the errors of any single model's projection.

  - Examples of these algorithms are as follows:

    - Random forest

    - Gradient-boosted trees

    - AdaBoost

The relationship between an *ML algorithm* and an *ML model* is analogous to the relationship between a recipe and the resulting dish. The ML algorithm is the procedure or the set of rules to follow, while the ML model is the end result after applying the algorithm to data.

In essence, ML algorithms are the building blocks that power the predictive and analytical capabilities of machine learning models. They define the way a model learns from data and subsequently how it makes predictions or classifications.

Selecting the appropriate ML algorithm requires careful examination of the data's characteristics, the desired outcome (such as classification, regression, or clustering), and considerations like data volume and feature intricacy. Continuous refinement is paramount in any ML endeavor. To keep model results optimized and up to date, you would need to consistently collect feedback, refresh your training data, retrain your model, and optimize your system to heighten both precision and accuracy.

Machine Learning Model Predictions Confidence

Machine learning models, when making predictions, usually accompany these outcomes with a confidence level. This confidence level serves as a quantified measure, representing the model's trustworthiness or certainty associated with a particular prediction. For instance, in image classification, when a model labels an image as a "cat," it might additionally provide a confidence score, say, 0.95, indicating a 95% certainty in its assessment.

The importance of understanding this confidence level encompasses several aspects:

- **Informed Decision-Making**: In high-stakes scenarios like medical diagnoses, actions or conclusions might be derived from model predictions only if the associated confidence surpasses a predefined threshold.
- **Model Interpretability and Trustworthiness**: For stakeholders or end users, a clearer comprehension of confidence levels offers insights into instances where the model's predictions can be trusted and where additional scrutiny might be needed.
- **Error Analysis and Model Refinement**: Instances where the model exudes high confidence yet blunders in its predictions can be pivotal in discerning potential areas for model improvement or understanding its limitations.

- **Calibration and Accuracy Alignment**: While a model's high confidence score might seem reassuring, it's pivotal to realize that high confidence doesn't invariably equate to accuracy. There could be scenarios where models falter in their predictions despite exhibiting high confidence. Techniques like calibration can be employed to align a model's confidence scores more congruently with its true accuracy.

In essence, the confidence level in predictions doesn't just serve as a metric; it plays a crucial role in understanding, validating, and optimally utilizing machine learning models in diverse real-world applications. As such, stakeholders should approach these confidence scores judiciously, considering them within the broader context of the application and the model's inherent limitations.

Machine Learning Inference

Once a machine learning **model** is trained, the next step is to deploy it to serve a specific function, be it classifying images, predicting stock prices, or any other task. This process of using a pre-trained model on new data to make predictions or classifications is called machine learning inference.

Inference differs from training in several key ways:

- **Purpose**: While model training is about learning patterns from data, inference is about applying those patterns to make decisions on new data.
- **Computational Needs:** Training machine learning models demands substantial computational power, often sourced from GPUs (Graphics Processing Units) optimized for tasks in gaming, artificial intelligence, and scientific simulations, along with considerable memory and time it takes due to the necessity to process vast datasets and iteratively adjust model parameters. To mitigate these high requirements, many opt for pre-trained models, which we'll also use to minimize GPU and memory consumption. While inference is less resource intensive since it uses already trained models, possibly via cloud services like Amazon SageMaker, edge-based ML inference is essential for real-time applications seeking low latency, and it notably benefits from these pre-trained models.

- **Frequency**: Training for ML models might occur once or is periodically updated to keep the dataset fresh, while inference happens every time a prediction or classification is needed (on-demand in nature using the pre-trained model).
- **Location**: While training often occurs in data centers with powerful computational resources (like AWS cloud), inference can happen anywhere - from these data centers to edge devices like smart home hubs or other edge IoT devices (like medical IoT devices or aviation IoT devices). This is particularly important for applications where data needs to be processed in real time or where data transfer to a central location is impractical.

In essence, the training phase is where the model learns, and the inference phase is where the model applies its knowledge. For many businesses and applications, inference happens far more frequently than training and is the primary avenue by which value (insights, decisions, automation) is derived from ML models.

Within the realm of AWS and IoT, the power of inference emerges as a game changer. As devices amass a wealth of data at the edge, the capability to analyze and act upon this data instantly - without the necessity to relay it to a central server - ushers in transformative possibilities. This synergy between IoT and ML, accentuated by on-the-spot inference, marks the cutting edge in technological progression, fostering intelligent decision-making, elevated user engagements, and streamlined systems.

Edge ML with AWS IoT Greengrass

AWS IoT Greengrass facilitates edge computing, allowing direct inference on edge devices and reducing dependency on cloud communication. This is essential for ML tasks, especially in network-limited IoT environments. Greengrass lets developers deploy and manage ML models on edge devices for faster responses and lower data costs. It supports models from TensorFlow and MXNet and offers a modular design for custom integrations. Now, let's explore an example of using a pre-trained model for "image classification" inference on this platform.

Image Classification with AWS IoT Greengrass (Using Neural Network Model)

This simulation sends an image to AWS IoT Greengrass for processing. Once received, the Greengrass component subjects the image to analysis using a pre-trained **ResNet-50 model** optimized for supervised learning. The result, an "image confidence score," is transmitted to AWS IoT Core via MQTT protocols. The confidence score ranges from 0.x to 1.0, with values closer to 1.0 indicating a stronger match by the model (i.e., 100% match).

What Is ResNet-50 Model?

ResNet-50 is a convolutional neural network (CNN) architecture, specially designed for "Deep Residual Learning for Image Recognition." ResNet-50 is specifically named because it has 50 layers in total, making it a relatively deep neural network.

Consider this in the context of our pre-established edge gateway, the AWS IoT Greengrass device (*UbuntuGGv2*), discussed in previous chapters. Powered by the Greengrass core, it conducts ML inference on the image within a designated directory. As a real-world application, envision a camera placed in a wildlife habitat capturing the image of an animal, especially if it's an endangered species.

The system employs ML inference to identify this species, quickly uploading this invaluable data to cloud storage. More than just storage, this data is crucial for analytics that can drive conservation strategies for endangered animals. For a visual architecture of this simulation overview, see Figure 8-1.

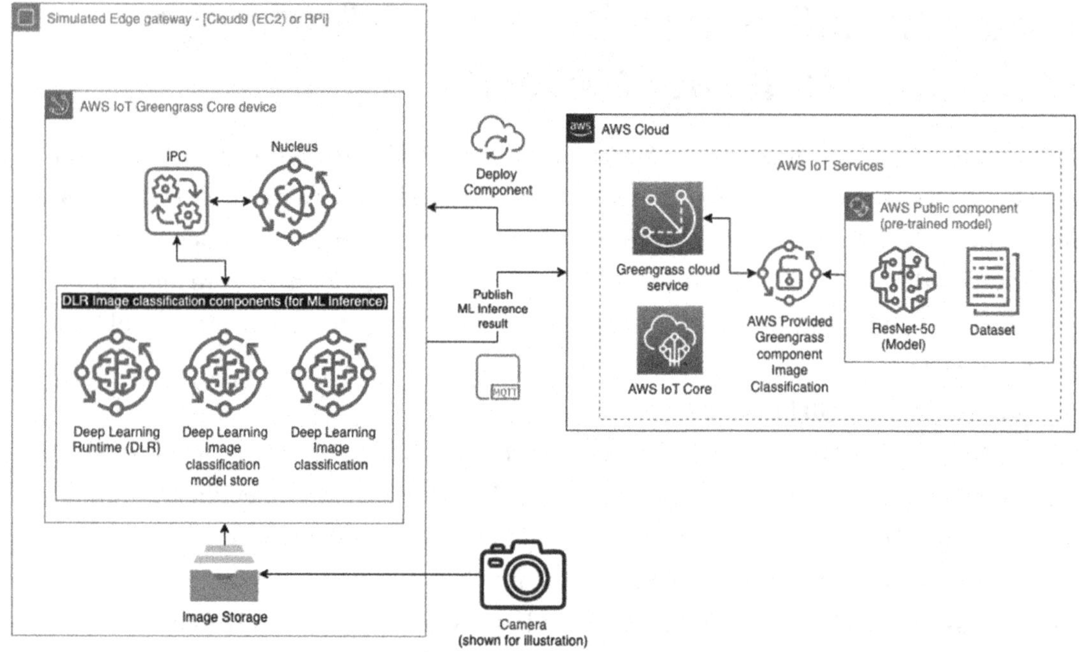

Figure 8-1. *Simulated image classification architecture diagram*

Set Up Image Classification Component

We will use the AWS IoT Greengrass core device (*UbuntuGGv2*) that we created in an earlier chapter; make sure Greengrass is running by running the following command in the terminal:

```
sudo systemctl status greengrass.service
```

We should see output similar to Figure 8-2 showing us it's running; if it *not* running, substitute *"status"* with *"start"*.

```
syed-book:~ $ sudo systemctl status greengrass.service
● greengrass.service - Greengrass Core
     Loaded: loaded (/etc/systemd/system/greengrass.service; enabled; vendor preset: enabled)
     Active: active (running) since Tue 2023-09-05 23:02:20 UTC; 14h ago
   Main PID: 217551 (sh)
      Tasks: 310 (limit: 19160)
     Memory: 2.3G
        CPU: 16min 26.747s
     CGroup: /system.slice/greengrass.service
             ├─217551 /bin/sh /greengrass/v2/alts/current/distro/bin/loader
             └─217556 java -Dlog.store=FILE -Dlog.store=FILE -Droot=/greengrass/v2 -jar /greeng
```

Figure 8-2. *AWS IoT Greengrass service status*

Execute the following command to establish a folder structure and upload the *image.jpg* file in that directory. Retrieve *image.jpg* from the Chapter 8 section of the book's GitHub repository. We'll utilize this file for ML inference in this simulation (see Figure 8-3).

```
mkdir -p $HOME/ml/image/
```

It is crucial to place the file "*image.jpg*" into the newly created folder (*$HOME/ml/image/*) (see Figure 8-3). Failure to do so will prevent ML inference, resulting in error messages in the logs. As discussed in Chapter 6, this will cause the component to enter a "*broken*" life cycle state, necessitating a restart of the component to resolve the issue.

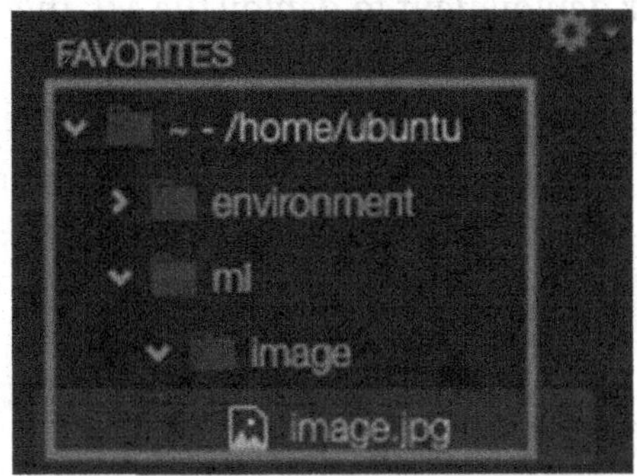

***Figure 8-3.** Placing the image in the created folder*

Monitor logs in the terminal as well so we can see what is actually happening at the edge.

```
sudo tail -F /greengrass/v2/logs/greengrass.log
```

Now that we have placed the file in the folder, let's head over to the AWS IoT Greengrass console and deploy our "*Deep Learning Runtime (DLR) image classification*" component.

From the AWS IoT console, navigate to "*Manage*" and then "*Deployments*" and select our previous deployment – in this case, "*Deployment for UbuntuGGv2Group*" – and click "*Revise*" (see Figure 8-4).

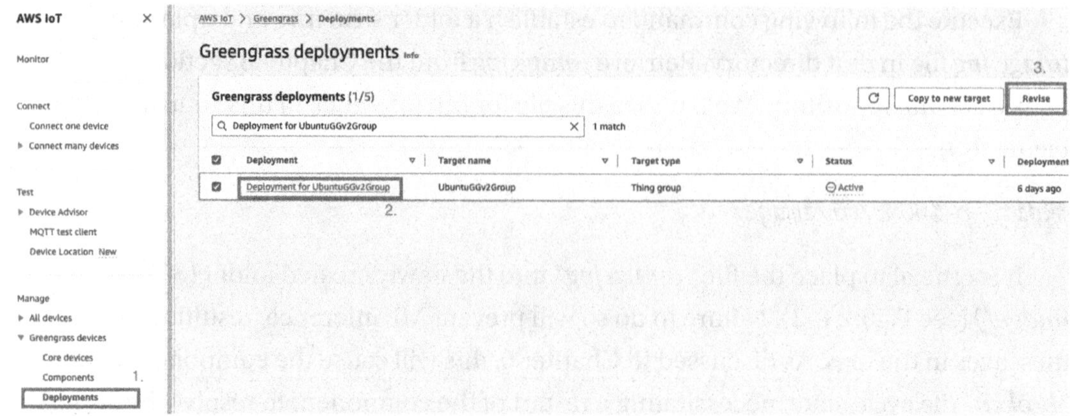

Figure 8-4. *Revising our deployment to deploy the ML inference component*

Navigate to the Component selection screen, and under the Public components filter "*DLRImageClassification*", select and navigate to next (see Figure 8-5).

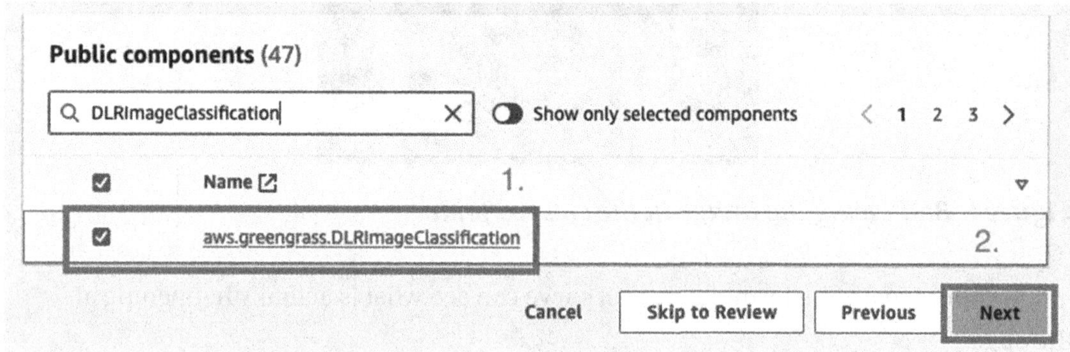

Figure 8-5. *Selecting DLR Image Classification*

Just like in our Greengrass chapter, we will need to configure the component and select and configure the component (see Figure 8-6).

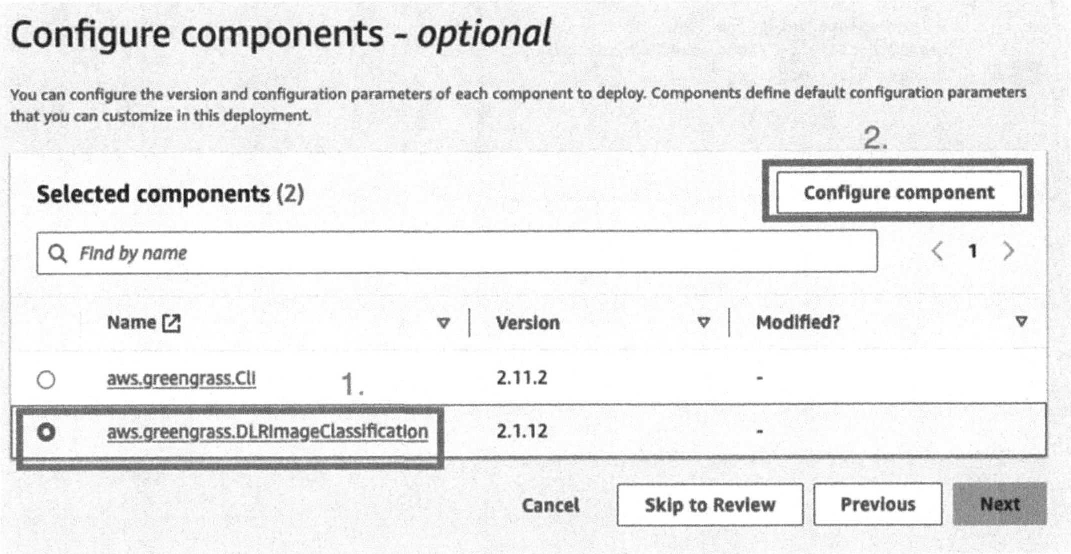

Figure 8-6. *Configuring the component*

For the "*configuration to merge*" process, please include the following JSON configuration parameters (see Figure 8-7); you can also obtain this from Chapter 8 of the book's GitHub repository. Ensure you provide a valid folder path tailored to your specific setup, whether it's a Raspberry Pi (RPi) or another environment like Cloud9 Ubuntu. For our *Cloud9 Ubuntu* setup, the path should be as given here:

```
{
    "InferenceInterval": "30",
    "ImageDirectory": "/home/ubuntu/ml/image/",
    "ImageName": "image.jpg"
}
```

In this configuration, we are just setting up how often to infer which directory and image name to use.

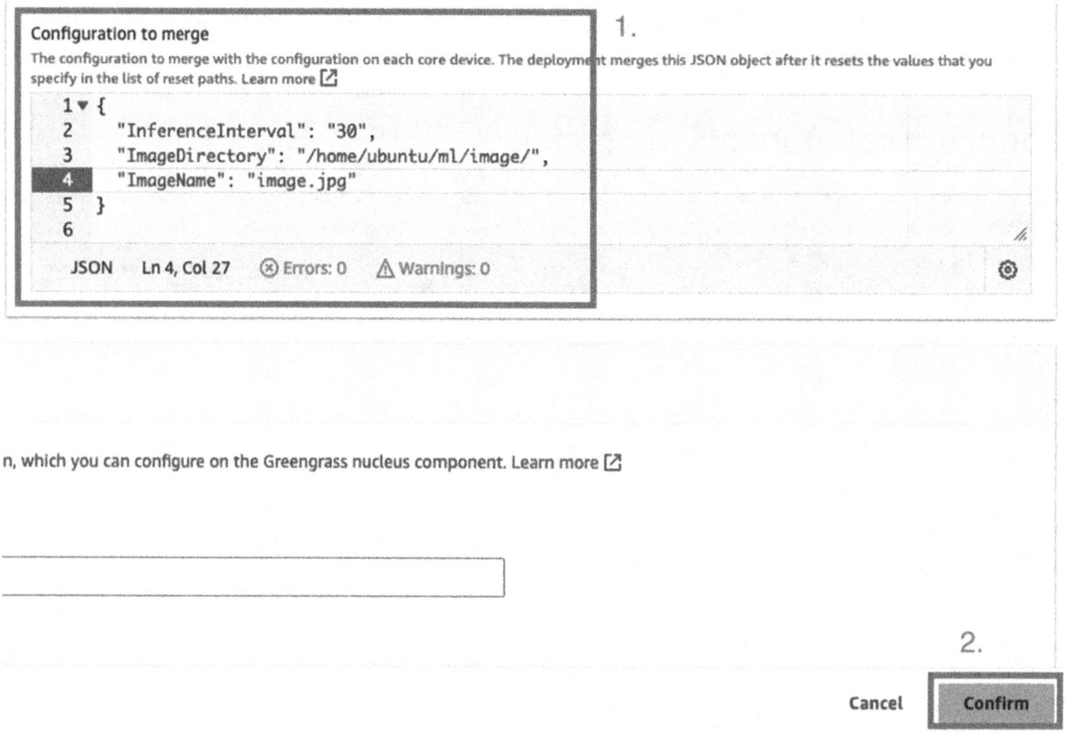

Configuration to merge

The configuration to merge with the configuration on each core device. The deployment merges this JSON object after it resets the values that you specify in the list of reset paths. Learn more

```
{
    "InferenceInterval": "30",
    "ImageDirectory": "/home/ubuntu/ml/image/",
    "ImageName": "image.jpg"
}
```

JSON Ln 4, Col 27 Errors: 0 Warnings: 0

n, which you can configure on the Greengrass nucleus component. Learn more

Cancel Confirm

Figure 8-7. Configuration to merge for – aws.greengrass.DLRImageClassification

Proceed ahead and deploy (keeping the rest of the settings as default) to our Greengrass core device. We will see in the Greengrass logs that the component was deployed successfully (see Figure 8-8).

```
2023-09-07T22:47:30.696Z [INFO] (aws.greengrass.DLRImageClassification
te=STOPPING, newState=INSTALLED}
```

Figure 8-8. *DLR Image Classification successfully deployed*

To view the inference results in the AWS IoT Core MQTT Client, subscribe to the topic: *ml/dlr/image-classification*. The inference outcome will appear in the MQTT test client every 30 seconds (refer to Figure 8-9). If you choose to change and use a different image, remember to reload the Greengrass component after the replacement. Why? The DLR Image Classification component caches the image for ML inference. Reloading the component after an image change ensures the cache is refreshed. You can use the following command to reload/restart.

```
sudo /greengrass/v2/bin/greengrass-cli component restart  --names "aws.greengrass.DLRImageClassification"
```

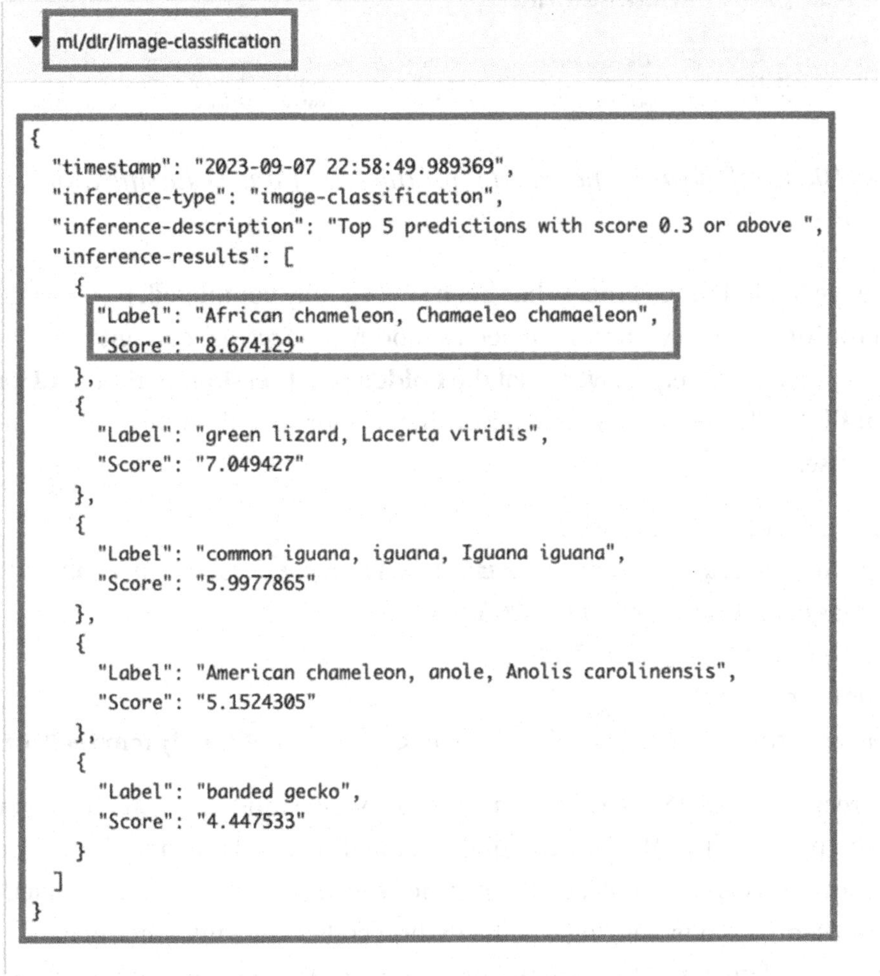

ml/dlr/image-classification

```
{
  "timestamp": "2023-09-07 22:58:49.989369",
  "inference-type": "image-classification",
  "inference-description": "Top 5 predictions with score 0.3 or above ",
  "inference-results": [
    {
      "Label": "African chameleon, Chamaeleo chamaeleon",
      "Score": "8.674129"
    },
    {
      "Label": "green lizard, Lacerta viridis",
      "Score": "7.049427"
    },
    {
      "Label": "common iguana, iguana, Iguana iguana",
      "Score": "5.9977865"
    },
    {
      "Label": "American chameleon, anole, Anolis carolinensis",
      "Score": "5.1524305"
    },
    {
      "Label": "banded gecko",
      "Score": "4.447533"
    }
  ]
}
```


Figure 8-9. *MQTT telemetry in the AWS IoT MQTT test client*

After the component is successfully installed and operational, you can verify the logs for the *DLR Image Classification* component. Execute the following command in the terminal to view the inference results being posted to AWS IoT:

```
sudo tail -F /greengrass/v2/logs/aws.greengrass.DLRImageClassification.log
```

If you are not getting ML inference results and have modified the configuration, you can always check using the following command what configuration parameters are used by the component and look for the "*aws.greengrass.DLRImageClassification*" component (see Figure 8-10):

```
sudo /greengrass/v2/bin/greengrass-cli component list
```

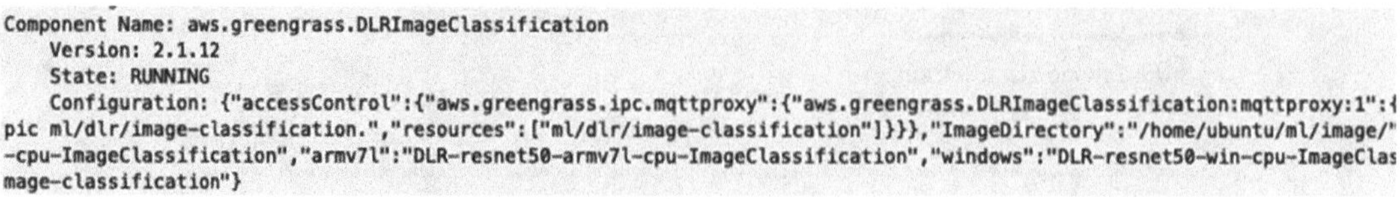

```
Component Name: aws.greengrass.DLRImageClassification
    Version: 2.1.12
    State: RUNNING
    Configuration: {"accessControl":{"aws.greengrass.ipc.mqttproxy":{"aws.greengrass.DLRImageClassification:mqttproxy:1":{
pic ml/dlr/image-classification.","resources":["ml/dlr/image-classification"]}}},"ImageDirectory":"/home/ubuntu/ml/image/"
-cpu-ImageClassification","armv7l":"DLR-resnet50-armv7l-cpu-ImageClassification","windows":"DLR-resnet50-win-cpu-ImageClas
mage-classification"}
```

***Figure 8-10.** Configuration parameter for the DLR Image Classification component*

The edge ML inference process has been successfully completed. If you want to adapt the inference to your unique needs, modify the "*recipe*" content with the command provided here. Be aware that the **bolded text (version, region, and name of output file)** will need to be altered according to your specific configuration and the version in use.

```
aws greengrassv2 get-component \
    --arn arn:aws:greengrass:us-east-1:aws:components:aws.greengrass.DLRIma
    geClassification:versions:2.1.12 \
    --recipe-output-format JSON \
    --query recipe \
    --output text | base64 --decode > myCustomImageClassificationRecipe.json
```

The "recipe" is a JSON file referencing the ResNet-50 model, which is extensively trained and provided by AWS (saving computational cost and time required to train with dataset). You can personalize ML inference settings by refining the "artifact," which represents the business logic in the Python code where inference occurs. Additionally, update the S3 location (within the recipe) where your Python file is stored. This adjustment enables the integration of your unique "custom inference," as it's commonly called.

What You Have Learned

In this chapter, we delved deeply into the vast domain of machine learning (ML), elucidating its core principles and pragmatic uses. Here's a streamlined recap:

1. **Diverse ML Algorithms:** We navigated through a range of ML strategies, highlighting supervised learning, deep learning (encompassing CNNs and RNNs), unsupervised learning (e.g., K-means clustering), reinforcement learning, semi-supervised learning, and transfer learning. Such algorithms are pivotal in addressing a multitude of real-world dilemmas.
2. **Algorithm-Model Nexus:** Grasping the intricate relationship between ML algorithms and models is vital. Topics like decision insight, model transparency, trustworthiness, error evaluation, model enhancement, calibration, and accuracy synchronization were discussed to ensure models predict responsibly and effectively.
3. **Inference in ML:** We drew a distinction between ML training and inference, emphasizing its relevance. Our deep dive into AWS IoT Greengrass showcased the smooth integration of ML inference on the edge, amplifying real-time responsiveness and efficacy.
4. **DLR's ResNet-50 Overview:** We tapped into ResNet-50, a specialized deep-learning framework for image categorization. It stands out with its profound layering for feature derivation, residual learning mechanisms, skip pathways for streamlined backpropagation, and unparalleled feature extraction proficiencies.
5. **Mastery in Image Recognition with ResNet-50:** Its structural depth and ability to extract distinct features make ResNet-50 a leader in image recognition tasks. It thrives in diverse applications, from object identification in photos to pattern discernment in medical imagery or species recognition in ecological monitoring.

6. **A Commitment to Precision:** Adopting the DLR Image Classification built on ResNet-50 has guaranteed us unmatched precision and dependability in classifying images. This architectural cornerstone exemplifies the advancements that leading-edge models bring to edge computing and IoT infrastructures.

In conclusion, we executed ML inference at the edge using an image by employing the AWS publicly provided DLR Image Classification component, leveraging a large, trained ML model against images.

Summary

To sum up, this chapter has furnished us with an enriched comprehension of the essentials in ML, predictive modelling, edge-based inference, and the power of ResNet-50 in image classification. Such insights lay a robust groundwork for diving deeper into the evolving universe of machine learning and artificial intelligence.

CHAPTER 9

Business Intelligence and Real-Time Insights by Using Timestream Data

As we explore the vast technological landscape, we come across a range of topics, ranging from basic IoT devices and sophisticated smart home innovations to the forefront of edge devices, IIoT assets, and the role of machine learning at the IoT edge. Although they may seem distinct, these diverse realms are bound together by a common thread: the rich tapestry of data they weave. When we harvest this data judiciously, it reveals critical business insights and acts as a compass directing us toward a sustainable future.

In today's world, it is more crucial than ever to prioritize sustainability. The environmental consequences of our actions necessitate a re-evaluation of our growth strategy. As a result, governments across the globe are taking action, with revolutionary transformations taking place in public transportation and fleet management systems.

The introduction of IoT in public transportation is a significant development. Picture buses and trains equipped with advanced sensors, transmitting a wealth of data, such as their precise location, cruising speed, and fuel consumption. This isn't just a bunch of numbers; it's the pulse of a transportation system, offering valuable insights into its efficiency, health, and environmental impact.

We turn to AWS services like Amazon Timestream to harness this wealth of data. Designed explicitly for time-series data, Timestream offers the scalability and efficiency required to handle the torrent of information flowing from IoT devices. It captures, stores, and retrieves data, ensuring that every data point from our transportation systems is meticulously logged and available for analysis.

S. Rehan, *AWS IoT With Edge ML and Cybersecurity*, https://doi.org/10.1007/979-8-8688-0011-5_9

Raw data, irrespective of its volume, requires interpretation to unlock its true value. This is where business intelligence (BI) tools, such as Amazon QuickSight, play a crucial role. By utilizing its advanced data visualization capabilities, QuickSight can transform the vast streams of time-stamped information from Timestream into insightful dashboards, graphs, and charts. These visual aids not only facilitate a better understanding of the current condition of transportation systems but also aid in predictive analytics, paving the way for proactive solutions and sustainable strategies.

In the subsequent sections of this chapter, we will delve into the intricacies of integrating IoT with AWS services like Amazon Timestream and visualization tools like Amazon QuickSight.

Simulating Real-Time Bus Operations to Generate Business Intelligence Insights

Let's examine the simulation architecture we will be constructing in this chapter (refer to Figure 9-1).

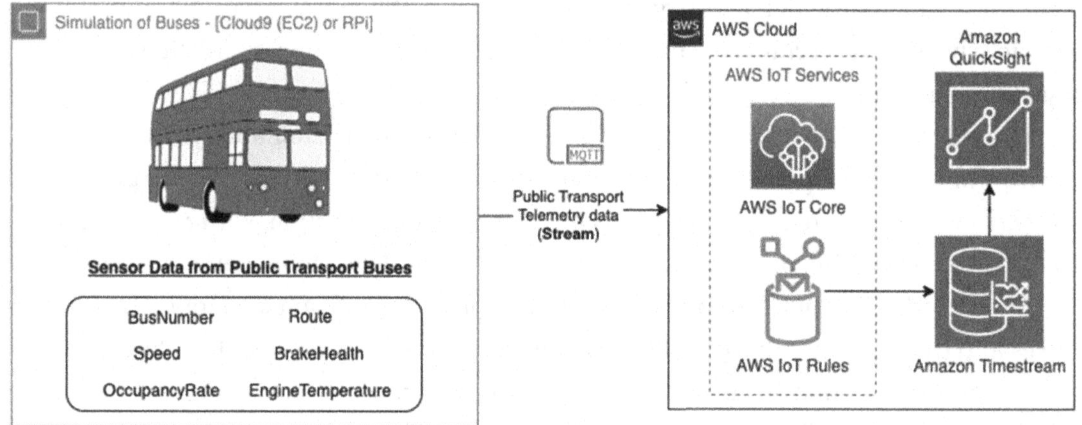

Figure 9-1. *Public transport buses simulation architecture*

Sensory data we will publish to AWS IoT Core from the buses:

1. **Bus Number**
    - **Benefit**: Allows for unique identification of each bus.
    - **Reason for Using**: Helps track individual buses, ensures data isn't mixed up, and analyzes patterns for sustainable operations.

2. **Route Taken**
    - **Benefit**: Provides insight into the bus's current and historical routes.
    - **Reason for Using**: Useful for route optimization, understanding traffic patterns, reducing fuel consumption, and promoting sustainable transit.
3. **Speed at the Time of Data Transmission**
    - **Benefit**: Monitors the speed of the bus in real time.
    - **Reason for Using**: Promotes fuel-efficient driving, reduces emissions, and ensures driver compliance with speed limits.
4. **Brake Health**
    - **Benefit**: Monitors the health of the brakes.
    - **Reason for Using**: Predictive maintenance based on brake conditions ensures timely replacements, reducing resource waste and ensuring safety.
5. **Occupancy Rate**
    - **Benefit**: Indicates how full the bus is.
    - **Reason for Using**: Assists in optimizing routes based on demand, reducing the need for empty or near-empty runs, thereby promoting sustainability.
6. **Engine Temperature**
    - **Benefit**: Monitors the health and efficiency of the bus's engine.
    - **Reason for Using**: By catching overheating early, we can ensure efficient fuel use and reduce emissions. Predictive maintenance based on engine temperature reduces downtimes.

Integrating sensory data points has the potential to revolutionize urban mobility. As environmental concerns become more pressing, it's crucial for our transit systems to evolve with intelligence and sustainability. The use of real-time data ensures passenger safety, reduces our environmental impact, and cuts operational costs. With the addition of predictive maintenance, we're ushering in a new era of efficient and eco-friendly public transport.

Real-Time Telemetry in AWS IoT Core

In order to set up our IoT device in AWS IoT Device Management, we are using a script to simulate the functioning of five public transport buses. Unlike the manual creation process we discussed in previous chapters, we have chosen to automate the process using a script. To obtain the script required for this task, you can refer to Chapter 9 of the book's GitHub repository (*script: createStreamingThing.sh*).

Place the code in your environment and execute the following commands:

```
chmod +x createStreamingThing.sh
./createStreamingThing.sh
```

What we are doing here is making the script executable and running it; when the script runs, it will do the following (see Figure 9-2):

- Create a folder in your home folder for "bus"
- Create an IoT thing
- Create an IoT thing certificate associated with our thing and activate the certificate
- An associate certificate with "*myFirstDemoNonProductionPolicy*", which we created in an earlier chapter (*policy not to be used in production, for learning purposes only*)

Upon success, you will see similar output.

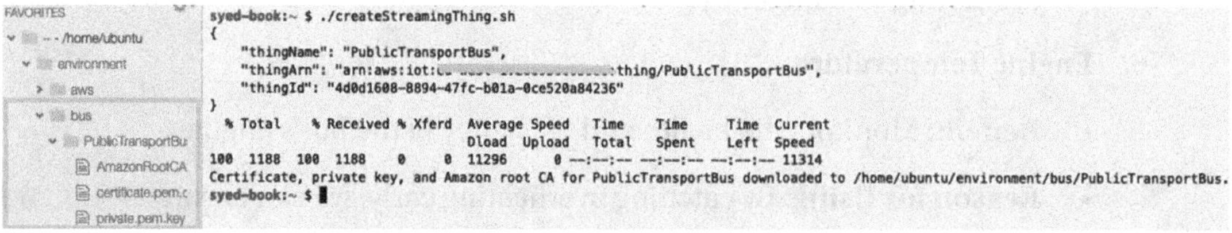

Figure 9-2. *Folder and IoT thing created*

Within the */home/ubuntu/environment/bus/**PublicTransportBus*** directory (created by the script), create a file named "*busSimulation.py*". If you're using a Raspberry Pi instead of Cloud9, ensure you place it inside the "*PublicTransportBus*" folder as your path may differ. Fill the file with the content provided here. As an alternative, download the file from the GitHub repository linked to Chapter 9 of the book. Don't forget to replace the placeholder "*REPLACE_HERE*" with your AWS IoT endpoint URL.

To obtain the endpoint address, use the following command:

```
aws iot describe-endpoint --endpoint-type iot:Data-ATS
```

Buses Simulation file (*busSimulation.py*) content:

```
import json
import random
import time

import boto3
from AWSIoTPythonSDK.MQTTLib import AWSIoTMQTTClient

# AWS IoT Core endpoint
iot_endpoint = "REPLACE_HERE"  # Replace with your AWS IoT Endpoint URL,
use command: aws iot describe-endpoint --endpoint-type iot:Data-ATS

# AWS IoT Thing Name
thing_name = "PublicTransportBus"

# Path to the certificates and private key in the same folder as the script
cert_path = "./certificate.pem.crt"
key_path = "./private.pem.key"
root_ca_path = "./AmazonRootCA1.pem"

# Initialize AWS IoT MQTT Client
mqtt_client = AWSIoTMQTTClient(thing_name)
mqtt_client.configureEndpoint(iot_endpoint, 8883)
mqtt_client.configureCredentials(root_ca_path, key_path, cert_path)

# Connect to AWS IoT
mqtt_client.connect()

# List of buses
buses = [
    {"busNumber": "Bus101", "route": "Route A"},
    {"busNumber": "Bus102", "route": "Route B"},
    {"busNumber": "Bus103", "route": "Route C"},
```

```
    {"busNumber": "Bus104", "route": "Route D"},
    {"busNumber": "Bus105", "route": "Route E"},
]

def generate_bus_data(bus):
    return {
        "busNumber": bus["busNumber"],
        "route": bus["route"],
        "speed": random.randint(0, 60),
        "occupancyRate": random.uniform(0, 1),
        "engineTemperature": random.randint(50, 150),
        "brakeHealth": random.choice(["Good", "Moderate", "Poor"]),
    }

# Infinite loop to publish random bus data
while True:
    for bus in buses:
        bus_data = generate_bus_data(bus)
        mqtt_client.publish(
            "/awsiotbook/publicTransport/busData", json.dumps(bus_data), 1
        )
        print(f"Published: {json.dumps(bus_data)}")
        time.sleep(
            10
        ) # Wait for 10 seconds before publishing the next data for
          another bus
```

Once we have placed the content or file from Chapter 9 of the book's GitHub repository, run the following command in the terminal to start sending streaming data (*make sure you have replaced the AWS IoT endpoint URL with the "**REPLACE_HERE**" placeholder*):

```
cd /home/ubuntu/environment/bus/PublicTransportBus
python3 busSimulation.py
```

Using the AWS IoT MQTT test client, subscribe to the topic: */awsiotbook/publicTransport/busData*.

Telemetry data will be transmitted to this topic every ten seconds (see Figure 9-3).

▾ /awsiotbook/publicTransport/busData


```
{
  "busNumber": "Bus101",
  "route": "Route A",
  "speed": 55,
  "occupancyRate": 0.4917903821548434,
  "engineTemperature": 143,
  "brakeHealth": "Moderate"
}
```


***Figure 9-3.** MQTT telemetry data for buses simulation*

With the streaming data now established, our next steps involve setting up the Amazon Timestream database. Following that, we'll create the AWS IoT Rule. Lastly, we'll integrate the Timestream data with Amazon QuickSight BI in the subsequent sections.

Real-Time IoT Telemetry with Amazon Timestream

Search and navigate to Amazon Timestream service (see Figure 9-4).

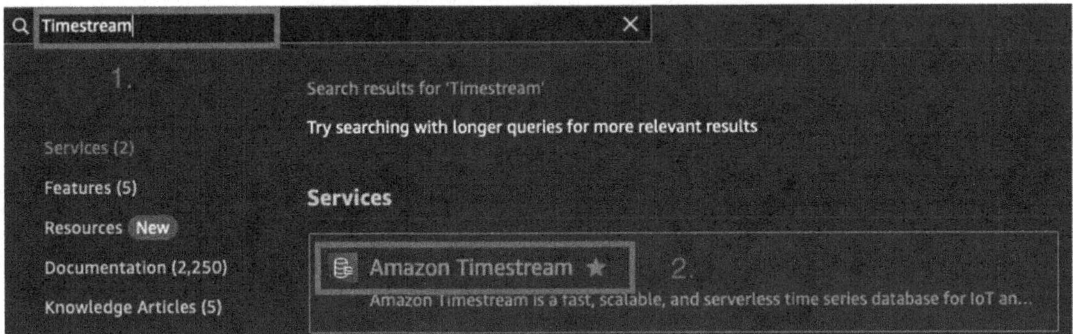

***Figure 9-4.** Searching for Amazon Timestream*

Select and *create a database* (see Figure 9-5).

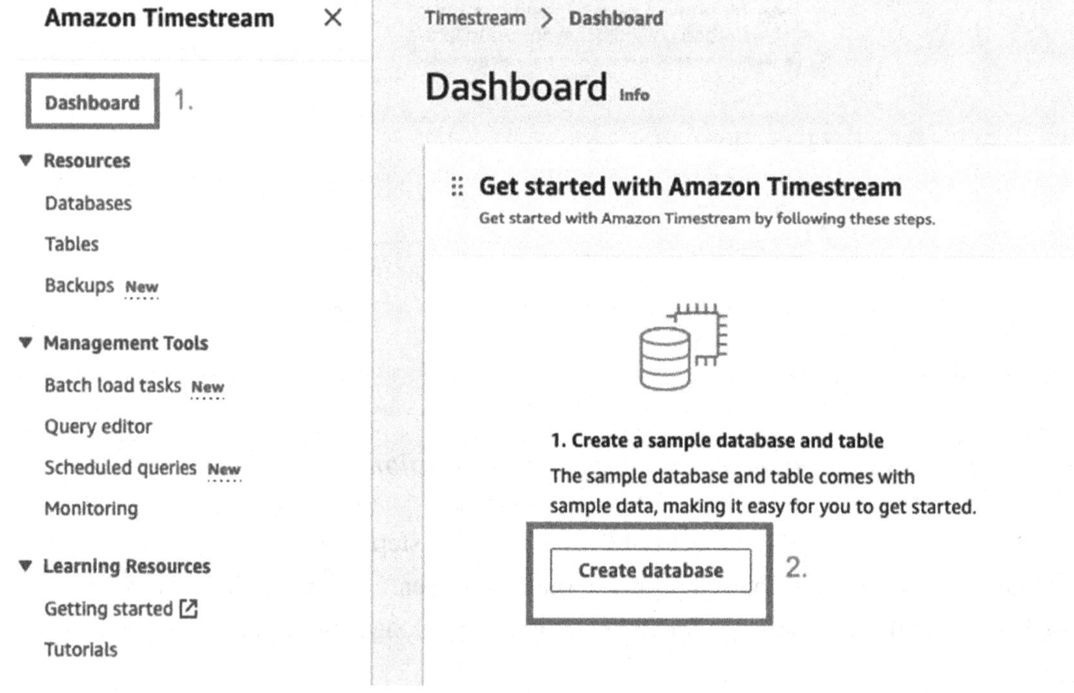

Figure 9-5. *Creating a database in Amazon Timestream*

Select "*Standard database*" and name it "*PublicTransportTelemetry*". Leave the rest of the details as default and select "*Create database*" (see Figure 9-6).

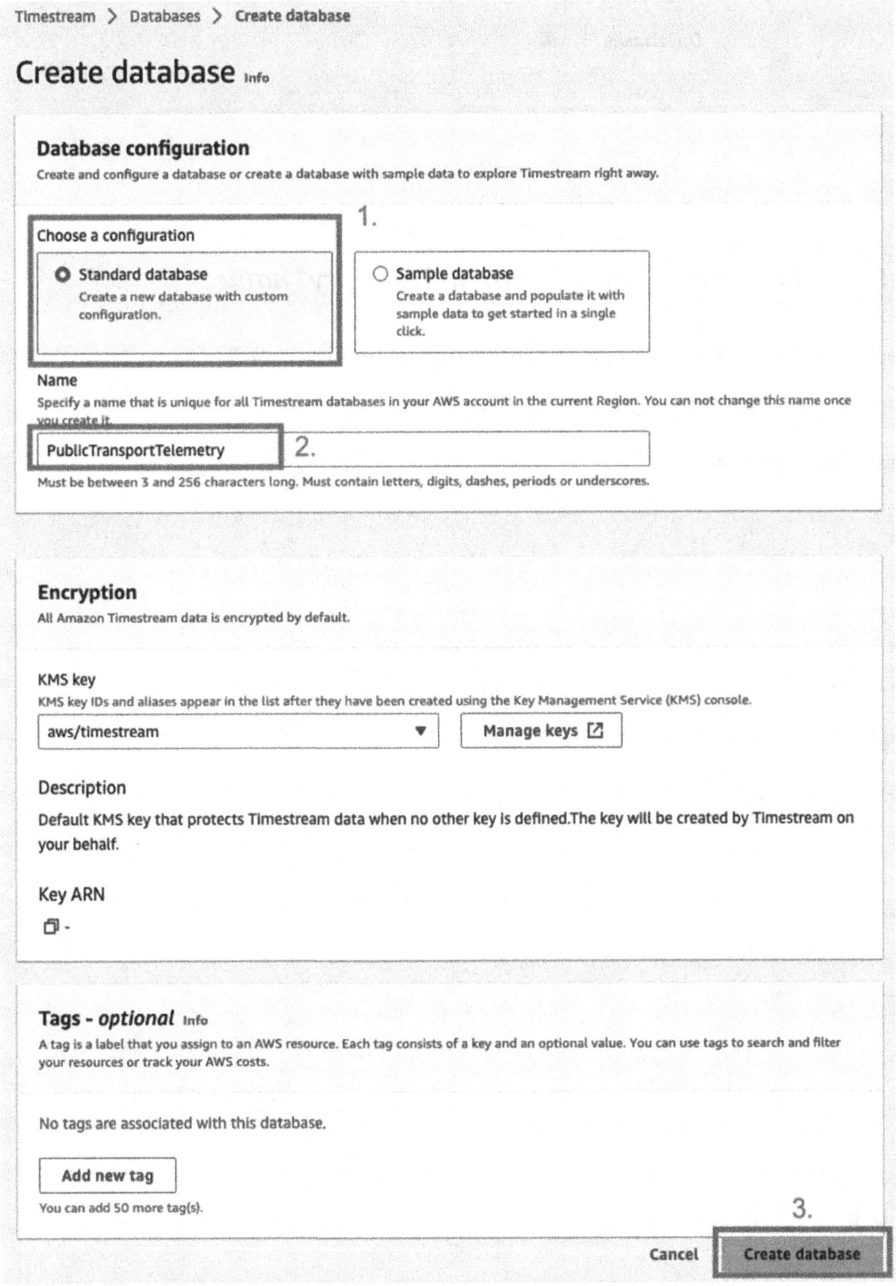

***Figure 9-6.** Creating "PublicTransportTelemetry" database*

Once created, click on the newly created database name (see Figure 9-7).

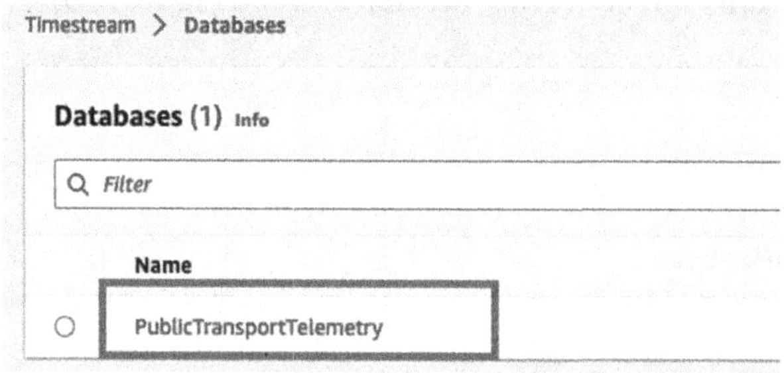

Figure 9-7. Click on the "PublicTransportTelemetry" name.

Select "*Tables*" and then click "*Create table*" (see Figure 9-8).

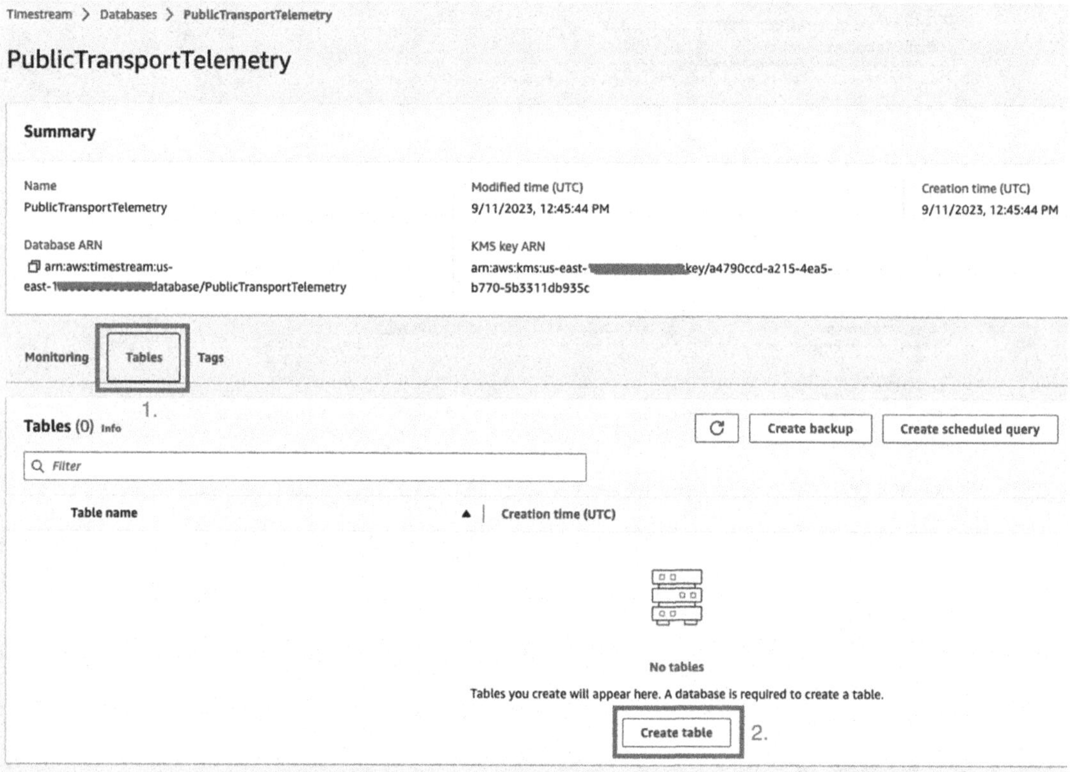

Figure 9-8. Creating the table

Set up the table by using the following details:

- For Table name: *busDataTbl*
- For Partition key configuration, select *Default partitioning*

Leave the rest of the settings as default and select "*Create table*" (see Figure 9-9); once the table is created, you should get a notification of the successful creation of the "*busDataTbl*" table (see Figure 9-10).

Database name
Choose the database where this table will be created.
PublicTransportTelemetry
Table name
Specify a table name that is unique within this database. You can not change this name once you create it.
busDataTbl
Must be between 3 and 256 characters long. Must contain letters, digits, dashes, periods or underscores.
1.
Schema settings - *new* Info
A Schema specifies the expected data model of the table. Specify how your data will be stored and distributed using partition keys. With custom partition keys, you can run queries that are faster and more efficient.
Partition key configuration
Choose to create a custom partition key or use Timestream's default partition key.
2.
Custom partitioning
This is useful when the primary access pattern of the queries is filtering over a high cardinality dimension or measure.
Default partitioning
This is useful when the primary access pattern of queries is measure based filtering. The values of 'measure_name' attribute is used as the partition key to partition the data.
You can't add or remove a partition key after the table has been created. You can find the key on the table's details page after the table has been created.

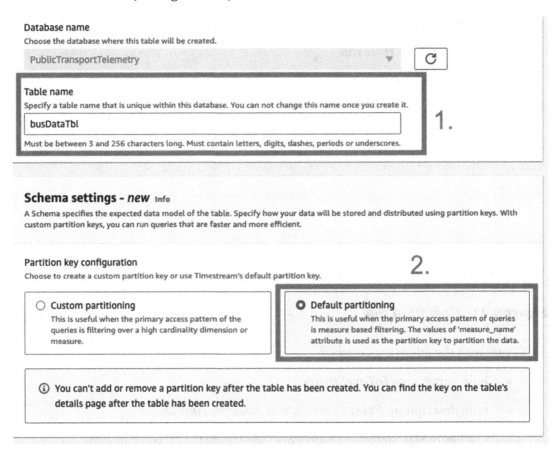

Figure 9-9. *Only select these two and leave the rest of the settings as default.*

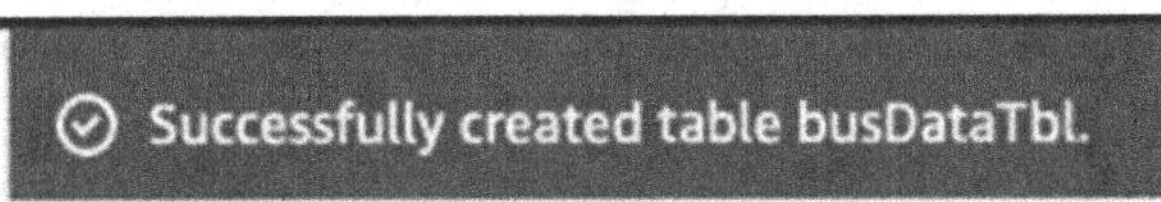

Figure 9-10. *Upon successful creation of the table*

Create AWS IoT Rule for Data Routing

As we have the Timestream database and table in place, let's set up the routing by sending data from IoT Core to Amazon Timestream; first, create AWS IoT Rule by navigating to the following.

From the AWS IoT Core console (see Figure 9-11):

- Select *Message routing*
    - Select *Rules*
        - Select *Create rule*

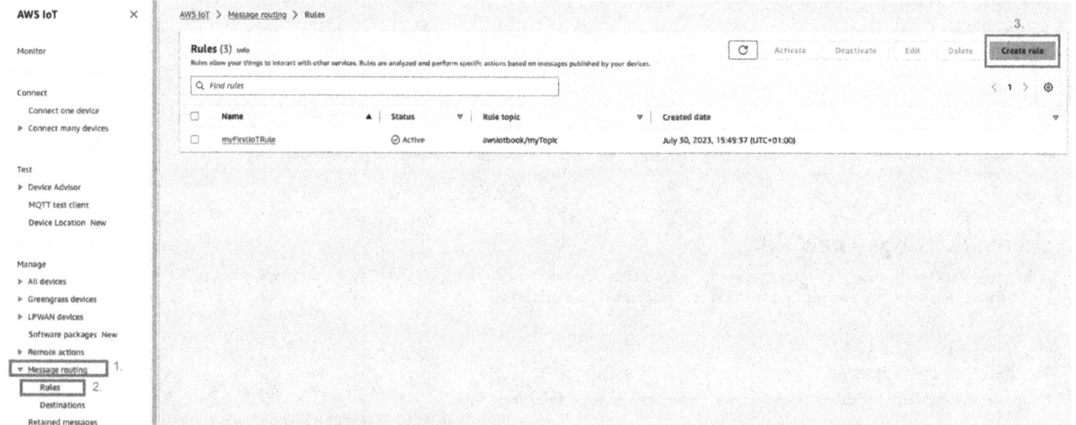

Figure 9-11. *Creating a rule*

Create with the following details:

- Rule name: *sendToTimeStream*
- Rule description: *Rule to send data to Amazon Timestream*
- Configure SQL statement as follows (see Figure 9-12) (you can also obtain this SQL statement from Chapter 9 of the book's GitHub repository):

```
SELECT busNumber, route, speed, occupancyRate, engineTemperature,
brakeHealth FROM '/awsiotbook/publicTransport/busData'
```

In Attach rule actions for Action 1, follow these:

- Select "*Timestream table*" for action
- For the database name, select "*PublicTransportTelemetry*"
- For the table name, select "*busDataTbl*"
- For dimensions, add *six new dimensions* with their corresponding *values*:

Dimension Name	**Values**
busNumber	*${busNumber}*
route	*${route}*
speed	*${speed}*
occupancyRate	*${occupancyRate}*
engineTemperature	*${engineTemperature}*
brakeHealth	*${brakeHealth}*

- For IAM role, select "*Create new role*" and give the role name: "*timestreamrole*"
- Add Error action; select "*Republish to AWS IoT topic*" and give the topic "*/awsiotbook/timestream/error*" leaving the rest of the settings as default, but for IAM role, select the following role: "*timestreamrole*" (see Figure 9-12)

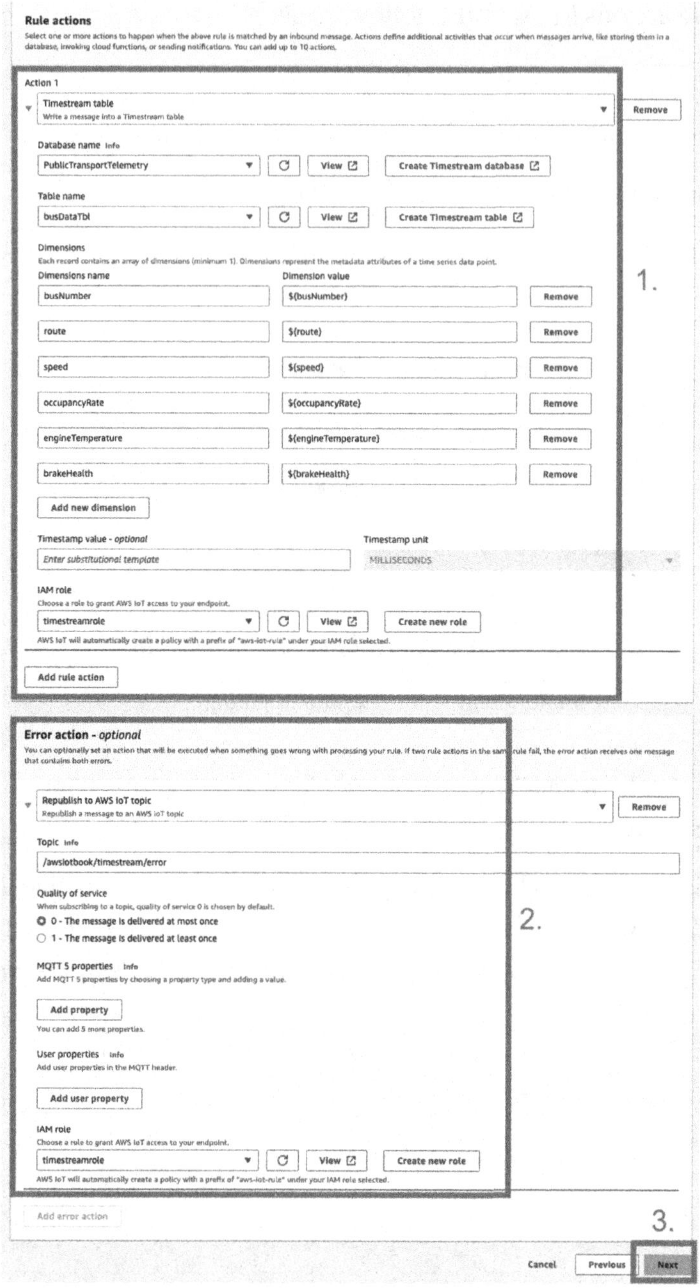

***Figure 9-12.** Creating a rule for Timestream data*

In the Review and Create screen, check that everything is as expected and select "*Create*".

Query Amazon Timestream for Live Data

Let's execute a query on our *"busDataTbl"* table to confirm the successful receipt of the data stream and validate the arriving data.

From the Amazon Timestream console, click *Tables* (under *Resources*) and select our table "*busDataTbl*"; click "*Actions*" and select "*Query table*" from the drop-down (see Figure 9-13).

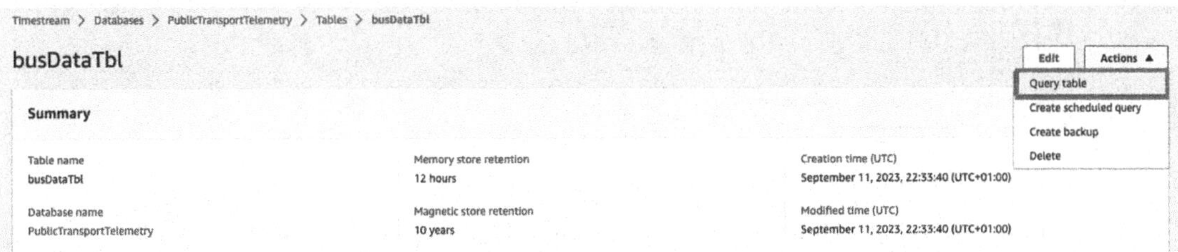

Figure 9-13. *Selecting Query table*

Use the default populated query and click "*Run*" (see Figure 9-14); we will see our data arriving and being saved in the Timestream database table with a timestamp (if the query is not populated, click on the database located in the left navigation pane and then select "*Preview Data*").

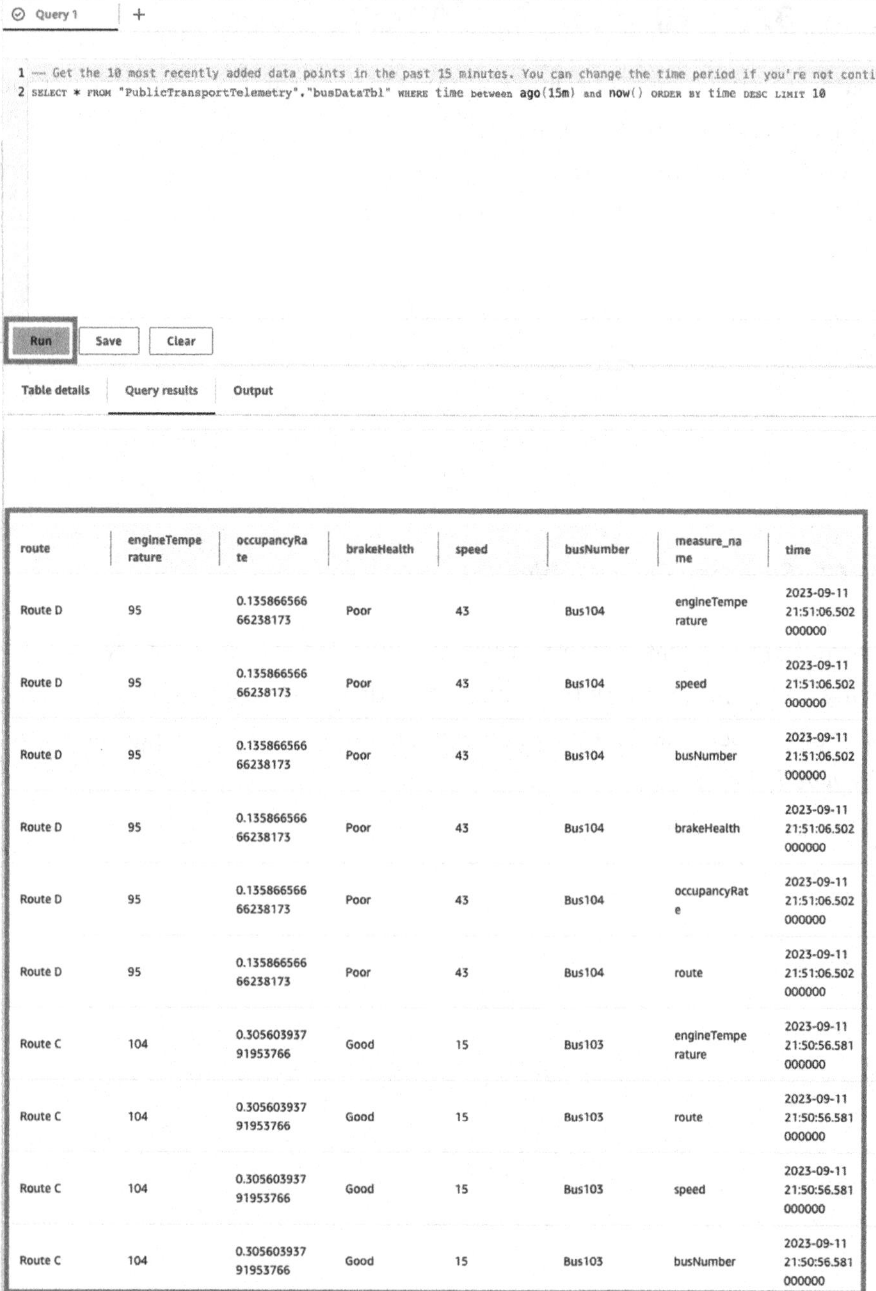

route	engineTemperature	occupancyRate	brakeHealth	speed	busNumber	measure_name	time
Route D	95	0.13586656666238173	Poor	43	Bus104	engineTemperature	2023-09-11 21:51:06.502000000
Route D	95	0.13586656666238173	Poor	43	Bus104	speed	2023-09-11 21:51:06.502000000
Route D	95	0.13586656666238173	Poor	43	Bus104	busNumber	2023-09-11 21:51:06.502000000
Route D	95	0.13586656666238173	Poor	43	Bus104	brakeHealth	2023-09-11 21:51:06.502000000
Route D	95	0.13586656666238173	Poor	43	Bus104	occupancyRate	2023-09-11 21:51:06.502000000
Route D	95	0.13586656666238173	Poor	43	Bus104	route	2023-09-11 21:51:06.502000000
Route C	104	0.30560393791953766	Good	15	Bus103	engineTemperature	2023-09-11 21:50:56.581000000
Route C	104	0.30560393791953766	Good	15	Bus103	route	2023-09-11 21:50:56.581000000
Route C	104	0.30560393791953766	Good	15	Bus103	speed	2023-09-11 21:50:56.581000000
Route C	104	0.30560393791953766	Good	15	Bus103	busNumber	2023-09-11 21:50:56.581000000

Figure 9-14. *Data being saved in our Timestream table*

Let's proceed ahead and set up our Amazon QuickSight dashboard.

Amazon QuickSight

You might need to "sign up for QuickSight" due to its role as a BI tool. With many companies delegating their "analytics and analysis" to specialized entities, a variety of options are available. Opt for the one that aligns with your needs. For the majority, the "default" settings will be appropriate. Ensure your selected *region matches* what you've been using throughout this book. Provide your QuickSight account name and email. Don't forget to choose "*Amazon Timestream*" to grant access and enable auto-discovery for these resources, as seen in Figures 9-15a and 9-15b.

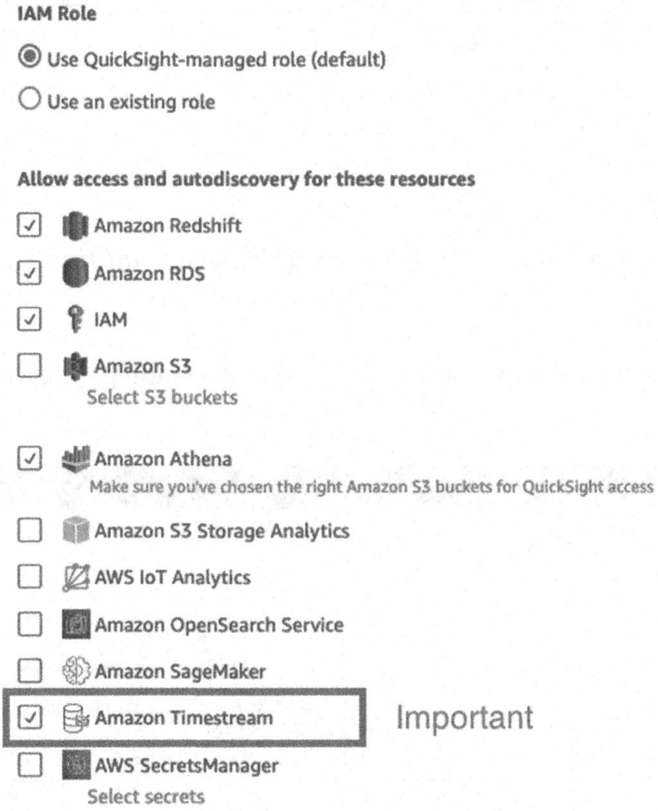

Figure 9-15a. *Selecting Amazon Timestream (first-time setup screen)*

Returning Amazon QuickSight Users (Not for First-Time Users) *(Adding Permissions)*

If you have used *Amazon QuickSight* previously, then you will need to select your profile from the top right; click "*Manage QuickSight*", select "*Security & permissions*" and then click "*Manage*" (see Figure 9-15b), and add "*Amazon Timestream*" as seen in Figure 9-15a. For returning users, once permission is done, click the "QuickSight" logo on the top left to return to "dashboard".

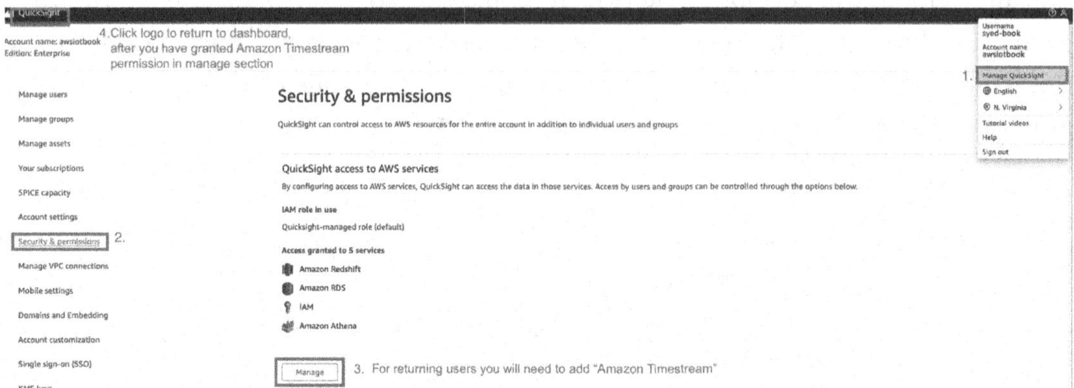

Figure 9-15b. *Returning users to Amazon QuickSight – adding Amazon Timestream*

After completing the setup, you'll be directed to the landing page; select "*Datasets*" (see Figure 9-16).

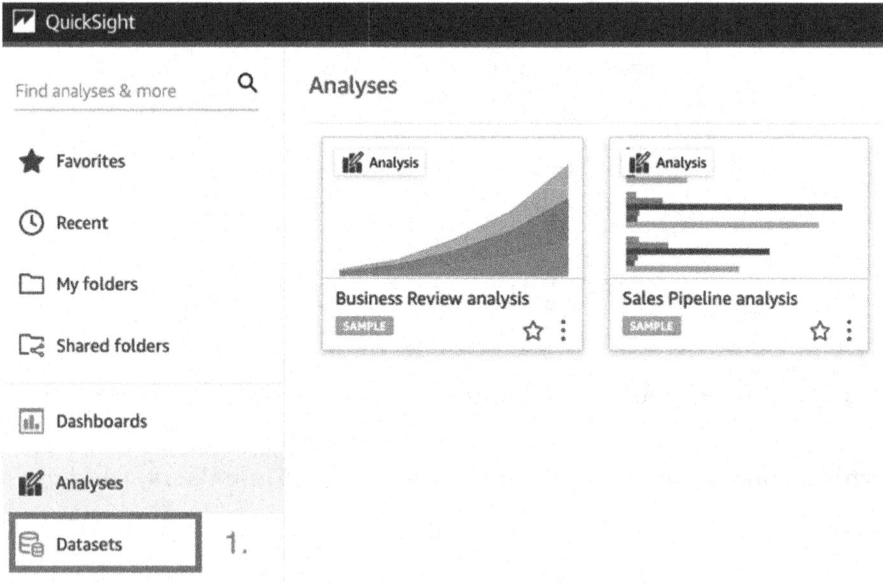

Figure 9-16. *Selecting Datasets*

In the Datasets screen, select "*New dataset*" and then click "*Timestream*" (see Figure 9-17).

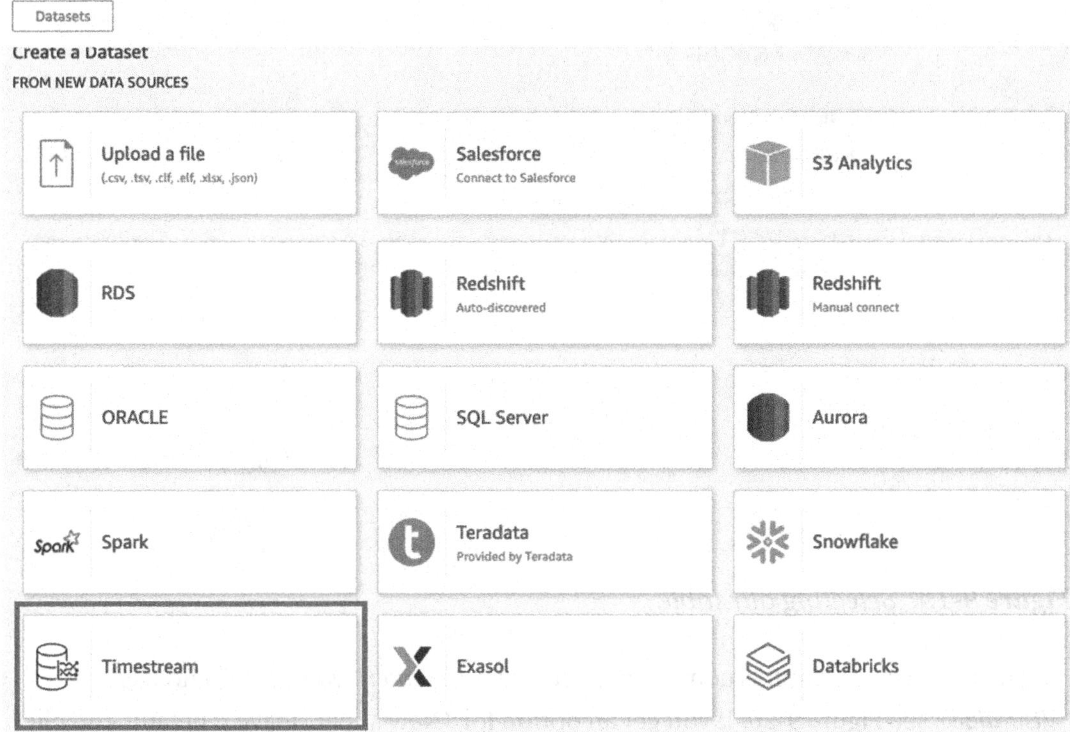

Figure 9-17. *Creating Timestream dataset*

In the "*New Timestream data source*" for the data source name, enter our database name "*PublicTransportTelemetry*" and select Validate connection; upon successful validation, you will get a green tick to confirm success; finally, click "*Create data source*" (see Figure 9-18).

New Timestream data source

Data source name 1.

PublicTransportTelemetry

✓ Validated 2.

3. Create data source

Figure 9-18. *Validating and creating data source for our Timestream DB*

QuickSight will access our Timestream database and display the "busDataTbl" table. Simply select it and then click "Select", as shown in Figure 9-19.

Figure 9-19. *Selecting our table*

Once dataset creation is complete, select "*Directly query your data*" and click "*Visualize*"; see Figure 9-20. If you get an option for "New sheet", leave it default and click "Create".

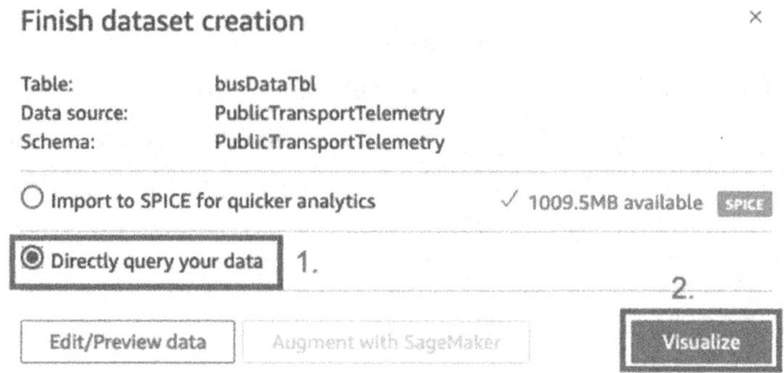

Figure 9-20. *Creating a visualization*

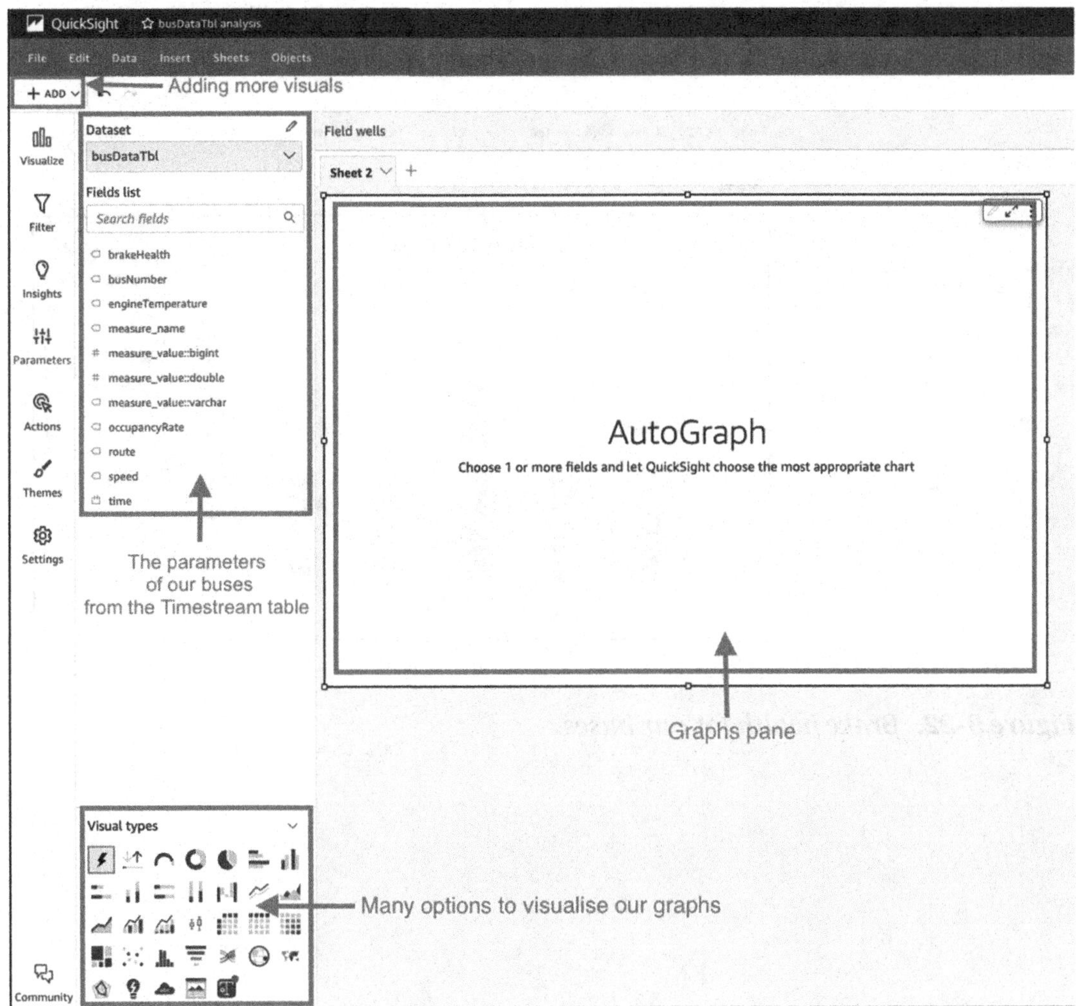

Figure 9-21. *QuickSight visual setup screen*

Let's create some graphs to delve deeper into our data. First, we'll examine the "*brakeHealth*" parameter for our "*busNumber*", as shown in Figure 9-22.

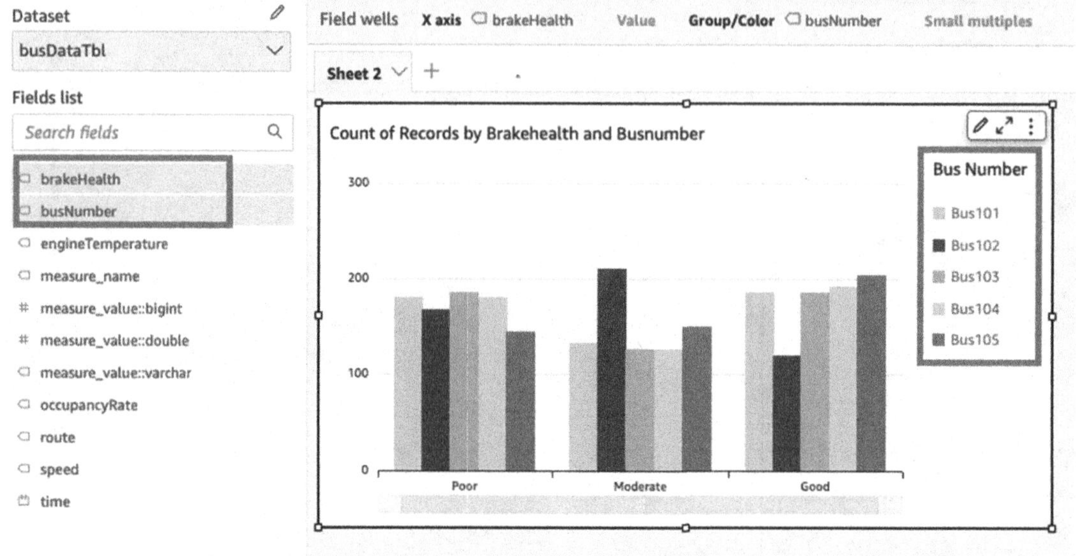

Figure 9-22. *Brake health for our buses*

Add more visuals by selecting "*+ADD*" and adding visuals; we can select "*speed*" and "*busNumber*" parameters and visualize them (see Figure 9-23).

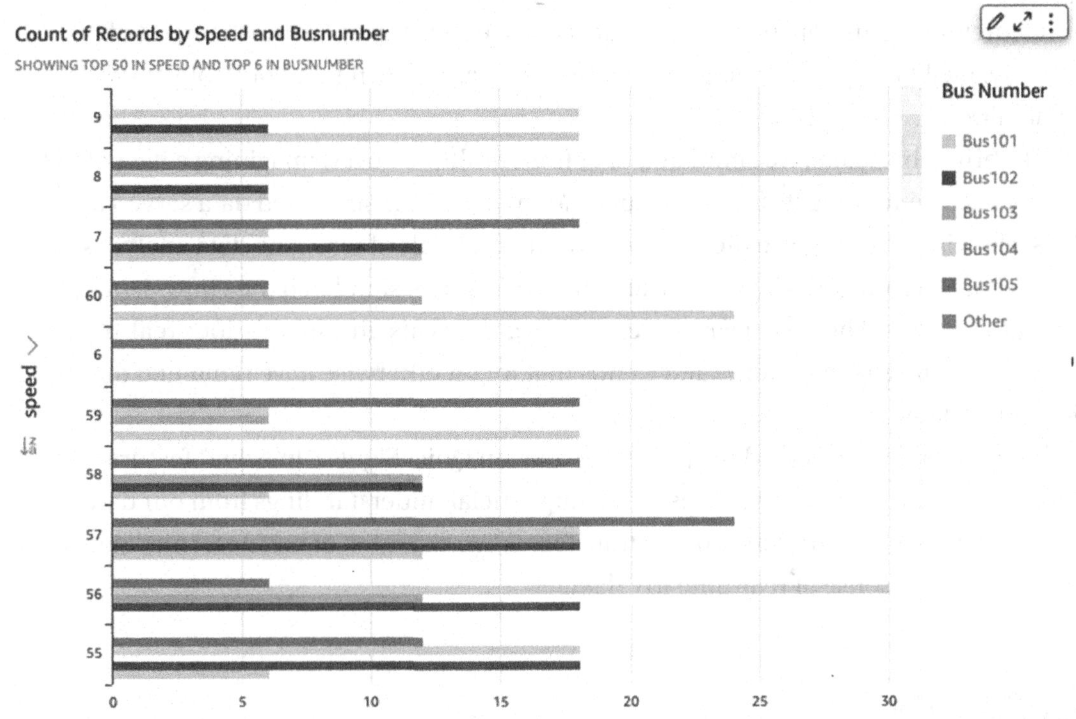

Figure 9-23. *Bus speed during their route with bus numbers*

Similarly, Amazon QuickSight offers features like "Insights." By selecting this and choosing our table parameters, QuickSight will automatically generate insights. This can help identify buses generating an excessive amount of data, which might indicate sensor faults, as depicted in Figure 9-24.

TOP 3 BUSNUMBERS

Top 3 busNumbers for total count of records are:
Bus101 with 660
Bus103 with 654
Bus102 with 654

Figure 9-24. *QuickSight generated insights*

What You Have Learned

In this chapter, we delved into a real-world scenario by simulating data from a fundamental urban transportation mode: buses. Public buses are the lifeblood of any city, facilitating the movement of its residents and playing a pivotal role in urban dynamics.

To bring this to life, we simulated data from multiple buses, imagining a fleet of five buses, each generating its unique set of random data. This simulated data served as a lens, allowing us to explore the intricacies and potentials of real-time data analytics.

Using Amazon QuickSight, we transformed this raw, simulated data into visually engaging graphs. These visual representations gave us insights into various real-time parameters, revealing patterns and trends that might otherwise have remained obscured in tabular data.

Moreover, we harnessed the power of Amazon QuickSight's "Insights" feature. This tool automates the analysis process, gleaning crucial understandings from our data.

Such capabilities underscore the transformative potential of business intelligence tools in making sense of real-time IoT data.

Summary

In this enlightening BI chapter, we navigated through a simulated real-world scenario focusing on a fundamental aspect of urban life: "*bus transportation.*" Recognizing the crucial role of buses in urban mobility, we simulated data from a hypothetical fleet of five buses, each generating unique random data. This simulation allowed us to delve deep into the world of real-time data analytics, illuminating its complexity and potential.

We utilized Amazon QuickSight to translate this simulated data into intuitive and visually compelling graphs, aiding in the unearthing of significant patterns and trends hidden within the raw data. The insightful "Insights" feature of Amazon QuickSight further automated our analysis, offering crucial and in-depth understandings of our data.

As we wrap up this chapter, the seamless integration of Timestream data with Amazon QuickSight stands out as a beacon of insight, transforming raw data into valuable, actionable knowledge for businesses and highlighting the immense potential for further exploration and understanding in this domain.

CHAPTER 10

Cybersecurity with AWS IoT

As we embark on the final chapter of this book, we venture deeper into an essential facet of IoT and connected devices. The threat is ever-present in a digital landscape teeming with potential threats, ranging from automated systems to individuals harboring malicious intentions. These adversaries might seek to exploit computing power, hijack IoT devices, or even compromise common Internet-connected devices such as laptops or Wi-Fi routers. In light of these potential threats, the importance of robust security cannot be overstated.

In AWS, there's a popular saying: "*Dance like no one is watching, and secure like everyone is.*" It encapsulates the inherent vulnerabilities of daily-use devices and the associated risks when connected to the Internet or local networks. The data churned out by our IoT devices, be they Industrial IoT (IIoT) setups, smart home appliances, or others, is of substantial value. Therefore, shielding these devices with the utmost security standards is vital. Leveraging the capabilities of the AWS cloud emerges as a prudent step in this direction.

This chapter will delve into the fundamentals of the Zero Trust principles, illustrating how to integrate them using AWS IoT services. We will spotlight features such as the AWS IoT Device Defender, highlighting the machine learning detection capabilities it brings to the table. We'll also discuss the AWS IoT Device Defender's capability to conduct audits on your fleet using AWS-recommended best practices. Moreover, we will explore AWS Security Hub, a remarkable service that offers a panoramic view of all your IT and IoT assets through a unified dashboard. In conclusion, we will outline effective strategies for managing compromised IoT devices, providing insights on averting a cascading impact on the broader device fleet without igniting a domino effect

S. Rehan, *AWS IoT With Edge ML and Cybersecurity*, https://doi.org/10.1007/979-8-8688-0011-5_10

Zero Trust and AWS IoT

With the digital transformation era in full swing, the expansion of interconnected devices, notably IoT (Internet of Things) and IIoT (Industrial Internet of Things), underscores a pressing need for robust cybersecurity models. Traditional perimeter-based defense, which predominantly trusts entities within corporate boundaries, is ill-equipped for today's challenges. This inadequacy stems from the reality that threats can emerge both externally and internally, particularly in IoT-rich environments.

What Is Zero Trust

Zero Trust is more than a technological solution; it's a foundational shift in our approach to cybersecurity, as delineated in the NIST (National Institute of Standards and Technology) of the United States' Special Publication 800-207 on Zero Trust Architecture (ZTA). Central to this philosophy is the premise: "Never trust, always verify." Every entity – whether a user, device, or application – undergoes rigorous validation, regardless of its origination point.

In the intricate fabric of IoT, where devices pervade various aspects of daily life, and IIoT, where connected machinery and sensors drive industrial operations, the principles of Zero Trust become paramount. Given the incessant communication among these devices, the window for potential security breaches widens, thereby accentuating the need for the Zero Trust model.

NIST 800-207 Guideline on Zero Trust Architecture (ZTA)

The National Institute of Standards and Technology (NIST) crystallizes the Zero Trust approach through its 800-207 documentation, outlining the Zero Trust Architecture (ZTA). This framework, especially pertinent in IoT and IIoT contexts, is rooted in seven foundational tenets:

1. **Unique Resources Classification:** Every data source, IoT device, or IIoT machinery is deemed a unique resource.

2. **Secure Communication:** Safeguard all communication channels, irrespective of network topology, especially crucial in IoT and IIoT landscapes with vast data transfers.

3. **Session-Based Access:** Implement access restrictions based on distinct sessions. Before any interaction – be it with an IoT thermostat or an IIoT-driven conveyor belt – trust must be authenticated, using the least privilege principle.

4. **Dynamic Policy Access:** Leverage adaptive policies that encapsulate a myriad of factors, from user identity to IIoT equipment demands, and the broader contextual backdrop.

5. **Continuous Monitoring and Updates:** Every asset, from the simplest IoT device to complex IIoT systems, is under scrutiny. Mechanisms, akin to Continuous Diagnostics and Mitigation (CDM), provide real-time oversight and timely redressal of threats by applying updates.

6. **Dynamic Authorization:** Foster iterative authentication and authorization processes, a cycle of access, threat assessment, policy evolution, and ceaseless trust re-evaluation.

7. **Data-Informed Decisions:** Use the voluminous data generated, especially in data-rich environments like IoT and IIoT, to perpetually fine-tune and enhance security postures.

Principles from AWS for implementing Zero Trust security

1. Combining identity and network capabilities when feasible

2. Beginning with specific use cases

3. Implementing Zero Trust based on the importance of systems and data

Transitioning to Zero Trust involves evaluating your workload to identify where this security model would be most advantageous. This means reconsidering identity, authentication, and factors like device condition to improve security. AWS provides essential Zero Trust features through its IoT, identity, and networking services. AWS IoT offers services for a reliable foundation that includes strong identity, restricted privileges, conditional access based on device health, continual updates, secure remote access, device management, and security monitoring to facilitate Zero Trust implementation.

AWS IoT and Aligning to NIST 800-207 Principles

- **Unique Resources Classification, Secure Communication, Session-Based Access, Dynamic Authorization**

  Per NIST 800-207's Zero Trust philosophy, it's essential to uphold a device's unique identity. Reflecting this, AWS IoT requires every IoT and IIoT device to have a distinct identity, adhering to strict security standards. With AWS IoT, all communications are inherently secure; every interaction by default, whether between devices or between devices and cloud services, is authenticated and authorized over a secure TLS communication path.

  When a device connects, it authenticates its distinct identity using mechanisms like X.509 certificates, security tokens, or other credentials. The AWS IoT security framework supports this through unique certificate-based device authentication, complemented by authorization using IoT policies and encryption via TLS 1.2 and 1.3.

  Furthermore, within the AWS IoT context and the broader Zero Trust model, the "*least privilege*" access principle is paramount. This principle specifies what operations a device is permitted to perform after connecting to AWS IoT Core, mitigating potential risks from breached authenticated identities. Such rigorous security measures are made possible by implementing AWS IoT policies.

- **Continuous Monitoring and Updates, Data-Informed Decisions, Dynamic Policy Access**

  Based on the NIST 800-207 guidelines, it's essential to comprehensively gather data on devices, network infrastructure, and communications to fortify security measures. AWS IoT Device Defender enables users to harness this IoT device data for continuous security enhancement.

AWS IoT Device Defender assists in identifying issues by offering detailed and historical data about devices, covering aspects like cloud-side metrics (e.g., chatty device behavior) and device-side metrics (e.g., open ports), as well as tracking past or current device violations (alarms). Moreover, its integrated mitigation tools provide capabilities to address audits and detect alarms. This includes actions such as quarantining devices, performing security best practices audits, rectifying failed guidelines, modifying default policy versions, and updating device certificates. Enhancing this further, AWS IoT Device Management's feature – AWS IoT Jobs, as discussed in a previous chapter – can be utilized to apply updates on a violating and noncompliant device, bringing it back to its original state.

Cybersecurity with AWS IoT Device Defender

AWS IoT Device Defender is a crucial part of the AWS cybersecurity suite, specifically designed for the Internet of Things (IoT) ecosystem. This service is fully managed and works to secure IoT configurations by continuously monitoring device behaviors and ensuring they comply with strict security best practices. By utilizing advanced machine learning models, it can also quickly identify and respond to suspicious activities or deviations from the norm. Along with its comprehensive alerting and mitigation capabilities, AWS IoT Device Defender is an indispensable tool for organizations seeking to enhance their IoT/IIoT security posture.

AWS IoT Device Defender Overview

AWS IoT Device Defender is a comprehensive IoT security service that continually ensures the safety of your IoT configurations. This fully managed service provides tools to

- Identify and address security concerns
- Audit device fleets against security best practices
- Continuously monitor devices for abnormal behavior
- Alert and respond to security threats

- Create security profiles using your custom predefined rules to create threshold measure
- Create a machine learning (ML)-based security profile where thresholds are learned based on device patterns and you can just define data points to alert and data points to clear device violation

Key Features of AWS IoT Device Defender

1. **Audit**
    - Inspects device-related resources (e.g., X.509 device certificates, IoT policies, Client IDs) to ensure compliance with AWS IoT security guidelines
    - Identifies noncompliant configurations, like multiple devices sharing an identity or overly permissive policies
2. **Rules Detect**
    - Continuously monitors devices for suspicious activities using vital security metrics from the device and AWS IoT Core.
    - Allows users to define normal behaviors for a group of devices. If a device acts outside of these defined behaviors and breaches the threshold, an alert is generated.
3. **ML Detect**
    - Utilizes machine learning to determine device behaviors, drawing from both cloud-side, device-side metrics and even custom metrics (number type at the time of writing).
    - Refreshes device behavior models every day, based on the most recent 14-day data, ensuring current and accurate monitoring.
    - Automatically identifies operational and security anomalies without user-defined thresholds by learning using historic data and applying ML patterns.
    - Dynamically adjusts to new device data, minimizing false positives.

- **ML Model**: An ML model in this context refers to a machine learning construct designed to monitor specific behaviors set by the user. This model learns from the metric data patterns of selected device groups and subsequently establishes three anomaly confidence levels: high, medium, and low. It then identifies anomalies by evaluating the metric data input for individual devices. Within ML Detect, each ML model is tailored to assess a singular metric-based behavior.

4. **Confidence Level**

   - ML Detect categorizes anomalies into three confidence levels: *high*, *medium*, and *low*.
     - **High Confidence Level:** Indicates lower sensitivity, typically resulting in fewer alarms
     - **Low Confidence Level:** Suggests high sensitivity, often leading to more frequent alarms
     - **Medium Confidence Level:** Strikes a balance between the two

5. **Mitigation**

   - Supplies relevant data about a device to assist in investigations, including metadata, statistics, and historical alerts
   - Offers built-in mitigation actions to address issues identified during audits or detected anomalies by security profiles

6. **Dimension**

   Dimensions allow you to fine-tune the scope of a behavior. For instance, you can set a topic filter dimension to apply behaviors to matching MQTT topics.

7. **Alarm**

   If a device anomaly arises, an alarm is sent through CloudWatch or SNS. This, and its specifics, appears in the AWS IoT console, which logs device alarm histories. Alarms also sound when devices either halt unusual behaviors or pause reporting for extended periods.

Alarm Verification States

Once an alarm is generated, it can be verified as

- **True Positive**
- **Benign Positive**
- **False Positive**
- **Unknown**

Each state can have an accompanying description. These states enable easy organization and filtering of AWS IoT Device Defender alarms. By leveraging these states and descriptions, teams can efficiently decide on follow-up actions: act on True Positives, ignore Benign Positives, or probe deeper into Unknowns. Initially, every alarm is set to the Unknown state.

- **Alarm Suppression:** You can manage Detect alarm notifications by toggling behavior notifications. While suppressing alarms doesn't halt Detect's evaluations (it still marks anomalous behaviors), these suppressed alarms aren't sent as SNS notifications. Instead, they're only available via the AWS IoT console or API.

8. **Alerting**
   - Sends notifications of alarms through various AWS services such as AWS IoT console, Amazon CloudWatch, and Amazon SNS

9. **Metrics**
   - AWS IoT Device Defender Detect utilizes metrics to pinpoint unusual device behaviors by contrasting the reported metric values with your predefined expectations (thresholds).
   - **Cloud-Side Metrics:** The system detects irregularities within the AWS IoT network using cloud-side metrics. Examples include the count of authorization failures or the volume and size of messages a device communicates via AWS IoT.

- **Device-Side Metrics:** AWS IoT Device Defender Detect gathers, consolidates, and oversees metrics produced by AWS IoT devices. These metrics can encompass aspects like the active ports on a device, data bytes or packets transmitted, and the device's TCP connections.
- **Custom Metrics:** As of the current update, AWS IoT Device Defender Detect supports custom metrics of the "Number" type.

Cybersecurity in Real-World Applications

Six common scenarios often discussed by customers:

1. Impersonation attack
2. Exploitation of cloud infrastructure
3. Denial-of-service attack
4. Crypto-jacking through IoT devices
5. Ransomware attacks on IoT devices
6. Protecting intellectual property

Let's explore each scenario, referencing real-world examples for clarity. We'll examine how the AWS IoT Device Defender can assist in these contexts, emphasizing the distinct metrics (be they cloud, device, or custom) suitable for its *security profile,* be it the *Rules Profile* or *ML Detect.*

1. Impersonation Attack

Impersonation attacks occur when attackers masquerade as trusted entities to gain access to AWS IoT cloud services, applications, and data, or to take control of IoT devices. When attackers impersonate trusted entities using pilfered credentials, connectivity metrics tend to surge. This is often because the stolen credentials are either invalid or concurrently in use by a legitimate device. Unusual patterns in authorization failures, connection attempts, or disconnections can be indicative of potential impersonation activities.

Real-World Use Case

In a smart city infrastructure, a traffic light controller system starts sending irregular signals, causing traffic anomalies at an intersection. Upon investigation, it was discovered that an attacker had impersonated a maintenance device's identity, gaining unauthorized access to the controller. The attacker used stolen credentials from a previous data breach. This caused the genuine maintenance device to experience connection issues, as the duplicated credentials led to frequent disconnects and reconnection attempts. The traffic anomalies were a result of the attacker testing the system's responsiveness to unauthorized commands, showcasing the vulnerabilities of not securing device identities properly.

Required metrics for this use case:

Metric type	Metric name	Reasoning
Cloud	Authorization failures	When attackers use stolen identities to masquerade as trusted entities, connectivity metrics typically surge due to credential conflicts. Elevated authorization failures, connection attempts, or disconnects can indicate potential impersonation.
Cloud	Connection attempts	
Cloud	Disconnects	
Device side – custom	Client ID Verifier	Using a numeric Client ID Verifier during connection can further refine the verification process to determine authentic devices from impersonators. If this verifier is generated from compiled code, impersonators likely won't have access to it. This aids in the identification, verification, and rectification stages.
Cloud	Source IP	We can improve our differentiation process by extracting IP addresses from the devices, which can then be used during our investigation and verification phases.

2. Exploitation of Cloud Infrastructure

Exploitative actions on AWS IoT cloud services are often manifested when there's excessive publishing or subscribing to topics, resulting in a surge in message volume or unusually large message sizes. This can stem from lax security policies or device vulnerabilities being leveraged for unauthorized control. A notable consequence of such abuses is a spike in AWS service costs.

Real-World Use Case

In a factory setting, an IoT sensor responsible for monitoring equipment health starts transmitting data at ten times its usual frequency. Additionally, the size of the data packets sent is far larger than typical readings. Upon investigation, it is discovered that a security loophole in the sensor's firmware allowed an external party to hijack its functions. Not only was this an attempt to overload the cloud storage and processing infrastructure, but it also caused a substantial uptick in AWS costs for that billing period.

Required metrics for this use case:

Metric type	Metric name	Reasoning
Cloud	Number of messages received	When attackers use stolen identities to masquerade as trusted entities, connectivity metrics typically surge due to credential conflicts. Elevated authorization failures, connection attempts, or disconnects can indicate potential impersonation.
Cloud	Number of messages sent	
Cloud	Message size	
Cloud	Source IP	Using a numeric Client ID Verifier during connection can further refine the verification process to determine authentic devices from impersonators. If this verifier is generated from compiled code, impersonators likely won't have access to it. This aids in the identification, verification, and rectification stages.

3. Denial-of-Service Attack

Denial-of-service (DoS) attacks relentlessly bombard a device or network with excessive traffic or system requests, aiming to render it nonfunctional and inaccessible to legitimate users. The unique interconnected nature of IoT devices makes them prime targets for these attacks, and they can even be maliciously repurposed to instigate DoS attacks on other systems.

Real-World Use Case

A prominent hospital's smart temperature monitoring system, which ensures the safe storage of critical medicines and vaccines, starts experiencing unprecedented downtime. The system becomes inaccessible, unable to relay vital temperature data, posing a significant risk to the efficacy of the stored medical supplies.

Upon investigation, it was discovered that the monitoring devices had been targeted in a well-orchestrated DoS attack, initiated through a compromised smart HVAC system within the same network. The attackers exploited vulnerabilities in the HVAC system to flood the temperature monitoring system with a surge of traffic, causing it to crash repeatedly. This scenario showcases the potential risks and cascading effects of DoS attacks in a critical IoT-enabled infrastructure.

Required metrics for this use case:

Metric type	Metric name	Reasoning
Device side	Packets out	DoS attacks often manifest as increased outbound communications from a device. Depending on the attack type, there might be a surge in the number of outgoing packets, bytes, or both.
Device side	Bytes out	
Device side	Destination IP	By specifying the IP addresses or CIDR ranges your devices should connect to, any deviation in the destination IP can signal unauthorized communication from your devices.
Device side	Listening TCP ports	A DoS attack often hinges on a robust command and control infrastructure. Malware on your devices gets directives about attack targets and timings. Consequently, this malware might listen on ports not typically utilized by your devices.
Device side	Listening TCP port count	
Device side	Listening UDP ports	
Device side	Listening UDP port count	

(*continued*)

Metric type	Metric name	Reasoning
Cloud side	Number of messages received	A rapid increase in incoming messages or a significant change in message size can signal a DoS threat. Setting appropriate thresholds mapped against your IoT devices' usual behavior pattern is essential here.
Cloud side	Message size	
Cloud side	Source IP	Potentially suspicious source IP.

4. Crypto-jacking Through IoT Devices

As cybercriminals seek out more powerful hardware, devices equipped with ASIC (Application-Specific Integrated Circuit) chips have become prime targets. These chips, specifically designed for particular tasks, are prevalent in high-performance systems such as Bitcoin mining rigs, advanced graphics cards, and certain HVAC controllers. Moreover, ASICs have started to appear in consumer IoT devices like high-end home routers, smart cameras, and select entertainment systems. Cybercriminals compromise these devices to harness the potent capabilities of ASICs for illicit crypto-mining operations, unbeknownst to the device owners. Such unauthorized activities can severely degrade the device's performance due to a spike in CPU and memory usage. Compromised devices also often communicate with external mining networks, presenting an even greater security concern.

Real-World Use Case

In a bustling metropolitan office, the Building Management System (BMS) – responsible for overseeing functions like temperature regulation, lighting control, and security mechanisms – begins to face unexpected performance slowdowns. Alarmed by this, the IT team dives deep to uncover the root cause and finds that specific devices, such as advanced HVAC controllers, security cameras, and smart lighting systems, are operating at almost their full capacity. This anomaly, especially during off-peak times, raises eyebrows. Upon deeper inspection, they identify crypto-mining malware silently working on these devices, discreetly accumulating cryptocurrency and redirecting the proceeds to an obscured external wallet.

These incidents underscore the vulnerability of sophisticated BMS devices, particularly those equipped with ASIC chips. ASICs, tailored for high-speed computational tasks, are often embedded in advanced HVAC controllers and other smart systems to enhance their efficiency and responsiveness. Their computational prowess, however, also makes them attractive targets for crypto-jacking. This highlights the pressing need to bolster security measures for systems equipped with such potent chips against looming cyber threats.

Required metrics for this use case:

Metric type	Metric name	Reasoning
Device side	Destination IP	For crypto-mining, network communication is essential. By maintaining a strict list of approved IP addresses for device communication, we can easily detect and prevent unintended activities.
Device side – custom	CPU usage	Cryptocurrency mining involves rigorous computational tasks that significantly strain the device's CPU. Elevated CPU utilization might signal potential crypto-mining operations.
Device side – custom	Memory usage	Prolonged engagement in data-intensive tasks can lead to increased memory consumption. A surge in memory usage might hint at underlying activities like cryptocurrency mining.
Device side – custom	ASIC chip temperature	Constant computational efforts can cause the ASIC chip to heat up substantially. An unusual rise in ASIC chip temperature could be indicative of active crypto-mining processes.
Device side – custom	Voltage	Cryptocurrency mining typically requires increased power consumption. A sudden surge in voltage might indicate intensive mining activities, and it's essential to investigate, both to confirm mining operations and to determine potential system faults.
Cloud side	Source IP	Potentially suspicious source IP detection.

5. Ransomware Attacks on IoT Devices

Despite their transformative potential, IoT devices are vulnerable to pervasive cybersecurity threats, including malware and ransomware. Ransomware, a particularly malevolent form of cyberattack, can encrypt critical data on devices, essentially holding them hostage. Users are then denied access to their own devices or data until they pay a demanded ransom.

Real-World Use Case

At a popular casino, players suddenly find multiple slot machines freezing, displaying a message demanding a ransom payment in cryptocurrency. These casino machines, integral to the establishment's revenue, are rendered inoperable. IT personnel quickly deduced that the machines, being part of the IoT spectrum, were infiltrated by ransomware. The attack not only interrupts the casino's operations, causing significant financial loss due to downtime, but also threatens to leak confidential data about the casino's operations and high-profile patrons unless the ransom is paid. This incident underscores the importance of robust cybersecurity measures, especially in IoT devices that handle sensitive and financial data.

Required metrics for this use case:

Metric type	Metric name	Reasoning
Device side	Destination IP	Network and remote attacks account for many IoT device breaches. Maintaining a strict list of approved IP addresses can help pinpoint unusual destinations, which might indicate malware or ransomware intrusions.
Device side	Listening TCP ports	Many malware threats initiate a command-and-control server to relay execution commands to a device. Identifying this central server, crucial for malware and ransomware activities, can be achieved by closely observing open TCP/UDP ports and their frequencies.
Device side	Listening TCP port count	
Device side	Listening UDP ports	
Device side	Listening UDP port count	

6. Protecting Intellectual Property

Protecting intellectual property (IP) is paramount, especially in an era dominated by digital advancements. Intellectual property theft targets invaluable assets like trade secrets, proprietary software, and specific hardware blueprints. Especially vulnerable are the manufacturing stages, where proprietary software or hardware designs are implemented in devices. Beyond physical theft, the digital domain presents risks such as illicit software duplication, unauthorized access to device certificates, or unintended cloud access due to lenient IoT policies.

Real-World Scenario

Consider a cutting-edge robotics firm specializing in AI-driven industrial robots. As they begin manufacturing their latest model, blueprints and software codes are shared across their global facilities. Unknown to them, an employee in one facility siphons off these intellectual assets and sells them to a competitor. While the robots are in production, the competitor launches a strikingly similar model at a fraction of the price, potentially jeopardizing the original firm's market standing and profits. The breach underscores the significance of stringent IoT policies and periodic audits to prevent such security lapses.

Required metrics for this use case:

Metric type	Metric name	Reasoning
Cloud side	Source IP	If a device is stolen, its IP address would diverge from the standard supply chain's expected range.
Cloud side	Number of messages received	An attacker might exploit a device for cloud-based IP theft, leading to a surge in message counts or sizes from the AWS IoT cloud. This spike can signal a potential security threat.
Cloud side	Message size	

Investigation Process

When addressing cybersecurity concerns in IoT devices, customers typically adopt a systematic investigation process. The goal is to restore device anomaly and determine appropriate response strategies.

While the process might differ depending on the device type (IoT or IIoT) and use case, the following diagram illustrates a common logic flow pattern I've often seen among AWS customers (refer to the flow chart).

Investigation Flow Process

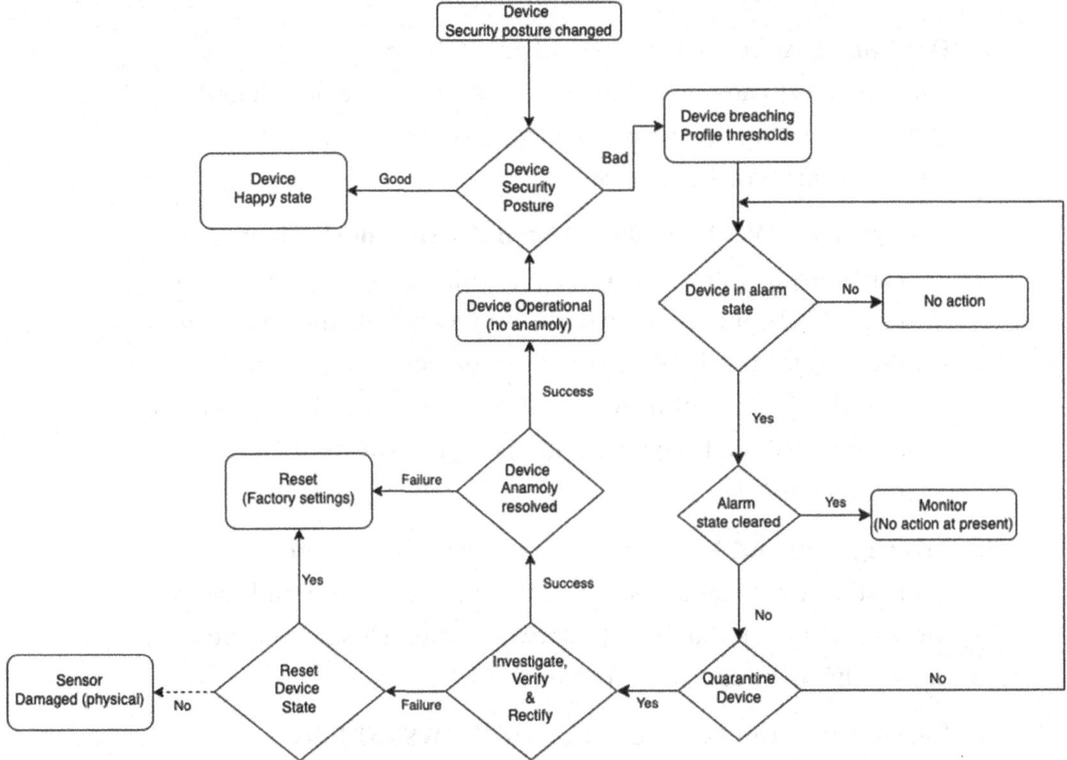

Flow chart: Common investigative pathways often followed by customers

To ensure our IoT devices maintain the highest level of security and reliability, we will adopt a structured approach using AWS IoT Device Defender. Here's our process:

1. **Profiles and Continuous Monitoring**: Through AWS IoT Device Defender, we can establish a comprehensive security profile, outlining acceptable thresholds tailored to specific use cases and organizational needs. This profile will serve as our benchmark for gauging and ensuring consistent device behavior.

2. **Alarm Activation and Notification**: When a device's actions stray from our defined profile metric thresholds, signifying a potential anomaly, an alarm is activated. Instantaneously, our security team and administrators receive notifications via Amazon SNS (email or text), prompting swift intervention.

3. **Quarantine Action**: In the wake of an alert, our security team/administrators can move the suspicious device to a designated Quarantine Group, ensuring its isolation to prevent potential repercussions on other devices.

    - **Optional: AWS Lambda-Assisted Quarantine:** We have the capability to automate device relocation to the Quarantine Group using AWS Lambda. Yet we recommend proceeding with *caution.* While automated responses offer efficiency, they can also mistakenly quarantine legitimate devices due to false positives, leading to operational disruptions. *Human oversight is thus recommended.*

4. **Investigation and Analysis**: With the device sequestered in quarantine, our team can securely inspect it using methods we've previously covered, such as the secure tunnel. This step is critical in identifying the anomaly's origin.

5. **Remediation and Remote Actions with AWS IoT Jobs**: Leveraging AWS IoT Jobs, we can remotely administer necessary rectifications to the device. This might involve firmware updates, configuration adjustments, or even device reboots. AWS IoT Jobs offers us the ability to return the device to peak performance without needing physical access.

6. **Restoration**: Once rectified and verified as secure, the device exits the quarantine and re-enters the general fleet, ensuring its efficient and safe collaboration with fellow devices.

Hands-On Scenario Overview

In our previous exploration of "Cybersecurity in Real-World Applications," we touched upon six distinct scenarios. Although each scenario follows the same mitigation processes for devices, they're differentiated by the unique metrics captured through AWS IoT Device Defender. These metrics span three categories: cloud side, device side, and custom.

To provide a rounded view, we've selected three scenarios that exemplify the diversity of these metrics and the associated mitigation techniques. For reference, the sample code tailored to all six scenarios - encompassing the specific metrics outlined in the previous section - is available for download. You can find this in Chapter 10 of the book's GitHub repository, with each code labeled according to its scenario name.

1. **Exploitation of Cloud Infrastructure**: This scenario primarily uses cloud-side metrics, with mitigation managed manually.
2. **Denial-of-Service Attack**: Here, the focus is on both device-side and cloud-side metrics, with manual intervention being the preferred mitigation approach.
3. **Crypto-jacking Through IoT Devices**: In this scenario, we'll delve into device-side and custom metrics. While automated mitigation using AWS Lambda is demonstrated, it's worth noting that automated mitigation is generally not the recommended path.

Establishing a Quarantine Group for Advanced Device Cybersecurity

As part of our commitment to ensuring optimal device security, we will establish a designated "*Quarantine Group*." This entity will serve as a secure isolation chamber that can temporarily accommodate devices that may have been compromised. Within this protective realm, we have the necessary resources to thoroughly investigate, validate, and rectify any anomalies or issues that may raise device alarms or breach standard device guidelines. Once we have identified and addressed the concerns, the device is ready to transition out of quarantine and reintegrate seamlessly into its native environment, in full compliance with all device standards.

Quarantine Group and Its Policy

Before diving into the intricacies of AWS IoT Device Defender's security profiles, there are some foundational tasks that must be completed. These include creating a Quarantine Group and defining its governing policy.

Create a policy by navigating to the AWS IoT Core console, and from the "*Manage*" section, select (see Figure 10-1)

- *Security*
    - *Policies*
        - *Create policy*

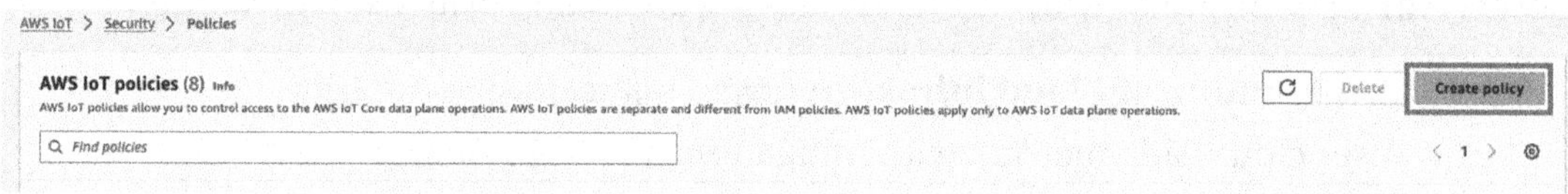

Figure 10-1. *Creating a policy*

In the "*Create policy*" screen, populate as follows (see Figure 10-2):

- Policy name: *Quarantine_Policy*
- Under Policy document:
    - Policy effect: "*Deny*"
    - Policy action: "*"
    - Policy resource: "*"
- Once done, click "*Create*"

In this policy, any device assigned this policy will have by default "*Deny*" action within the AWS IoT Core realm.

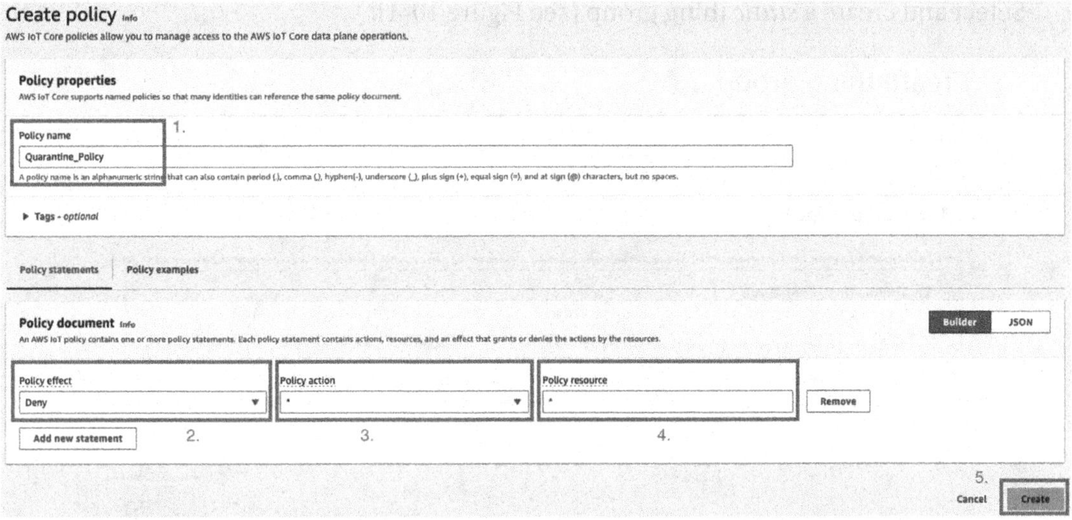

Figure 10-2. *Quarantine Policy details*

Next, let's create a "*Quarantine Group*" and assign the "*Quarantine Policy*" to it.

From the AWS IoT Core console, navigate to the "*Manage*" section, and then select (see Figure 10-3)

- *Thing groups*
    - *Create thing group*

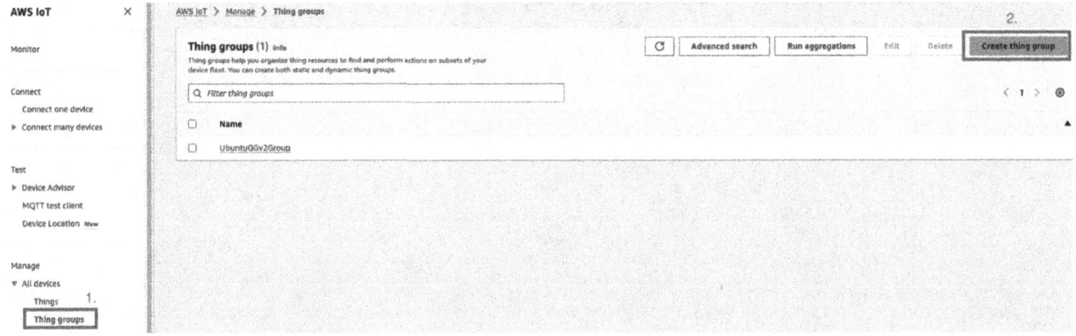

Figure 10-3. *Creating a thing group*

Select and create a *static* thing group (see Figure 10-4).

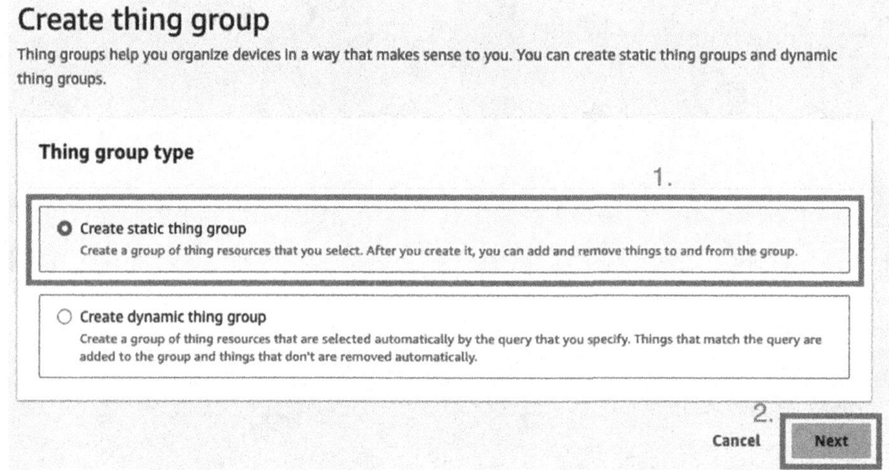

Figure 10-4. *Creating a static thing group*

In "*Create static thing group*", populate details as follows (see Figure 10-5):

- Thing group name: *Quarantine_group*
- Description: *This is a quarantine group for all violating/alarm-generating devices, which needs isolation from other fleet.*
- Once done, click "*Create thing group*".

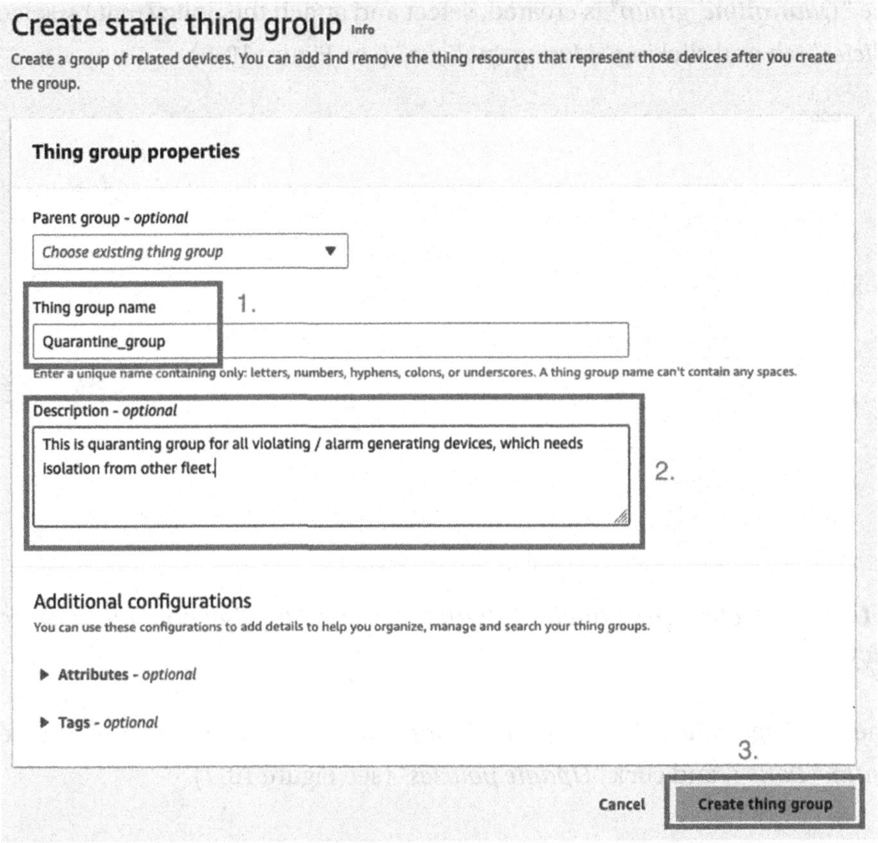

Figure 10-5. *Populating thing group details*

Once "*Quarantine_group*" is created, select and attach the policy to it by selecting the "*Policies*" tab and clicking "*Manage policies*" (see Figure 10-6).

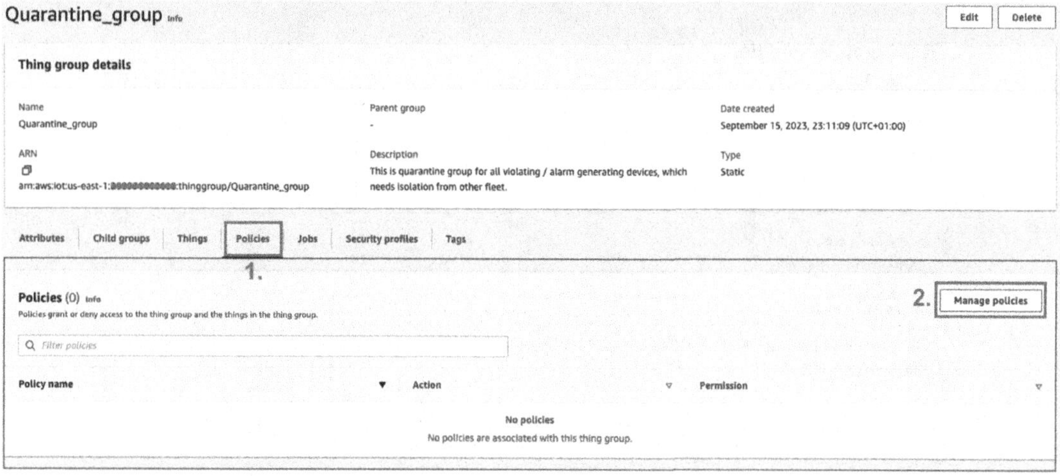

Figure 10-6. *Selecting the Policies tab and clicking Manage policies to attach the policy*

In the "*Manage policies*" pop-up, click "*Add policy*", select our recently created "*Quarantine_Policy*", and click "*Update policies*" (see Figure 10-7).

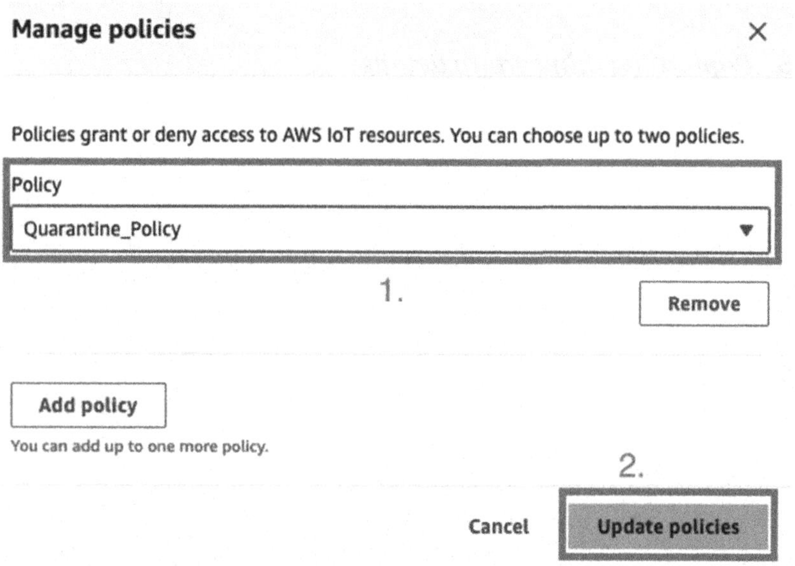

Figure 10-7. *Selecting Quarantine_Policy and updating*

Once we have attached this policy to our group, we can see "*Permission*" will show denied for all "*Action*".

Setting Up Notifications with Amazon SNS

From the AWS Console "*Unified search bar*", search for *SNS* and navigate to the service console (see Figure 10-8).

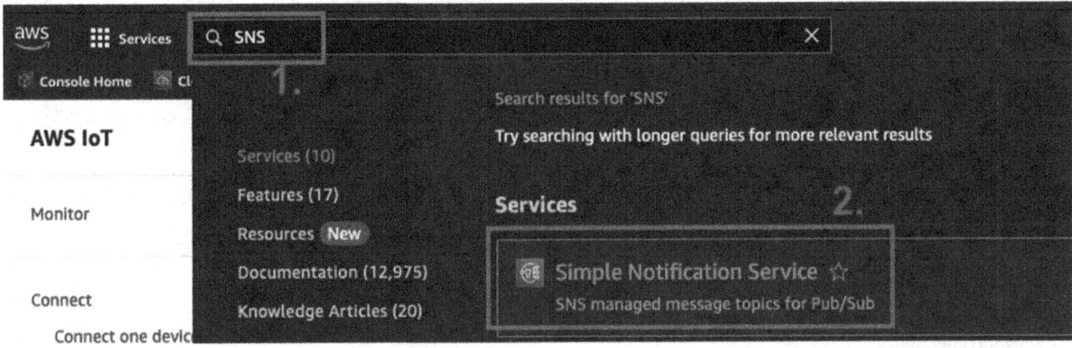

Figure 10-8. *Selecting SNS service*

Select Topics from the Amazon SNS sidebar and "*Create topic*" (see Figure 10-9).

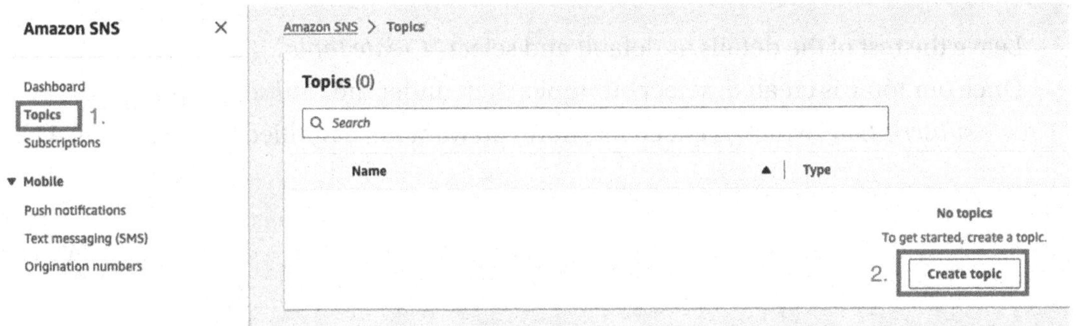

Figure 10-9. *Creating a topic in Amazon SNS*

In the Create topic screen, select "Standard" topic type and populate details as follows (see Figure 10-10).

- Name: *AWSIoTbookSNSNotification*
- Display name: *AWSIoTbookNotify*

Create topic

Details

Type Info
Topic type cannot be modified after topic is created

1.

○ FIFO (first-in, first-out)
- Strictly-preserved message ordering
- Exactly-once message delivery
- High throughput, up to 300 publishes/second
- Subscription protocols: SQS

● Standard
- Best-effort message ordering
- At-least once message delivery
- Highest throughput in publishes/second
- Subscription protocols: SQS, Lambda, HTTP, SMS, email, mobile application endpoints

Name 2.
AWSIoTbookSNSNotification
Maximum 256 characters. Can include alphanumeric characters, hyphens (-) and underscores (_).

Display name - *optional* Info
To use this topic with SMS subscriptions, enter a display name. Only the first 10 characters are displayed in an SMS message.
AWSIoTbookNotify
Maximum 100 characters. 3.

***Figure 10-10.** Creating a topic in Amazon SNS*

Leave the rest of the details as default and select "*Create topic*".

Once our topic is created, select our topic; then under the "*Subscriptions*" tab, click "*Create subscription*", which is effectively how you want to be notified (see Figure 10-11).

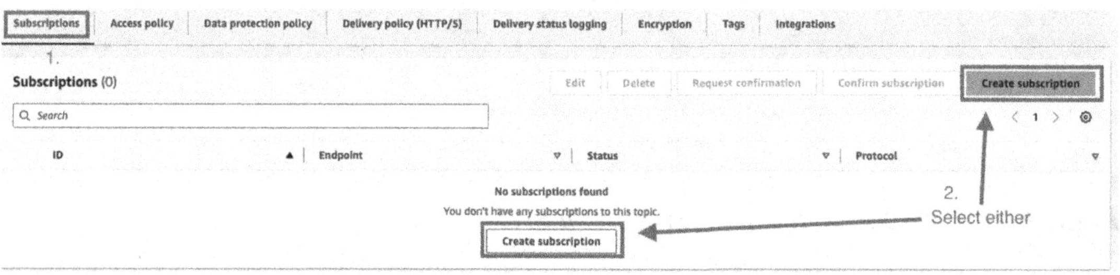

***Figure 10-11.** Creating a subscription (how you want to be notified)*

In the "Create subscription" window, retain the default Topic ARN (which serves as the unique identifier for the topic, with ARN denoting Amazon Resource Name). Fill out the remaining fields as described here (see Figure 10-12):

- For Protocol, select *Email*
- Endpoint: *<enter your email address> (note: you will need to verify this to receive alerts)*
- Leave the rest of the settings as default
- Click "*Create subscription*"

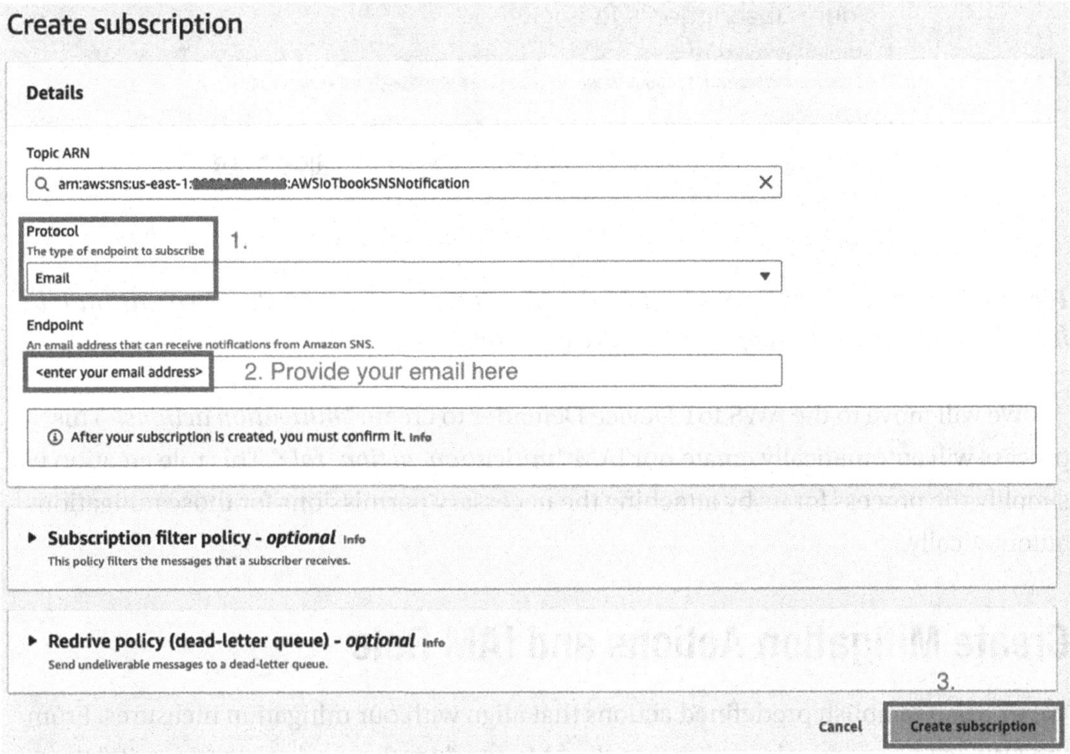

Figure 10-12. *Creating an email subscription*

Until you verify your email, you won't receive any alerts. Upon successful verification, you'll encounter the message as depicted in Figure 10-13.

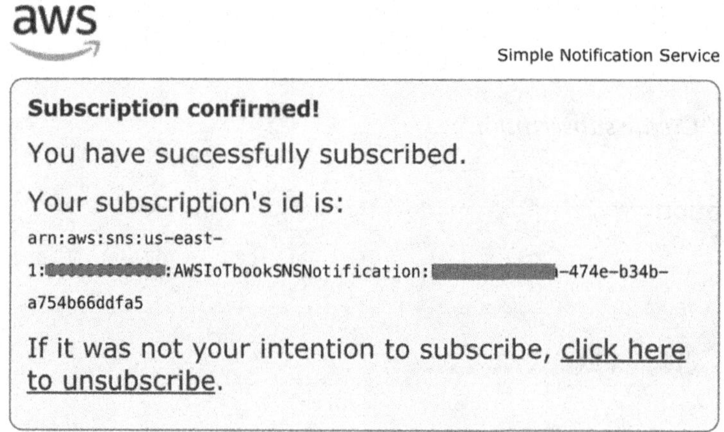

Figure 10-13. *Verification is required to receive alerts. Successful verification will be acknowledged and displayed in the browser*

We will move to the AWS IoT Device Defender to create "*mitigation actions*." This process will automatically create our IAM "*mitigation_action_role*". This role creation will simplify the process for us by attaching the necessary permissions for those mitigations automatically.

Create Mitigation Actions and IAM Role

We will also establish predefined actions that align with our mitigation measures. From the AWS IoT Core console, navigate to the "*Manage*" section and select "*Security*", then "*Detect*", and, finally, "*Mitigation actions*" and click "*Create your first mitigation action*" (see Figure 10-14).

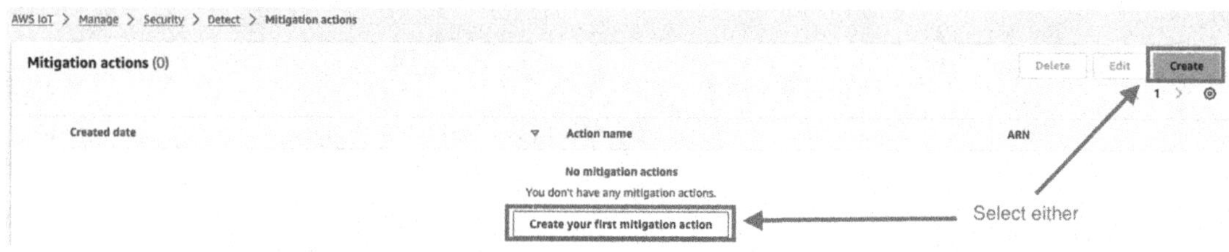

Figure 10-14. *Creating a mitigation action*

In the "*create a new mitigation action*" screen, populate/select details as follows (see Figure 10-15):

- Action name: "*Isolate_device*"
- Action type: "*Add things to thing group (Audit or Detect mitigation)*"
- Click "*Create role*" (step 3), and give the role name: "*mitigation_action_role*"
- Parameters: Select "*Quarantine_group*"
- Click "*Create*"

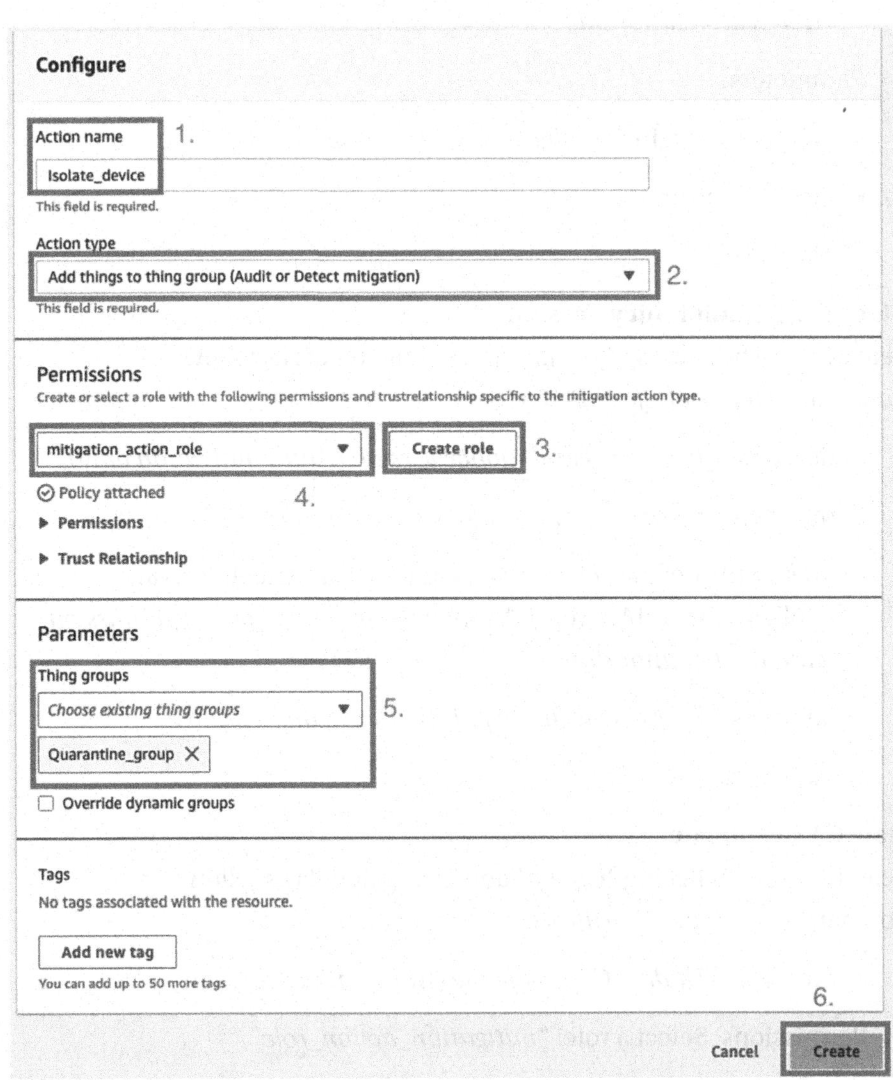

Figure 10-15. *Creating a role and an action for our mitigation action*

By following the same process, we will create a few more mitigation actions.

Enable IoT Logging

Repeat the step by clicking "*Create*" and giving details as follows:

- Action name: *"EnableIoTLogging"*
- Action type: *"Enable IoT logging (Audit mitigation only)"*
- Permissions: Select a role: "*mitigation_action_role*"
    - Leave the default selection as it is (so it can attach relevant policies to our IAM role): "*Attach the managed policy permission and trust relationship*"
- Parameters:
    - Roles for logging *"mitigation_action_role"*
    - Log level: *"Error"*
- Click "*Create*"

Replace the Default Policy Version

Repeat the step by clicking "*Create*" and giving details as follows:

Action name: *"replaceDefaultPolicy"*

- Action type: *"Replace default policy version (Audit mitigation only)"*
- Permissions: Select a role: "*mitigation_action_role*"
    - Leave the default selection as it is (so it can attach relevant policies to our IAM role): "*Attach the managed policy permission and trust relationship*"
- Parameters: Template: *<Empty policy> (leave this default)*
- Click *"Create"*

Update CA Certificate

Repeat the step by clicking "*Create*" and giving details as follows:

Action name: *"updateCACertificate"*

- Action type: *"Update CA certificate (Audit mitigation only)"*
- Permissions: Select a role: "*mitigation_action_role*"

    - Leave the default selection as it is (so it can attach relevant policies to our IAM role): *"Attach the managed policy permission and trust relationship"*
- Parameters: Action: *<Deactivate> (leave this default)*
- Click *"Create"*

Update Device Certificate
Repeat the step by clicking *"Create"* and giving details as follows:
Action name: *"updateDeviceCertificate"*

- Action type: *"Update device certificate (Audit mitigation only)"*
- Permissions: Select a role: *"mitigation_action_role"*
    - Leave the default selection as it is (so it can attach relevant policies to our IAM role): *"Attach the managed policy permission and trust relationship"*
- Parameters: Action: *<Deactivate> (leave this default)*
- Click *"Create"*

Publish Finding to SNS
Repeat the step by clicking *"Create"* and giving details as follows:
Action name: *"publishFindingToSNS"*

- Action type: *"Publish finding to SNS (Audit mitigation only)"*
- Permissions: Select a role: *"mitigation_action_role"*
    - Leave the default selection as it is (so it can attach relevant policies to our IAM role): *"Attach the managed policy permission and trust relationship"*
- Parameters: Topic: *"AWSIoTbookSNSNotification"*
- Click *"Create"*

Having set up our supplementary actions to address cybersecurity incidents for IoT devices, we must also implement a notification setup, and as we learnt so far in the book, every service needs IAM role to talk to each other. So we can be alerted promptly when an alarm or security profile threshold is breached; for this, we'll add IAM policy to our *"mitigation_action_role"*, leveraging the Amazon Simple Notification Service (SNS).

Checking Our IAM Policy for Fine-Grained Access

We have already used the mitigation action procedure mentioned previously to attach policies. However, it's always a good practice to ensure that our role does not have any additional policies than required. This is crucial as the IAM role is used for service-to-service communication, and it must be set up based on the principle of "least privilege."

From the AWS IAM console:

- Select Roles
  - Search a role: "*mitigation_action_role*" and then click on its name (see Figure 10-16).
  - In the "*mitigation_action_role*" screen, we can see the attached policies.

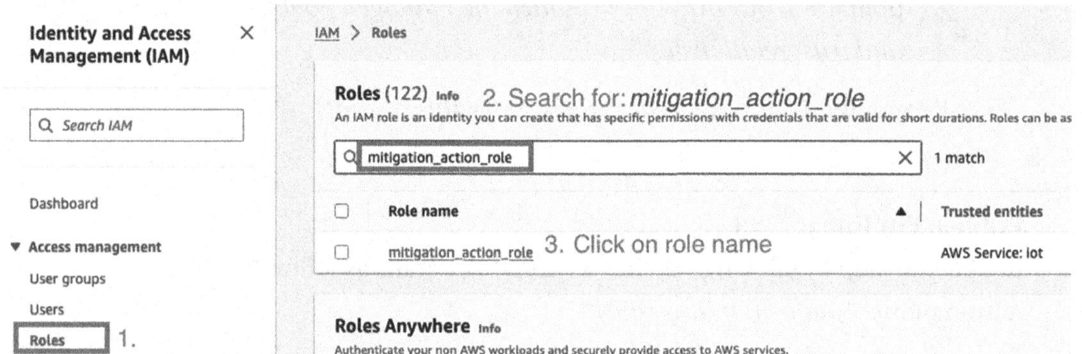

Figure 10-16. *Searching and clicking "mitigation_action_role"*

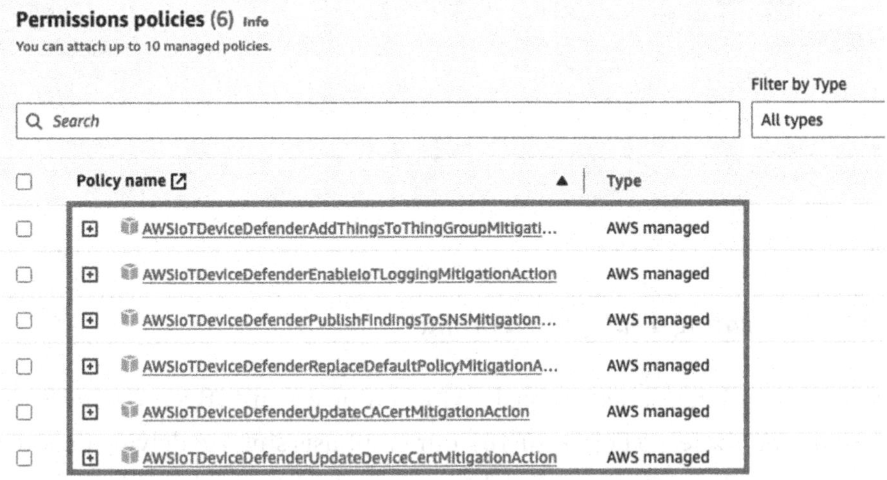

Permissions policies (6) Info
You can attach up to 10 managed policies.

Filter by Type: All types

Policy name	Type
AWSIoTDeviceDefenderAddThingsToThingGroupMitigati...	AWS managed
AWSIoTDeviceDefenderEnableIoTLoggingMitigationAction	AWS managed
AWSIoTDeviceDefenderPublishFindingsToSNSMitigation...	AWS managed
AWSIoTDeviceDefenderReplaceDefaultPolicyMitigationA...	AWS managed
AWSIoTDeviceDefenderUpdateCACertMitigationAction	AWS managed
AWSIoTDeviceDefenderUpdateDeviceCertMitigationAction	AWS managed

Figure 10-17. *Make sure to have these policies*

Now let's proceed to create our "*security profiles*."

Set Up AWS IoT Device Defender Profiles

We will start with our first scenario "*Exploitation of Cloud Infrastructure*" and walk through how to mitigate it. Let's set up our AWS IoT Device Defender profiles and create an IoT thing (by using provided scripts from Chapter 10 of the book's GitHub) to create this anomaly and see the alarm states.

The process for crafting rule-based profiles remains consistent across our scenarios. What varies are the specific metrics and their thresholds.

From the AWS IoT Core console, under "*Manage*"

- Select "*Security*" and then "*Detect*"
    - *"Security profiles"*
        - Click *"Create Security Profile"*.
            - *"Create Rule-based anomaly Detect profile"* (see Figure 10-18)

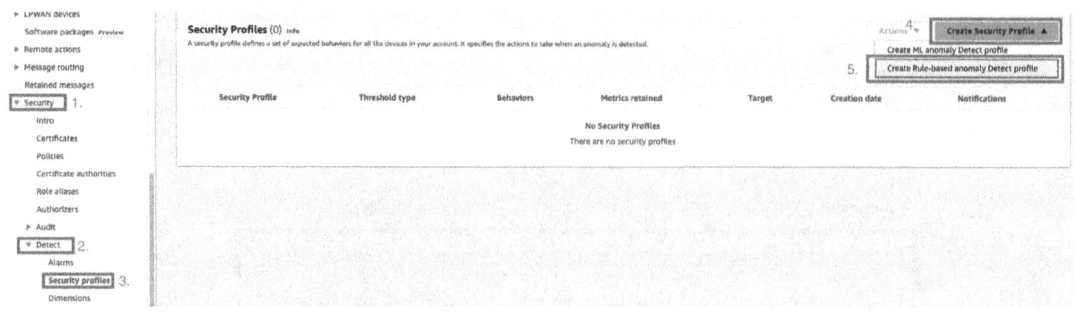

Figure 10-18. Creating a rule-based profile

With the foundational steps established for setting up an *"AWS IoT Device Defender Rules Detect profile"* (refer to Figure 10-18), our emphasis shifts to delving deeper into metric selection, understanding critical data points, and emphasizing the mitigation strategy. It's worth noting that while the foundational creation process is standard, the nuances in metric choice and response mechanisms (threshold data points) provide the customization needed for each unique rule profile.

Exploitation of Cloud Infrastructure (Cloud-Side Metrics, Manual Mitigation)

- **Create an AWS IoT Device Defender Rule-based anomaly Detect profile.**
    - Security Profile name: *"exploitCloudDetectProfile"* (see Figure 10-19)
    - Description: *"My cloud infrastructure exploitation detection profile"*
    - Target: *"All things"*
    - For SNS configuration:
        - Topic: *"AWSIoTbookSNSNotification"*
        - Role: *"mitigation_action_role"*
- Click *"Next"*.

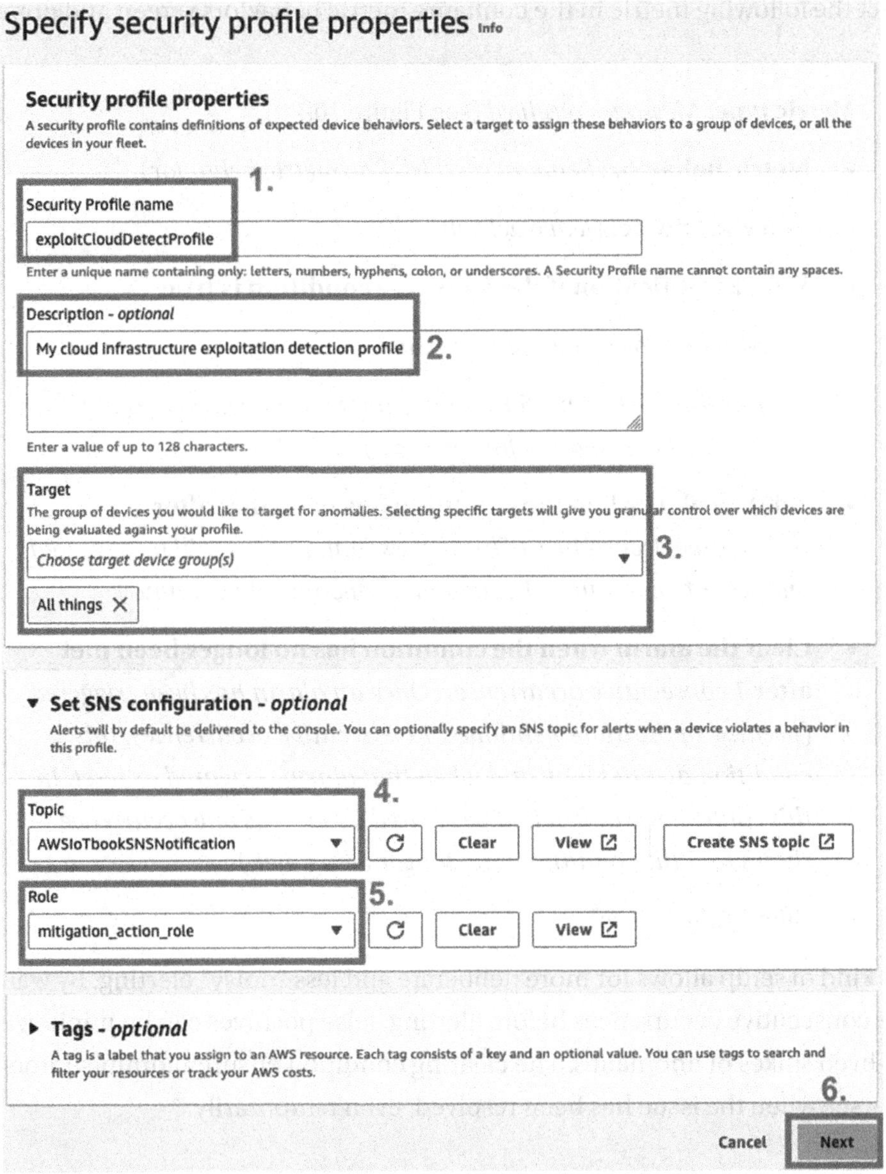

Specify security profile properties Info

Security profile properties

A security profile contains definitions of expected device behaviors. Select a target to assign these behaviors to a group of devices, or all the devices in your fleet.

1.

Security Profile name

exploitCloudDetectProfile

Enter a unique name containing only: letters, numbers, hyphens, colon, or underscores. A Security Profile name cannot contain any spaces.

Description - *optional*

My cloud infrastructure exploitation detection profile

2.

Enter a value of up to 128 characters.

Target

The group of devices you would like to target for anomalies. Selecting specific targets will give you granular control over which devices are being evaluated against your profile.

Choose target device group(s)

3.

All things ×

▼ Set SNS configuration - *optional*

Alerts will by default be delivered to the console. You can optionally specify an SNS topic for alerts when a device violates a behavior in this profile.

4.

Topic

AWSIoTbookSNSNotification

Clear View Create SNS topic

5.

Role

mitigation_action_role

Clear View

▶ Tags - *optional*

A tag is a label that you assign to an AWS resource. Each tag consists of a key and an optional value. You can use tags to search and filter your resources or track your AWS costs.

6.

Cancel Next

Figure 10-19. *Creating the rule-based profile "exploitCloudDetectProfile"*

Select the following metric in the configure metric behaviors screen and populate as follows:

- **Metric type:** *Messages received* (see Figure 10-20)
    - **Metric behavior:** *Send an alert (define metric behavior)*
    - **Behavior name:** *(leave default)*
    - **Send a notification if the following condition is true**
        - *Messages received is greater than*
        - *Absolute, 20, Time: 5 minutes (more than 20 messages are received in a span of five minutes)*
    - **Send an alert when the condition has been met after** *1 consecutive occurrence. (This means that an alert will be triggered only after five minutes, 1 consecutive five-minute window.)*
    - **Clear the alarm when the condition has no longer been met after** *1 consecutive occurrence. (Once an alarm has been triggered (because of the aforementioned 1 consecutive occurrence), this condition dictates how and when that alarm is cleared or reset. In this context, the alarm will be cleared as soon as one occurrence shows that the condition is no longer being met.)*
    - Click "*Add Metric*".

This kind of setup allows for more deliberate and less "noisy" alerting. By waiting for three consecutive occurrences before alerting, false positives can be minimized due to short-lived spikes or anomalies. The clearing condition ensures administrators can promptly see when the issue has been resolved, even temporarily.

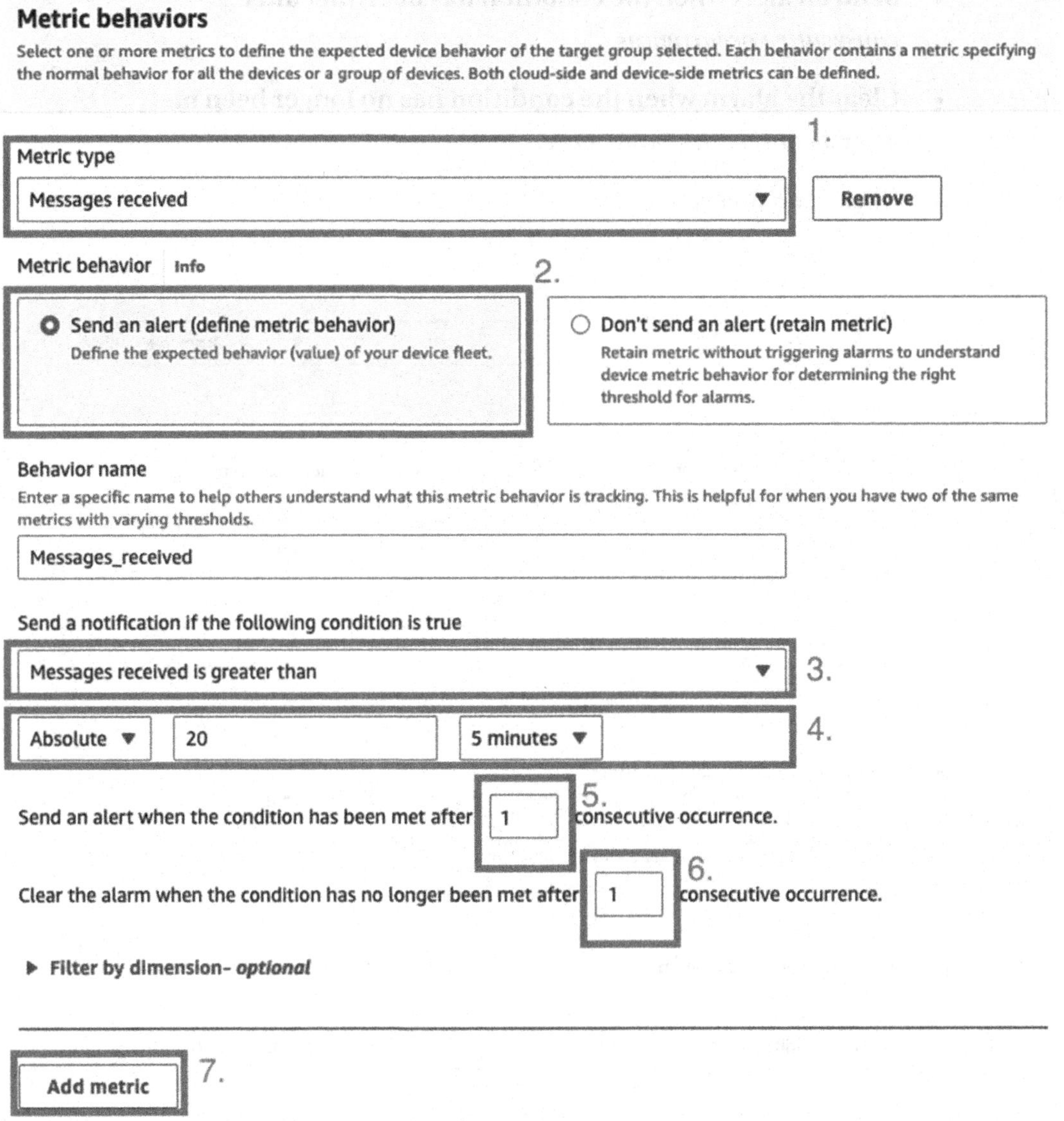

Metric behaviors

Select one or more metrics to define the expected device behavior of the target group selected. Each behavior contains a metric specifying the normal behavior for all the devices or a group of devices. Both cloud-side and device-side metrics can be defined.

1.

Metric type

Messages received ▼

Remove

Metric behavior Info

2.

Send an alert (define metric behavior)
Define the expected behavior (value) of your device fleet.

Don't send an alert (retain metric)
Retain metric without triggering alarms to understand device metric behavior for determining the right threshold for alarms.

Behavior name

Enter a specific name to help others understand what this metric behavior is tracking. This is helpful for when you have two of the same metrics with varying thresholds.

Messages_received

Send a notification if the following condition is true

Messages received is greater than ▼ 3.

Absolute ▼ 20 5 minutes ▼ 4.

5.

Send an alert when the condition has been met after 1 consecutive occurrence.

6.

Clear the alarm when the condition has no longer been met after 1 consecutive occurrence.

▶ Filter by dimension- *optional*

Add metric 7.

***Figure 10-20.** Creating the Messages received metric*

- **Metric type:** *Messages sent* (see Figure 10-21)
    - **Metric behavior:** *Send an alert (define metric behavior)*
    - **Behavior name:** *<leave default>*
    - **Send a notification if the following condition is true**
        - *Messages sent is greater than*
        - *Absolute, 20, Time: 5 minutes*

- **Send an alert when the condition has been met after** *2 consecutive occurrences.*
- **Clear the alarm when the condition has no longer been met after** *1 consecutive occurrence.*
- Click "*Add Metric*".

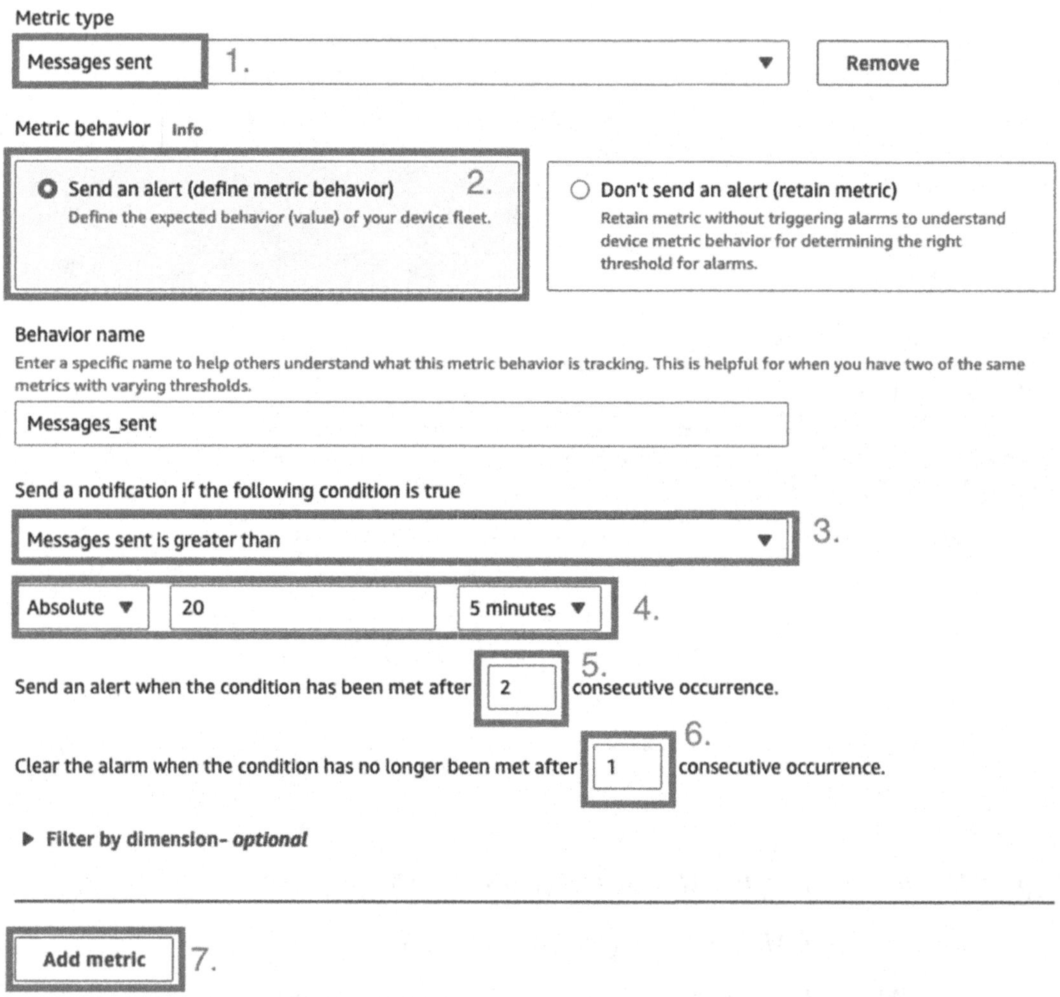

Figure 10-21. *Creating the Messages sent metric*

- **Metric type:** *Message size* (see Figure 10-22)
  - **Metric behavior:** *Send an alert (define metric behavior)*
  - **Behavior name:** *<leave default>*
  - **Send a notification if the following condition is true**
    - *Message size is greater than (in bytes)*
    - *Absolute, 100*
  - **Send an alert when the condition has been met after** *1 consecutive occurrence.*
  - **Clear the alarm when the condition has no longer been met after** *1 consecutive occurrence.*
  - Click "*Add Metric*".

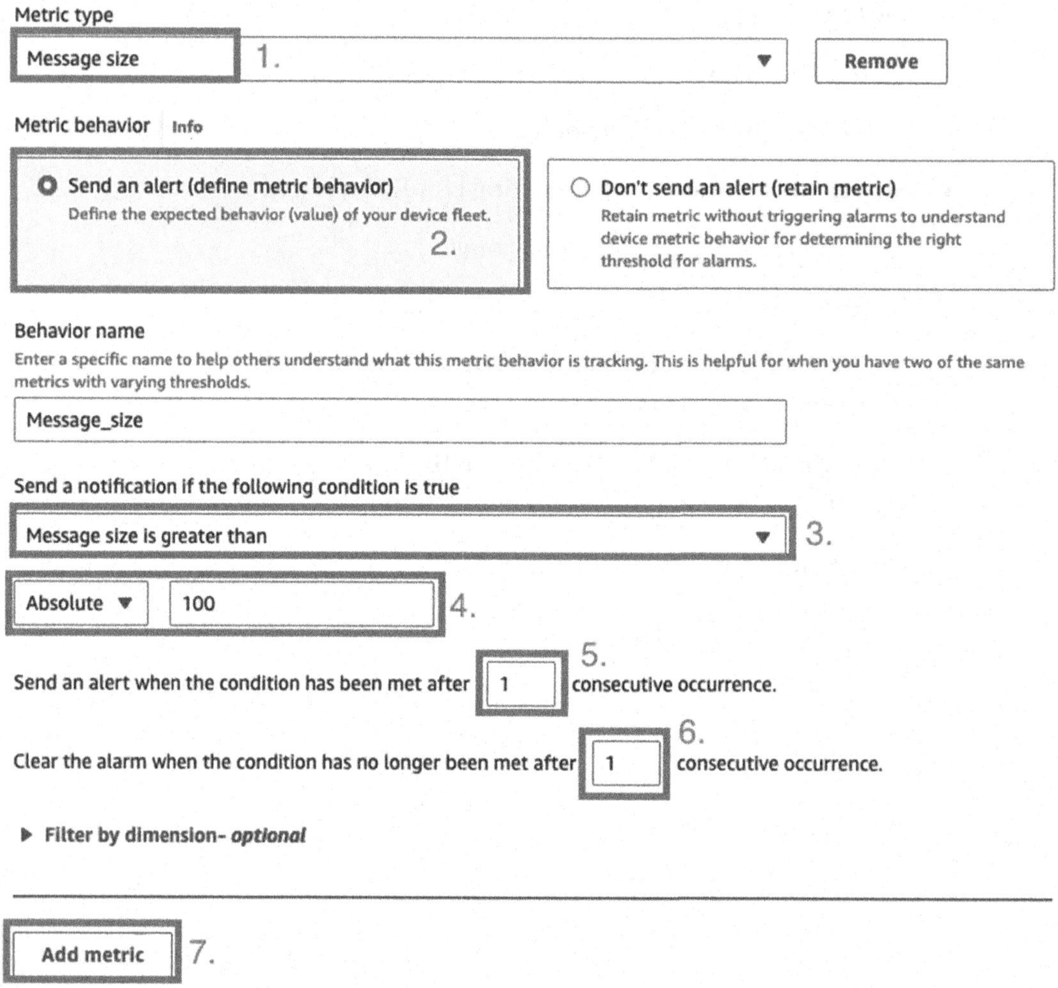

Metric type
Message size 1. Remove

Metric behavior Info

Send an alert (define metric behavior)
Define the expected behavior (value) of your device fleet. 2.

Don't send an alert (retain metric)
Retain metric without triggering alarms to understand device metric behavior for determining the right threshold for alarms.

Behavior name
Enter a specific name to help others understand what this metric behavior is tracking. This is helpful for when you have two of the same metrics with varying thresholds.
Message_size

Send a notification if the following condition is true
Message size is greater than 3.

Absolute 100 4.

Send an alert when the condition has been met after 1 consecutive occurrence. 5.

Clear the alarm when the condition has no longer been met after 1 consecutive occurrence. 6.

Filter by dimension- *optional*

Add metric 7.

Figure 10-22. *Setting up the Message size metric*

- **Metric type:** *Source IP* (see Figure 10-23)
    - **Metric behavior:** *Send an alert (define metric behavior)*
    - **Behavior name:** *<leave default>*
    - **Send a notification if the following condition is true**
    - *Source IP is not in CIDR set*
        - *192.168.100.14/24*

- **Send an alert when the condition has been met after** *1 consecutive occurrence.*
- **Clear the alarm when the condition has no longer been met after** *1 consecutive occurrence.*
- Click "*Next*".

Metric type
Source IP
Remove
Metric behavior Info
Send an alert (define metric behavior)
Define the expected behavior (value) of your device fleet.
Don't send an alert (retain metric)
Retain metric without triggering alarms to understand device metric behavior for determining the right threshold for alarms.
Behavior name
Enter a specific name to help others understand what this metric behavior is tracking. This is helpful for when you have two of the same metrics with varying thresholds.
Source_IP
Send a notification if the following condition is true
Source IP is not in CIDR set
192.168.100.14/24
Send an alert when the condition has been met after 1 consecutive occurrence.
Clear the alarm when the condition has no longer been met after 1 consecutive occurrence.
Filter by dimension- optional
Add metric
Cancel
Previous
Next

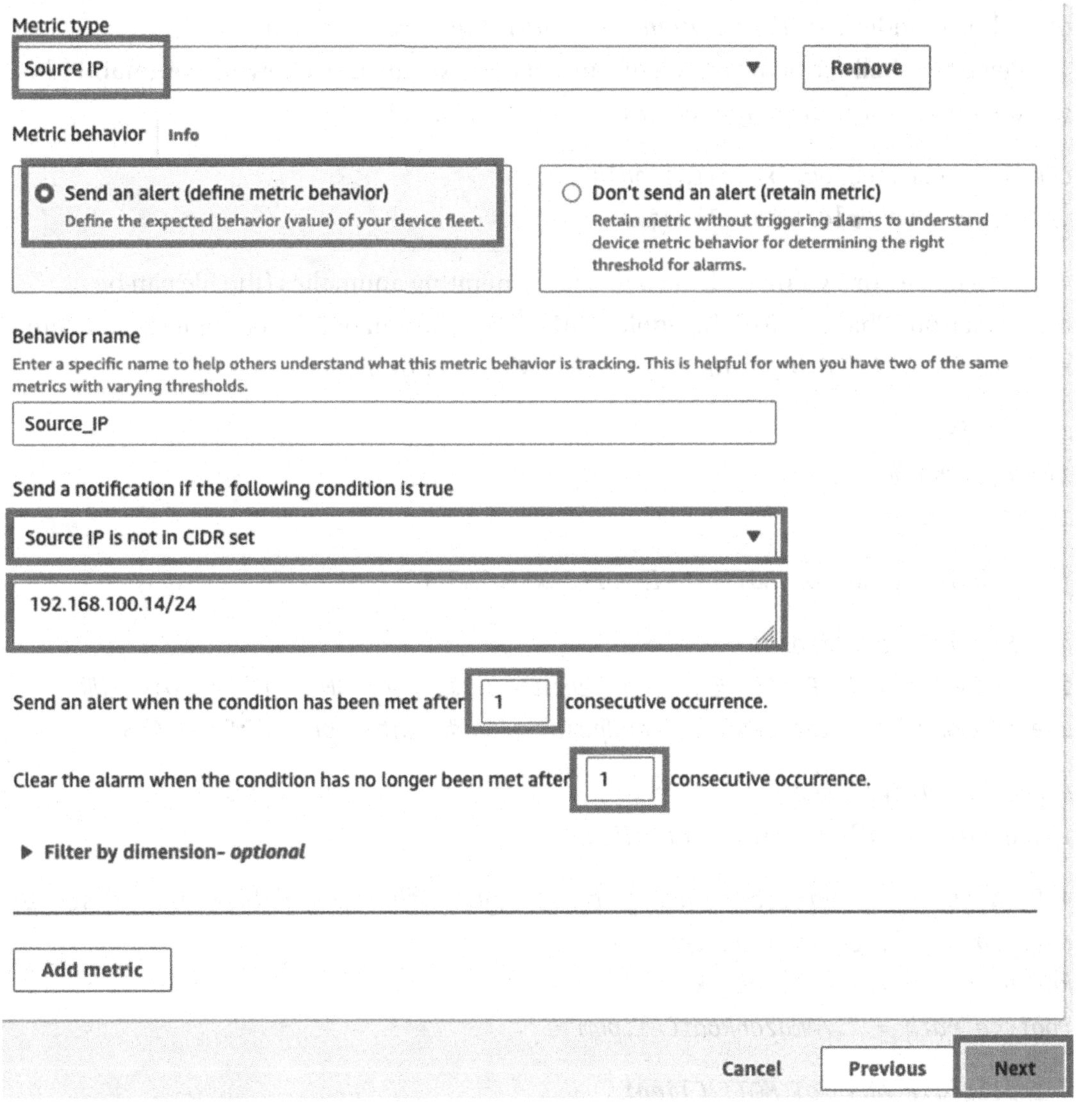

Figure 10-23. *Setting the Source IP metric*

In the "*Review and Create*" section, you can review and adjust metric behaviors. After clicking "Create", you can still go back and modify these settings. This allows you to tweak the consecutive occurrence values based on your environment and the frequency of device messages, even after the profile has been established.

You have the option to either manually set up an IoT thing or utilize the script provided to establish the IoT thing and its associated Python script. This Python script is designed to generate anomalies for this profile. You can access this script in Chapter 10 of the book, under the "*Exploitation-of-Cloud-Infrastructure*" folder.

Place the shell script in your environment and execute the following command (this will create the IoT thing name "*cloudExploitationThing*"):

```
chmod +x createCloudExploitationThing.sh
./createCloudExploitationThing.sh
```

Let's place our Python code now to start generating anomalies (the file can be obtained from Chapter 10 of the book's GitHub) or you can use the content shown here – make sure to "*REPLACE_HERE*" with your AWS IoT Endpoint:

```
import json
import random
import time

from AWSIoTPythonSDK.MQTTLib import AWSIoTMQTTClient

# AWS IoT Core endpoint
iot_endpoint = "REPLACE_HERE"  # Replace with your AWS IoT Endpoint URL,
use command: aws iot describe-endpoint --endpoint-type iot:Data-ATS

# AWS IoT Thing Name
thing_name = "cloudExploitationThing"

# Path to the certificates and private key in the same folder as the script
cert_path = "./certificate.pem.crt"
key_path = "./private.pem.key"
root_ca_path = "./AmazonRootCA1.pem"

# Initialize AWS IoT MQTT Client
mqtt_client = AWSIoTMQTTClient(thing_name)
mqtt_client.configureEndpoint(iot_endpoint, 8883)
mqtt_client.configureCredentials(root_ca_path, key_path, cert_path)
```

```
# Connect to AWS IoT
mqtt_client.connect()

def generate_metrics_data():
    # Ensure this message content always exceeds 100 bytes.
    message_content = "This message is crafted to be larger than 100 bytes
for demonstration purposes. Extra content here."

    return {
        "Message": message_content,
        "SourceIP": f"192.168.{random.randint(101,254)}.{random.
        randint(0,254)}",  # Simulating random source IP outside CIDR
        192.168.100.14/24
    }

# Infinite loop to publish metrics data
while True:
    metrics_data = generate_metrics_data()
    mqtt_client.publish(
        "/awsiotbook/deviceDefender/cloudExploitationMetrics",
        json.dumps(metrics_data),
        1,
    )
    print(f"Published: {json.dumps(metrics_data)}")
    time.sleep(10)  # Send message every 10 seconds
```

Once the file is placed, run the code with the following command to start generating the anomaly:

```
python3 cloudExploitationThing.py
```

We will see the output shown in Figure 10-24, generating the anomaly.

```
syed-book:~/environment/chapter10/Exploitation-of-Cloud-Infrastructure $ python3 cloudExploitationThing.py
Published: {"Message": "This message is crafted to be larger than 100 bytes for demonstration purposes. Extra
Published: {"Message": "This message is crafted to be larger than 100 bytes for demonstration purposes. Extra
Published: {"Message": "This message is crafted to be larger than 100 bytes for demonstration purposes. Extra
```

Figure 10-24. *AWS Cloud 9 terminal output*

We can see an email being dispatched upon device causing violation (see Figure 10-25).

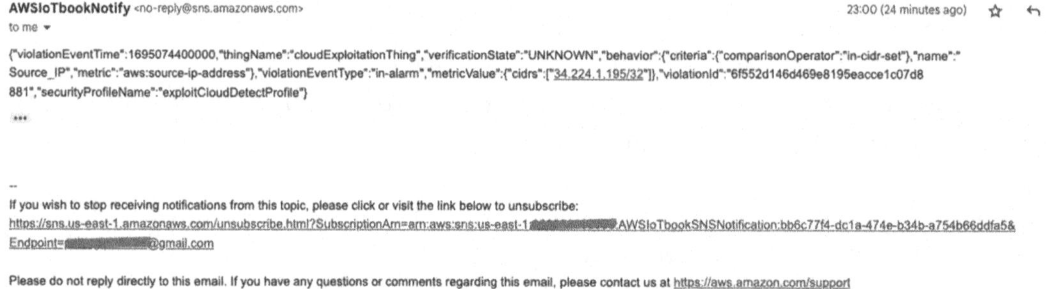

Figure 10-25. *Email notifying of an IoT thing creating violation*

View Alarm State and Mitigate Device

From the AWS IoT Core console, navigate to the "*Manage*" section, then

- Under Security
- Detect
- Alarms

We will be able to see things in the Alarm "*Active*" state, and we can start our "*mitigation action*" (see Figure 10-26).

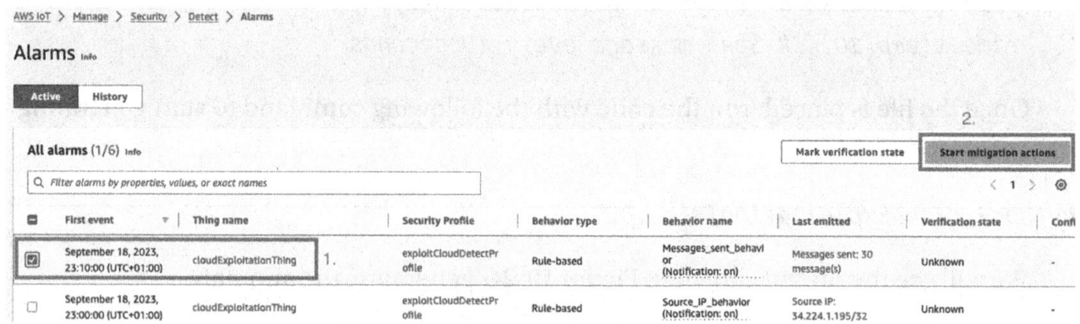

Figure 10-26. *Thing in Alarm state and mitigation action option*

After selecting "*Start mitigation actions*," our thing "*cloudExploitationThing*" will appear. We can choose the "*Isolate_device*" mitigation action and then click "*Start*" (see Figure 10-27). By doing this, we successfully isolate or quarantine the device in our "*Quarantine_group*," completely denying it AWS IoT access.

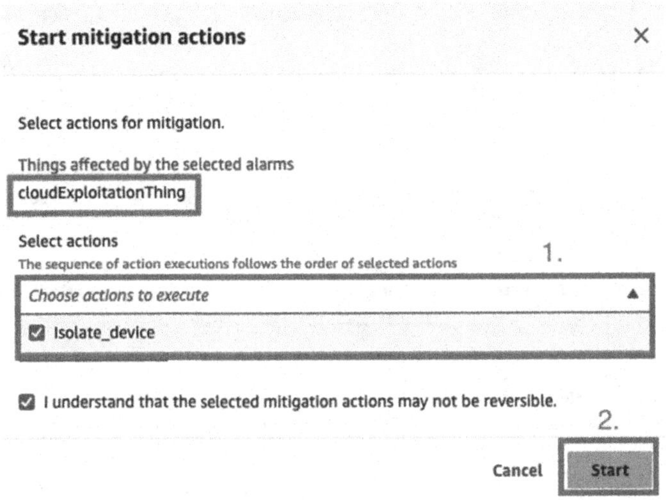

Start mitigation actions

Select actions for mitigation.

Things affected by the selected alarms

cloudExploitationThing

Select actions

The sequence of action executions follows the order of selected actions

1.

Choose actions to execute

Isolate_device

I understand that the selected mitigation actions may not be reversible.

2.

Cancel Start

Figure 10-27. *Starting mitigation action*

From the AWS IoT console, navigate to Thing groups (under the "*Manage*" section) and select "*Quarantine_group*", and from the "*Things*" tab, we will see our device in "*Quarantine_group*" (see Figure 10-28).

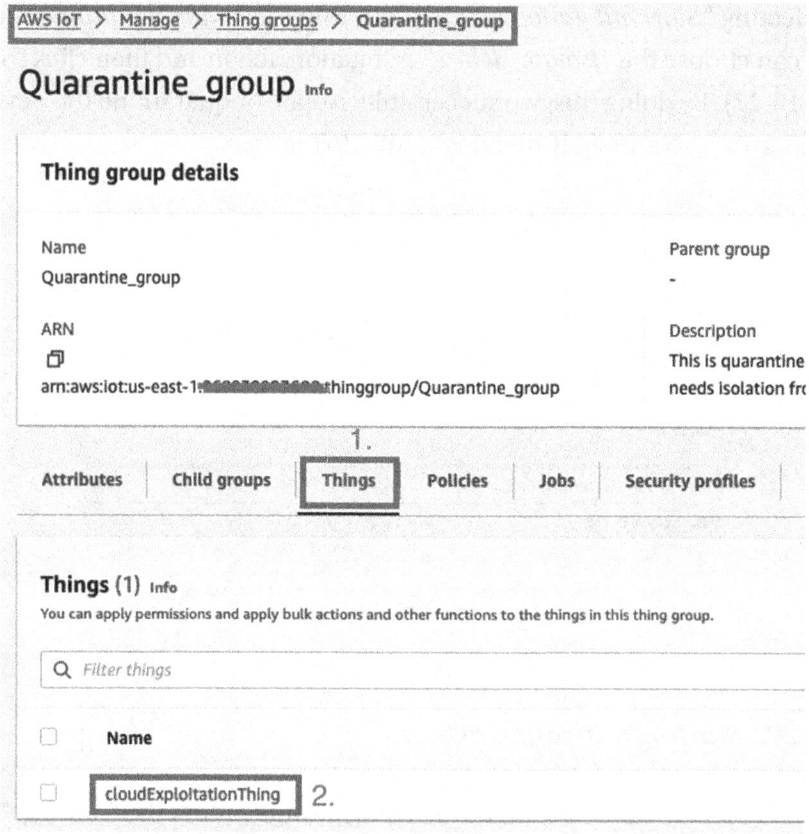

Figure 10-28. *We can see our device in the group.*

After quarantining the device, let's attempt to reconnect our "*cloudExploitationThing*" to AWS IoT Core. If it was connected earlier, disconnect and then try to reconnect. Upon trying, we will see that the connection request is denied, confirming that our mitigation action has been successful on denying any further connection request post quarantine action.

This isolation allows for a thorough "*investigation, verification, and rectification*" process. This process might involve establishing a secure SSH tunnel to the device or even restoring the device to its factory state using AWS IoT Jobs, techniques we've explored in earlier chapters. Once confident in the device's restored state, you can remove it from the "*Quarantine_group*" (as illustrated in Figure 10-29). Restarting the Python script afterward will permit the device to resume sending messages to AWS IoT Core (verify by subscribing to the topic: */awsiotbook/deviceDefender/cloudExploitationMetrics*).

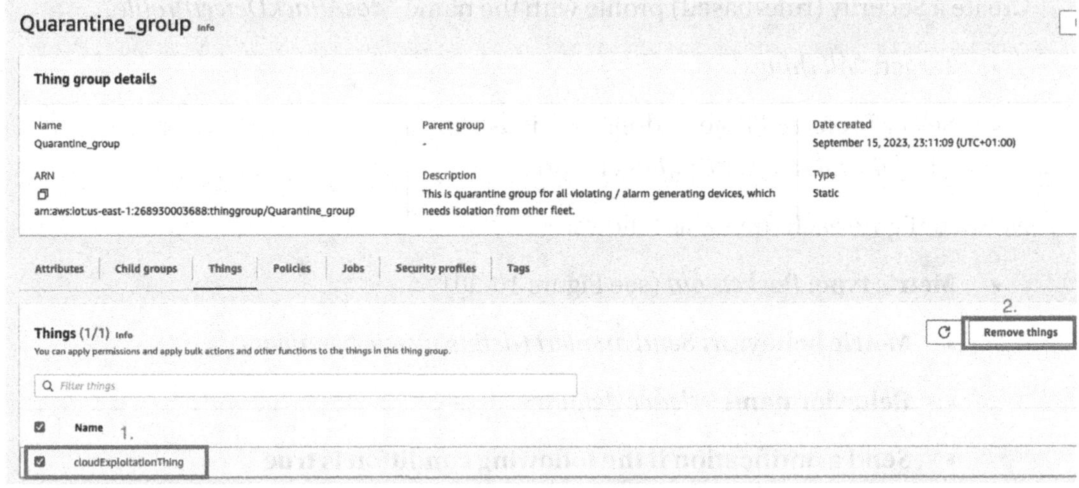

Figure 10-29. *Removing the device from the isolation (Quarantine)*

Denial-of-Service Attack (Device-Side and Cloud-Side Metrics, Manual Mitigation)

In simulating a DoS attack for our AWS IoT Device Defender profile, we'll incorporate ten metrics. This will provide a blend of device-side and cloud-side metrics, which, upon breaching their thresholds, will trigger an alarm.

Metric count	Metric type	Metric name
1	Device side	Packets out (outbound packets from a device)
2	Device side	Bytes out (outbound bytes from a device)
3	Device side	Destination IP (a device connecting to non-approved IPs)
4	Device side	Listening TCP ports (a device's open TCP ports count)
5	Device side	Listening TCP port count (number of TCP ports the device is listening on)
6	Device side	Listening UDP ports (number of UDP ports the device is listening on)
7	Device side	Listening UDP port count (a device's open UDP ports count)
8	Cloud side	Number of messages received
9	Cloud side	Message size
10	Cloud side	Source IP

Create a Security (rule-based) profile with the name *"dosAttackDetectProfile."*

- Target: *"All things".*
- Select Topic and Role as done previously in *"exploitCloudDetectProfile"* creation.

Now, configure each metric as follows:

- **Metric type:** *Packets out* (see Figure 10-30)
    - **Metric behavior:** *Send an alert (define metric behavior)*
    - **Behavior name:** *<leave default>*
    - **Send a notification if the following condition is true**
        - *Packets out is greater than*
        - *Absolute, 50*
    - **Send an alert when the condition has been met after** *1 consecutive occurrence.*
    - **Clear the alarm when the condition has no longer been met after** *1 consecutive occurrence.*
    - Click *"Add Metric".*

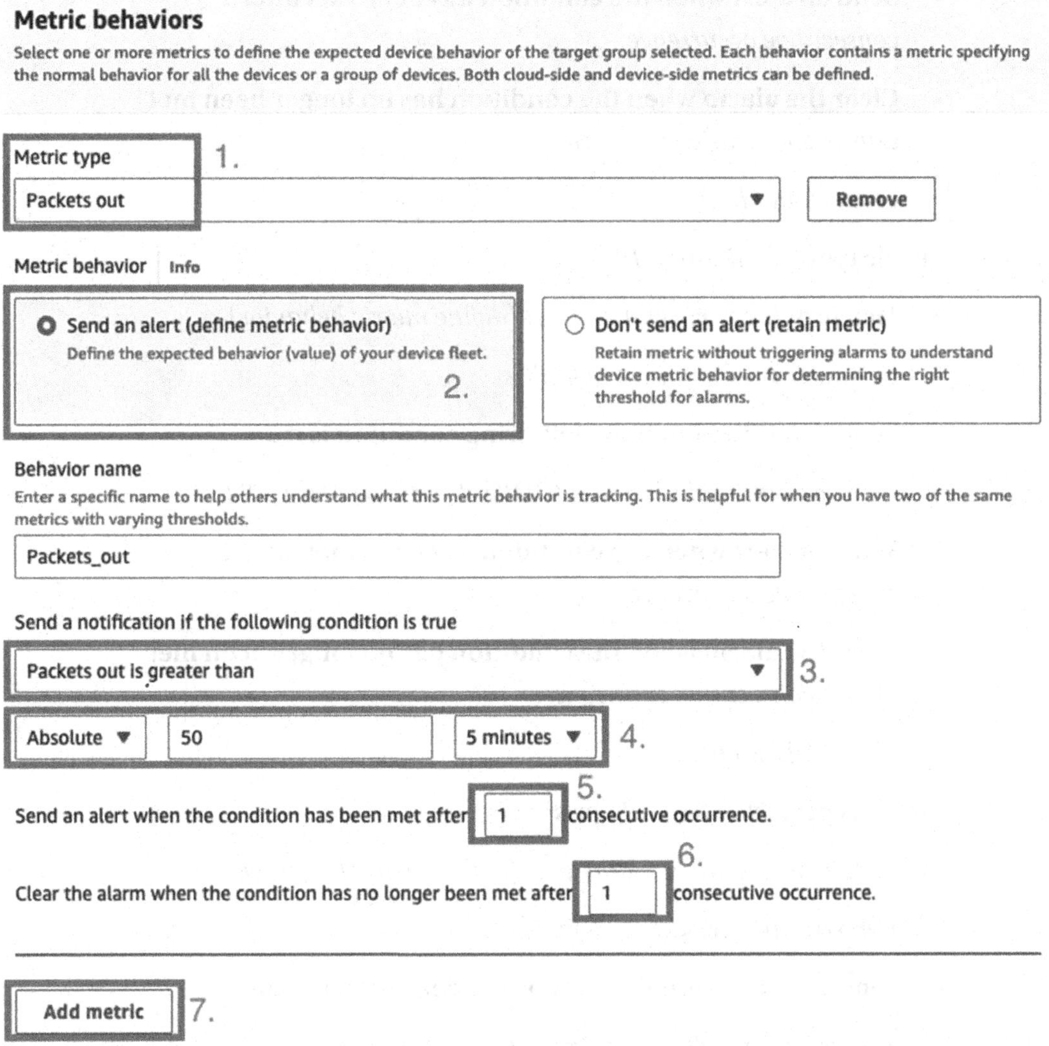

Metric behaviors

Select one or more metrics to define the expected device behavior of the target group selected. Each behavior contains a metric specifying the normal behavior for all the devices or a group of devices. Both cloud-side and device-side metrics can be defined.

Metric type 1.

Packets out ▼ Remove

Metric behavior Info

Send an alert (define metric behavior)
Define the expected behavior (value) of your device fleet. 2.

Don't send an alert (retain metric)
Retain metric without triggering alarms to understand device metric behavior for determining the right threshold for alarms.

Behavior name

Enter a specific name to help others understand what this metric behavior is tracking. This is helpful for when you have two of the same metrics with varying thresholds.

Packets_out

Send a notification if the following condition is true

Packets out is greater than ▼ 3.

Absolute ▼ 50 5 minutes ▼ 4.

Send an alert when the condition has been met after 1 consecutive occurrence. 5.

Clear the alarm when the condition has no longer been met after 1 consecutive occurrence. 6.

Add metric 7.

Figure 10-30. *Adding "Packets out" device-side metric*

- **Metric type**: *Bytes out*
    - **Metric behavior:** *Send an alert (define metric behavior)*
    - **Behavior name:** *<leave default>*
    - **Send a notification if the following condition is true**
        - *Bytes out is greater than*
        - *Absolute, 100*

- **Send an alert when the condition has been met after** *1 consecutive occurrence.*
- **Clear the alarm when the condition has no longer been met after** *1 consecutive occurrence.*
- Click "*Add Metric*".

- **Metric type:** *Destination IP*
  - **Metric behavior:** *Send an alert (define metric behavior)*
  - **Behavior name:** *<leave default>*
  - **Send a notification if the following condition is true**
    - *Destination IPs is not in CIDR set: 192.168.100.14/24*
  - **Send an alert when the condition has been met after** *1 consecutive occurrence.*
  - **Clear the alarm when the condition has no longer been met after** *1 consecutive occurrence.*
  - Click "*Add Metric*".
- **Metric type:** *Listening TCP ports*
  - **Metric behavior:** *Send an alert (define metric behavior)*
  - **Behavior name:** *<leave default>*
  - **Send a notification if the following condition is true**
    - *Listening TCP ports is in port set: 80,443,22*
  - **Send an alert when the condition has been met after** *1 consecutive occurrence.*
  - **Clear the alarm when the condition has no longer been met after** *1 consecutive occurrence.*
  - Click "*Add Metric*".

- **Metric type:** *Listening TCP port count*
    - **Metric behavior:** *Send an alert (define metric behavior)*
    - **Behavior name:** *<leave default>*
    - **Send a notification if the following condition is true**
        - *Listening TCP port count is greater than or equals: Absolute: 1*
    - **Send an alert when the condition has been met after** *1 consecutive occurrence.*
    - **Clear the alarm when the condition has no longer been met after** *1 consecutive occurrence.*
    - Click "*Add Metric*".
- **Metric type:** *Listening UDP ports*
    - **Metric behavior:** *Send an alert (define metric behavior)*
    - **Behavior name:** *<leave default>*
    - **Send a notification if the following condition is true**
        - *Listening UDP ports is in port set: 53, 123*
    - **Send an alert when the condition has been met after** *1 consecutive occurrence.*
    - **Clear the alarm when the condition has no longer been met after** *1 consecutive occurrence.*
    - Click "*Add Metric*".
- **Metric type:** *Listening UDP port count*
    - **Metric behavior:** *Send an alert (define metric behavior)*
    - **Behavior name:** *<leave default>*
    - **Send a notification if the following condition is true**
        - *Listening UDP port count is greater than or equals: Absolute: 1*
    - **Send an alert when the condition has been met after** *1 consecutive occurrence.*

- **Clear the alarm when the condition has no longer been met after** *1 consecutive occurrence.*
- Click *"Add Metric".*

- **Metric type:** *Messages received*
    - **Metric behavior:** *Send an alert (define metric behavior)*
    - **Behavior name:** *<leave default>*
    - **Send a notification if the following condition is true**
        - *Messages received is greater than: Absolute: 100*
    - **Send an alert when the condition has been met after** *1 consecutive occurrence.*
    - **Clear the alarm when the condition has no longer been met after** *1 consecutive occurrence.*
    - Click *"Add Metric".*
- **Metric type:** *Source IP*
    - **Metric behavior:** *Send an alert (define metric behavior)*
    - **Behavior name:** *<leave default>*
    - **Send a notification if the following condition is true**
        - *Source IP is not in CIDR set: 192.168.99.0/24*
    - **Send an alert when the condition has been met after** *1 consecutive occurrence.*
    - **Clear the alarm when the condition has no longer been met after** *1 consecutive occurrence.*
    - Click *"Add Metric"*
- **Metric type**: *Message size*
    - **Metric behavior:** *Send an alert (define metric behavior)*
    - **Behavior name:** *<leave default>*
    - **Send a notification if the following condition is true**
        - *Message size is greater than or equals: Absolute: 150*

- **Send an alert when the condition has been met after** *1 consecutive occurrence.*
- **Clear the alarm when the condition has no longer been met after** *1 consecutive occurrence.*
- Click "*Next*".

Now that we have a security profile in place, obtain the script "createsimulatedDoSAttackThing.sh" and its associated Python script "simulatedDoSAttackThing.py" (obtain from Chapter 10 of the book's (*folder: Denial-of-service-attack*) GitHub or use the content from here for Python script).

Create our IoT thing by using following command:

```
chmod +x createsimulatedDoSAttackThing.sh
./createsimulatedDoSAttackThing.sh
```

Retrieve the file from the book's GitHub. If you choose to create a new file instead, populate it with the content provided here, ensuring you replace "REPLACE_HERE" with your specific AWS IoT Endpoint:

```
import json
import random
import time

from AWSIoTPythonSDK.MQTTLib import AWSIoTMQTTClient

# AWS IoT Core endpoint
iot_endpoint = "REPLACE_HERE"

# AWS IoT Thing Name
thing_name = "simulatedDoSAttackThing"

# Path to the certificates and private key in the same folder as the script
cert_path = "./certificate.pem.crt"
key_path = "./private.pem.key"
root_ca_path = "./AmazonRootCA1.pem"
```

```
# Initialize AWS IoT MQTT Client
mqtt_client = AWSIoTMQTTClient(thing_name)
mqtt_client.configureEndpoint(iot_endpoint, 8883)
mqtt_client.configureCredentials(root_ca_path, key_path, cert_path)

# Connect to AWS IoT
mqtt_client.connect()

def generate_anomaly_metrics():
    # Simulating values that breach the AWS IoT Device Defender metrics.
    message_content = "This is a message content crafted to breach the
    message size threshold. It is intentionally verbose and redundant
    to ensure that the content size exceeds 150 bytes. This is done to
    simulate a potential anomaly in the IoT Device Defender metrics."

    return {
        # Device side metrics
        "PacketsOut": random.randint(51, 100),  # Exceeds the
        threshold of 50
        "BytesOut": random.randint(101, 200),  # Exceeds the
        threshold of 100
        "DestinationIP": "10.0.0.10",  # Outside of CIDR 192.168.100.14/24
        "ListeningTCPPorts": [80, 443, 22],
        "ListeningTCPPortCount": 3,
        "ListeningUDPPorts": [53, 123],
        "ListeningUDPPortCount": 2,
        # Cloud side metrics
        "NumberOfMessagesReceived": 150,  # Exceeds the threshold of 100
        "MessageSize": len(message_content),  # Exceeds the threshold of
        150 bytes
        "SourceIP": f"10.{random.randint(0,255)}.{random.randint(0,255)}.
        {random.randint(0,255)}",  # Outside of CIDR 192.168.99.0/24
        "Message": message_content,
    }
```

```
# Infinite loop to publish metrics data
while True:
    anomaly_metrics = generate_anomaly_metrics()
    mqtt_client.publish(
        "/awsiotbook/deviceDefender/dosMetrics", json.dumps(anomaly_
        metrics), 1
    )
    print(f"Published: {json.dumps(anomaly_metrics)}")
    time.sleep(10)  # Send message every 10 seconds
```

Run the file with following command:

```
python3 simulatedDoSAttackThing.py
```

After executing the script, alarms will begin to trigger immediately for metrics like Source IP. For time-based metrics, expect alarms to surface after a five-minute interval (see Figure 10-31).

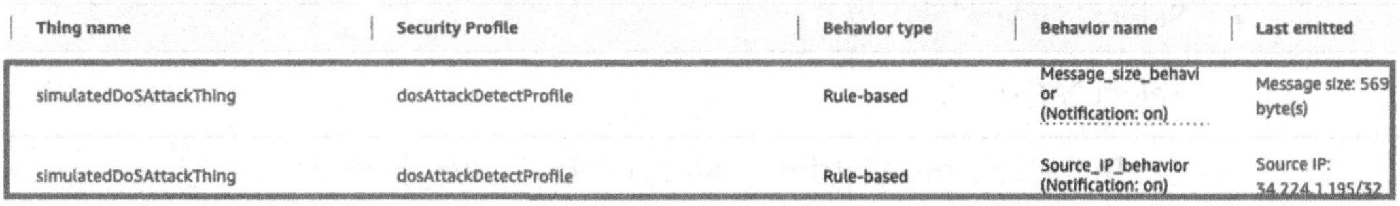

Thing name	Security Profile	Behavior type	Behavior name	Last emitted
simulatedDoSAttackThing	dosAttackDetectProfile	Rule-based	Message_size_behavior (Notification: on)	Message size: 569 byte(s)
simulatedDoSAttackThing	dosAttackDetectProfile	Rule-based	Source_IP_behavior (Notification: on)	Source IP: 34.224.1.195/32

Figure 10-31. *Alarm raised for our DoS simulated thing*

Similar to our previous security profile, we have the option to "*Quarantine the device*". Subsequently, we can proceed with the "*Investigation, verification, and rectification*" steps, restoring the device once it's rectified.

Crypto-jacking Through IoT Devices (Device-Side and Custom Metrics, Automated Mitigation)

Let's explore our final scenario, which predominantly involves custom device-side metrics, given the nature of the attack: *crypto-mining.*

Metric count	Metric type	Metric name
1	Device side	Destination IP
2	Device side (custom)	CPU usage
3	Device side (custom)	Memory usage
4	Device side (custom)	ASIC Chip temperature
5	Device side (custom)	Voltage
6	Cloud side	Source IP

Create a Custom Metric

We will need to create our four custom metrics; to do this, let's navigate from the "*Manage*" section:

- Select "*Security*".
    - Select "*Detect*".
    - Select "*Metrics*".
        - In the Custom Metrics section, click "*Create*" (see Figure 10-32).

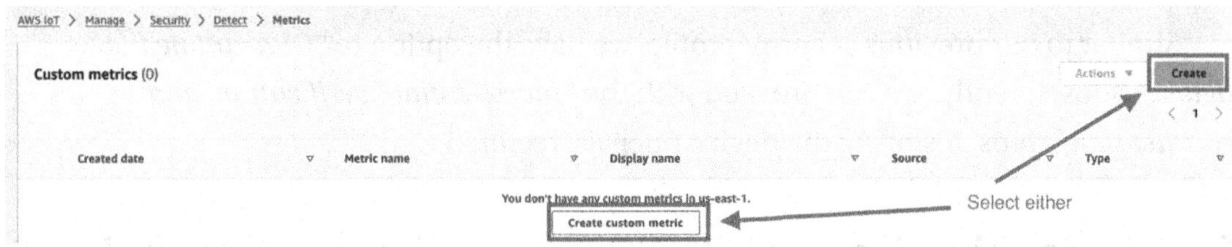

***Figure 10-32.** Creating a custom metric*

Set up the custom metrics using the details provided here (see Figure 10-33):

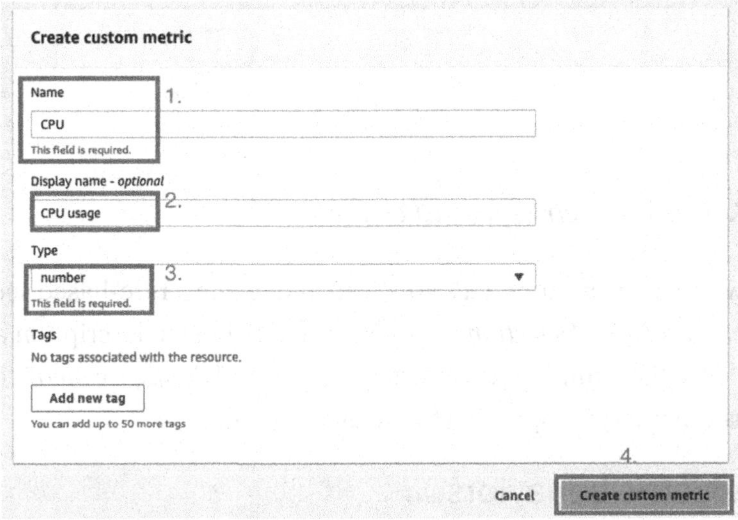

***Figure 10-33.** Creating a custom metric*

Name: CPU
Display name: CPU usage
Type: *number*
Then **click** "*Create custom metric*".
Repeat the process again for rest of the metrics as follows:
Name: Memory
Display name: Memory usage
Type: *number*
Then **click** "*Create custom metric*".
Name: ChipTemperature
Display name: ASIC Chip temperature
Type: *number*
Then **click** "*Create custom metric*".
Name: Voltage
Display name: Voltage
Type: *number*
Then **click** "*Create custom metric*".
We will see our newly created custom metrics (see Figure 10-34).

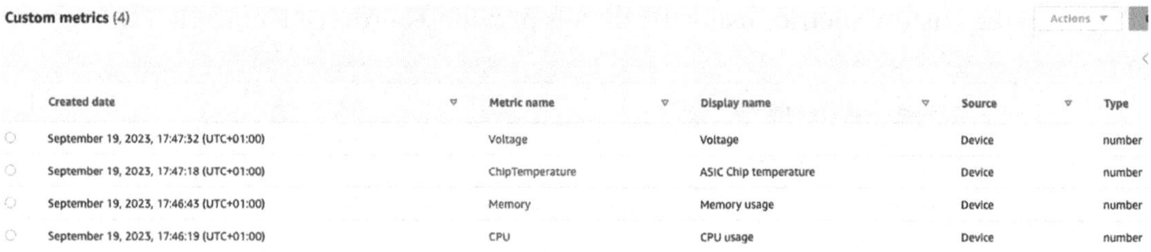

Figure 10-34. *Custom metrics we just created*

Now that we have the metrics, let's go ahead and create a rule-based security profile and name it "*cryptoJackingDetectionProfile*"; give your chosen description and target to "*All things*". Select SNS configuration as prior profiles. In "*Configure metric behaviors*", we will see our custom metrics appearing (see Figure 10-35).

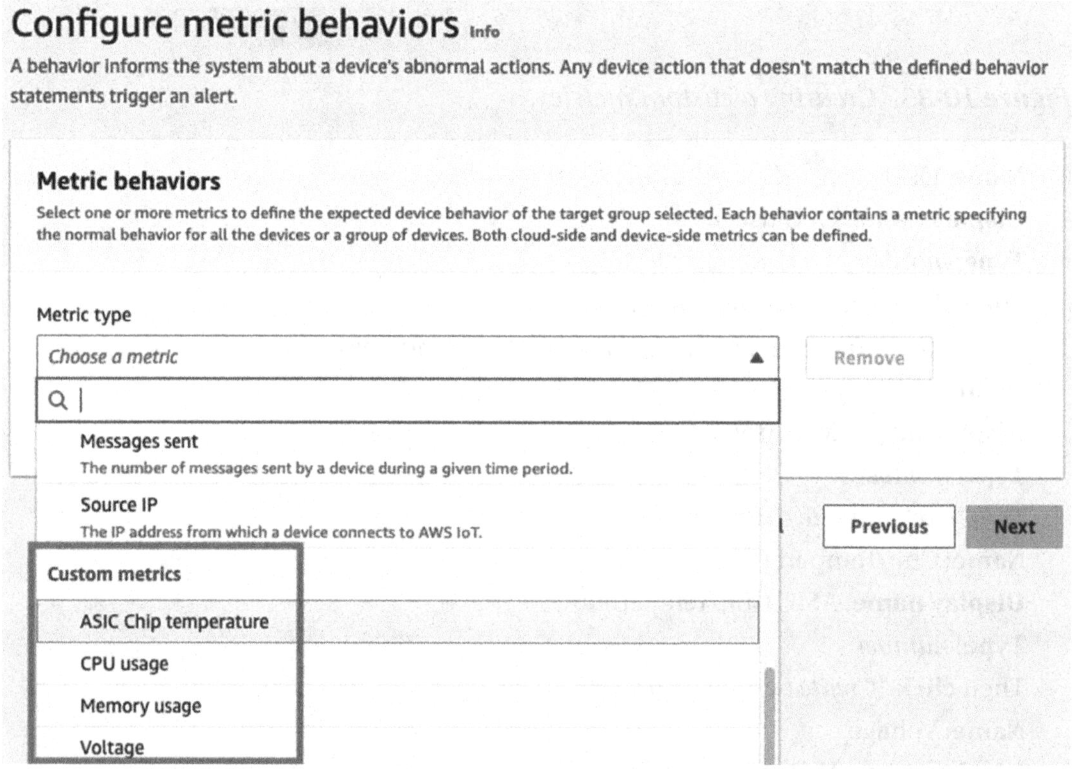

Figure 10-35. *Custom metrics we will use in our security profile*

Create the metric behaviors as follows:

- **Metric type (Device)**: *Destination IPs*
    - **Metric behavior:** *Send an alert (define metric behavior)*
    - **Behavior name:** *<leave default>*
    - **Send a notification if the following condition is true.**
        - *Destination IPs is not in CIDR set: 192.168.101.0/24*
    - **Send an alert when the condition has been met after** *1 consecutive occurrence.*
    - **Clear the alarm when the condition has no longer been met after** *1 consecutive occurrence.*
    - Click *"Add Metric".*
- **Metric type (Custom):** *CPU*
    - **Metric behavior:** *Send an alert (define metric behavior)*
    - **Behavior name:** *<leave default>*
    - **Send a notification if the following condition is true.**
        - *CPU Usage is greater than or equals: Absolute: 80, 5 minutes*
    - **Send an alert when the condition has been met after** *1 consecutive occurrence.*
    - **Clear the alarm when the condition has no longer been met after** *1 consecutive occurrence.*
    - Click *"Add Metric".*
- **Metric type (Custom)**: *Memory*
    - **Metric behavior:** *Send an alert (define metric behavior)*
    - **Behavior name:** *<leave default>*
    - **Send a notification if the following condition is true.**
        - *Memory Usage is greater than or equals: Absolute: 75, 5 minutes*

- **Send an alert when the condition has been met after** *1 consecutive occurrence.*
- **Clear the alarm when the condition has no longer been met after** *1 consecutive occurrence.*
- Click *"Add Metric".*

- **Metric type (Custom)**: *ChipTemperature*
  - **Metric behavior:** *Send an alert (define metric behavior)*
  - **Behavior name:** *<leave default>*
  - **Send a notification if the following condition is true.**
    - *ASIC Chip temperature is greater than or equals: Absolute: 100, 5 minutes*
  - **Send an alert when the condition has been met after** *1 consecutive occurrence.*
  - **Clear the alarm when the condition has no longer been met after** *1 consecutive occurrence.*
  - Click *"Add Metric".*
- **Metric type (Device)**: *Source IP*
  - **Metric behavior:** *Send an alert (define metric behavior)*
  - **Behavior name:** *<leave default>*
  - **Send a notification if the following condition is true.**
    - *Source IPs is not in CIDR set: 192.168.99.0/24*
  - **Send an alert when the condition has been met after** *1 consecutive occurrence.*
  - **Clear the alarm when the condition has no longer been met after** *1 consecutive occurrence.*
  - Click *"Add Metric".*
- **Metric type (Custom):** *Voltage*
  - **Metric behavior:** *Send an alert (define metric behavior)*

- **Behavior name:** *<leave default>*
- **Send a notification if the following condition is true.**
    - *Voltage is greater than: Absolute: 3, 5 minutes*
- **Send an alert when the condition has been met after** *1 consecutive occurrence.*
- **Clear the alarm when the condition has no longer been met after** *1 consecutive occurrence.*
- Click "*Next*".

In the "*Review and Create*" screen, we will see our metric behavior and create the profile.

Now that we have the profile in place, let's run the IoT thing creation script and python script (obtained from Chapter 10 of the book's GitHub – *folder: Crypto-jacking-through-IoT-Devices*). If you created the file manually, you can use the content from here.

Let's first create our IoT thing (place the script in your environment and run the command):

```
chmod +x createsimulateCryptoJackingThing.sh
./createsimulateCryptoJackingThing.sh
```

For the Simulation Python script (download the file from GitHub: *simulateCryptoJackingThing.py*) or for manual creation, use the content as follows:

```
import json
import random
import time

from AWSIoTPythonSDK.MQTTLib import AWSIoTMQTTClient

# AWS IoT Core endpoint
iot_endpoint = "REPLACE_HERE"  # Replace with your AWS IoT Endpoint URL

# AWS IoT Thing Name
thing_name = "simulateCryptoJackingThing"

# Path to the certificates and private key in the same folder as the script
cert_path = "./certificate.pem.crt"
key_path = "./private.pem.key"
```

```
root_ca_path = "./AmazonRootCA1.pem"

# Initialize AWS IoT MQTT Client
mqtt_client = AWSIoTMQTTClient(thing_name)
mqtt_client.configureEndpoint(iot_endpoint, 8883)
mqtt_client.configureCredentials(root_ca_path, key_path, cert_path)

# Connect to AWS IoT
mqtt_client.connect()

def generate_cryptojacking_metrics():
    return {
        "DestinationIP": f"10.{random.randint(0,255)}.{random.
        randint(0,255)}.{random.randint(0,255)}",  # Always outside of CIDR
        192.168.101.0/24
        "CPUUsage": random.uniform(81, 100),  # Always greater than 80
        "MemoryUsage": random.uniform(76, 95),  # Always greater than 75
        "ASICChipTemperature": random.randint(101, 120),  # Always greater
        than 100
        "Voltage": random.uniform(3.1, 3.5),  # Always greater than 3
    }

# Infinite loop to publish cryptojacking metrics
while True:
    cryptojacking_metrics = generate_cryptojacking_metrics()
    mqtt_client.publish(
        "/awsiotbook/deviceDefender/cryptojackingMetrics",
        json.dumps(cryptojacking_metrics),
        1,
    )
    print(f"Published: {json.dumps(cryptojacking_metrics)}")
    time.sleep(10)  # Send message every 10 seconds
```

Once the file is in place, let's run using the following command and see Alarm states being raised:

```
python3 simulateCryptoJackingThing.py
```

Once five minutes has passed, we will see Alarms appearing and our device being detected by Security Profile "*cryptoJackingDetectionProfile*" (see Figure 10-36).

September 19, 2023, 18:25:00 (UTC+01:00)	simulateCryptoJackingThing	cryptoJackingDetectionProfile	Rule-based

Figure 10-36. *Alarm being generated for our simulated device*

Machine Learning with ML Detect

So far, we looked at rule-based "*Security Profile*"; let's create "*ML anomaly Detect profile*" (see Figure 10-37).

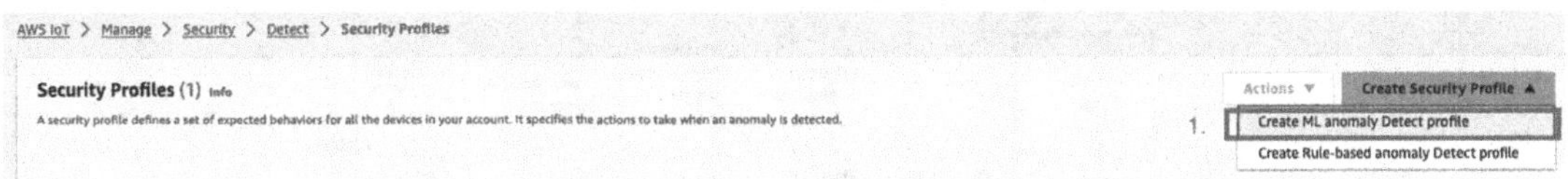

Figure 10-37. *Creating an ML-based security profile*

Populate the details as follows (see Figure 10-38):

- Target: *"All things*
- Security Profile name: *"awsiotbookMLProfile"*
- Description: *"My First ML Detect profile"*
- Metrics, select from the drop-down. Select "*All Cloud side metrics"* as well as "*All Device side metrics"* (you can also select Custom metrics if you prefer to add them too).

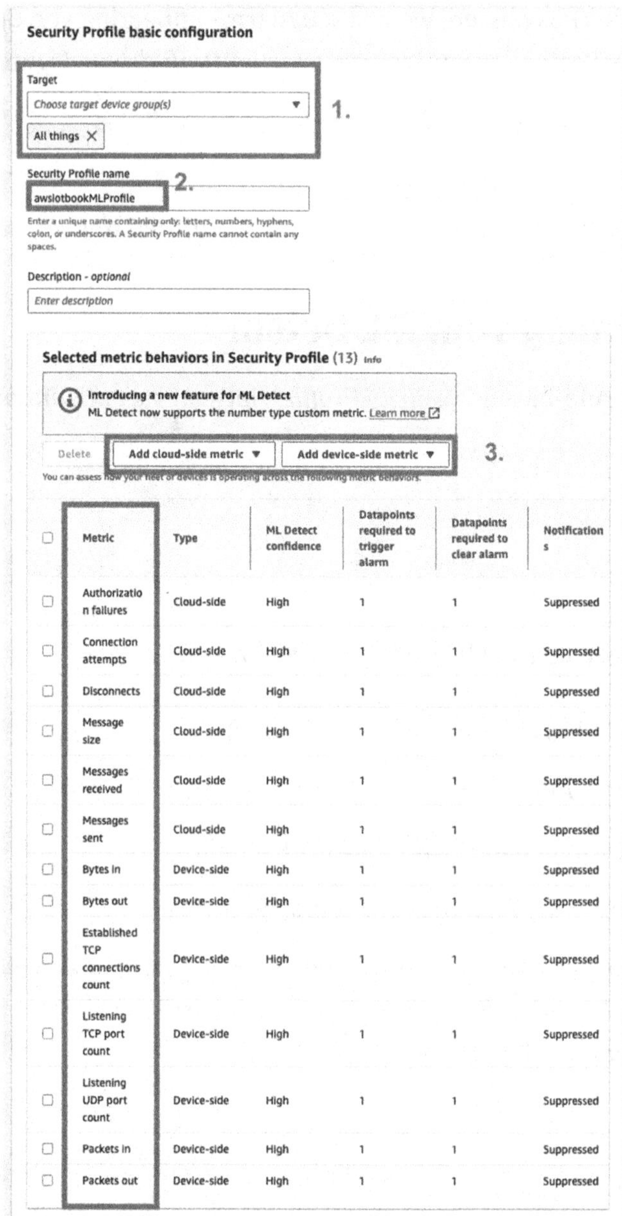

Figure 10-38. *ML detects metric selection*

In the Edit metric behaviors screen, we will have options to adjust the following (see Figure 10-39) and update the metric values accordingly:

ML Detect Confidence: The confidence level indicates the sensitivity of the ML model to anomalous behavior. High confidence results in fewer alarms due to low sensitivity, while low confidence leads to more alarms because of high sensitivity.

Datapoints to Trigger Alarm: Specifies how many data points are needed to activate an alarm.

Datapoints to Clear Alarm: Defines the number of data points required to deactivate an alarm.

Notifications: You can manage alarm notifications via Amazon SNS by choosing between Not Suppressed or Suppressed behaviors. While suppressing doesn't halt ML Detect's evaluations, suppressed alarms aren't sent as Amazon SNS notifications. Such alarms are only accessible via the AWS IoT console or specific APIs.

Type: AWS IoT Device Defender offers three standard metrics: cloud-side (reported by AWS IoT cloud services), device-side (reported by devices), and custom metrics (what we created earlier).

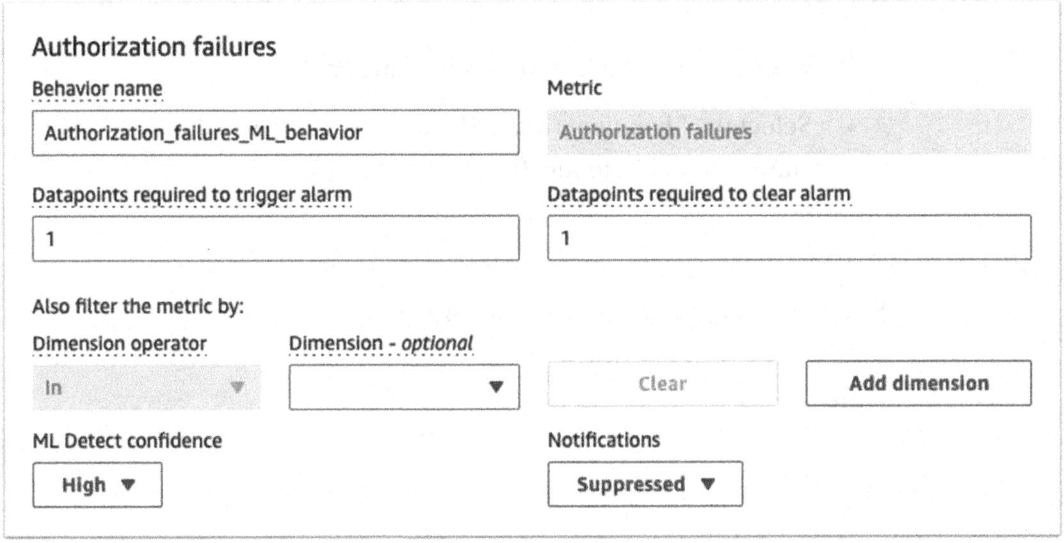

Figure 10-39. *ML Detect Metric behavior screen*

Unlike rules-detect, there's no need to modify the algorithm. The Machine Learning component of the profile automatically identifies data anomalies for each metric. If an anomalous pattern is detected, an alarm is raised. Additionally, when data points are altered, the ML model adapts to accommodate your settings; we will keep the settings default and create the profile.

Points to Note

As of the time of writing, the following data requirements apply before the ML Detect profile will be activated:

- Each metric behavior needs 14 days of training data to construct an ML model.
- Each metric behavior requires a minimum of 25,000 data points to build the ML model.
- The model is updated with new data points every 24 hours.
- If the model doesn't receive data for an extended period, it will deactivate the ML model.

From the AWS IoT Core console, navigate under the "*Manage*" section:

- Select "*Security*".
    - *"Detect"*
        - *"Security profiles"* - select *"awsiotbookMLProfile"*.
            - Select the "*Behaviors and ML training*" tab to see the status of the ML model (see Figure 10-40).

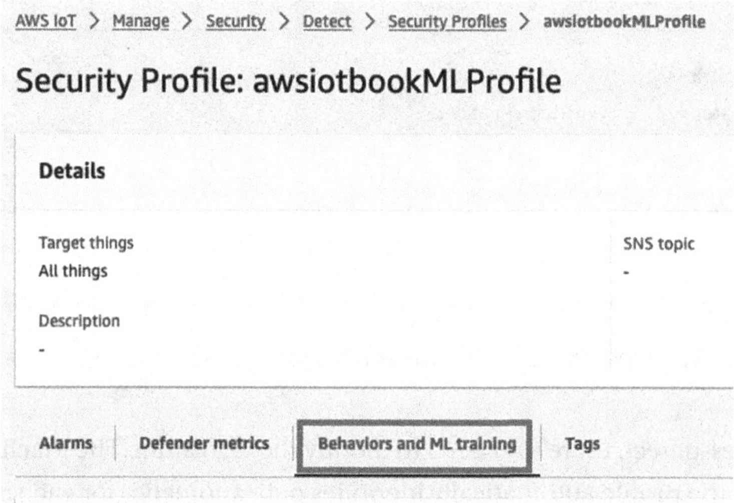

Figure 10-40. *ML model status for all metrics*

Let's examine the differences between the "*Pending build*" (see Figure 10-41) and "*Active*" (see Figure 10-42) ML models as well as understand the "*Expired*" model (see Figure 10-43).

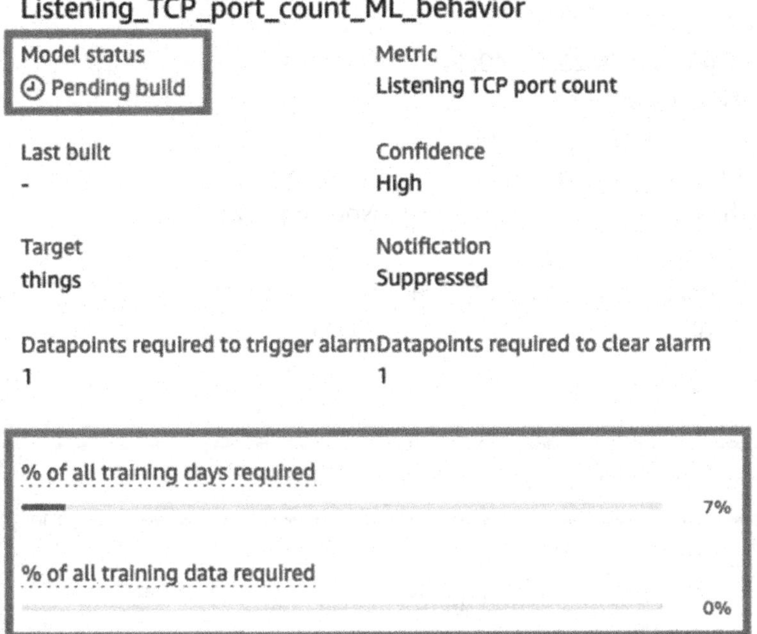

Figure 10-41. *ML Model Pending build*

Disconnects

Model status Active	Metric Disconnects
Last built August 08, 2023, 05:40:34 (UTC+01:00)	Confidence High
Target things	Notification Not suppressed
Datapoints required to trigger alarm -	Datapoints required to clear alarm -

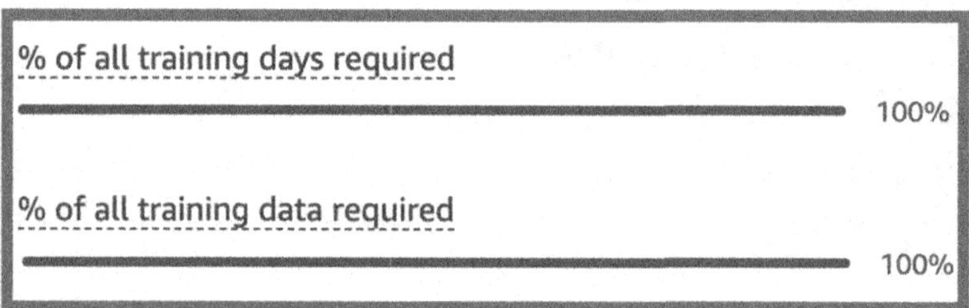

Figure 10-42. ML Model Active

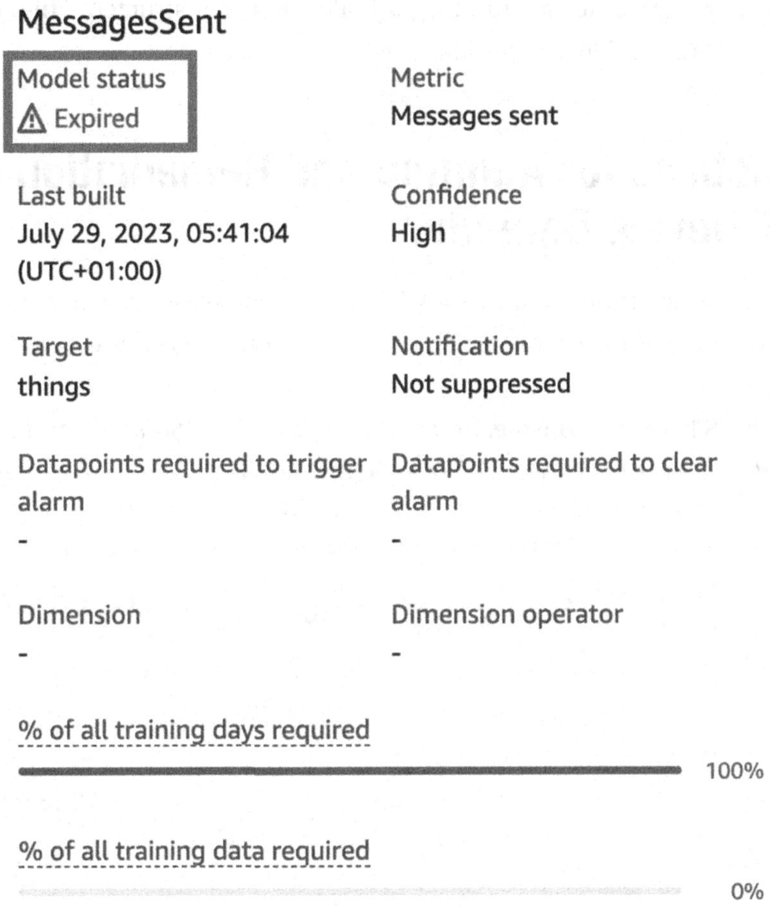

MessagesSent

Model status ⚠ Expired	Metric Messages sent
Last built July 29, 2023, 05:41:04 (UTC+01:00)	Confidence High
Target things	Notification Not suppressed
Datapoints required to trigger alarm -	Datapoints required to clear alarm -
Dimension -	Dimension operator -

% of all training days required 100%

% of all training data required 0%

Figure 10-43. *Model expired*

To test your newly created ML, detect profile, and build the model, you can use "*createsimulatedMLDetectThing.sh*" to create the MLDetectThing and also the Python script "*simulatedMLDetectThing.py*" to send the required metrics to build this model (obtain the files from Chapter 10 of the book's GitHub repository – *folder: MLDetect*).

To create the AWS IoT thing (place the file in your environment):

```
chmod +x createsimulatedMLDetectThing.sh
./createsimulatedMLDetectThing.sh
```

Execute and send metrics (place the file in the relevant folder) and execute the Python script:

```
python3 simulatedMLDetectThing.py
```

With this, we observe the data model gradually being constructed. This concludes the IoT Device Defender Security profiles section.

Best Practices for Auditing and Remediation with AWS IoT Device Defender

Now that our learning phase is complete, it's time to tighten the policies that were kept lenient for educational purposes. The best tool for this task is the AWS IoT Device Defender Audit.

From the AWS IoT Core console, under "*Manage*", select "*Security*" and then "*Audit*" and click "*Automate IoT security audit*" (see Figure 10-44).

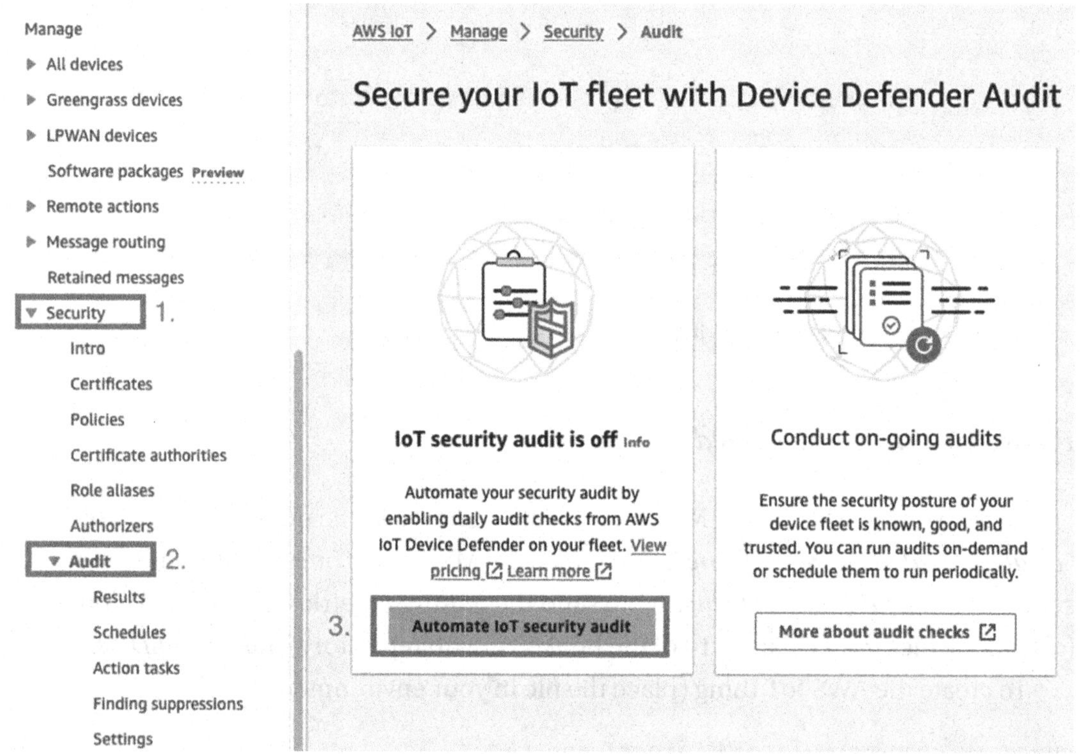

Figure 10-44. *Enabling Automated IoT security audit*

While still in the "*Audit*" section, click "*Schedules*". You will notice an audit scheduled to run daily, which is a recommended practice. However, for now, we will initiate an ad hoc audit; click "*Create*" (see Figure 10-45).

AWS IoT > Manage > Security > Audit > Schedules

Scheduled audits (1) Actions ▾ Create 1.

Name	Recurrence
AWSIoTDeviceDefenderDailyAudit	Daily

Figure 10-45. *Creating an audit*

At the time of writing, you will find 16 best practices recommended by AWS IoT, derived from our customers' feedback (see Figure 10-46). This list is continuously updated and refreshed for our AWS IoT customers, aligning with the latest best practices and security guidelines.

AWS IoT > Manage > Security > Audit > Audit Results > Audit Create

Create a new audit

Available checks (16)

Check name	Severity	Resource type
Authenticated Cognito role overly permissive	Critical	Cognito pool
CA certificate key quality	Critical	CA certificate
CA certificate revoked but device certificates still active	Critical	CA certificate
Device certificate key quality	Critical	Device certificate
Device certificate shared	Critical	Device certificate
Intermediate CA revoked for active device certificates	Critical	Issuer certificate
IoT policy overly permissive	Critical	Policy
Role alias overly permissive	Critical	Role alias
Unauthenticated Cognito role overly permissive	Critical	Cognito pool
Conflicting MQTT client IDs	High	Client ID
CA certificate expiring	Medium	CA certificate
Device certificate expiring	Medium	Device certificate
IoT policy potentially misconfigured	Medium	Policy
Revoked device certificate still active	Medium	Device certificate
Role alias allows access to unused services	Medium	Role alias
Logging disabled	Low	Account settings

Figure 10-46. *AWS IoT provided best practices for audit*

In the "*Set Schedule*" section, choose "*Run audit now (once)*" and click "*Create*". After the audit finishes, the status will display as "complete". This can take between five and ten minutes, as it performs an in-depth audit of all your IoT assets.

Once audit completes, we can see the number of noncompliant practices (see Figure 10-47).

AWS IoT > Manage > Security > Audit > Audit Results

Audit results (20+)

Name	Date	Status	Summary
On-demand 1.	September 19, 2023, 21:41:39 (UTC+01:00)	Not compliant	6 of 16 non-compliant

***Figure 10-47.** Audit compliance result*

Select the "*On-demand*" audit and see the noncompliant checks and on what metrics (see Figure 10-48).

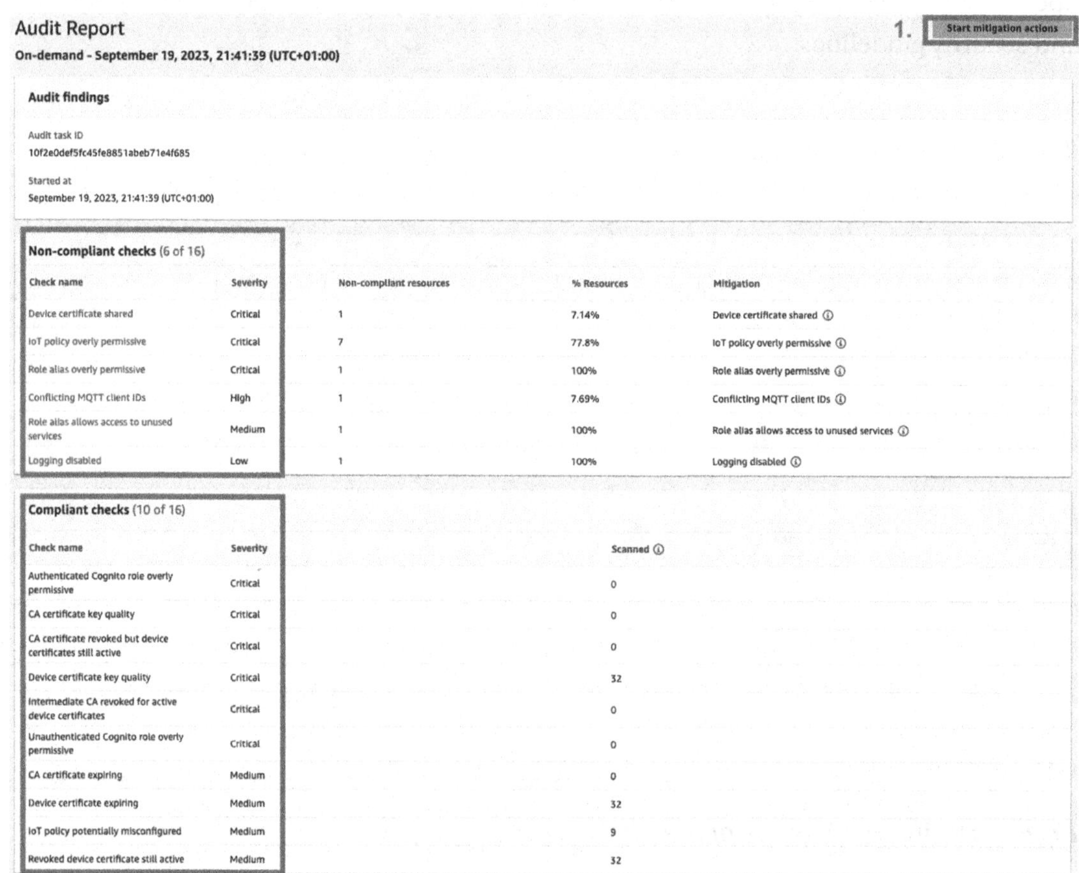

***Figure 10-48.** Noncompliant resources results*

If we select "*IoT policy overly permissive*", we will see our educational Demo policy we created in our earlier chapter (*myFirstDemoNonProductionPolicy*) (see Figure 10-49); now is the time to lock down our security posture by using mitigation actions we created earlier.

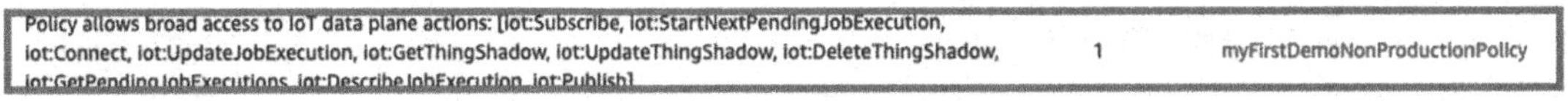

Policy allows broad access to IoT data plane actions: [iot:Subscribe, iot:StartNextPendingJobExecution, iot:Connect, iot:UpdateJobExecution, iot:GetThingShadow, iot:UpdateThingShadow, iot:DeleteThingShadow, iot:GetPendingJobExecutions, iot:DescribeJobExecution, iot:Publish]	1	myFirstDemoNonProductionPolicy

Figure 10-49. *AWS IoT Device Defender Audit Result - Non compliant check of IoT Policy is overly permissive*

Select "*Start mitigation actions*" to rectify the noncompliant assets and select from the drop-down "action codes" and "reason codes" (see Figures 10-50a and 10-50b).

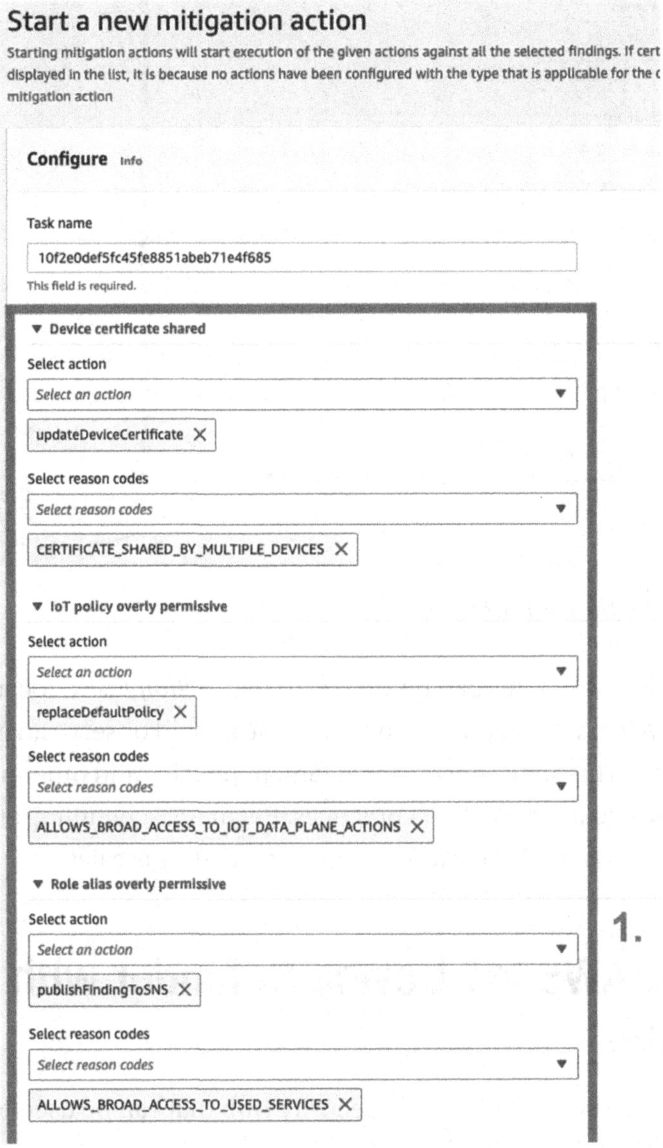

Start a new mitigation action

Starting mitigation actions will start execution of the given actions against all the selected findings. If cert displayed in the list, it is because no actions have been configured with the type that is applicable for the c mitigation action

Configure Info

Task name

10f2e0def5fc45fe8851abeb71e4f685

This field is required.

▼ Device certificate shared

Select action

Select an action

updateDeviceCertificate ✕

Select reason codes

Select reason codes

CERTIFICATE_SHARED_BY_MULTIPLE_DEVICES ✕

▼ IoT policy overly permissive

Select action

Select an action

replaceDefaultPolicy ✕

Select reason codes

Select reason codes

ALLOWS_BROAD_ACCESS_TO_IOT_DATA_PLANE_ACTIONS ✕

▼ Role alias overly permissive

Select action

Select an action

publishFindingToSNS ✕

Select reason codes

Select reason codes

ALLOWS_BROAD_ACCESS_TO_USED_SERVICES ✕

1.

Figure 10-50a. *Mitigation actions*

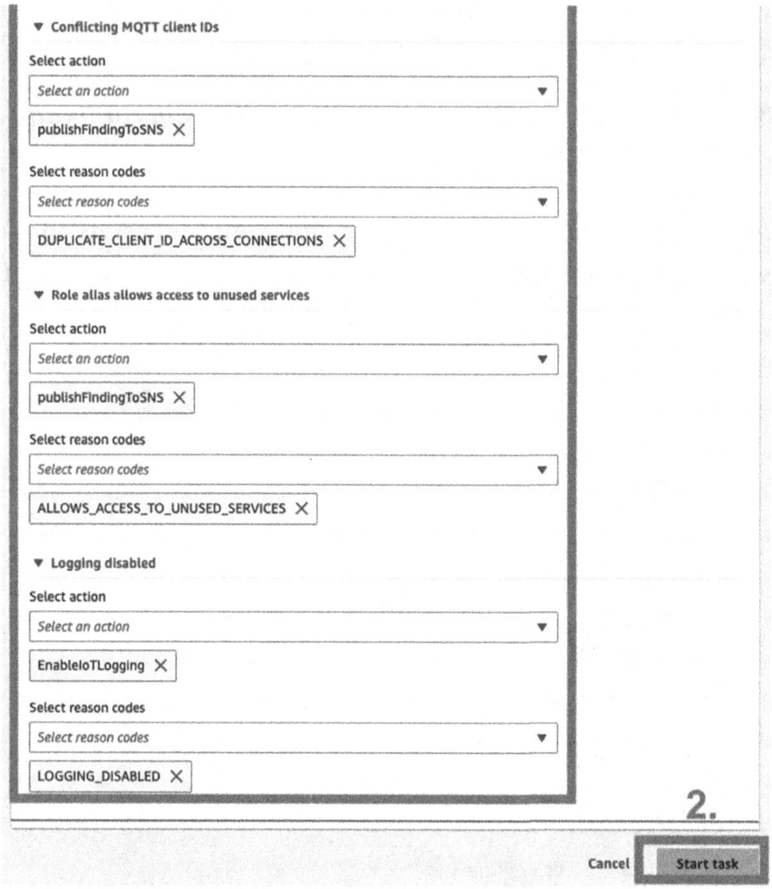

▾ Conflicting MQTT client IDs
Select action
Select an action
publishFindingToSNS ✕
Select reason codes
Select reason codes
DUPLICATE_CLIENT_ID_ACROSS_CONNECTIONS ✕
▾ Role alias allows access to unused services
Select action
Select an action
publishFindingToSNS ✕
Select reason codes
Select reason codes
ALLOWS_ACCESS_TO_UNUSED_SERVICES ✕
▾ Logging disabled
Select action
Select an action
EnableIoTLogging ✕
Select reason codes
Select reason codes
LOGGING_DISABLED ✕
2.
Cancel Start task

Figure 10-50b. *Mitigation actions (2)*

After completion, the status can be viewed in the "*Action tasks*" located under the "*Detect*" section. When we run our ad hoc again, we should observe an audit status labeled "*compliant*". This status ensures that lenient policies and other noncompliant issues are addressed to align with best practices. Regularly scheduling audits is crucial to proactively address potential security concerns before they escalate.

Integrating AWS IoT Device Defender with AWS Security Hub

AWS has a dedicated service called AWS Security Hub that can be used in augmenting AWS IoT Device Defender findings.

What Is AWS Security Hub

AWS Security Hub is a service provided by Amazon Web Services (AWS) that provides a comprehensive view of the security state of your AWS resources. It is designed to centralize and prioritize security findings from across AWS services and third-party tools, helping you to monitor security alerts and conduct security investigations more effectively.

Here are some key features of AWS Security Hub:

- **Aggregated Security Findings**

  AWS Security Hub collects and aggregates findings from AWS services such as AWS IoT Device Defender, Amazon GuardDuty, Amazon Inspector, and Amazon Macie, as well as from various AWS partner security solutions providing single pane of glass.

- **Compliance Standards**

  It continuously monitors your environment using automated security checks based on the AWS best practices and industry standards, such as the Center for Internet Security (CIS) AWS Foundations Benchmark.

- **Security Standards Insights**

  Security Hub provides insights into your security posture and helps identify resources that are not in compliance with security best practices.

- **Prioritized Findings**

  It helps you prioritize your security tasks by correlating findings across services and providers and prioritizing them to help you focus on the most critical issues.

- **Integration with Other Services**

  Security Hub integrates with various other AWS services and third-party tools, allowing you to manage and monitor security findings more effectively.

- **Custom Insights and Actions**

  You can define custom insights to help you identify and respond to security trends and patterns and take automated actions using Amazon CloudWatch Events.

In essence, AWS Security Hub offers a unified, centralized view of your security alerts and compliance status across your AWS environment, enabling easier management and monitoring of your security and compliance.

Integrate AWS IoT Device Defender with AWS Security Hub

Integrating AWS IoT Device Defender with AWS Security Hub is straightforward. Upon your first visit to the AWS Security Hub page, you will be given the option to enable checks against "*Security standards*" (see Figure 10-51). Select all of them, as they encompass a wide range of security checks, and click "*Enable Security Hub*".

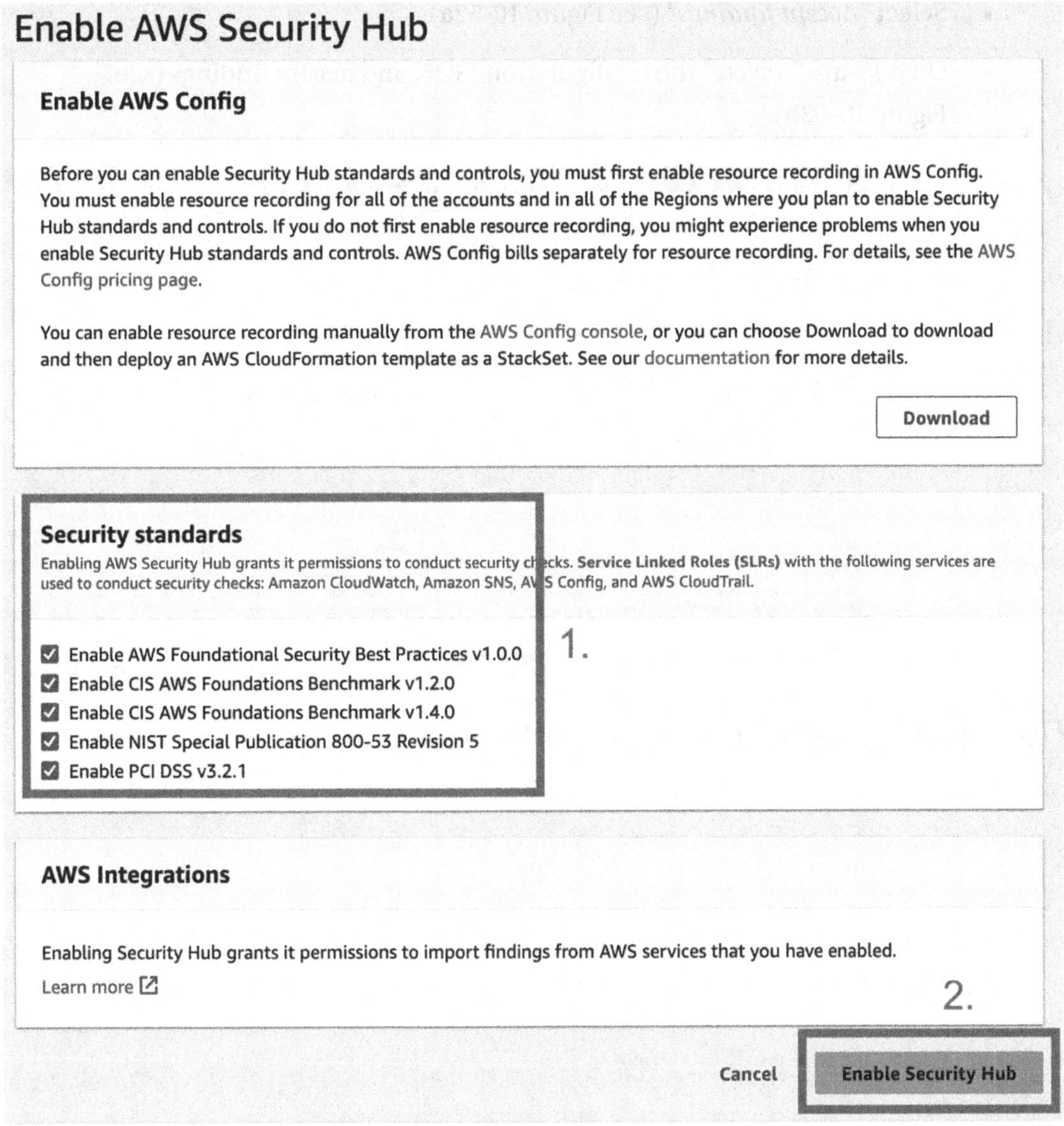

Enable AWS Security Hub

Enable AWS Config

Before you can enable Security Hub standards and controls, you must first enable resource recording in AWS Config. You must enable resource recording for all of the accounts and in all of the Regions where you plan to enable Security Hub standards and controls. If you do not first enable resource recording, you might experience problems when you enable Security Hub standards and controls. AWS Config bills separately for resource recording. For details, see the AWS Config pricing page.

You can enable resource recording manually from the AWS Config console, or you can choose Download to download and then deploy an AWS CloudFormation template as a StackSet. See our documentation for more details.

Download

Security standards

Enabling AWS Security Hub grants it permissions to conduct security checks. Service Linked Roles (SLRs) with the following services are used to conduct security checks: Amazon CloudWatch, Amazon SNS, AWS Config, and AWS CloudTrail.

1.

- [x] Enable AWS Foundational Security Best Practices v1.0.0
- [x] Enable CIS AWS Foundations Benchmark v1.2.0
- [x] Enable CIS AWS Foundations Benchmark v1.4.0
- [x] Enable NIST Special Publication 800-53 Revision 5
- [x] Enable PCI DSS v3.2.1

AWS Integrations

Enabling Security Hub grants it permissions to import findings from AWS services that you have enabled.

Learn more

2.

Cancel Enable Security Hub

Figure 10-51. *Enabling security checks*

Let's select the integration option; from the AWS Security Hub Console, select "*Integrations*" (see Figure 10-52a):

- For filter integrations: search for "*iot*".
- From the Search output, look for the following:
  - *AWS: IoT Device Defender – Audit*
  - *AWS: IoT Device Defender - Detect*

- Select "*Accept findings*" (see Figure 10-52a).
- On pop-up, "*review*" the configuration JSON and accept findings (see Figure 10-52b).

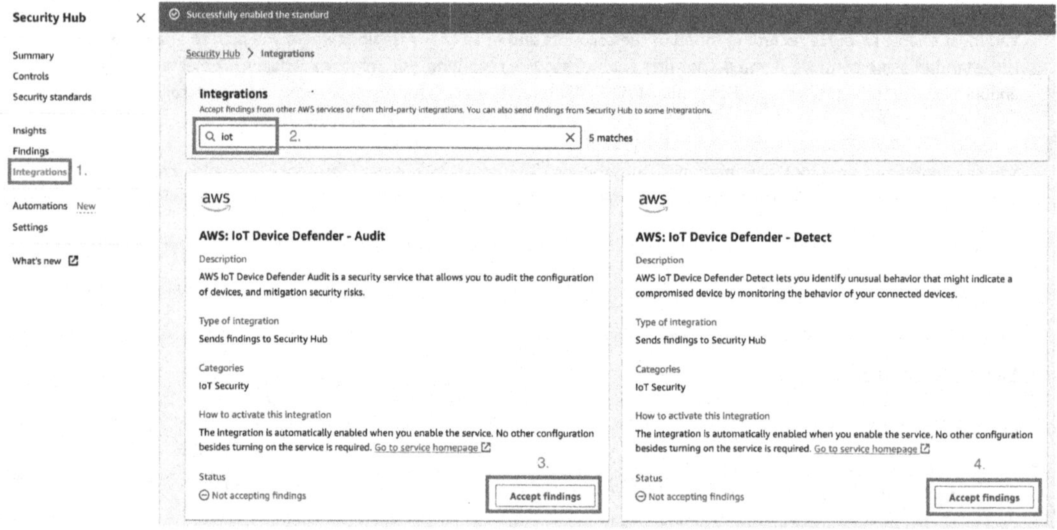

Figure 10-52a. *Searching and accepting findings*

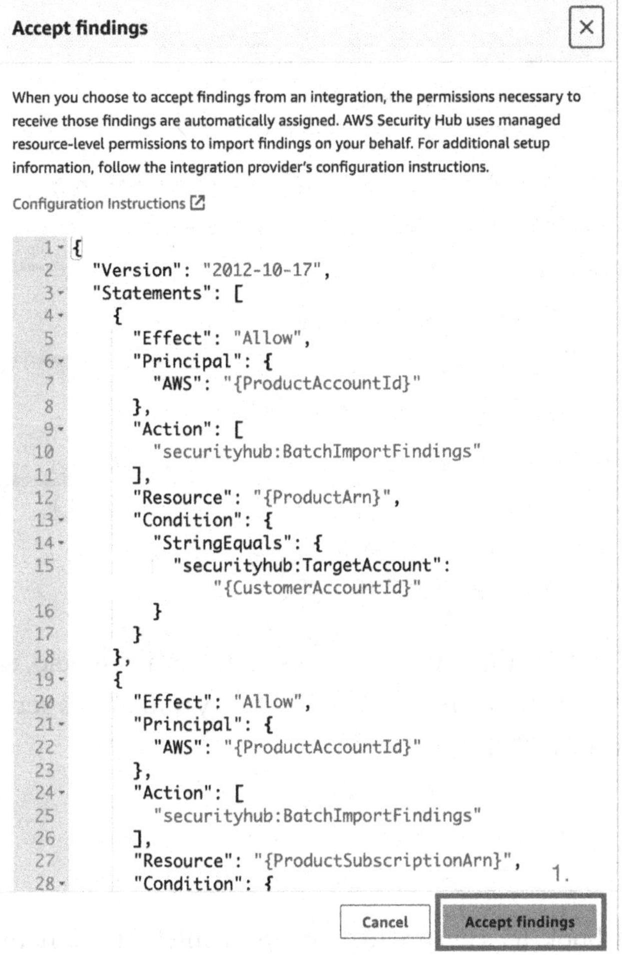
Accept findings
When you choose to accept findings from an integration, the permissions necessary to receive those findings are automatically assigned. AWS Security Hub uses managed resource-level permissions to import findings on your behalf. For additional setup information, follow the integration provider's configuration instructions.
Configuration Instructions
{
"Version": "2012-10-17",
"Statements": [
{
"Effect": "Allow",
"Principal": {
"AWS": "{ProductAccountId}"
},
"Action": [
"securityhub:BatchImportFindings"
],
"Resource": "{ProductArn}",
"Condition": {
"StringEquals": {
"securityhub:TargetAccount": "{CustomerAccountId}"
}
}
},
{
"Effect": "Allow",
"Principal": {
"AWS": "{ProductAccountId}"
},
"Action": [
"securityhub:BatchImportFindings"
],
"Resource": "{ProductSubscriptionArn}",
"Condition": {
1.
Cancel
Accept findings

***Figure 10-52b.** Reviewing configuration and accepting findings*

Along with other security check findings, we will also receive our IoT data here. We can filter the data using a plethora of "filter" options provided and organize it by order of severity too (see Figure 10-53).

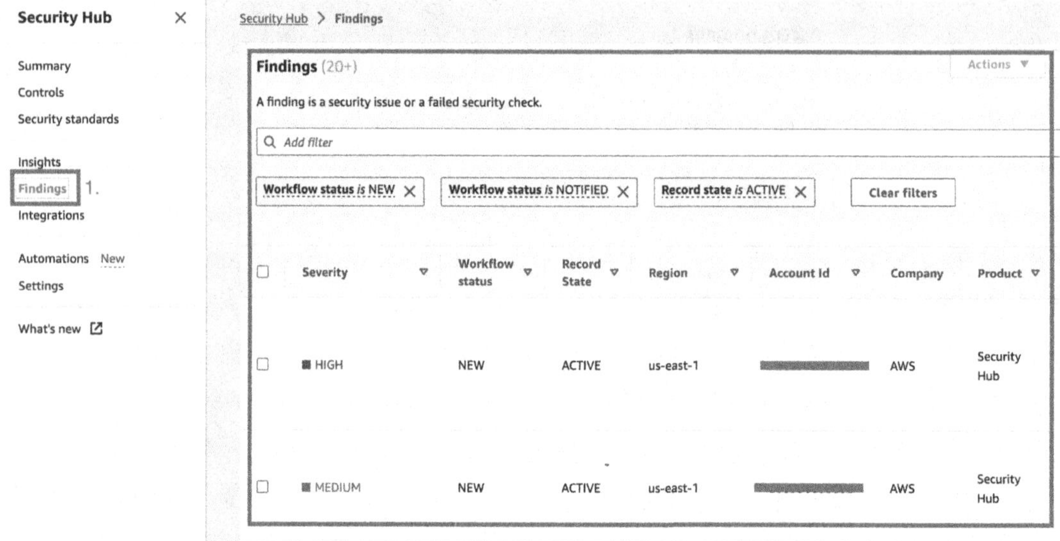

Figure 10-53. *AWS Security Hub findings*

With this, we conclude this chapter. Cybersecurity is a vast field, and AWS offers numerous tools to enhance security. AWS continually updates its services and tools to stay ahead of the security threats curve.

Clean Up

As we conclude the book, let's ensure to wrap up cleanly by terminating all AWS Cloud9 or EC2 instances set up for educational purposes. Additionally, delete IAM roles, policies, and other ancillary creations made throughout this book if not being used further for learning purposes. This prudent cleanup helps in avoiding extra costs and ensures that no unused resources are left active, reinforcing good security practices.

What You Have Learned

In this comprehensive chapter titled "Cybersecurity with AWS IoT," we undertook a deep dive into the multifaceted world of cybersecurity. Our exploration encompassed various critical subjects, ensuring you have a well-rounded understanding.

- **Introduction to Zero Trust**: We commenced our exploration by demystifying the foundational concept of Zero Trust. This included not only understanding its principles but also grasping its pivotal role in contemporary cybersecurity paradigms.
- **Aligning with NIST 800-207**: Our discussions extended into the recognized standards of NIST 800-207, detailing the guidelines they set forth. We further bridged the knowledge gap by drawing connections between these universally acclaimed guidelines and AWS IoT, illustrating how they can harmoniously align.
- **Deep Dive into AWS IoT Device Defender**: This segment was dedicated to unraveling the multitude of features offered by AWS IoT Device Defender. We meticulously dissected its capabilities, ensuring you're equipped to harness its full potential.
- **Real-World Cybersecurity Scenarios**: To ensure the applicability of our discussions, we ventured into real-world cybersecurity use cases. This deep dive aimed to showcase the practical challenges faced and how AWS IoT Device Defender could be a valuable ally. By examining how to identify and isolate anomalies through its sophisticated "Rules" and "ML" anomaly security profiles, you are now empowered to tackle real-world challenges head-on.
- **Responding to Customer Feedback:** Valuing and acting upon customer feedback are crucial. Therefore, we dedicated a section to address the main concerns expressed by customers during my interactions with them. We explored complex scenarios, from impersonation attacks to DoS attacks, offering both an overview and a hands-on approach. This blend of theory and practice ensures a holistic understanding, bridging the gap between knowledge and its real-world application.
- **Harnessing Amazon SNS for Timely Alerts**: Recognizing threats in real time can be the difference between a minor hiccup and a significant catastrophe. We explored Amazon SNS's capabilities in this context, elucidating how it can be a cornerstone in alerting mechanisms, notifying stakeholders of breaches in near real time.

- **Exploring "ML Detect" in Device Defender**: In the age of AI and ML, it was imperative to delve into the *"ML Detect"* feature. This segment illuminated its prowess in fortifying cybersecurity measures, ensuring that you can leverage cutting-edge technology in your defense strategies.
- **Best Practices**: Knowledge without direction can be overwhelming; we learned the *"Best Practices for Auditing and Remediation with AWS IoT Device Defender."* This section was curated to provide you with a clear road map, ensuring that your IoT ecosystems are not just secure but also optimized for efficiency and proactive security audits.
- **Concluding with AWS Security Hub:** AWS has vast arsenal of security services. Thus, we concluded the chapter with one very popular service, *"AWS Security Hub,"* which can give you complete overview of security insights and findings along with your other AWS services that may contain anomalies or permissive polices.

Summary

In this enriching chapter on cybersecurity with AWS IoT, a thorough navigation through the world of cybersecurity in IoT realm was undertaken. The journey began with a clear demystification of the foundational concept of Zero Trust. This exploration emphasized its pivotal role and principles in modern cybersecurity paradigms, laying a solid foundation for understanding advanced topics.

The dialogue was extended to align with the esteemed standards of NIST 800-207. This part was instrumental in detailing the established guidelines and illustrating the synergy between these guidelines and AWS IoT, ensuring that the readers are well versed with the standards for effective cybersecurity measures.

An extensive analysis into the AWS IoT Device Defender was carried out, offering a deep understanding of its multifaceted features. This segment empowered the readers to harness the full potential of this tool, ensuring they are equipped to handle real-world cybersecurity challenges effectively.

The chapter also ventured into exploring practical cybersecurity scenarios. This exploration aimed to showcase the applicability of AWS IoT Device Defender in identifying and isolating anomalies, thereby providing a robust understanding and hands-on experience for tackling real-world cybersecurity issues.

We explored complex scenarios, offering both theoretical insight and a practical approach to various types of attacks such as impersonation and DoS attacks.

Further, the chapter navigated through the capabilities of Amazon SNS in providing timely alerts. This exploration highlighted the importance of near real-time notification in preventing significant security breaches, ensuring that stakeholders are promptly informed of any breaches.

In the realm of AI and ML, an insightful segment on the "ML Detect" feature was included. This section illuminated its prowess in fortifying cybersecurity measures, ensuring that the cutting-edge technology of "machine learning" is leveraged in defense strategies.

Concluding the chapter, an integration of AWS IoT Device Defender with the AWS Security Hub was provided. This closing section underscored its role in offering complete security insights and findings alongside other AWS services, ensuring a secure and robust AWS environment.

In essence, the chapter furnished a holistic, in-depth, and practical understanding of various crucial aspects of cybersecurity, enabling effective handling of real-world cybersecurity challenges with confidence and expertise.

Index

S. Rehan, *AWS IoT With Edge ML and Cybersecurity*, https://doi.org/10.1007/979-8-8688-0011-5

D

E